Communism in
Eastern Europe

Communist Eastern Europe

Communism in Eastern Europe

Second Edition

Edited by Teresa Rakowska-Harmstone

MANCHESTER UNIVERSITY PRESS

Published in the United Kingdom by Manchester University Press.
Oxford Road, Manchester M13 9PL.

British Library cataloguing in publication data:

Communism in Eastern Europe–2nd ed.
1. Communism–Europe, Eastern
I. Rakowska-Harmstone, Teresa
335.43'0947   HX239

ISBN 0-7190-1704-1
ISBN 0-7190-1705-X Pbk

Manufactured in the United States of America

Contents

Preface

The format of the book and the general purpose remain substantially unchanged in the new edition, but each chapter was updated and revised in the light of the changes that took place in Eastern Europe since the publication of the original edition, namely to cover the late 1970s and the early 1980s, especially the events in Poland and their impact in Eastern Europe. By mutual consent Andrew Gyorgy withdrew from the editorship, leaving the undersigned as the sole editor. Regrettably also, Robert R. King was not available to update the Bulgaria and Romania chapters. Fortunately, however, replacement contributions were secured from Patrick Moore (Bulgaria) and Walter Bacon, Jr. (Romania). It was decided also to drop the chapter on Eurocommunism because in the 1980s its importance declined and its relevance to East European parties faded. Jiri Valenta agreed to provide instead a new contribution: "The Soviet Union and Eastern Europe: Crisis, Intervention, and Normalization." The editor has, in addition, provided a general introduction.

Special thanks—for both editions—are due to Janet Rabinowitch, senior sponsoring editor of Indiana University Press. Her support, good judgment, and superb editorial skills were indispensable in making this volume a better book than it would otherwise have been.

T.R-H.

Preface to First Edition

The success of a volume like *Communism in Eastern Europe* depends on the interplay of several factors and on the cooperation of a number of colleagues. The editors gratefully acknowledge the patience and support of their co-authors and of the publisher, Indiana University Press, who agreed from the inception of this project with the two principal underlying assumptions:

(1) That there is a need for a comprehensive, lucid, and technically accurate general textbook in the field of East European politics designed for junior-senior as well as graduate courses in the fields of politics and international affairs; and

(2) That the volume should be organized around two types and patterns of approaches, namely, individual country-by-country case-studies, buttressed by certain significant *functional* chapters illuminating the key supranational and interregional problem areas of East Central Europe.

Consequently, our book is divided into twelve chapters, eight of which are individual country studies, while four present a broad panorama of such regionally oriented subjects as the role and function of Eastern Europe in world politics; the economic development of the area; the impact of contemporary Eurocommunism; and certain key aspects of current political and leadership changes in Eastern Europe. The individual authors were asked by the editors to focus on the following key subjects: the geopolitical background of the country involved; the size and distinctive characteristics of the population; the relevant features of the nation's historic development, with particular emphasis on the turbulent interwar period of dictatorships and semidictatorships throughout the region; and various psychological and sociological forces which have helped shape the last three decades. Other factors considered were the political party structures—the dominant right-wing elements as well as the slowly emerging underground leftist groups—which set the stage for a fullfledged Communist "takeover."

Our colleagues and fellow authors were also requested to consider in some detail, as part of the structural focus of a typical "country" chapter, the current state of cultural affairs, human rights, dissenters and defectors, and—in general—issues related to the theory and practice of human rights. These important considerations lead inevitably to discussion of the scope, intensity, and overall effectiveness of political opposition in the given East European country, its chances of asserting itself and of having its voice heard. Such issues have been particularly interesting in connection with recent Hungarian and Polish developments, and probably least relevant in the German Democratic Republic and Bulgaria.

A review of the recent past and of current developments inevitably foreshadows a cautious preview of possible future events in the countries of East Central Europe, and both our individual country and functional chapters do speculate about certain contingencies broadly related to the future of the Soviet control of the eight East European countries, and their more than 150 million inhabitants. Of course, such future predictions and ideological forecasts have to be restrained and careful by definition, given the tenuous "balance-of-power" position and geopolitical character of most of Eastern Europe.

While the book considers broadly the evolution of this region since the end of World War II in 1945, it deals primarily with the events of the 1970s and with projections for the 1980s. In Soviet political terms, the stress is on post-Khrushchev developments, i.e., the 1964–79 period. Among the main themes treated are nationalism; intra-bloc political and economic integration through WTO and CMEA; Eurocommunism; and detente. It is hoped that the volume will strike a useful balance between the myriad long- and short-term issues confronting Eastern Europe, one of the world's more conflict-ridden political regions.

Because so many languages are involved in this book, diacritical and accent marks have been deleted from foreign words. The short bibliography at the end of each country chapter is intended as a guide to further reading, not as a list of sources on which the chapter is based.

T.R.-H.

A.G.

Introduction

Teresa Rakowska-Harmstone

Contrary to Western preconceptions, Eastern Europe is neither homogeneous nor monolithic. The region is, in fact, a mosaic of peoples and cultures of ancient and highly differentiated origins and varied historical experience often marked by bitter intraregional conflicts. It is only the "communism" of the title of this book that imposes a unity on the area. The Communist systems of Eastern Europe to be studied here were not the product of spontaneous, indigenous growth but a result of the post–World War II settlement, based on the realities of political and military power, which advanced the East—represented by the Soviet Union—into the heart of Europe. In all but two of the countries under review, Communist systems were introduced by the Soviet armed forces, notwithstanding the fact that in Czechoslovakia the Communist party received the most votes in the first postwar (and the last free) elections of 1946. The two exceptions are Albania and Yugoslavia, where communism emerged in the wake of a civil war and a genuine revolution. But on the whole, the establishment of Communist regimes after World War II represented a major historical discontinuity for the countries of the region.

The so-called Eastern Europe of today is the East Central Europe of the interwar period; the German Democratic Republic includes the core of Prussia and Saxony. These are truly "The Lands Between" (to borrow the title of a well-known book[1]), through which runs Europe's great East-West cultural division dating from the split of the Roman Empire in the fourth century, the Western half dominated henceforth by Catholic Rome and the Eastern part by Orthodox Byzantium. In modern times the influence of Byzantium was supplanted by that of Imperial Russia in the northeast and by the Ottoman Empire in the southeast Danube basin and the Balkans. The Roman heritage of Western Christianity and culture was carried on in the North by the Polish-Lithuanian Kingdom until it was partitioned by Russia, Prussia, and

1

Austria in the eighteenth century, and in the Southwest by the Habs-
burgs' Dual Monarchy. The Germans, Poles, Czechs, Slovaks, and
Hungarians have been on the Western side and the Romanians, Bulgarians, and Albanians on the Eastern side of the great cultural division.
The line runs right through the middle of modern Yugoslavia, dividing
the Catholic Croats and Slovenes from the Orthodox Serbs, Montenegrins, and Macedonians, as well as from the Moslems of Bosnia and of
Albanian Kosovo.

In ethnolinguistic terms, the Poles, Czechs, Slovaks, Croats,
Slovenes, Serbs, Montenegrins, Macedonians, Bulgarians, and Bosnian Moslems are all Slavs; the Hungarians (Magyars) are the descendants of Eastern nomadic peoples; the Albanians of ancient Illyrians;
and the Romanians, apparently, of ancient Dacians and Latin-speaking
Roman settlers.

National memories are cherished equally by the peoples of the region, such as the Poles and the Hungarians who had historical states
prior to the twentieth century, by those such as the Croats or the
Bulgarians whose medieval kingdoms fell to foreign conquest, and by
those such as the Romanians whose national identity grew out of convergence of related people. All have translated national historical traditions into fervent nationalism, which, early in this century, helped to
destroy the empires among which they had been divided. Most were
able to realize their national aspirations in the states that emerged in
East Central Europe in the interwar period, although some of them, the
Croats and the Slovaks among others, remain frustrated to this day.
But after World War II all found themselves again under foreign domination, this time by the Soviet Union; only two of the countries, Yugoslavia and Albania, succeeded in striking out on their own. "Fraternal"
(working) class ties are supposed to be at the basis of the unity of
Soviet bloc states ruled now by Communist parties, but nationalism
has remained as the region's major and most disruptive force. It has
been the main source of intrabloc conflicts and of resistance to bloc
integration policies promoted by the Soviet Union. As the touchstone
of popular loyalties, it has also been crucial in the efforts of Communist
regimes to generate domestic legitimacy.

In power now for more than thirty-five years, the Communist regimes all share basic systemic principles modeled on the Soviet system, even though there is much differentiation in detail. The key
political principle is the leading role of the party, which means that the
party has a monopoly of political power, appropriated on the strength
of its ideologically defined role as the "vanguard" of the working class.
Here ideology is a substitute for the sanction of periodic popular approval: because of its "advanced social consciousness," it is assumed

that the party has the only correct knowledge of the "objective laws" governing historical progress, which entitles it to a monopoly of power and gives its decisions the force of universal laws. This premise has several immediate practical consequences.

First, assuming that the meaning of constitutionalism as understood in the West is the imposition of restraints on, and the institutionalization of, the exercise of political power, Communist systems are preconstitutional. Although they all have formal constitutions, these serve to provide a legal framework, a *Rechtstaat*, for the party's governance of society but place no restraints whatsoever on the party's power; thus there is no framework for its institutionalization, no *Politischerstaat*.[2] Because political power is not institutionalized, neither is political succession; a leadership struggle is substituted for the constitutional transfer of power. Elections (with one-party or party-led bloc candidates) and legislatures (which meet to give formal assent to party decisions) have socialization, mobilization, and support-building functions, which should not be confused with the more familiar western role of representing popular sovereignty.

Second, the maintenance of a monopoly of power requires the existence of coercive mechanisms whose powers are only subject to the party's political will: the police in the first instance but ultimately also the armed forces, the internal function of which is the "defense of socialism," i.e., the defense of the party's power. Third, because the party's rule is legitimated by ideology, the system cannot tolerate any ideological challenge. It thus requires also the monopoly of communications and consequently the imposition of censorship. Fourth, the party's monopoly of power precludes the existence of subsystem autonomy. Any political and social organizations not initially controlled by the party are either destroyed or eventually subordinated to the party's will. The latter has been the case with Eastern Europe's churches, for example, except for Poland's Roman Catholic church, which has proved too strong. Because no social groups are allowed to express independent viewpoints—by definition, no social conflict exists in Communist societies (only madmen, counterrevolutionaries, or imperialist agents can be in opposition to the party)—the system has no institutionalized mechanisms for conflict resolution.

All Communist regimes have duplicate institutional structures: there is a party bureaucracy and a parallel state bureaucracy. The first makes decisions and supervises their implementation; the second carries them out. The relationship between the party and the state apparatuses largely circumscribes the arena of Communist politics. The state's subordination to the party's will or, in other words, the exercise by the party of its leading role, is safeguarded by a number of intricate mechanisms: the principle of "democratic centralism" (decisions flow from the top down); the principle of *nomenklatura* (all important appointments are subject to the party's decision or approval); incorporation of top government and social leaders into the party decision-making bodies; maintenance of parallel structures as noted above; and the "eyes and ears" role played by party cells, which unite party members in all political, administrative, economic, and social institutions and organizations in the country. In practice, the dividing line between party functionaries as decision makers and state bureaucrats as executors is blurred, not the least because everybody in any position of authority is also a party member. Despite the absence of formal pressure groups, special interests find expression in factional struggles within key bureaucracies. Other control mechanisms are the procuracy and the courts (there is no Western-type independent judiciary), which enforce "socialist legality," and the secret police, who enforce political conformity.

Communist regimes are mobilizing regimes, but they lack mechanisms for change in response to pressures generated by their own policies' interaction with a given society's social forces and political culture. In East European countries efforts to introduce change have operated under double constraints. The first obstacle has been the indivisibility of the party's leading role, which has made unacceptable the type of change attempted by the Hungarian revolution of 1956, by the Prague Spring of 1968, or by Poland's Solidarity of 1980–81. Regardless of safeguards offered to preserve the system, these efforts at reform breached the systemic principles outlined above and threatened the survival of ruling elites. Within each country's political culture a range of accommodations might well be feasible (the examples of Czechoslovakia in 1968 and of Yugoslavia are indicative), if it were not for the second constraint: the presence, power, and determination of the Soviet Union.

For East Europeans, Soviet influence and policy in the region have a historical echo. The USSR is the twentieth century's double anachronism: its political system follows the blueprint of a nineteenth-century ideology, superimposed on the world's last surviving multi-ethnic empire. Yet the Soviet Union sees the East European regional subsystem as an extension of the Soviet "family of nations" and as the nucleus of the "world socialist system." Given the heterogeneous historical and cultural background of Eastern Europe, the pressures for change there cannot but be on a collision course with the systemic requirements described above and with bloc integration policies pursued by the Soviet Union.

The pressures for change in Eastern Europe have been felt in three major areas, although their focus and intensity have varied from country to country and over time. The demands for some recognition, at least, of political pluralism and civil and human rights have proved futile, as the history of the region since World War II demonstrates, and prospects were no better in 1984 than they were in 1948. The push for economic reforms has been dictated by the imperatives of economic growth and performance and consumer satisfaction, but any change that would undercut the power of the Communist party has proved largely impossible, except in Yugoslavia, which is free of Soviet constraints, and in Hungary, which has been performing a balancing act between the command and the "socialist market" economic models. The pressures for national self-determination in multiethnic systems have foundered on the same shoals, again with the exception of Yugoslavia, where the party's leading role was diluted in the 1960s by economic reforms and liberalization. In Yugoslavia *de facto* autonomous republican parties have emerged that run the country on the basis of a collective consensus. The Yugoslav and Romanian examples show that nationalism is not necessarily incompatible with the leading role of the party, provided that concessions to nationalism do not also include concessions to pluralism.

As Andrzej Korbonski has astutely noted in the Poland chapter[3] and in his other works, every type of nation-building crisis identified by Almond and Powell[4] has occurred in Communist Eastern Europe, sometimes in one and the same country. With the exception of the German Democratic Republic—a rump of the German nation—and multi-ethnic Yugoslavia, few of the countries suffer from an identity crisis, but all, to a greater or lesser degree, have undergone a legitimacy crisis and related crises of penetration and participation. Many have also experienced a distribution crisis. Poland currently is in the acute stage of every one of the aforementioned crises except for that of identity. At the other extreme, Hungary and perhaps Bulgaria have been the most successful in resolving, at least for the time being, the problems that generate these crises.

In the search for legitimacy, which has been crucial for East European Communist regimes, identification with nationalism has been indispensable. Yugoslavia and Albania have left the bloc altogether. If it were not for geostrategic reasons, Romania might have done the same. Romania's assertion of nationalism as the proper basis of communism, and of national interest in foreign policy, has proved highly dysfunctional to bloc integration. Other regimes have adopted an astute and selective use of national symbolism for legitimation purposes, in most cases with considerable success (for obvious reasons the GDR has had a problem in this regard). Even in Poland, the use of the national army to destroy political opposition in the name of national survival (General Jaruzelski's coup of December 1981) has facilitated the party's task.

"Goulash communism" has been the other important prop of Communist legitimacy, its effectiveness dependent on the regime's ability to deliver the goods. Hungary has been most successful in this regard, as were for a time, post-1968 Czechoslovakia, the German Democratic Republic, and Bulgaria.

On the whole, political instability has characterized post-1945 Eastern Europe. The degree of instability has been proportionate to the gap in historical continuity between the system and the society, and between communism and the national political culture. Coercion, either internal or through outside intervention, has been essential for the maintenance of communism. But, after more than thirty-five years of Communist rule, the Soviet Union and its system have had an impact. The national consensus has been undermined by a cleavage between society as a whole and the Communist "New Class," which, in the interest of self-preservation, favors maintenance of the status quo and opposes change. Also, negative traits pervasive in Soviet society have seeped slowly but relentlessly into East European societies at large. These include social alienation—from the party, the government, and political pursuits in general; endemic alcoholism; and such survival mechanisms as corruption, theft, bribery, influence peddling, snitching on neighbors and coworkers, contempt for the law, and an ability to bypass, subvert, and hoodwink the authorities.

The combined use, by the Soviet Union, of the carrot-and-stick technique and manipulation of the self-preservation instincts of the countries' Communist elites has resulted in a progressive, albeit slow, integration of East European polities into the Soviet state system. Moscow orchestrates interparty contacts, overseas synchronization of state structures, and coordinates foreign policy. Coordinated economic planning and sectoral integration proceeds within the CMEA. Last but not least, the success of military integration can best be measured by the changing nature of the sequence of intervention: in Hungary in 1956 the Soviet armed forces had to intervene alone: in 1968 in Czechoslovakia the intervention was carried out formally by Warsaw Pact members (with Romania's abstention); in 1981 in Poland the intervention was accomplished internally, by Polish hands, in the form of a military coup.

NOTES

1. Alan Palmer, *The Lands Between; A History of East-Central Europe Since the Congress of Vienna* (New York: Macmillan, 1970).

2. George Brunner, "The Functions of Communist Constitutions," *Review of Socialist Law,* no. 2, 1977.

3. Below, pp. 50–85.

4. Gabriel A. Almond and G. Bingham Powell, Jr., *Comparative Politics: Systems, Process, and Policy* (Boston: Little Brown, 1966), pp. 35–37.

1

Eastern Europe in World Perspective

Vernon V. Aspaturian

As the world nears the turn of the century, the importance and visibility of the countries of Eastern Europe, both as a collective entity and as individual international actors, are likely to increase and the foreign policy activity of the East European states is correspondingly bound to be more complicated. The relationship of individual East European states to the Soviet Union at any given time will remain the single most important and uncomplicated variable conditioning the international behavior of the states in the region. In spite of Soviet desires to the contrary, the Soviet connection will be forced to compete with other conditioning factors and determinants and the Soviet variable will continue to erode slowly. Whether the erosion will be sufficient to bring about a fundamental restructuring of Soviet-European relationships by the year 2000 cannot be precisely forecast on the basis of existing trends. The ultimate character of the resolution of the festering and boiling "Polish problem" and the unresolved succession issues generated by Brezhnev's death will play important roles in shaping future relationships.

Until comparatively recent times, Eastern Europe did not exist as a distinct geographical, regional, or political concept; its role on the world stage was marginal. Today, Eastern Europe is recognized as one of the major geo-political regions of the world. Before World War II and particularly before World War I, global or world politics were essentially colonial and imperial politics and the exclusive province of a handful of Great Powers, all located in Europe except for the United States and Japan. Eastern Europe, like most of the non-European world, was essentially an object of great-power politics rather than an actor on the European stage, to say nothing of the world stage. Knowledge of, not to mention contact with, the world beyond its immediate proximity was nil, except for the awareness of a vast and generous America to which millions of East Europeans migrated after 1900.

Similarly, the outside world was only dimly aware of the nations and few states of Eastern Europe that existed in the late nineteenth and early twentieth centuries. Subsumed for centuries as parts of the four great empires of the East—the German, Hapsburg, Russian, and Ottoman—the nations of Eastern Europe possessed little international or world visibility as distinctive national personalities. The region was even remote and unfamiliar to Western Europe, with the exception of Hungary, as part of the Dual Monarchy, and Poland, whose disappearance from the diplomatic scene was briefly interrupted by Napoleon's creation of the Grand Duchy of Warsaw, which helped to keep Poland alive as a submerged but nevertheless distinctive national personality. As for Czechs and Slovaks, Romanians, Croats, Slovenes, Serbs, Bosnians, Macedonians, Montenegrins, Bulgarians, Albanians, Estonians, Latvians, Lithuanians, Belorussians, and Ukrainians, to say nothing of nuances like Uniates and Hussites, Ghegs and Toscs, Ruthenians and Szeklers, or Masurians and Kaschubes, they were indiscriminately perceived as Austro-Hungarians, Russians, Turks, or indeterminate Slavs by all but a handful of scholars, poets, and statesmen who knew better.

As recently as 1938, at the height of the Sudeten crisis, an exasperated and outraged Prime Minister Neville Chamberlain referred to Czechoslovakia and the Sudeten crisis in a public radio broadcast as "a quarrel in a far away country between people about whom we know nothing"; it was "horrible, fantastic, incredible," he said, that Britain should somehow be concerned.[1] And yet Czechoslovakia is the westernmost country of contemporary Eastern Europe, nestled in the center of the European continent; its control, Bismarck had assured the Germans, ensured the mastery of all Europe.

During and after World War II, the countries of Eastern Europe moved out of the mists of remoteness and were conceptually united with Western Europe as part of Europe in the cultural, as distinct from the geographic, sense. But because of Soviet occupation and control, the countries and nations of Eastern Europe were again congealed into a single gray mass, rarely disaggregated into their individual personalities. For the world beyond Europe and America, Eastern Europe was as remote and distant as were the Congo and Burma to East Europeans. As late as 1956, Eastern Europe and East Europeans were perceived even by educated Africans and Asians as an undifferentiated mass; to some degree this accounted for the relative indifference of the emerging Third World to their fate as satellites of the Soviet Union. This indifference was illustrated by the voting behavior of Third World countries in the U.N. General Assembly at the time of the Hungarian uprising in 1956.

Thus, during the past century, the status and role of Eastern Europe in the international community have passed through a number of phases, corresponding to the changing structural self-perception of its role in the world community and the reciprocal perception by the outside world. These phasal roles can be sequentially summarized as a general movement from objects of international politics, to instruments and pawns, to subjects and actors, first on the European stage and then on the world stage, in a number of capacities.

Until about 1850, Eastern Europe was largely an object over which four great empires contended; after 1850, some parts of Eastern Europe, as they became independent, were in turn instruments and pawns of the Great Powers; during the interwar period, the newly independent countries of Eastern Europe assumed the role and status of actors and subjects in the international community, an evolution that was arrested first by Nazi Germany and then by the Soviet Union after World War II. Eastern Europe as a geographical-regional concept did not make its appearance until after World War I, when the succession states were carved out of the German, Hapsburg, and Russian empires, of which most of the area was a part. The southern part of contemporary Eastern Europe was subject to the Ottoman Empire for centuries. It is ironic that this relatively less developed sector of Eastern Europe under Ottoman rule was the first to proliferate into independent states, a process that was largely completed before World War I. Ottoman Europe and its successor states in Europe, however, were generally described as part of a subregion, the Balkans, sometimes called Southeastern Europe and, before 1914, often considered part of the Near East.

After World War I the "northern tier" and the "southern tier" of Eastern Europe were united into a single geographical-regional concept. After World War II the geographical concept of Eastern Europe merged with the ideological concept to form the contemporary political-regional concept. Since about 1957, in spite of its association with the USSR and in some respects because of it, Eastern Europe has emerged as one of the major geo-political regions of the world, whose states function in part as members of a distinct grouping or bloc and in part as individual and separate actors on the world stage. Whether as part of a group or in their individual capacities, the states of Eastern Europe are perceived by themselves and by others as actively engaged in diplomatic, political, economic, and military activities on a global scale.

The parochialism of Eastern Europe is a thing of the past. While the region does not function as a world power, either as a group of states or as individual states, it does act in a global context with a world perspective. This is true of every state in the region, even the smallest. Who would have dreamed, for example, even twenty-five years ago, that a bizarre relationship like the now defunct Beijing-Tirana axis could have existed? That Albania would become aware of China is understandable, but that China would find the tiny speck that is Albania on the fringes of Eastern Europe and proclaim her a political-ideological ally against both "imperialism" and "revisionism," resulting in a wide array of economic, cultural, political, and military interactions between them, is, in its strange way, a remarkable tribute to the visibility of Eastern Europe on the world scene.

The status of Eastern Europe as one of the major geo-political regions of the world was given quasi-official recognition by the United Nations when it was informally stipulated that at least one nonpermanent member of the Security Council should be elected from the states of this region on a rotating basis. Geographical Eastern Europe and political Eastern Europe are not perfectly congruent. For all practical purposes, Eastern Europe today means Communist Europe, except for the USSR. This conception excludes Greece, Turkish Thrace, Finland, and the European non-Russian republics of the Soviet Union, which are geographically a part of Eastern Europe, and correspondingly includes the German Democratic Republic and the former German provinces of Pomerania and Silesia (now parts of Poland), which traditionally were not considered a part of the geographical area.

Since the concept of Eastern Europe has also been burdened with a cultural characteristic, some nations and states of Eastern Europe, particularly those whose history, culture, and religion were Western-oriented, resented inclusion in a broader unit that seemed to separate them from Western Europe and to associate them with Byzantine/Ottoman Europe and the Balkans, an area that was considered backward. Thus, before World War II countries like Poland, Czechoslovakia, Hungary, and Germany (the northern tier) preferred to be identified with another subregional concept, Central Europe, separate and distinct from Eastern Europe (the Soviet Union) and Southeastern Europe (the Balkans).

In 1983 the aggregate population of Eastern Europe numbered nearly 137 million and was distributed among eight states and more than a dozen distinct nationalities, whose history and tradition of mutual animosity, hostility, and conflict need not be recorded here.[2] Two major Christian religions dominate the region: Latin Christianity in the North and Byzantine Christianity in the South, with pockets of Protestant sects, Uniate Catholics, and Moslem groups. Two major alphabets, the Latin and the Cyrillic, correspond to the Catholic-Byzantine cleavage. Extensive Jewish communities once existed in Poland, Czechoslovakia, Hungary, and Romania, but as a result of the holocaust, only small residual Jewish communities can be found in Eastern Europe today. The paramount language group is Slavic, divided between West Slavic and South Slavic. Four of the states, embracing ten nations, are Slavic, whereas the remaining states each represent a distinct language grouping.[3]

Thus, in spite of the political-ideological homogeneity that characterizes contemporary Eastern Europe, it is a remarkably diverse aggregation of states and nations in terms of traditional characteristics. It has been the traditional diversities rather than the perceived homogeneities that have shaped the Eastern European past and have determined its political fate to be more often an object of the international system than a subject, individually and collectively.

Since the beginning of the nineteenth century, when the first nations of Eastern Europe emerged as independent states out of the four empires of which they were a part, they have never been capable, individually or collectively, of resisting either German or Russian encroachment on their political existence. Even as the Ottoman Empire was forced into retreat from Southeastern Europe, the emerging states and nations were quickly reduced to pawns or objects of the two great European nations—Russians and Germans—in rivalry with one another for dominance in the region. The Germans were presented not only by Prussia and its successor, the German Empire, but also by the Hapsburg Empire, which technically speaking was not *the* German state, but a German dominated state (especially before 1867), constitutionally organized as a Dual Monarchy (Austro-Hungarian) and masquerading as a multinational state.

Because of the relatively small size, inexperience, weakness, and mutual rivalries of the Eastern European nations, they were vulnerable to the manipulation and exploitation of the Germans and Russians and were forced or cajoled to gravitate into the sphere of one or the other of the two great nations. The most notable exception in the eighteenth century was Poland, which attempted to vie with both as an equally great or imperial nation, but without much success. Since Poland refused to seek the protection or patronage of either the Germans or the Russians and thus threatened both, it was Poland's fate to be dismembered. The smaller nations of Southeastern Europe that emerged later managed to preserve their formal independence by deliberately seeking or accepting the protection of the Hapsburg or Romanov empires. From 1850 to World War II, for a variety of reasons, the German influence was more dominant than the Russian. After World War I, because both Germany and Russia were weak pariah states, Eastern Europe was blessed with real autonomy under the remote and benign protection of France, but with the resurgence of German power after 1933, the countries fell one by one into the German orbit, with Poland once again subjected to partition.

EASTERN EUROPE IN WORLD DIPLOMACY
BETWEEN THE WARS

During the brief interwar period, the countries of Eastern Europe functioned in the European community as *separate* actors rather than as a regional unit or part of a political grouping, and as *independent* actors rather than as subjects and pawns of larger states. Although all of the East European states were members of the League of Nations and maintained diplomatic relations with a modest spectrum of states outside Europe, their international activity was restricted largely to Europe; they played little or no role on the global stage, except for Poland, which became a semipermanent member of the League Council and had pretensions of being more than a parochial East European state. The only non-European state with which the East European countries developed extensive contacts and relationships was the United States, not only because of President Wilson's role in determining the fate and shape of Eastern Europe, but also because millions of immigrants from the Hapsburg and Russian empires were drawn from the subject nationalities that became the new states of Eastern Europe.

It should be recalled in this connection that "global" politics as such did not exist between the wars. The international community consisted of about 60 states (as contrasted to nearly 160 today), of which no fewer than 30 were in Europe and 21 in the Western Hemisphere. Not a single authentic independent state existed on the continent of Africa (except for Ethiopia before 1936), while the entire Asian continent accounted for barely half a dozen independent states. Hence the Eurocentric character of East European diplomatic activity corresponded not only with international realities but East European interests as well. Europe was still the epicenter of the diplomatic universe and the closest approximations to "global" politics were colonial and imperialist rivalries of the major powers. For all practical purposes the East European states were insulated from the outside world by colonial enclosures and geographical distance.

With the rise of Fascism in Italy, and particularly with the advent of Hitler in Germany and the re-entry of Moscow into the general stream of European diplomacy after the completion of the First Five-Year Plan, it appears in retrospect that the countries of Eastern Europe enjoyed independence and autonomy only because the traditional great powers—Germany and Russia—had been weakened.

Unfortunately, the countries of Eastern Europe did not take the opportunity of the interwar period to submerge their differences and design ways in which to preserve their autonomy collectively against a possible resurgence of German and Russian power, which they would be unable to resist individually. Instead, irredentism, revisionism, and revanche prevailed, as typified by the Hungarian cry "Nem, Nem, Soha!" ("No, No, Never"), a reference to the Treaty of Trianon, which dismembered Hungary and reduced her to a nondescript Balkan-type state. The revisionism of the discontented East European countries (Hungary, Bulgaria, and Poland to some degree) was fueled and inflamed by the revisionist aspirations of Germany and Italy, while the restiveness of nationalities who found themselves as part of a binational or multinational state, instead of their own nation-state (Slovaks in Czechoslovakia and Croats in Yugoslavia), was also exploited and manipulated by both Hitler and Mussolini. It was an unfortunate coincidence that precisely those states that were the targets of the revisionist powers were also the ones with the most serious domestic nationality or minority problems (Czechoslovakia, Yugoslavia, and Romania).

Rivalries, animosities, and hatreds separated the winners and losers of World War I, but even among winners and losers there were serious mutual demands and claims.

The new successor states and those largely satisfied with the settlements after World War I (Poland, Czechoslovakia, Yugoslavia, Romania, and Greece), as a rule, allied themselves with France, the most powerful state in Europe, and entered into local alliances with one another, directed against the irredentism and revisionism of Austria, Hungary, and Bulgaria. The Little Entente (Czechoslovakia, Yugoslavia, and Romania) and the Balkan Entente (Romania, Yugoslavia, Greece, and Turkey) represented not only the independence of the East European states in their behavior but also their dependence on France. These local alliances, furthermore, represented efforts at collective action to fill the power vacuum in the area, while simultaneously reflecting the deep cleavages that separated the small countries from one another and rendered them vulnerable to penetration, manipulation, and control by the Great Powers.

It seemed only natural, as the *status quo* states of Eastern Europe looked to France for support and protection, that the revisionist states of Eastern Europe would increasingly rely upon Germany and Italy to support their revisionist aspirations. Within a few years after Hitler's advent to power—and particularly after the annexation of Austria—Hungary and Bulgaria gravitated toward Berlin and Rome. As France's willingness and ability to protect her East European clients diminished after the Sudeten crisis and Munich, Hitler, in effect, was given a free hand in Eastern Europe. Even *status quo* states like Romania and Yugoslavia sought the protection of German might, not only against their local tormentors but against the Soviet Union as well. Even before the Anschluss and Munich, France's alliance with Moscow appeared to Eastern Europe to nullify whatever protection France had afforded them against the USSR, which increasingly posed a threat to all of Eastern Europe, not only in traditional territorial terms but also because of the revolutionary threat to their social systems.

Thus, except for Czechoslovakia and Poland, which were the immediate targets of Germany, all of the states of Eastern Europe became client or potential client states of Germany, subject to barter and manipulation as Berlin saw fit. As the arbiter of Eastern Europe's destiny, Hitler first made an arrangement with Stalin, demarcating spheres of influence in the region, with entire states and provinces bartered away to Moscow in exchange for a benign neutrality in the war between Germany and the Allied Powers. Germany then posed as an "honest broker" arbitrating disputes between her clients (most notably the division of Transylvania between Hungary and Romania), and dismembered Yugoslavia and Greece, redistributing their territory in 1941 among their neighbors. Croats and Slovaks found satisfaction in the creation of their own states under German patronage; Hungary and Bulgaria exulted in their territorial acquisitions, while Czechs, Poles, and Serbs were deprived of their statehood.

Although Germany altered the entire political and territorial landscape of Eastern Europe, this arrangement proved to be temporary. Once Germany was defeated and the Soviet Union appeared on the scene to claim the entire area as her exclusive zone of ideological, political, economic, and military influence, Eastern Europe once again was subject to territorial and demographic convulsions, and while the new landscape of Eastern Europe did not resemble that created by Hitler, neither did it resemble very much that of the prewar period. Three states—Latvia, Lithuania, and Estonia—disappeared into the jaws of the Soviet Union, while a new state, the German Democratic Republic, was created. Slovakia and Croatia disappeared as independent states, whereas Austria, Czechoslovakia, and Yugoslavia were reconstituted, the first, as it existed before 1938; the second, somewhat truncated by the Soviet annexation of the Carpatho-Ukraine; and the third, slightly expanded at Italy's expense. Hungary was pressed back into her 1937 frontiers, as was Bulgaria, but Poland and Romania suffered extensive territorial losses to the Soviet Union. Poland was compensated for her losses with Pomerania, Silesia, and part of East Prussia, while Romania had to be content with the restoration of all Transylvania to her control.

The Soviet Union annexed about 200,000 square miles of territory in Eastern Europe and moved its borders westward by about 200 miles, whereas the boundaries of "Eastern Europe" were now pressed beyond Central Europe and into the easternmost frontiers of Western Europe, as the western frontier of East Germany extended beyond 10 degrees longitude, west of Hamburg and little more than 150 miles east of the Rhine. More fundamental than the territorial changes were the ideological and socioeconomic convulsions that rocked the region, as Eastern Europe assumed not only a new profile but also a new identity, as an aggregated appendage of the Soviet state and an extension of the Soviet sociopolitical order and Soviet military power.

EASTERN EUROPE AS A WORLD ACTOR

Between 1945 and 1949, Eastern Europe once again became an arena of contending Great Powers, but this time the powers were the USSR and the United States, since only the latter had the power to offer itself as a protector of Eastern Europe against the territorial, ideological, sociopolitical, and military onslaught from the East. But since the United States did not have any immediate, tangible vital interest in Eastern Europe, but rather an abstract ideological-political interest and an overall strategic interest in its rivalry with the Soviet Union, it was not prepared to take the risks or to make the sacrifices that Moscow was prepared to do in order to retain control over an area of traditional, vital, and immediate interest to her overall well-being. For the Soviet Union, Eastern Europe was simultaneously a defense *glacis;* a springboard for possible expansion westward; an ideological legitimization of her universal pretensions; a laboratory for the application of the Soviet model of development; a reservoir of human, natural, and economic resources to be exploited for Soviet recovery; a collection of diplomatic pawns and surrogates to be used in international politics; and a source of psychological and even quantitative comfort in international organizations and conferences, where the Soviet Union might otherwise be isolated and alone.

U.S. interest in Eastern Europe and charges of Soviet violations of the Yalta Agreement with respect to "free democratic institutions" and "free elections," when combined with an unexpected American passion for the reunification of Germany, struck Stalin and the Soviet leaders as malign and designed to deprive the Soviet Union of her just deserts, to press her back within her pre-1939 frontiers, and to deny her the global role to which she was entitled as one of the major world powers. Although anticommunist ideological goals were certainly involved, the U.S. attempt to weaken the Soviet presence in Eastern Europe was directed primarily at depriving the Soviet Union of a forward geopolitical springboard for possible invasion or intervention in Central and Western Europe. Its objective then and now has been to remove, once and for all, the direct threat of Soviet intervention in Germany and Western Europe in response either to attempted Communist uprisings or takeovers within these individual countries or to vulnerabilities and openings that might entice the Soviet Union to move its own forces directly into the area. What the United States sought was a transformation of Eastern Europe from a potential Soviet springboard into a buffer zone between Soviet power and West-Central Europe.

Whether Eastern Europe is a buffer zone, a defense *glacis,* or a springboard for expansion is in the eye of the beholder and cannot be objectively measured. If Eastern Europe could function simultaneously as a defensive zone and a springboard for the Soviet Union, it could so function for the United States and Western Europe as well. Since Stalin was aware that the East European states were too weak and fragmented to function as an independent buffer zone between the USSR and the United States, assuming they were willing to do so (which was dubious), the Soviet leader saw in the U.S. demand for "free elections" a not-so-subtle attempt to mobilize the widespread anti-Soviet and anti-Russian sentiment in most of these countries. This would effectively nullify Roosevelt's concession to Stalin that the states of Eastern Europe would have to have "friendly governments," i.e., friendly to the USSR. Stalin knew that "free elections" were incompatible with "friendly governments" and so did the Truman Administration.

Although after 1948, except for Yugoslavia, the Soviet grip on Eastern Europe tightened with a seeming permanence, the countries of Eastern Europe once again became objects of contending powers rather than independent actors on the international stage. After 1956, when U.S. credibility as a contender with the Soviet Union for Eastern Europe diminished with the quashing of the Hungarian uprising, China attempted to convert Eastern Europe into an object of ideological contention between Moscow and Beijing, perceiving a possibility that the East European states might find it useful to employ China as a counterpoise against Moscow within the family of Communist states. But within the narrower confines of the Communist interstate fraternity, the East European states were allowed more latitude as subjects. They initially welcomed the usefulness of the Chinese connection, which they exploited to gain considerable autonomy "within" the Communist interstate system in return for not seeking greater autonomy outside the system.

Since 1956 and in spite of the invasion of Czechoslovakia in 1968 and the proclamation of the "Brezhnev doctrine," the international role and status of Eastern Europe as a collectivity and as individual states have increased perceptibly. It is important to recognize, however, that international visibility is not a one-dimensional phenomenon but a multidimensional one. Instead of a single role or identity in the world community developed to an intense pitch, East European activity in the world community assumed the pattern of accepting new roles and seeking several international environments in which to function. The latitude of activity for Eastern Europe as a whole and as individual states varies considerably as to both roles and environment. Each East European state has and continues to seek its own individual equilibrium with the Soviet Union and with every other East European state as well as with Eastern Europe as a whole, and this equilibrium varies considerably. Thus some East Europeans states have more roles to play than others, possess a different spectrum of identities, and function in a different set of environments.

The increasing involvement of Eastern Europe in the international community is not an unmixed blessing, as some East European states find that often they are involved involuntarily in global concerns in distant corners of the world because of their Soviet connection, and seemingly must maintain a foreign policy that is not too distinct from that of a great or super power. Thus, during the Czech Spring of 1968, one Czech writer was moved to complain: "We are a small country. . . . We should have a modest foreign policy, one conforming to our possibilities. I do not understand why we have to intervene in the affairs of Madagascar, Guatemala, or Nigeria."[4]

Yet, as Yugoslavia demonstrated after 1948, expanding one's involvement and activity in the international community results in the creation and discovery of new roles, new identities, new associations, and new constituencies, which can sustain and promote the interests of a small state in many dimensions. While it is true that many East European states resent being adjuncts of Soviet global concerns in the general international environment or pawns within the international Communist movement against China and other Communist heretics, in general, the expansion of Eastern Europe's international activities has on the whole been beneficial and will continue to be so. Pawns and clients do not always remain pawns and clients, as China, Yugoslavia, Albania, Romania, and even Cuba have demonstrated in different ways.

All of the states of Eastern Europe enjoy separate and independent membership in the United Nations and the general international system. This is the widest international movement in which they function as actors, but it is also an environment in which the intensity of their activity is restricted. During the Stalinist period, the East European states functioned as a bloc within the organization, never deviating from the Soviet position. They were permitted to function in U.N. agencies and activities only to the degree permitted them by Moscow and usually as surrogates of the Soviet Union on various committees and commissions. As a general rule, Eastern Europe and the Soviet Union boycotted almost all of the U.N. specialized agencies.

The overall global character of Eastern Europe's international behavior can perhaps be placed in proper perspective by comparing it with that of the behavior of all states in the international community. This comparison will take the form of examining the relative participation of individual East European countries in international organizations and in general diplomatic interaction. Some of the aggregate data employed are dated (1963–65) and are designed to give the most general type of measurement. The aggregate data for membership in international organizations in Table 1 provide the individual country's rank among the 122 states with such participation, the number of U.N. organizations to which it belongs, the number of memberships in other international organizations, and the total of all such memberships, as of 1965.

During the past two decades, however, membership activity in international organizations has increased considerably, especially that of individual countries. International and multilateral organizations have also multiplied in number, proliferated, and metastasized immensely during the last 25 years. Nearly 60 international or multilateral organizations affiliated with Comecon (CMEA) alone now exist, to say nothing of a wide array of other international associations. The variations that exist in the individual membership activity of Communist states, given the wide variety of international organizations, serve in some instances to give express definition to the international personalities of lesser Communist states and even suggest relative independence or latitude of freedom from Soviet direction. Except for the GDR (East Germany), Mongolia, and North Korea, the membership profile of the USSR in U.N. organizations is the most Spartan. Even Bulgaria belongs to one more organization than does the Soviet Union, which still refuses to join the Food and Agricultural Organization (FAO), to which all other Communist states belong except for the GDR. East Germany, Mongolia, North Korea, and Bulgaria most closely approximate the membership profile of the USSR and its two stunted clones, the Ukraine and Belorussia.

Table 1   Memberships in International Organizations

| Country | Rank | U.N. Organizations | | Other | Total |
		1965	(1983)		
USSR	59.5	9	(10)	29	38
Poland	48.5	12	(12)	30	42
Czechoslovakia	57.5	11	(12)	28	39
Hungary	70.5	8	(13)	26	34
Bulgaria	77	9	(11)	24	33
Romania	55.5	11	(16)	29	40
Yugoslavia	27	15	(17)	35	50
Averages	56	11	(—)	29	40
GDR	119	0	(9)	5	5
Albania	115	8	(8)	9	17
Cuba	82.5	12	(14)	20	32
Mongolia	117.5	6	(9)	4	10
China	121.5	0	(15)	2	2
N. Korea	121.5	0	(9)	2	2
Vietnam	120	0	(15)	3	3
U.S.A.	10	16	(17)	51	67
France	1	16	(17)	91	107
TOTAL COUNTRIES	122	—	(—)	—	—
Mean	—	13	(—)	27	40
Median	—	19	(—)	24	37

Source: C. L. Taylor and M. C. Hudson, *World Handbook of Political and Social Indicators,* second edition (New Haven: Yale University Press, 1972); *The World Fact Book— 1983* (Washington, D.C.: Central Intelligence Agency, 1983).

As Table 1 demonstrates, membership activity in 17 important U.N. organizations has increased for all Communist states since 1965, but particularly for those states that were not members of the U.N. in 1965: the GDR, Vietnam, and the People's Republic of China. Along with North Korea, which remains a nonmember, their membership in affiliated organizations rose from 0 to 15 for China and Vietnam, 0 to 9 for the GDR and North Korea, and from 6 to 9 for Mongolia.

As would be expected, the independent and politically unaffiliated Communist state, Yugoslavia, exhibited the widest degree of membership in 1983, with membership in all 17 associations and agencies. Romania followed closely behind with membership in 16. Albania brought up the rear with an unchanging membership in only 8 organizations, among the lowest of all U.N. members. Of the more than 160 members of the U.N. (excepting the mini-states), the Soviet Union, Mongolia, the GDR, and North Korea now rank well below the average and median in membership activity. For the Soviet Union, this purely quantitative index is an inadequate indicator of its diplomatic personality, but for other Communist countries, membership activity is a fair register of their relative latitude of autonomy and choice of options. For example, Yugoslavia (17), Romania (16), China (15), Vietnam (15), and Cuba (14), the Communist states with the highest rate of membership activity, are also precisely those Communist states that exhibit greatest freedom from Soviet control and domination. Only Albania (8) perversely seeks to demonstrate its independence in the opposite direction.

Moving on to general diplomatic interaction, measured in terms of diplomats sent, diplomats received, and number of missions abroad, out of 119 countries listed, the Soviet Union ranked eleventh in 1963–64. The countries of Eastern Europe, again excluding Albania and East Germany, exhibited remarkably high levels of activity for small and medium states, ranging from a rank of 19.5 for Czechoslovakia and Yugoslavia to 39 for Romania. As measured against the United States, ranking first with 100 missions abroad, the Soviet Union had 65 missions abroad, whereas East European countries (with the exception of Albania and East Germany) ranged from 40 for Romania to 57 for Yugoslavia and Czechoslovakia; the mean and median for all 119 countries were 31 and 25, respectively. The aggregate average number of missions abroad for Eastern Europe (except for Albania and East Germany) was 50, giving it an average aggregate ranking of 27.

The aggregated data in Table 2 are somewhat dated and require qualification. The number of states in the international community has risen to nearly 160 at the time of writing from 119 two decades earlier. The GDR, North Korea, China, and Vietnam have shown an extraordinary increase in diplomatic activity during this period. The GDR, for example, which had only 16 missions abroad in 1963–64, by 1981 had established some form of diplomatic relations with 131 countries. The diplomatic missions of other Communist countries have also dramatically increased in numbers, especially in the Third World and particularly in Africa where more than 50 members of the U.N. are located. As a result the rank order of most East European countries has probably risen appreciably.

The relatively wide disparity in activity between institutional membership and bilateral diplomatic contacts suggests that Moscow feels less threatened by bilateral diplomatic activity than by memberships in international organizations, and hence is more tolerant of the former than the latter. Membership in organizations involves affiliation, organizational commitment, and partial identification with noncommunist states, which may be employed as constituency support against the demands of Moscow, whereas bilateral diplomatic contact appears to be less threatening to Soviet influence, which has higher priority than

Table 2 Diplomatic Representation, 1963–64

Country	Rank	Diplomats Sent	Diplomats Received	Missions Abroad
USSR	11	1,345	732	65
Poland	21.5	386	301	55
Czechoslovakia	19.5	422	321	57
Hungary	35.5	264	209	42
Bulgaria	26.5	247	209	47
Romania	39	360	228	40
Yugoslavia	19.5	280	324	57
Average	27	327	265	50
GDR	83.5	153	186	16
Albania	85.5	56	59	15
Cuba	38	216	201	41
Mongolia	94	43	—	11
China	40.5	405	389	38
N. Korea	78	111	—	18
N. Vietnam	81	81	—	17
U.S.A.	1	2,782	1,418	100
TOTAL COUNTRIES	119	—	—	—
Mean		196	224	31
Median		102	172	25

Source: C. L. Taylor and M. C. Hudson, *World Handbook of Political and Social Indicators,* second edition (New Haven: Yale University Press, 1972).

any commitment that an individual East European state may have with another state. The Soviet Union is wary of any organizational commitments by its East European clients that might collide with commitments to Communist organizations or to the Soviet Union itself.

After 1956, Soviet and East European activity in the United Nations and in U.N.-associated organizations increased, and the spectrum of membership for the two, while similar, is by no means identical. Thus, as of 1983, of the major U.N.-affiliated organizations, the Soviet Union still did not belong to the FAO, whereas all of the East European states except Albania belonged; the USSR did not belong to GATT (General Agreement on Tariffs and Trade), whereas Czechoslovakia, Romania, Poland, Hungary, and Yugoslavia belonged. The financial and developmental organizations are still off limits to the Soviet Union and other East European states. Only Romania and Yugoslavia belong to the World Bank and the IFC. Romania and Hungary recently joined the Monetary Fund and along with Yugoslavia are the only East European states affiliated with that organization. Ironically, both Vietnam and China have joined all of the financial and developmental agencies, whereas North Korea and Cuba adhere to the general Soviet and East European profile on this score.

The character of the relationship between Eastern Europe and the Soviet Union inevitably raises the question of why a group of small East European states is so actively involved in the world at large. There are a number of loose hypotheses and theories purporting to explain the collective effort of the Communist states in world affairs, whether conceived globally or restricted to a particular region, such as Africa. There is first the "Soviet direction, coordination, or subordination theory" that emphasizes that East European international activity is little more than an adjunct of Soviet global behavior and that individual states are assigned missions and roles that will supplement or enhance Soviet interests. Related to this idea is the "division of labor hypothesis," based not so much on Soviet direction or coordination, but rather the product of each Communist state simply pursuing its own interests by performing those functions and services in which it specializes or excels. Thus, the first theory suggests that the primary inspiration is the Soviet Union and the priority of its interests, with the interests of the individual allied state being served only incidentally or secondarily. The second theory suggests the opposite, that the interests of the individual East European state are primary and Soviet interests are served only incidentally or coincidentally.

Then there is the "competitive theory," which also suggests a degree of autonomous and spontaneous action, whereby individual European states are involved in competition with one another to curry favor or support from Moscow or are involved in competition with states outside the Communist orbit. The behavior of East Germany fits in with this theory very well, but the explanatory power of the theory is almost entirely restricted to East Germany. A related theory, with more validity, can be called the "visibility" or "leverage" theory, which suggests that East European international activity is viewed as a means to gain a separate identity and visibility through increased contacts with the outside world, to build international constituency support, and hence to gain leverage in relations with the Soviet Union while ostensibly behaving in accordance with its desires.

The uneven and idiosyncratic behavior of East European states in the international community would seem to militate against an integrated theory of any kind. Each of the theories, of course, can serve to explain behavior on an *ad hoc* basis and indeed it would appear that East European international behavior is so disparate and deficient in regularity that generalizations would be inappropriate. Through methodological prestidigitation, theories and hypotheses can be metamorphosed into more mundane "explanations," applied eclectically and on an *ad hoc* basis. While less satisfying conceptually, they may nevertheless result in more appropriate analyses.

One can almost immediately discern some important behavioral differences among East European states that are explicable individually rather than within a pretentious paradigm. Thus, the activities of East Germany, Czechoslovakia, and Bulgaria resemble very much the pattern of orchestrated behavior that would strongly suggest Soviet direction, coordination, and subordination, as well as a rationally determined division of labor. These three countries also happen to be among the most subservient and obsequious in their relationships with Moscow for a variety of reasons. One knowledgeable East German has indeed stated that "Soviet bloc policy in the Third World, especially Africa, is coordinated in terms of general objectives through the foreign ministries of respective countries." According to this source, neither the Warsaw Treaty Organization nor Comecon is employed as a vehicle of coordination, except on very specific issues involving arms transfers or military assistance likely to affect the capabilities of the Warsaw Alliance. Similarly, if economic and technical assistance interferes with the coordinated planning objectives of Comecon, then the latter can also be involved. Furthermore, this source acknowledged that in fact a sort of division of labor does exist, which can be based on function, region, or time frame, or a combination thereof. Whether the coordination was imposed or the product of collaboration, the source did not elaborate upon.

On the other hand, certain East European states, notably Poland and to a lesser extent Hungary, are conspicuous by their virtual absence from Third World activities, while others, namely Romania and Yugoslavia, are with equal obviousness pursuing their own interests and are highly active in the Third World, but their activities appear not to be coordinated with those of Moscow and other East European states. Thus, we have at least three types of regularity in behavior:

1. Activity coordinated with Moscow's policies and interests (GDR, Czechoslovakia, Bulgaria);
2. Activity independent of Soviet policy and behavior (Romania, Yugoslavia);
3. Relative abstention from assistance activities in the Third World (Poland, Hungary).

It is nevertheless true that historically the global activity of the East European states first occurred because they were involved and manipulated by the Soviet Union in its global concerns. Individual states were used by Moscow as foils or as proxies in various activities.

For example, Czechoslovakia funneled arms first to Israel and then to Egypt; Bulgaria represented the Soviet position in various international bodies and conferences. Above and beyond the Soviet connection, adherence to Marxism-Leninism and the activity of East European Communist parties and leaders in the world Communist movement conditioned and socialized East European Communists to think "internationally" and to behave globally once they came to power. Soviet writers, for example, even cite the world Communist movement as a sort of socialization vehicle, conditioning the behavior of Communist states: "As a rule, before a given country becomes socialist, its Marxist-Leninist party already has a system of stable ties with fraternal parties in other countries, established in the course of its activity in the world Communist movement."[5]

As Communist states become members of the general interstate community, they retain their membership in the world Communist movement, the second general international environment in which they function. In this environment, acting out their roles as Communist parties rather than as states, they interact with other Communist parties, ruling and nonruling, the latter considered to be leaders of future Communist states. With the development of Titoism, Maoism, and then Eurocommunism, the world Communist movement has become a more doctrinally flexible environment, to the point where it can hardly be called a "movement" at all. More latitude for intensive identity-building is permissible for individual East European Communist parties in this environment because of the fragmentation or decentralization of the world Communist movement. Various groupings, including polarized aggregations, exist within this environment, whose outer parameters become more flexible, as intramovement groupings become tighter.

Aside from their identity as members of the general interstate system and the world Communist movement, Eastern Europe, as a whole or as individual states, belongs to a number of subsystems that are subordinate to either the general interstate system or the world Communist movement, or both.

Subsystems within the international Communist environments are as follows:

1. *The World Socialist System,* made up of the 14 self-identified Marxist-Leninist states, irrespective of mutual acceptance.
2. *The Socialist Community,* consisting of all Marxist-Leninist states except Albania, China, and possibly Yugoslavia.
3. *The Warsaw Treaty Organization,* a multilateral military alliance, ostensibly open to all European states, but in fact including only

the USSR and all East European states except Yugoslavia and
Albania.
   4. *The Council for Mutual Economic Assistance (CMEA),* an economic organization, purportedly aimed at "socialist integration"
and the establishment of an "international socialist division of
labor." All East European states, including Yugoslavia (as an "associate" member) but excluding Albania, belong, as do Mongolia,
Vietnam, and Cuba.

Subsystems within the general international environment to which
all or some East European states belong are the following:

   1. *Eastern Europe,* as a geographical-political region, which by
definition includes all East European Communist states.
   2. *Europe,* a cultural-civilization-racial-geographical concept, with
which East European states identify more and more, as Asian
Communist states identify more with the Third World and with
underdeveloped countries. As East European socioeconomic indicators approach those of Western Europe, the gap between East
and West Europe will become narrower and the gap between
Europe and Asian Communist states will broaden. The European
identity of the East European states, including the USSR, becomes increasingly more emphatic. The Helsinki Conference on
European Security, for example, was defined as a European conference, in which all East European states participated as separate members and not as part of a bloc. Romania and Yugoslavia,
for example, took positions at this conference substantially at
variance with the USSR.
   3. *The Third World,* made up primarily of the underdeveloped countries of Asia, Africa, and Latin America, but with which Yugoslavia and Romania have established special links, making them
quasi-members.
   4. *The Non-Aligned World,* closely approximating the above but
defined in terms of position between the two contending poles.
Marshal Tito and Yugoslavia have been founders and leading
members. Romania has also sought to affiliate itself with this
grouping, although Romania is aligned as a member of the Warsaw Pact. Romania, however, has been a fractious and dissident
member.
   5. *The Group of 77 (G-77),* a loosely organized Third World economic grouping.

Thus, it is clear that East European countries, far from behaving uniformly, belong to a number of groupings, some of them overlapping in membership. Even within the narrower Soviet bloc groupings (WTO and CMEA), some variations in behavior persist. Romania, for example, remains on excellent terms with Beijing, which has asserted that the other East European countries, except Yugoslavia and Albania, have reverted to being Soviet puppet states. Romania, furthermore, maintains friendly relations with Israel, departs from Soviet voting patterns in international organizations and conferences, and behaves as a maverick in a number of ways.

But Eastern Europe's role in the international community is not simply linked to the various groupings to which it belongs or the environments within which it operates. In many ways, Eastern Europe constitutes a cultural bridge between the Soviet Union and Western Europe, since some East European states and nations (Poles, Czechs, Slovenes, Croats, Hungarians, and East Germans) are more "western" than "eastern" in culture, tradition, and orientation. Eurocommunism may serve to reinforce the spiritual link between Western and Eastern Europe but within a Communist environment, just as the Helsinki movement has had the same effect outside the world of Communist states and powers.

The more identities and roles the countries of Eastern Europe develop and the more international environments they function within, the more diluted their identity as Communist states becomes and the more they tend to identify themselves as *European* and *developed* Communist states. These identities and roles are fostered by the East European economic, technical, and military assistance programs that are found in every continent. East European countries are involved in these programs in their individual capacities as developed states, as parts of international organizations, or as a function of their association with the Soviet Union. Commercial links with Western Europe, the United States, and Third World countries have steadily increased. Thousands of professional citizens of East European countries have experienced travel and work abroad in a diverse spectrum of countries. And, frequently, underdeveloped countries find it much easier to deal with small, less threatening developed Communist states than with the Soviet Union. While Moscow may view this as providing the USSR with surrogate access to areas where it might be unwelcome, it is also obvious that these links serve to strengthen the independent contacts of East European states with the outside world.

Important measures of Eastern Europe's status within the international community are the range and intensity of its associations and interactions with states in both Communist and noncommunist subgroups. Generally speaking, the more intense a country's identification with Communist subgroups and organizations and the more extensive its participation in such groups, the less likely it is to identify with or participate in noncommunist interstate groupings and organizations. In other words, the more integrated an Eastern European state is in Communist groupings, the less likely it is to function as an independent actor in the general international community. With respect to memberships and affiliations, Table 3 provides data that tend to support this observation. The table clearly illustrates the relative behavioral uniformity of five East European states (Poland, Czechoslovakia, German Democratic Republic, Hungary, Bulgaria), which (with minor exceptions) has associational profiles virtually identical to that of the Soviet Union. At the same time, the table delineates variances from Soviet behavior and shows the correspondence between the extent of affiliations with Communist organizations and the degree of association with noncommunist organizations. The distinction between the two in this analysis is simple: Communist organizations are those to which only Communist states belong, whereas noncommunist organizations are those to which both Communist and noncommunist states belong.

Although the term Eastern Europe is an aggregate category and thus conceals important variations and nuances in the individual international profiles of East European states, it is nevertheless true that individual East European states tend to be perceived in terms of stereotypes and hence as "typical" of Eastern Europe as a whole. This is particularly true of those East European states whose associational profiles coincide with the Soviet profile and can thus be defined plausibly as part of a "Soviet bloc." But, correspondingly, this is increasingly less true of Albania, Romania, and Yugoslavia, whose idiosyncratic international behavioral patterns are perceived as those of separate states in Eastern Europe rather than as part of "Eastern Europe." Romania's profile differs less significantly than that of Yugoslavia, whose noncommunist affiliations are more extensive and diverse and whose Communist affiliations are less intensive and less extensive. Albania's deviance is marked by severely limited affiliations in both Communist and noncommunist organizations.

At least five East European states can be defined as being essentially part of a "Soviet bloc," acting as such within both the Communist and general interstate environment. Even in terms of per capita GNP in 1981, the "Soviet bloc" exhibited a general uniformity, which distinguished it sharply from non-European Communist states and even from Albania and Yugoslavia. Of the eight Communist states in Eastern Europe, only Yugoslavia and Romania have successfully affiliated or identified themselves with noncommunist interstate groups, most notably the Third World, the Group of 77, and the nonaligned group, a behavioral trait shared with the non-European Communist states. In some interesting respects, the associational profiles of Romania and Yugoslavia correspond closely to those of Vietnam and China and share with North Korea and Cuba some points of common departure from the Soviet and East European norm. Thus all of the above states but China belong to the Group of 77; all claim some affiliation with the Third World and the nonaligned group of states. Romania, Yugoslavia, Vietnam, and China belong to the U.N. financial and developmental agencies (Romania does not belong to the IDA). Other interesting associational parallels are GATT membership (Hungary, Romania, Poland, Czechoslovakia, Yugoslavia, and Cuba) and Monetary Fund affiliation (Hungary, Romania, Yugoslavia, China, and Vietnam.) It is mainly because of the idiosyncratic behavior of Albania, Yugoslavia, and Romania in the international community that Eastern Europe is increasingly perceived even by the Third World as a collection of individual state-personalities rather than simply as a gray mass attached to Moscow. Furthermore, the unsuccessful attempts by Hungary, Poland, and Czechoslovakia to act independently of the Soviet Union can also be more clearly perceived as part of a single behavioral continuum, of which the successful assertion of autonomy in foreign affairs by Yugoslavia, Albania, and Romania is an integral part.

It is apparent that the differential patterns of foreign policy behavior in Eastern Europe reflect in some degree the basic geocultural cleavage of Eastern Europe into northern and southern tiers, or, more precisely, a north-central group and a southeastern group. Not only in behavioral patterns, but in terms of other indices as well, this distinction persists. There is even a vague and episodic movement in the direction of concerted action by Albania, Romania, and Yugoslavia in their relationship with Moscow, which waxes and wanes in accordance with perceptions of Soviet threats to intervene.

Bulgaria's behavioral pattern, however, interferes with what might otherwise be a tidy and precise demarcation between a subdued northern tier and a defiant southern tier in Eastern Europe. Bulgaria, the prototypical Balkan state, is Moscow's most loyal, faithful, and probably only voluntary client state in Eastern Europe, and apparently has no ambition to behave independently in foreign policy, a trait that distinguishes it from *all* other states in Eastern Europe where neither a *successful* nor an *unsuccessful* act of defiance has taken place.

Aside from membership and affiliation with interstate groups within the international community, other measurable indices of Eastern Europe's status and visibility in the international community are: (1) development of trade and commerce with different parts of the world; (2) participation in economic and financial assistance programs;

Table 3 Membership and Affiliation of Communist States in Interstate Organizations and Groupings[a]

Country	World Communist Environment										General Interstate Environment — U.N. and Affiliated Agencies																		Other Interstate Groupings					GNP Per Capita 1981
	WCM	WSS	Socialist Community	WTO	CMEA	EJINR	IBEC	IIB	USSR ALLIANCE	Other Alliance	United Nations	IFAD	IAEA	ILO	FAO	UNESCO	WHO	BANK	IFC	IDA	FUND	ICAO	UPU	ITU	WMO	IMCO	GATT	ICJ	Third world	Nonaligned States	G-77	Eastern Europe	Helsinki Europe	
USSR	X	X	X	X	X	X	X	X	—	X	X	—	X	X	—	X	X	—	—	—	—	X	X	X	X	X	—	X	—	—	—	X	X	$5,930
Ukraine	X	X	X	NR*	NR*	NR*	NR*	NR*	NR*	NR*	X	—	X	X	—	X	X	—	—	—	—	—	X	X	X	—	—	X	—	—	—	NR	—	—
Belorussia	X	X	X	NR*	NR*	NR*	NR*	NR*	NR*	NR*	X	—	X	X	—	X	X	—	—	—	—	—	X	X	X	—	—	X	—	—	—	NR	—	—
Poland	X	X	X	X	X	X	X	X	X	X	X	—	X	X	X	X	X	—	—	—	—	X	X	X	X	X	X	X	—	—	—	X	X	4,960
Czechoslovakia	X	X	X	X	X	X	X	X	X	X	X	—	X	X	X	X	X	—	—	—	—	X	X	X	X	X	X	X	—	—	—	X	X	8,970
GDR	X	X	X	X	X	X	X	X	X	X	X	—	X	X	—	X	X	—	—	—	—	—	X	X	X	X	—	X	—	—	—	X	X	9,750
Hungary	X	X	X	X	X	X	X	X	X	X	X	—	X	X	X	X	X	—	—	—	X	X	X	X	X	X	X	—	—	—	—	X	X	5,950
Bulgaria	X	X	X	X	X	X	X	X	X	X	X	—	X	X	—	X	X	—	—	—	—	X	X	X	X	X	—	X	—	—	—	X	X	3,820
Romania**	X	X	X	X	X	X	X	X	X	e	X	X	X	X	X	X	X	X	X	—	X	X	X	X	X	X	X	X	(X)	—	—	X	X	4,230
Yugoslavia	X	X	—	—	g	—	—	—	e	h	X	X	X	X	X	X	X	X	X	X	X	X	X	X	X	X	X	X	X	X	X	X	X	3,300
Albania	X	X	—	f	—	—	—	—	—	—	X	—	X	X	—	X	X	—	—	—	—	—	X	X	X	X	—	X	X	—	X	—	—	830[b]
Mongolia	X	X	X	—	X	X	—	—	X	X	X	X	X	—	X	X	X	—	—	—	—	—	X	X	X	—	—	X	(X)	—	—	—	—	667[c]
China	X	X	—	—	—	—	—	—	—	X	X	X	—	X	X	X	X	X	X	X	X	X	X	X	X	X	—	X	(X)	—	—	—	—	347
North Korea	X	X	—	—	—	X	—	—	X	—	—	—	X	X	X	X	X	—	—	—	—	X	X	X	X	—	—	X	(X)	?	X	—	—	786
Vietnam[b]	X	X	X	—	X	X	—	—	X	X	X	X	X	—	X	X	X	X	X	X	X	X	X	X	X	—	—	X	(X)	X	X	—	—	153
Cuba	X	X	X	—	X	X	—	—	X	—	X	X	X	X	X	X	X	—	—	—	—	X	X	X	X	X	X	X	X	X	X	—	—	1,372

NR = not recognized. * "Not Recognized as Separate Actors."

Notes:

[a] Data for U.N. as of 1982
[b] 1979
[c] 1976
[d] Associate member since 1964
[e] Nullified, 1949
[f] Withdrew, 1968
[g] Ceased participation in 1968
[h] Expired or nullified
[i] Withdrew 1966
[j] Observer status since June 1973
NR   Not recognized as separate actor
** Romania's participation in Communist organizations is substantially less intense than that of other East European states.

Legend

WCM: World Communist Movement
WSS: World Socialist System
WTO: Warsaw Treaty Organization
CMEA: Council of Mutual Economic Assistance
EJINR: Eastern Joint Institute of Nuclear Research
IBEC: International Bank of Economic Cooperation
IIB: International Investment Bank
IFAD: International Fund for Agricultural Development
IAEA: International Atomic Energy Association
ILO: International Labor Organization
FAO: Food and Agricultural Organization
UNESCO: U.N. Educational, Scientific, and Cultural Organization

WHO: World Health Organization
BANK: International Bank for Reconstruction and Development
IFC: International Finance Corporation
IDA: International Development Association
FUND: International Monetary Fund
ICAO: International Civil Aviation Organization
UPU: Universal Postal Union
ITU: International Telecommunications Union
WMO: World Meteorological Organization
IMCO: Inter-Governmental Maritime Consultative Organization
GATT: General Agreement on Tariffs and Trade
ICJ: International Court of Justice

Sources: *Treaties and Alliances of the World* (New York: Scribners, 1974), for data on U.N. memberships and affiliations. *The World Fact Book—1983* (Washington, D.C., 1983)

Table 4   Direction of East European Trade, 1960–81
(Millions of U.S. Dollars)

	Total Trade	Communist Countries					Noncommunist Countries		
		Total	USSR	Eastern Europe	Far East[a]	Other[b]	Total	Developed Countries	Less Developed Countries
1960									
Exports	7,625	5,525	2,819	2,101	398	208	2,100	1,523	578
Imports	7,761	5,556	2,955	2,084	351	166	2,206	1,712	495
1970									
Exports	18,158	12,545	6,610	4,953	331	647	5,613	4,134	1,478
Imports	18,522	12,500	6,803	4,909	232	556	6,021	4,835	1,186
1975									
Exports	45,213	30,116	15,565	12,211	—	2,344	15,097	10,312	4,785
Imports	51,229	30,550	16,304	12,269	—	2,024	20,679	17,132	3,547
1980									
Exports	86,169	54,899	29,940	20,523	—	4,436	31,370	22,611	8,659
Imports	91,190	56,046	32,254	20,433	—	3,359	35,144	26,171	8,973
1981									
Exports	83,947	53,119	29,609	18,727	—	4,783	30,825	20,329	10,499
Imports	86,955	55,513	33,191	13,387	—	3,935	31,442	23,539	7,903

[a] Includes data for China, North Korea, and Vietnam.
[b] Includes data for Albania, Cuba, Mongolia, and Yugoslavia, and for China, North Korea, and Vietnam after 1970
Source: *Handbook of Economic Statistics, 1982* (Washington, D.C., 1982).

(3) participation in military assistance programs; and (4) participation in technical and academic assistance programs.

It should be emphasized that in measuring Eastern Europe's participation in the activities mentioned above, no attempt will be made to disaggregate the data by individual countries. The aggregate data for Eastern Europe conceal wide variations in individual state behavior, and, in some instances, "Eastern Europe" may actually represent the activity of only one or two countries for a particular year or aid given to a particular region. Furthermore, not all East European countries have the same capacity or incentive to become involved in international activity, although it should be noted that all East European states are involved to some degree in all the activities described. The behavioral profile of Eastern Europe will be compared to that of the Soviet Union and China in order to place it within the behavioral context of the Communist world as a whole.

In the tables devised to measure East European international activity, the aggregate data for Eastern Europe include only Poland, Czechoslovakia, East Germany, Hungary, Bulgaria, and Romania, unless otherwise noted.

International Trade and Commerce

Table 4 provides data for the direction of trade, in terms of both exports and imports for five specific years during the period 1960–81.

The first observation to be made is that the total volume of exports and imports has increased steadily over the years, as measured in dollars. Between 1960 and 1981 imports rose over 13-fold, while exports increased more than 12-fold. As the volume of trade grew, the direction of East European trade shifted away from the Communist world, both developed and underdeveloped. In 1960, Eastern Europe's international trade could be described as essentially parochial, but less so than during the period before 1956. More than 70 percent of its small volume of trade was with the Soviet Union and within Eastern Europe, and only 7.6 percent was with the less-developed countries. By 1981, the Communist share of East European trade had dropped to 63 percent for exports and 64 percent for imports, while exports and imports to the less-developed countries had risen to 10.1 and 9.7 percent, respectively. Trade with the developed countries (United States, Western Europe, Japan) also increased at the expense of the Communist sector. It should be noted that variations in dollars are not always congruent with variations in volume, especially with reference to commodities like oil, whose world market price increased substantially. The expanded commerce of Eastern Europe has not been an unmixed blessing, since some countries have developed serious trade imbalances and have accumulated huge hard-currency debts. These imbalances and debts, in turn, have had a deleterious impact on the consumer and agricultural sectors of the domestic economy, most notably in Poland, but also in Romania and Czechoslovakia.[6]

Economic Assistance

For a part of the world that traditionally kept itself uninvolved in affairs beyond those of Europe, Eastern Europe has contributed more than a modest share of total Communist economic assistance to the less-developed countries, particularly when it is noted that both the Soviet Union and China have global pretensions, whereas Eastern Europe does not. What proportion of the East European involvement is simply an adjunct to Soviet policy (whereby the USSR reaps the political benefit and Eastern Europe pays the economic cost) and what share represents a genuine East European involvement designed to lessen its isolation, and hence vulnerability and dependence upon the USSR, is difficult to calculate. Suffice it to say that both processes are involved and, generally speaking, the greater the visibility of East European states in the international community, the greater the potential leverage they may have in their relations with the USSR.

Table 5 provides comparative data regarding the distribution of Communist economic assistance to major regions of the world in the form of credits and grants during the period 1954–81. Of the total amount extended during this period, Eastern Europe's contribution was 9.830

Table 5 Communist Economic Assistance to Less-developed Countries, 1954–81
(Millions of U.S. Dollars)

	1972		1975		1980		1981		1954–81	
	USSR	Eastern Europe	USSR	Eastern Europe	USSR	Eastern Europe	USSR	Eastern Europe	USSR	Eastern Europe
TOTAL	655	925	1,955	545	2,070	1,330	455	665	22,355	11,885
Middle East					—	675	55	—	7,925	4,495
North Africa					315	—	—	115	—	—
Sub-Saharan Africa					310	280	125	—	—	—
East Asia					—	40	—	—	260	665
Latin America					250	195	170	50	1,420	2,135
South Asia					1,195	135	100	250	6,625	1,370
OTHER					—	—	—	250	—	250

Source: *Soviet and East European Aid to the Third World, 1981* (Washington, D.C., 1983).

Table 6 Communist Military Agreements and Arms Deliveries to the Third World,
1955–81
(Millions of U.S. Dollars)

	Agreements Concluded				Equipment Delivered			
Year	Total	USSR	Eastern Europe	China	Total	USSR	Eastern Europe	China
TOTAL	74,860	67,400	6,315	1,145	53,700	48,075	4,705	920
1955–79	52,770	47,340	4,285	1,145	39,665	35,340	3,405	920
1980	14,000	14,000	—	—	6,815	6,290	525	—
1981	8,090	6,060	2,030	—	7,220	6,445	775	—

Sources: *Communist Aid Activities . . . 1954–79* and *Soviet and East European Aid . . .
1981.*

billion dollars or 29.8 percent of the total, which was more than half of
the Soviet share and nearly double that of the Chinese. Although East
European assistance went to some 22 countries in Africa, 5 in East
Asia, 15 in Latin America, 10 in the Middle East, and 6 in South Asia,
i.e., nearly 60 countries, the assistance was highly uneven from one
year to the next. To illustrate this unevenness, in 1974, one third of all
aid went to Africa, and Romania alone accounted for 54 percent of all
East European aid for that year. Romania's stepped-up activity in economic assistance is also a good illustration of East European aid that is
not a conscious adjunct of Soviet policy but represents individual
Romanian initiative in pursuit of its own economic and political interests.

As Table 5 demonstrates, over the entire period, the Middle East,
North Africa, and South Asia have received the greatest amount of
assistance from Moscow and Eastern Europe, whereas Africa has been
the principal recipient of Chinese aid. Again, it must be emphasized
that these aggregate figures conceal a highly uneven distribution in
numbers of countries receiving assistance and amounts received, as
well as in numbers of East European countries granting aid and the
amounts granted.

Military Assistance

Military assistance to the less-developed countries can be measured
in three dimensions: (a) arms agreements and exports; (b) military
assistance personnel stationed abroad; (c) military personnel from
abroad being trained. East European military assistance, when compared to economic assistance, is comparatively modest. Table 6 shows
that of the nearly 54 billion dollars of Communist arms exports to less-
developed countries during the period 1955–81, more than 89 percent
was delivered by the USSR, with only 8.8 percent coming from East-

Table 7 Communist Military Personnel in the Third World
(thousands)

	1965	1970	1975	1979	1981
TOTAL	3,730	10,635	9,425	16,240	57,380
USSR and					
Eastern Europe	3,635	10,125	8,220	15,865	18,205
North Africa	605	1,020	1,005	2,835	4,600
Sub-Saharan Africa	400	965	1,580	3,990	5,300
East Asia	520	0	0	0	0
Latin America	0	0	35	110	225
Middle East	1,500	7,820	4,900	4,780	5,925
South Asia	610	320	700	4,150	2,155
China	95	510	1,205	375	—
Sub-Saharan Africa	70	410	1,165	305	—
East Asia	25	0	0	0	—
Middle East	0	75	0	0	—
South Asia	0	25	40	70	—
Cuba				34,315	39,175
North Africa				15	50
Sub-Saharan Africa				33,045	36,910
Latin America				255	1,715
Middle East				1,000	500

Sources: *Communist Aid Activities . . . 1954–79* and *Soviet and East European Aid . . . 1981.*

ern Europe. China's increment was a bare 2 percent. Nearly 90 percent of arms assistance went to Middle Eastern countries in recent years. Again, the principal beneficiaries, donors, and amounts varied considerably over the entire period.

In 1981, of 57,380 military specialists from Communist countries stationed abroad in 34 less-developed countries, 16,280 were from the Soviet Union, 1,925 from Eastern Europe, and 39,175 were from Cuba. The East European contingent probably corresponded approximately to Eastern Europe's share of arms exports, i.e., about 10 percent. The distribution of military technicians abroad is similar to the distribution of arms exports since (with the exception of Cuban personnel) Soviet and East European military personnel are engaged principally in the training of indigenous personnel in the use, assembly, and maintenance of military equipment. Of the more than 39,000 Cubans abroad in 1981, most were concentrated in Ethiopia and Angola, and the Cuban contingent accounted for over 80 percent of the more than 6-fold increase in Communist military personnel abroad from 9,425 in 1975 to 57,380 in 1981 (Table 7).

Military personnel from the less-developed countries are to be found in all East European countries, but again in proportions more modest

Table 8 Military Personnel from Less-developed Countries
Trained in Communist Countries, 1955–81

	Total	USSR	Eastern Europe	China
TOTAL	55,080	45,585	6,345	3,150
Middle East	18,875	16,370	2,505	—
North Africa	4,150	3,580	555	15
Sub-Saharan Africa	14,750	10,840	1,205	2,705
Latin America	780	780	—	—
East Asia	9,300	7,590	1,710	—
South Asia	7,225	6,425	370	430

Sources: *Communist Aid Activities . . . 1954–79* and *Soviet and East European Aid . . . 1981.*

than East European economic assistance. During the period 1955–81, military personnel came from 19 African countries, 7 Middle Eastern, 5 South Asian, and 2 East Asian countries. Of the 55,000 military personnel being trained from the less-developed countries over more than a two-decade period, Eastern Europe was host to little more than 11 percent while the Soviet Union trained nearly 85 percent of the total (Table 8).

Economic and Academic Personnel

The East European presence in the less-developed countries is most effectively represented by economic assistance personnel stationed abroad. The East European share of all Communist economic technicians in the less-developed countries is truly extraordinary when compared to the Soviet and Chinese effort. The larger number of East European states and the fact that some of them are more highly developed and modernized than the Soviet Union enables the East European states to diversify and specialize in their assistance programs. The total of Communist technicians in the less-developed countries during the period 1970–75 was 244,960, of whom 47,200 (17.4 percent) were from Eastern Europe, 78,390 (32 percent) from the Soviet Union, and 118,950 (48.6 percent) were Chinese. The Chinese effort was concentrated in East Africa and included workers as well as "technicians."

The Chinese presence declined significantly in 1976 to 20,465 whereas the East European contingent nearly doubled to 26,000 and accounted for more than 37 percent of Communist economic technicians for that year, and an even more impressive 57.3 percent of the combined Soviet and East European contingent, stationed in more than 40 countries. Table 9 provides comparative data for the distribution of Communist economic assistance personnel for selected years,

Table 9 Communist Economic-Technical Personnel
in Less-developed Countries, 1960–81

	1960	1965	1970	1975	1979	1970–76	1981
TOTAL	6,285	17,720	23,930	58,330	93,690	244,960	118,760[a]
USSR	4,245	9,285	10,645	17,975	32,635	78,390	95,635
North Africa	0	885	2,420	3,110	7,450		45,870
Sub-Saharan Africa	300	1,735	1,585	2,995	5,640		14,730
East Asia	180	395	150	25	35		60
Latin America	5	5	30	355	340		930
Middle East	1,470	3,705	3,935	8,400	13,785		27,150
South Asia	2,290	2,560	2,525	3,090	5,385		6,795
Eastern Europe	1,080	4,070	5,215	14,870	48,195	47,620	
North Africa	0	1,755	2,285	9,915	30,395		
Sub-Saharan Africa	190	765	755	1,235	4,800		
East Asia	90	115	65	30	55		
Latin America	65	70	150	275	255		
Middle East	560	800	1,295	3,025	12,135		
South Asia	175	565	665	390	560		
China	960	4,365	8,070	25,485	12,860	118,950[b]	
North Africa	0	80	465	595	930		
Sub-Saharan Africa	55	2,535	6,505	22,625	9,325		
East Asia	190	425	100	35	160		
Europe	0	0	0	70	125		
Latin America	0	0	0	70	155		
Middle East	700	435	745	1,310	1,135		
South Asia	15	890	255	780	1,030		
Cuba							23,075
North Africa							5,250
Sub-Saharan Africa							9,435
East Asia							760
Latin America							4,640
Middle East							3,650
South Asia							100

[a] Includes Eastern Europe.
[b] Includes Chinese laborers on construction projects.
Sources: *Communist Aid Activities . . . 1954–79* and *Soviet and East European Aid . . .
1981.*

1960–81, as well as overall totals for the period, 1970–76. This table
shows the steady increase of the East European contingent to nearly 40
percent of the total in 1976. Again, it should be emphasized that aggregate data conceal the unevenness of participation and distribution by
donor, recipient, and region. For example, in 1976, some 10,000 East
European economic technicians were in Libya alone, drawn from no
fewer than five countries (Poland, Hungary, Bulgaria, Czechoslovakia,
and East Germany).

By 1981, the total Soviet and East European contingent of economic personnel had reached the unprecedented number of 96,000, operating in 75 countries. Meanwhile, Chinese personnel had virtually disappeared with the completion of China's major construction projects. More than half of the Soviet-East European technicians were from Eastern Europe. Some 23,000 Cuban personnel worked alongside other Soviet bloc personnel. Two-thirds of the Soviet and East European technicians were working in Arab and other countries that pay in hard currency for these services. In particular, this activity has been financially lucrative for East European countries.

It appears from the data that Eastern Europe is much more comfortable and has better capability in providing economic assistance than military assistance, given the dramatic difference in absolute and relative levels of assistance between the two areas. Of course, the data could be interpreted to suggest a rational division of international labor, with the Soviet Union carrying the military assistance burden and Eastern Europe assuming a larger share of the economic assistance effort. A detailed analysis of the East European economic assistance programs, however, would show that many of the projects are of direct economic benefit to the East European countries involved, with the political benefit being a spillover or side-effect, rather than the main incentive. This is true not only of Romanian programs, but of other East European countries' programs as well.

For the past two decades, the Soviet Union and Eastern Europe have conducted an ambitious academic assistance program for Third World countries. During the period 1955–79, nearly 120,000 students from less-developed countries were reached by these programs. By the end of 1976, some 48,500 students had returned from the Soviet Union and Eastern Europe, about one-third of them from the countries of Eastern Europe. In the same year, over 36,000 students were still studying in the Soviet Union and Eastern Europe, with the East European share double that of the previous three years. Table 10 shows that the number of students departing for the Soviet Union and Eastern Europe steadily increased from 1965 to 1981.

Approximately 72,000 students from the Third World were enrolled in Soviet and East European universities at the end of 1981, with nearly one-half in Eastern Europe. Africa provided the largest contingent (about 50 percent). Students from socialist-oriented countries were favored, with more than one-third drawn from these states. Most academic training is free of charge and students are provided with full subsistence, including transportation. The East European proportion has been increasing, with some 5,800 going to Eastern Europe and 8,000 to the USSR in 1979.

Table 10   Academic Students From the Third World
in Communist Countries, 1965–81
(thousands)

	1965	1970	1975	1979	1981*
TOTAL	15,915	21,415	28,435	55,345	72,090
USSR	10,435	12,695	17,920	30,970	72,090
North Africa	170	610	1,555	1,825	4,485
Sub-Saharan Africa	4,895	6,260	8,040	12,865	30,320
East Asia	1,250	270	220	25	15
Latin America	935	1,640	2,190	2,860	6,800
Middle East	2,125	2,790	3,615	6,760	4,500
South Asia	1,060	1,125	2,300	6,635	11,820
Eastern Europe	5,025	8,720	10,410	24,025	
North Africa	325	680	1,040	1,605	
Sub-Saharan Africa	2,475	3,445	4,230	10,795	
East Asia	720	375	115	10	
Europe	0	0	0	10	
Latin America	305	780	890	2,150	
Middle East	955	2,985	3,410	6,405	
South Asia	245	455	725	3,050	
China	455	0	108	350	
North Africa	15	0	0	35	
Sub-Saharan Africa	260	0	70	205	
East Asia	75	0	0	0	
Europe	0	0	0	5	
Latin America	0	0	10	0	
Middle East	5	0	15	10	
South Asia	100	0	10	95	

*Data for 1981 combine Soviet and East European figures.
Sources: *Communist Aid . . . 1979* and *Soviet and East European Aid . . . 1981.*

   Of course, the education of foreign students is a chancy business,
and the Soviet-East European experience has been very mixed. The
results, far from improving the image of the Soviet Union and Eastern
Europe, may have actually damaged it. The net consequence depends
not only upon the treatment of the students by the host society, but also
upon the quality of the education, and the reception the students receive at home and abroad when they display their Communist
academic credentials.
   Aside from the political effects, the extensive interaction between
Eastern Europe and the outside world, particularly the Third World,
cannot but have enhanced the visibility of countries of Eastern Europe
on the world scene, as a region as well as separate personalities. Hundreds of thousands of East Europeans and citizens from remote areas
of the world have had contact with one another at various levels and in

Table 11 Academic, Technical, and Military Trainees Departing from Less-developed Countries to Communist Countries, 1970–76

	1970	1973	1976	Total 1970–76
Total Trainees	7,845	11,755	16,350	80,475
USSR and E. Europe	7,535	11,260	16,135	77,110
China	310	495	25	3,365
Academic	3,645	5,375	7,965	36,060
USSR and E. Europe	3,645	5,275	7,905	35,605
China	0	100	65	455
Technical	1,650	3,715	5,320	24,395
USSR and E. Europe	1,650	3,715	5,265	24,220
China	0	0	55	175
Military	2,250	2,665	3,065	21,020
USSR and E. Europe	2,240	2,270	2,965	18,285
China	310	395	100	2,735

Source: *Handbook of Economic Statistics, 1977.*

various parts of the world. Thousands of East European citizens have visited and worked in a wide spectrum of countries, and a corresponding number of citizens from all corners of the globe have visited or have been trained in Eastern Europe. Table 11 provides data for the comparative distribution of trainees from the Third World departing for Communist countries. It shows that more than 77,000 trainees departed for the Soviet Union and Eastern Europe during the period 1970–76 alone.

CONCLUSIONS

Although the developmental gap between Western Europe and Eastern Europe remains substantial, it has been decreasing rapidly, and Eastern Europe as a whole is generally viewed as part of the developed world and as an integral part of Europe. To be sure, in the traditional trifurcation of the world, Eastern Europe has been consigned to the "Second World," which is an ideological category embracing all Communist states, developed and less developed, but developmental identities increasingly appear to be supplanting ideological identities from the perspective of both developed and underdeveloped states, irrespective of ideology. The traditional tripartite division of the world, based on ideological outlook and alignments, is giving way to new divisions of the world along developmental-continental-civilizational-racial lines. Beijing has already declared both the "Communist camp" and the traditional "Second World" as defunct and has restructured the globe into a new tripartite division, with Eastern Europe and Western

Table 12 Eastern Europe in Development Context, 1963–81

Country Region	Population (Thousands)			Total GNP (Millions of Dollars at Market Prices)		GNP Per Capita (Dollars)		
	1963	1975	1981	1965	1981	1963	1975	1981
World	3,175,000	4,069,067	4,577,000	6,120,000	11,600,000	821	1,396	2,540
Developed	919,327	1,039,355	1,220,060	5,170,000	9,280,000	2,381	4,288	7,600
Underdeveloped	2,255,696	3,031,027	3,356,940	950,000	2,320,000	185	404	690
USSR	225,000	254,300	270,000	1,230,000	1,587,000	1,678	3,130	5,930
USA	189,200	213,631	230,000	1,800,200	2,925,500	4,255	6,490	12,730
European Community	287,484	317,724	272,000	1,480,000	2,420,000	2,059	3,800	8,910
WTO E. Europe	98,478	106,238	110,000	1,230,000	670,000	1,351	2,562	6,096
Bulgaria	8,078	8,741	8,900	19,400	34,000	928	1,930	3,820
Czechoslovakia	13,900	14,804	15,300	88,900	137,000	1,962	3,870	8,970
GDR	17,000	16,885	16,700	102,300	162,900	1,845	3,270	9,750
Hungary	10,100	10,541	10,700	41,800	63,700	1,309	2,210	5,950
Poland	30,600	34,022	35,900	111,900	178,000	1,127	2,300	4,960
Romania	18,800	21,245	22,400	43,900	94,700	936	2,101	4,230
Yugoslavia	19,000	21,346	22,500	22,600	51,800	602	1,510	3,300
Albania	1,762	2,411	2,846	—	2,150	464	497	830
Asian Communist								
States	751,219	986,119	1,119,499	—	576,600	106	292	659
Mongolia	917	1,444	1,809	—	1,200	818	554	665
China	716,000	934,600	1,032,000	120,000	328,000	129	293	320
N. Korea	11,500	16,500	18,802	7,100	16,200	273	388	786
Vietnam	15,300	24,323	57,036	—	8,400	140	52	153
Cuba	7,502	9,252	9,852	—	13,900	731	633	1,372

Sources: *World Military Expenditures and Arms Trade 1963–1973* (Washington, D.C.: USACDA, 1974); *World Military Expenditures and Arms Transfers, 1966–1976* (Washington, D.C.: USACDA, 1977); *Handbook of Economic Indicators, 1982.*

Europe lumped together as part of a new "Second World," as distinct from a "First World," consisting solely of the United States and the USSR, and a "Third World," consisting of all the developing countries of Asia, Africa, and Latin America:

> In this situation of "great disorder under heaven," all the political forces in the world have undergone drastic division and realignment through pro-longed trials of strength and struggle. A large number of Asian, African, and Latin American countries have achieved independence one after another, and they are playing an even greater role in international affairs. *As a result of the emergence of social-imperialism, the socialist camp which existed for a time after World War II is no longer in existence* [author's emphasis]. Owing to the law of the uneven development of capitalism, the Western imperialist block, too, is disintegrating. Judging from the changes in international relations, the world today actually consists of three parts, or three worlds, that are both interconnected and in contradiction to one another. The United States and the Soviet Union make up the First World. The developing countries in Asia, Africa, Latin America, and other regions make up the Third World. The developed countries between the two make up the Second World.[7]

Although the polemical and self-serving character of Beijing's re-categorization of the world is evident, it is also equally apparent that Beijing's image of the world is basically developmental in design. The data in Table 12 show the progressive developmental convergence that has taken place between Eastern Europe and Western Europe and the progressively widening gap between Eastern Europe and the Asian Communist states and the entire underdeveloped world in general. These developmental trends have generated universal perceptions of a world in which developmental cleavages assume a higher saliency than ideological differences. Thus the average per capita GNP for Western Europe in 1981 was $8,910 and for WTO Eastern Europe $6,096, whereas the average per capita GNP for the underdeveloped countries stood at $690 and that for the non-European Communist states averaged out at $660. Even more graphically, Eastern Europe with its 135 million people generated a GNP ($724 billion) larger than that for the five non-European Communist states ($591 billion) with a total population of over one billion people. If the data for the Soviet Union are included, the gap between European and non-European communism becomes even more conspicuous.

As a developed part of the world, Eastern Europe, in spite of its already widespread involvement, may be perceived increasingly as not carrying its share of the burden to assist the less-developed countries. The six Warsaw Pact countries accounted for 2.4 percent of the world's population in 1981, but generated 5.7 percent of its gross national product and accounted for 4.8 percent of all exports. On the other hand, Eastern Europe contributed only 1.24 percent of all capital aid to less-developed countries and delivered about 1.82 percent of all arms exports.

Irrespective of the separate identity that the countries of Eastern Europe as a region and as individual personalities have succeeded in developing over the past two decades, the connection with the Soviet Union remains the dominant world image of Eastern Europe. And this is likely to remain so for some time, given the vital stake that Soviet leaders perceive in maintaining their paramountcy in the region. As noted earlier, Eastern Europe is important to the Soviet Union for a number of reasons, the two most important being strategic and ideological. These two purposes of the Soviet presence in Eastern Europe are distinct and independent, yet not easy to disaggregate by both the Soviet leaders and the outside world. The relative priority of these two important purposes, as between one another and other purposes, has changed over time in response to circumstances, events, and perceptions, both Soviet and external.

The purely strategic security purpose of the Soviet presence in Eastern Europe is the most easily understandable and appreciated, but it is not always easy to distinguish from the ideological purpose, which has both defensive and expansionist implications. The crux of the matter is whether Soviet leaders perceive security in traditional territorial, economic, and military terms, or whether they perceive security in ideological terms, i.e., the defense, expansion, validation, and legitimization of a distinctive sociopolitical order inspired by a particular ideology, rather than the simple preservation or promotion of the territorial and economic interests of the Soviet state.

Eastern Europe has historically constituted an invasion channel from the West into Russia, and similarly, it has served as an invasion conduit from Russia into Central and Western Europe. As an important buffer region made up of small, relatively weak states that are divided from one another by ancient historical animosities, it traditionally has been manipulated and exploited by neighboring great powers for their own ends. Eastern Europe, by itself, remains incapable of filling the power vacuum that inevitably develops in this region, and it has been the fate of East Central Europe to become the sphere of influence of one of the great powers. Since World War II, it has become a part of the Soviet sphere, where it functions as the Soviet Union's single most important geographical defense zone.

Hence, it is not likely that the Soviet leaders will permit Eastern Europe to break away in the foreseeable future. As events in Czechoslovakia demonstrated in 1968, they are prepared to intervene, if necessary, to prevent any significant erosion of their East European empire, although the costs in terms of Soviet international prestige may rise with successive interventions.

The Soviet presence in Eastern Europe thus guarantees, at the minimum, a denial of the region to any other great power; currently, the pertinent great power is West Germany, because Eastern Europe has traditionally been a sphere of influence of either Germany or Russia. Two of the Soviet leaders' great concerns about West Germany's Ostpolitik, initiated by Chancellor Ludwig Erhard in 1965–66 and extended by Chancellors Kurt Kiesinger and Willy Brandt, were that the policy threatened to loosen the bonds between Eastern Europe and the Soviet Union and that it appeared to represent a bid by West Germany to revive its traditional interest in the area.[8] A policy that served to entice the East European states into developing closer relations with West Germany, it encouraged the autonomous defiance of Romania, particularly in the realm of foreign policy. More importantly, it reinforced these internal developments in Czechoslovakia that might have removed the nation from the Soviet orbit.[9]

The strategic aspects of the Soviet presence in Eastern Europe can be viewed separately from the ideological and political aspects, since they are not irrevocably interrelated with any specific ideological purpose or political system; but they cannot be separated when measuring the overall importance of Eastern Europe to the Soviet Union. In a psychological sense, Soviet control of Eastern Europe also serves to validate Moscow's credentials as a regional power, as a leader of a group of states, and as a leader of one of the two principal alliance and political systems in the world. It is important to bear in mind that the United States and the Soviet Union are the only two alliance leaders in the world today, and that a certain amount of prestige is derived from that role. Furthermore, much of the Soviet Union's prestige in international affairs derives from the fact that it is the leader of a group of states.

Thus, the second general purpose of the Soviet presence in Eastern Europe is essentially political and ideological in character, although the ideological aspect has been assuming an increasingly symbolic context. These ideological and symbolic purposes are becoming progressively residual but nevertheless continue to be important for the short run, since the ideological element in Soviet behavior has been eroding for many years and probably will continue to do so. The Soviet Union appears to have no real future as the leader of a universal Communist movement, because China's emergence as a rival has effectively arrested that role. Before the emergence of China as a rival, the policies of the United States had, in many ways, also blocked the expansion of Soviet or Communist power, but in different ways.

In the short run, then, the existence of Eastern Europe as a bloc of Communist states modeled on the Soviet system—and the word "Communist" is emphasized—continues to validate the Soviet Union's credentials as an ideological and revolutionary power, as well as the residual center of a world revolutionary movement.

Eastern Europe thus is not only an imperialistic extension of the Soviet Union, it is also an extension of the Soviet Union's social system; and as the first and most important extension of the Soviet system beyond the borders of the Soviet Union, it represents the residue of Moscow's former ecumenical pretensions. All of the Communist states in Eastern Europe came into being under various forms of Soviet sponsorship. They were all cast from the Soviet mold, and in one way or another represented the first step in universalizing the Soviet system. All have been beneficiaries of Soviet protection, as well as victims of Soviet domination. It might be said that while the Communist regimes have been the beneficiaries of Soviet protection, the populations have been the victims of Soviet domination.

The Communist states of Eastern Europe are, in effect, miniature alter egos of the Soviet Union; and when the Soviet leaders look at Eastern Europe, they find contentment only if it reflects a reasonable facsimile of themselves. The integrity, viability, and even existence of the Soviet system depend upon the maintenance of the Communist regimes in Eastern Europe; and thus, for psychological reasons alone, the overthrow of any Communist regime in Eastern Europe, even the Albanian, would constitute a threat to the Soviet system. It is important to bear in mind that the Soviet Union does not consider itself to be merely a state; it considers itself as a representative of a particular form of social and economic organization that has universal validity and application. And the East European states are subordinate not simply to Soviet foreign policy; their internal structures are also in some degree subordinate to Soviet will.

On the other hand, East European states (with perhaps the exception of Bulgaria) resent being viewed as extensions of the Soviet system and increasingly perceive themselves as permanent entities, pursuing roads to socialism separate, distinct, and away from Soviet communism and toward the positions of Eurocommunist parties in Western Europe. The advent of Eurocommunism in Western Europe thus may set into motion trends and forces that may convert East European communism, with its separate roads, into a distinctive form of communism that may become a potential bridge between Eurocommunism and Soviet communism, rather than a mere extension of the latter. Of course Soviet power remains decisive in this area and the East European states must pursue their separate roads with prudence and caution.

The defensive function of the Soviet presence in Eastern Europe has been almost universally recognized as valid, certainly by the United States, and has been justified amply by both history and logic. But the second purpose has been a matter of concern to the West, particularly the United States—the function of the Soviet presence in Eastern Europe as a possible first step in the communization of all Europe. As far as Western Europe and the United States were concerned, of course, the ideological-expansionist aspect of the Soviet presence in Eastern Europe dwarfed all other considerations. Since, in Soviet calculations, the defensive and offensive functions of the Soviet presence in Eastern Europe are intricately intertwined, the Soviet leaders seem inherently incapable of disassociating responses that threaten their security from those designed to blunt their ideological offensive. Hence as long as only the United States, Western Europe (especially West Germany), and China remain the principal external champions and supporters of greater freedom for Eastern Europe, the perception of threat will tend to dominate in Moscow.

As an increasingly active participant in the international community of nearly 150 states, and given its recognition as a group of developed, modernized European states of some magnitude, Eastern Europe becomes increasingly incongruous as a group of states still subservient to another state, in a world full of small, exotic, and underdeveloped states subservient to no one.[10] Furthermore, one East European state, Poland, is a substantial state by any objective standard. With an ethnically homogeneous population of about 3.6 million, it ranks as the fifth largest nation in Europe (excluding the Soviet Union), after Germany, Italy, France, and Great Britain. Its aggregate GNP in 1981 was $111 billion, among the largest in the world, and about as large as that of India with over 250 million people. That a nation of this magnitude can still be subservient to another state toward the end of the twentieth century staggers the imagination, and it is only a matter of time until a condition that is merely incongruous in the world community becomes intolerable, as the rise of Solidarity in 1980 dramatically demonstrated. Given the national paranoia of the Soviet leadership, Poland and Eastern Europe's hopes for full emancipation can only be furthered by associating themselves with groupings and cultivating constituencies in the world community that can articulate an interest in their freedom without projecting a threat to Moscow. Since the Soviet Union is eager to earn the approbation of countries in the Third World, in the event of future Soviet misbehavior in Eastern Europe, the Soviet leadership may be more sensitive to criticism and condemnation from this direction. Moreover, it can hardly rebut such disapprobation as threatening to its security. Both Yugoslavia and Romania have followed this route, and it appears that North Korea and Vietnam are also enhancing their identification with noncommunist groupings in order to insulate themselves from the threat of Soviet or Chinese domination.

NOTES

1. Quoted from the radio broadcast, as recorded by Columbia Records in "I Can Hear It Now," compiled and narrated by Edward R. Murrow.

2. The total includes Yugoslavia and Albania. The population of the 6 East European Warsaw Pact states was 111 million in 1983.

3. The West Slavic languages are Polish, Czech, and Slovak; the South Slavic are Slovene, Serbo-Croatian, Bulgarian, and Macedonian. The ten Slavic nations are Poles, Czechs, Slovaks, Slovenes, Croatians, Serbians, Bosnians, Montenegrins, Macedonians, and Bulgarians; the four non-Slavic nations are Hungarians, Romanians, Albanians, and Germans.

4. As reported in "The Train Jan Prochazka Missed," *Literaturnaya gazeta*, May 19, 1972.

5. *The World Socialist System and Anti-Communism* (Moscow, 1972), p. 79.

6. As East European (and Soviet) trade with the outside world has expanded, its hard currency deficit has grown correspondingly. Poland's deficit is particularly serious. The following table charts the increasing deficit. The increasing foreign indebtedness of Eastern Europe also increases the interdependence between Eastern Europe and the noncommunist world.

Net Hard Currency Debts in Millions of U.S. Dollars

Country	1970	1973	1975	1980 (est.)
Bulgaria	.7	.8	1.8	2.7
Czechoslovakia	.3	.8	1.5	3.6
GDR	1.0	2.1	3.8	11.8
Hungary	.6	.9	2.1	7.5
Poland	.8	1.9	6.9	24.5
Romania	1.2	2.0	3.0	9.2
TOTAL	4.6	8.5	19.1	59.3
USSR	1.7	3.6	7.5	9.5

Source: *Handbook of Economic Statistics, 1982.*

The increasing foreign indebtedness of Eastern Europe also increases the interdependence between Eastern Europe and the noncommunist world.

7. From a speech by Vice-Premier Teng Hsiao-ping before the U.N. General Assembly, April 10, 1974, in *Peking Review,* April 19, 1974, p. 6.

8. For an excellent survey, see Andrew Gyorgy, "Ostpolitik and Eastern Europe," in Charles Gati, editor, *The International Politics of Eastern Europe* (New York: Praeger Publishers, 1976), pp. 154–172.

9. For further amplification, see Vernon V. Aspaturian, "Has Eastern Europe Become a Liability to the Soviet Union?" in Gati, *The International Politics of Eastern Europe*, pp. 17–36; V. V. Aspaturian, "The Aftermath of the Czech Invasion," *Current History*, November 1968; V. V. Aspaturian, "Soviet Aims in East Europe," *Current History*, October 1970.

10. For an excellent analysis of international influences on East European behavior, see Andrzej Korbonski, "External Influences on Eastern Europe," Gati, *The International Politics of Eastern Europe*, pp. 253–274.

2 Poland

Andrzej Korbonski

A social scientist asked to analyze political developments in a country over a certain period is faced, first of all, with the task of selecting an approach that is likely to yield some useful and interesting results. This task, complicated to begin with, becomes even more complex when the country in question happens to be Poland, an East European Communist state which for more than thirty-five years has been undergoing dramatic political and socioeconomic changes; which thus far has defied easy generalizations and classifications; and which continues to be a country of sharp and growing contrasts.

The choice of an approach is obviously largely determined by the questions one seeks to answer. In this case, the major question concerns essentially the performance of the country's political system. To put it somewhat differently: what makes the Polish system work? In order to answer this question, one must delve into a discussion of such issues as the country's political structure and dynamics, its leadership and elite patterns, socioeconomic and cultural trends, and last but not least, its foreign policy, including its relations with the Soviet Union, the hegemonial power in the region.

The approach that appears most suited for analyzing the political system of contemporary Poland is the "developmental" approach derived from the pioneering work of Gabriel Almond.[1] This approach is based on the assumption that the process of political development is characterized by a number of essential "criteria," "requirements," and "challenges." Thus, all societies passing through the process of political development are bound to deal with at least four developmental requirements—nation-building, state-building, participation, and distribution. Also, all societies undergoing this process have to cope with several crises arising out of the conflicts between the developmental criteria mentioned above. The five crises or challenges most frequently faced are those of identity, legitimacy, penetration, participation, and distribution. For example, a society that has successfully passed through the stages of nation- and state-building must, sooner or later, resolve the problem of popular participation by providing the populace with institutional arrangements for the articulation of its demands and grievances. Similarly, a well-integrated political system must face at some point the problem of distribution by ensuring a decent standard of living for its people, who otherwise can challenge the legitimacy of the system. Almond has suggested that "the way in which political systems encountered these challenges and problems, their order and sequence, and the choices made by elites by confronting them and solving them [go] far toward explaining the peculiar characteristics of [their] structures, cultures and capability profiles."[2]

The greatest virtue of Almond's approach is that, especially in its revised form, it was "precisely designed to deal with the problem of changes and it was also clearly independent of any particular historical context. . . . [It] could be applied to a primitive stateless tribe, a classical Greek city-state, or to a modern nation-state."[3] It follows that it is also suitable for the study of political change in Poland, where the impact of such variables as leadership and international environment, as well as the national political culture, was particularly strong. Moreover, the framework permits one to examine the process of change without prejudging its ultimate outcome or goal. Hence, in addition to looking at factors causing or inducing "change," "modernization," or "development," we are also able to consider influences affecting the process of "political decay" or deterioration in the level and quality of performance of the political system which seemed to have occurred in Poland with some regularity.

Any political system may also be viewed as being composed of several elements, all of which are undergoing a process of change. Some of these systemic components may be changing at rapid rates, while others may be transformed slowly. Samuel Huntington distinguishes five major components of any political system—culture, structure, groups, leadership, and policies—and suggests that the process of political change is ultimately strongly influenced by the interplay between these components—their type and rate of change and the combination in which they occur.[4] Thus, I propose to analyze the process of political change in Poland since the end of the 1960s by focusing, on the one hand, on the five developmental challenges or crises identified by Almond, and on the other, on the five systemic components analyzed by Huntington. Since the emphasis is going to be on the most recent developments, the early period in postwar Polish history will receive a rather summary treatment; it has been extensively studied and discussed in Western literature.

THE FIRST THIRTY-FIVE YEARS

The one developmental challenge that postwar Poland, in contrast to
several other East European countries, did not have to face was that of
national identity. While the process of nation-building in Poland had
not been successfully accomplished during the interwar period and the
problem of hostile national minorities prevented the achievement of
full national integration, the country emerged from World War II as a
homogeneous nation-state. The Nazi mass genocide of the Jewish
population, the expulsion of the Germans from the newly acquired
territories in the west, and the enforced incorporation of Poland's eastern provinces into the Soviet Union resulted in Poland becoming ethnically (and religiously) quite homogeneous, probably for the first time
in its long history.

While this phenomenon is usually taken for granted, there is little
doubt that it had considerable and lasting impact on postwar developments in Poland. The major beneficiaries appeared to be the
country's new Communist rulers, who were spared from having to deal
with the kinds of ethnic and national conflicts that influenced political
processes in Yugoslavia, Czechoslovakia, and Romania, all of which
continued to harbor substantial minorities inherited from the precommunist period.

The process of national integration was further reinforced by the
mass dislocations and migrations during and immediately after the war.
The wartime eastward expulsion of the Polish population inhabiting
territories incorporated into the German Reich, followed by the mass
postwar settlement of the "Recovered Territories" in the west, did go a
long way toward reducing the strong regional antagonisms that had
characterized prewar Poland. These antagonisms were the result of
striking regional and local differences that had been caused by more
than 150 years of Russian, German, and Austrian rule.

While the postwar emergence of an ethnically homogeneous and
nationally integrated Poland undoubtedly strengthened the hand of the
Communist rulers at least in the initial period, it will be argued below
that in the long run it was likely to aggravate some of the other developmental crises, especially those of political penetration and legitimacy. The former crisis implied that the Communist regime had not
been able successfully to penetrate Polish society, which meant that
large parts of it remained essentially outside the control of the government. The crisis of legitimacy suggested that despite tremendous efforts to generate some voluntary acceptance of, if not obedience to, the
new political system, the Communist rulers failed, by and large, to
achieve that particular objective. Both crises were due in large measure to the striking persistence of certain features of the country's

political culture, among which nationalism continued to play an important role.

The crises or challenges of penetration and legitimacy are usually closely related to the process of state-building. The latter can be identified in the Polish context with the Communist seizure of power that took place in the period 1944–48. The takeover in Poland did not differ significantly from that in some of the other countries in the region: as aptly described by Zbigniew Brzezinski, it represented a synthesis of certain socioeconomic reforms and a fairly substantial degree of Soviet-sponsored terror and violence.[5]

There were two features of the Communist takeover of Poland whose impact still affects political developments in that country today, more than thirty-five years after the event. One feature was a comprehensive land reform initiated in 1944, which succeeded, on the one hand, in politically neutralizing the peasants, who at that time represented about two-thirds of the country's population, and on the other, in strengthening the peasant class, which subsequently became a major thorn in the Communists' side. The other special feature was the establishment of the Oder-Neisse line and the incorporation and settlement of former German territories with which the new rulers strongly identified themselves. The need to uphold the incorporation of the freshly acquired areas, whose status remained uncertain until 1970, united both friends and foes of the new regime, and also made the process of takeover somewhat easier, as the incoming Communists portrayed themselves as defenders of Poland's national interest. That the new borders made the country even more dependent on the Soviet Union was not generally recognized at that time.

The process of Stalinization (1948–53) that followed the seizure of power might be viewed simply as a continuation of the process of state-building, whereby the Communist polity attempted to penetrate Polish society and to establish total control over it. Here again, the various stages and methods in the gradual establishment of the Soviet political, economic, and societal models followed the traditional path and did not deviate greatly from the policies pursued by the other countries in the region.

However, as in the case of the takeover process, there were some interesting departures from the model, which were to have major repercussions in the future. One of these departures was the relative absence of the high degree of terror and violence that had characterized the Sovietization process in Bulgaria, Czechoslovakia, and Hungary. To be sure, all resistance to the imposition of the Stalinist model was brutally suppressed, yet in the final analysis the various purges of the party and of society at large claimed relatively few victims. An overwhelming majority of those who suffered persecution and imprisonment survived and reappeared after Stalin's death to play a major role in the country's affairs in the late 1950s and beyond.

The same was true with regard to collectivization of agriculture, anti-church policy, and other policies aimed at restructuring Polish society *à la russe*. In each case the pressure from above appeared considerably milder than in the other satellites. The process of Sovietization in Poland turned out to be less bloody and harsh than elsewhere in Eastern Europe.

The first major challenge to the legitimacy of the system took place in 1956. The reasons for the failure of the Communist polity fully to penetrate Polish society—a major contributory factor in the crisis—were convincingly summarized by Brzezinski. According to him, the ability of each East European regime to deal with the consequences of de-Stalinization depended on the intensity of the socioeconomic crisis within the country, the degree of alienation of the working class and the intelligentsia from the rulers, the extent of the given regime's involvement in anti-Titoist policies, and the availability of alternative leadership.[6] Poland and Hungary were much more affected by the above crises than the other countries in the region, and both went through major upheavals in the fall of 1956: a bloody revolt in Hungary and a bloodless changeover in Poland. The latter brought Wladyslaw Gomulka back to power and was accompanied by a series of political and economic changes, among which the collapse of agricultural collectivization was by far the most significant. Gomulka, one of the chief engineers of the postwar Communist takeover, fell victim to Stalinist purges, and his elevation to leadership represented a major break with the past. Although the double crisis of penetration and legitimacy did not last long, it was clear that Poland's politics would never be the same and that the sharp challenge to the supposedly impregnable system would not remain without an echo.

The next decade and a half witnessed an unsuccessful attempt at what may be called "system maintenance" or "consolidation." The regime's efforts to acquire even a modicum of legitimacy failed, most signally in March 1968, when university students and intellectuals rose up in protest against government censorship and increasingly restrictive cultural policy. Thereafter the country entered a period of political stagnation and decay, with the chasm between the rulers and the ruled becoming gradually wider. The explosion of December 1970, when the workers on the Baltic coast rioted in protest against a drastic increase in retail prices and succeeded in bringing down the Gomulka regime, represented the second major double crisis of legitimacy and penetration, the impact of which is still felt today.

The third developmental challenge, that of participation, did not make its appearance until relatively late in the period under discussion. Beginning in 1956, the Polish regime attempted to expand the scope of popular participation at various levels, but until the early 1970s, the progress had not been significant. It may be argued, in fact, that the overthrow of Gomulka in December 1970 represented not only a crisis of legitimacy and penetration but also a crisis of participation, and that in this respect it illustrated rather well the notion of mass politicization leading to social frustration and political instability because of the absence of channels for meaningful participation.[7]

One may generalize, however, that in Poland, throughout most of the period under discussion, the frustration, anomie, and alienation from the system were related more closely to the questions of distribution and welfare than to participation or even legitimacy. In other words, economic demands tended to take precedence over political desiderata, and while both of them probably merged in the first systemic crisis of October 1956, there was no doubt that economic grievances were responsible for the second major challenge to the regime in December 1970. Altogether, despite the impressive progress in industrialization and economic development, the living standard of the Polish population has been growing at a rate slower than in most of the other people's democracies, contributing still further to economic and political discontent.

Thus, on the eve of the seventies Poland was in disarray. Although the political system managed to maintain itself and to withstand the various crises and challenges, its performance was clearly below par and its future uncertain. Except for a very brief period in 1956–57, the Communist regime did not succeed in generating popular acceptance and legitimacy, and by the end of the 1960s it had lost a good deal of support even among its traditional followers. By the same token, the political system was unable to penetrate deeply Polish society, with the result that large segments of the latter, especially the peasantry and the youth, and, as it became abundantly clear in December 1970, also the industrial working class, remained to a considerable degree outside the control of the regime, whose extractive capacity was thereby considerably impaired. This, in turn, had serious repercussions on the performance of the economic system, which failed not only to secure a modest living standard for the majority of the population but also to sustain a moderate rate of economic growth, to guarantee that a better life would be achieved before long.

The replacement of Gomulka by Edward Gierek in December 1970 seemed to inaugurate a new era in recent Polish history. From the start, Western observers, taking their cue most likely from the personal background and experience of the new leader, proclaimed the incoming regime as "dynamic," "pragmatic," and "technocratic," which implied a major contrast to its predecessor and carried a promise of better things to come.

For the first few years these predictions appeared to be largely validated. To begin with, the country's stagnating economy entered a period of rapid growth, stimulated mostly by massive injections of Western credits and technology. Simultaneously, Polish peasants, relieved finally of the heavy burden of compulsory deliveries, responded by sharply expanding their output. Politically, the new regime also assumed a middle-of-the-road stance by bringing into leading positions men largely unencumbered by ideological dogmatism or rampant nationalism. They tended to be younger and better educated, further reinforcing the view that pragmatism and rationality were to be the chief determinants of policy at the expense of dogmatism and dilettantism.

In foreign policy, too, the new team departed significantly from its predecessor. In addition to the continued betterment of relations with West Germany, initiated by the treaty signed in Warsaw on the eve of Gomulka's ouster in December 1970, Gierek made a major effort to improve relations with France, the United States, and other Western countries. His major purpose appeared to be to secure Western credits, which would propel Poland toward rapid industrial modernization. Closer to home, Poland's relations with the Soviet Union were developing satisfactorily and gave Moscow little cause for concern, as Gierek took great pains to reassure the Kremlin that his overtures to the West represented no threat to Soviet hegemony in the region.

Hence, as suggested earlier, it appeared as if a new era had indeed dawned upon Poland, which became permeated with a new spirit of dynamism in sharp contrast to the stagnation and decay of the late 1960s. The honeymoon, however, proved to be short-lived and, for all practical purposes, it was over on the fifth anniversary of Gierek's accession. From then on, the political and economic situation deteriorated rapidly, reaching bottom in June 1976, when the regime, making the same mistake as in December 1970, announced a drastic increase in the prices of key foodstuffs. It was then immediately confronted by several major workers' riots and a threat of a general strike, and was forced to retreat and withdraw the increase within twenty-four hours. While the government survived, it had suffered a serious defeat from which it could not and did not recover. In the summer of 1976 a group of intellectuals—including the well-known "revisionists" Adam Michnik and Jacek Kuron—founded a Workers' Defense Committee (*Komitet Obrony Robotnikow*) to assist the repressed workers, marking the beginning of an alliance between intellectuals and workers, a new element in the contemporary Polish political matrix. In the systemic context, the establishment of KOR was a momentous development because of its decision to "go open." KOR was harassed but not suppressed, and its existence encouraged the emergence of an open, albeit illegal opposition. By 1980 opposition groups proliferated, as did their publications, which circulated outside the official censorship system.

From 1976 to 1980 the Gierek regime attempted unsuccessfully to maintain itself in power against growing pressures emanating from both the workers and intellectuals. Poland's economic situation continued to deteriorate and despite indications that the country was facing an imminent crisis, no attempt was made to introduce the long overdue economic reforms or to deal with other political and social issues that gave rise to the rapidly expanding dissident movement. Despite the strong support of Moscow, which apparently considered Gierek to be a valuable intermediary vis-a-vis Western Europe, especially in the post-Afghanistan period, the Polish leader began to encounter growing opposition within his own party, increasingly frustrated by a lack of progress on all fronts. Thus, in the summer of 1980, in the face of multiple challenges by groups that had supported it only a decade ago, the image of a pragmatic, dynamic, and relatively popular regime was replaced by one that bore a striking resemblance to its predecessor under Gomulka, characterized by uncertainty, lack of direction, internal strife, and stagnation. Problems of corruption and incompetence endemic to Communist systems reached staggering proportions in Gierek's Poland. These were accompanied by blatant abuse of power and open cynicism on the part of party and state bureaucrats not only at the top but at lower levels and in regional administration, where they affect the populace more directly.

POLAND IN THE 1980s

When on July 1, 1980 the Gierek regime announced still another increase in meat prices, no one, not even the most astute observers of the Polish scene, East or West, anticipated that this event would trigger the single most important political crisis in postwar Poland, comparable in its domestic and international impacts to the Titoist heresy of 1948, the Hungarian revolt of 1956, and the Prague Spring of 1968.

Not surprisingly, Polish workers in different parts of the country reacted angrily to the price increase and many of them struck in protest. The government apparently expected this and initially, at least, managed to settle the various strikes by offering the workers higher wages to compensate for the price rise. What was clearly not expected was the fact that the strikes continued to spread from one part of the country to another and that gradually they acquired a mass and coordinated character.

In August the strike wave reached the Baltic port city of Gdansk where ten years earlier, in December 1970, the local shipyard workers had risen against the Gomulka regime. Once again the shipyard workers, headed this time by Lech Walesa, took the lead in organizing workers from other Gdansk factories and presented the regime with a set of twenty-one demands. The government negotiators, who until then had been quite successful in settling strikes in individual factories, were forced for the first time to deal with an interfactory strike committee that claimed to speak on behalf of several hundred thousand workers from different branches. The old formula of "divide and rule," which worked in the past, failed and the Gierek regime, threatened by strikes elsewhere on the Baltic coast as well as in the crucial coal-mining region of Silesia, ultimately accepted the twenty-one demands submitted by the workers.

While most of the demands dealt with detailed bread-and-butter issues of particular interest to the striking workers, there were at least four points whose acceptance by the government represented an unprecedented surrender by an ostensibly Marxist-Leninist regime. To begin with, the government formally acknowledged the birth of an "independent and self-governing" trade union that began to call itself Solidarity *(Solidarnosc)* and which the regime had to recognize as an equal partner in the negotiations, acting as an authentic spokesman and articulator of workers' interests. Moreover, the government affirmed Solidarity's right to strike, which represented another *novum* in the annals of international Communism. Two additional demands dealt with relaxation of censorship and granting of further concessions to the Catholic church. The regime accepted these demands and signed an agreement with Solidarity in Gdansk on August 31, 1980, thus opening what appeared to be a new era in Polish politics.

The subsequent eighteen months until December 1981 witnessed a power struggle between Solidarity, determined to see the implementation of the Gdansk agreement, and the regime, fighting for survival in the face of a serious political and economic crisis that threatened the very existence of communism in Poland. In September 1980 Gierek was replaced as party leader by Stanislaw Kania, hitherto an obscure *apparatchik,* and a few months later the defense minister, General Wojciech Jaruzelski, took over the Premiership of the government. Wholesale personnel turnover in the top party and government bodies accompanied these changes.

Within a short time of its birth, Solidarity reached an estimated total membership of about 10 million, which in a country of 35 million inhabitants represented a truly impressive achievement and a testimony to the movement's overwhelming popularity among the population. Within its ranks Solidarity counted one million party members, which accounted for about one-third of total Communist party membership, illustrative of the latter's growing decline and disarray. During its first year in existence, the chief task of Solidarity was to legitimize itself and, once this was accomplished, to achieve not only the fullest possible implementation of the August 1980 accords but also such workers' demands as the five-day working week. In order to reach these objectives Solidarity did not hesitate to use the strike weapon. But despite much talk and apparent concessions by the government, little real progress took place in the implementation of the August 1980 agreements.

During that time Solidarity behaved essentially as a labor union or an interest group articulating traditional workers' demands in the context of the existing political system. While the borderline between politics and economics in Communist states has always been rather nebulous, at least until the summer of 1981 there were no clear indications that the Polish working class was getting ready to challenge the Kania-Jaruzelski regime. On the other hand, the creation of Rural Solidarity in the spring of 1981, the continuing close collaboration between Solidarity, the Catholic church, and the intellectuals, and the growing number of strikes and other disputes in various parts of the country reflected the progressive and unmistakable decline in the authority of the party and the government, both of which were losing support even among their strongest followers.

The Polish Communist party was clearly in ferment and was facing growing demands from its rank and file for greater liberalization and democratization. The leadership responded by finally calling an Extraordinary Ninth Party Congress that met in July 1981 ostensibly to elect a new leadership and ratify various political and economic reforms demanded by the population. For the first time in the history of Polish communism, most of the delegates to the Congress were elected democratically. They, in turn, proceeded to elect a new party leadership that, except for a handful of individuals, excluded leading personalities of the past identified with both conservative and liberal wings. The freshly elected Central Committee consisted of new and inexperienced members who, although most likely well-intentioned and highly motivated, proved no match for the few surviving veterans as well as the many remaining *apparatchiki* who obviously had no intention of fulfilling the high sounding provisions of the reform program approved by the Ninth Congress and who, right from the start, began to manipulate the newly elected members. It soon became clear that the personnel and other changes resulting from the Congress were purely cosmetic and that the real power in the party remained in the hands of a small oligarchy determined to hold on to it at all costs.

Solidarity held its first (and last) national congress in September–October 1981. By that time the movement had undergone some significant changes, and it hardly resembled the fledgling organization born in the Gdansk shipyard some twelve months earlier. The changes were qualitative as well as quantitative. In the fall of 1981 Solidarity was behaving less and less like a traditional interest group and more and more like a political pressure group, ready and willing to challenge the existing regime. Some of the new stance was due to a growing realization that the government would never grant voluntarily the various demands put forward by the union and that further pressure was needed to force it to do so. Moreover, until and unless the government consented to greater participation by Solidarity in political and economic decision making, the Polish working class would continue to be deprived of political power sharing despite its obvious numeric strength and popularity. The workers were becoming impatient and frustrated with what they perceived to be a total lack of progress in implementing their demands. At the same time many of them assumed a new stand that might be described as overconfident and even arrogant: they interpreted the government's reluctance to act as a sign of weakness and growing disarray. Many of the declarations and speeches delivered at the Solidarity Congress reflected the rising militancy of both the leadership and the rank and file. The very broad spectrum of views that began to be articulated under Solidarity's umbrella, and excessive emphasis on grass-roots democracy, made it increasingly difficult for the leadership to control the members and locals, and, internally, to maintain consensus on policies.

Thus the fall of 1981 witnessed an increasing polarization of Polish polity and society. On the one side was the Communist party led, after Kania's ouster, by General Jaruzelski, who, by retaining both his premiership and Defense Ministry, became at least formally the single most powerful leader in the Communist world, and who, unlike his predecessor, showed little inclination to capitulate to workers' demands. On the other side was Solidarity—frustrated and militant and less and less amenable to control by the relatively moderate leaders such as Walesa. In the middle was the Catholic church, still hoping to mediate between the adversaries, and, of course, the large masses of the Polish people, who by that time were becoming strongly critical of both sides, primarily because of the catastrophic and rapidly de-

teriorating economic situation. The stalemate between Solidarity and
the Jaruzelski regime could not last: in early November, following an
abortive meeting between Walesa, Jaruzelski, and Archbishop Glemp,
who succeeded Cardinal Wyszynski as head of the Polish church, the
deadlock appeared complete.

One other actor, the Soviet Union, was watching the developments
in Poland with growing concern. There is no doubt that the Kremlin
was taken by surprise by the events of the summer of 1980 and by the
Gdansk agreement establishing Solidarity. Moscow's initial reaction to
the unfolding crisis was relatively moderate and most likely reflected
considerable uncertainty about the best way of containing the Polish
disease and preventing it from spreading elsewhere in Eastern Europe.
In addition to criticizing Solidarity and putting pressure on the Polish
leadership to settle the crisis, Moscow began gradually to apply less
subtle measures such as joint military maneuvers under the aegis of the
Warsaw Pact, visits to Warsaw of high-ranking Soviet officials, and
increasing references to the Brezhnev doctrine contained in harshly
critical statements regularly issued by the Soviet leadership.

Although throughout the entire critical period there was a constant
fear of a possible Soviet military intervention *a la* Hungary and
Czechoslovakia, the invasion never materialized. One may speculate
that the Kremlin concluded at some point that a military solution would
have been too costly: unlike the Czechoslovak army, the Polish troops
were expected to resist, necessitating a large-scale military deployment
that in 1980–81 would have proved highly burdensome in light of the
continuing Soviet involvement in Afghanistan and on the Sino-Soviet
border. Moreover, while there was no doubt regarding Soviet military
victory, the latter was likely to be followed by a lengthy occupation
that would be extremely costly in economic terms. Finally, a military
intervention would antagonize not only Washington but, above all,
Western Europe, which the Kremlin has been courting assiduously in
an effort to decouple it from the United States.

On the other hand, the anticipated spillover of the Polish crisis into
the neighboring countries did not occur despite the fears of Czechoslovakia and East Germany, which as Soviet proxies have been engaged in
a vicious campaign against Solidarity. Presumably the main reason for
the indifference of the East European workers toward their Polish
brethren was the disastrous economic situation in Poland: faced with a
situation of greater freedom but empty shelves and long lines in front of
shops, Poland's neighbors opted for full bellies. Hence it soon dawned
on Moscow that the crisis could be relatively easily contained, isolating
Poland from the rest of the Warsaw Pact and reducing or even eliminating the need for a Soviet invasion.

While the Soviet leadership decided against direct intervention, it may be taken for granted that the Kremlin was consulted about, and gave its blessing to, the imposition of martial law by the Jaruzelski regime on December 13, 1981. To everyone's surprise, the military takeover proved remarkably easy and despite its great numeric strength and seeming mass popular support, Solidarity put up only token resistance, especially after the arrest and internment of Walesa and the rest of the leadership. Within a few days the Polish military appeared to be in full control of the situation. However, it soon became obvious that although it proved easy to defeat Solidarity and assume control, the Polish *junta* had little or no idea how to restore normalcy to the country, which at the end of 1981 stood at the threshold of political and economic collapse.

The subsequent two years witnessed desperate attempts by the Jaruzelski regime to normalize the situation—without visible success. While Solidarity was formally destroyed, efforts to replace it with officially sanctioned unions failed rather dismally and the Polish working class in 1984 remained as alienated as before. The same applied to the other major social classes—the peasants and the intelligentsia. The ruling party lost close to one-third of its membership and if it could be said to rule at all, it was only courtesy of the military, which despite the official lifting of martial law in July 1983 continued to control the "commanding heights" in the country. The Catholic church, which tried to maintain its mediating role after December 1981, was not very effective despite the return visit to Poland of Pope John Paul II in June 1983, which was clearly intended (unsuccessfully as it turned out) to speed up the process of national reconciliation. Although some progress was achieved in the economic sphere, the overall situation remained difficult and both the gross national product and the standard of living in the mid-1980s continued to stagnate. Hence it was not surprising that the Jaruzelski regime was probably supported by not more than five to ten percent of the population and that the gap between the rulers and the ruled in Poland remained as wide as ever.

What had happened and what factors were responsible for this unexpected turnabout in the fortunes of a regime that had begun so auspiciously years before? Consideration of a dozen or so systematic variables mentioned at the outset of this chapter may prove helpful in explaining what took place.

CULTURE

Culture, as a systematic component, is defined by Huntington as embracing "the values, attitudes, orientations, myths and beliefs relevant to politics and dominant in society."[8] In this context, the concept includes not only mass perceptions and beliefs, many of them with roots established long before the Communist takeover, but also both the official ideology advocated and disseminated by the ruling elite and the antiregime attitudes articulated by political dissenters.

Perhaps the most striking aspect of the cultural variable in Polish politics has been the remarkable persistence of what may be termed "traditional" values, despite the massive socialization and re-socialization campaigns conducted by successive regimes since the end of the war. At the risk of oversimplification, the most relevant of these aspects appear to be basic distrust and disobedience of political or governmental authority; emphasis on egalitarian values and equality; fervent, if not rampant, nationalism; and attachment to certain traditional institutions and social arrangements and structures.

In talking to members of the ruling elite, one often hears the complaint that "building communism in a country such as Poland is an impossible task." It can be presumed that over the years, the Polish Communist leaders must have become increasingly frustrated with their inability to lay strong foundations for a new political and social system, eyeing with some envy the situation in Bulgaria, Czechoslovakia, East Germany, and Romania, where the obedient population had seemingly accepted and become reconciled to the new order.

There is no doubt that deeply rooted mistrust and dislike of authority have been largely responsible for the failure of the Communist system to penetrate Polish society. It can be argued that although the antiauthoritarian attitudes go back several centuries, they acquired their modern expression during the 150-year period of partitions, further reinforced by 6 years of German occupation during World War II. The fact remains that in the first half of the 1980s the average Pole, in contrast to his neighbors, most likely considered the Communist regime essentially illegitimate and imposed from the outside. To be sure, one could expect a similar attitude toward almost any Polish regime, yet the fact that it was a Communist government that, in addition, was imported from the East, made its mass acceptance impossible. Centuries of resistance against foreign domination left marks on the Polish psyche that thirty years of Communist indoctrination did little to eradicate.

Whether one chooses to call it attachment to freedom, rugged individualism, lack of discipline, or simply proclivity to anarchy, the Polish people have steadfastly refused to accept the Communist system as legitimate. This has been as true for the educated classes—traditionally the bastion of independent thought and action—as for the peasants and workers, until recently assumed to be much more malleable and obedient.

There are several interesting corollaries to this phenomenon. First of all, it must be emphasized that the resistance to the system stems only partly from the fact that it happens to be a Communist one. It does not necessarily mean that a democratic system of whatever shape or form would have been universally accepted. On the contrary, traditional Polish political culture tended to be, if not anti-, then at least non-democratic, embodying to a large degree the values of the old gentry, which were highly elitist, nonegalitarian, and particularistic. These traits seemed to have survived long after the Communist takeover and explain the persistence of deep social cleavages between various segments of Polish society: intelligentsia and workers; workers and peasants; urban and rural dwellers.

A recent striking change in the Polish political and social environment that has greatly impaired the ability of the regime to exercise its authority has been the significant muting of the above conflicts. The process has been slow in coming. German occupation policies did little to reduce the traditional cleavages: directed primarily against the urban intelligentsia, they tended to spare the workers and peasants; indeed, the latter benefited greatly from a sharp rise in food prices. This policy was largely followed by the Communists during the takeover period: land reform benefited the peasants, the industrial working class was elevated to an apparent privileged status, and the intelligentsia continued to suffer. It is not surprising, therefore, that on the eve of Stalinization, the cleavages among the three major classes appeared as wide as ever, and the fact that the Stalinist *Gleichschaltung* policies were directed against *all* classes did little to reduce the existing chasms.

One of the most interesting and significant aspects of the bloodless coup of October 1956 was the emergence of a united front against the Stalinist regime, spearheaded by the intelligentsia, including university students, but also strongly supported by the workers and even the peasants. To be sure, the alliance was short-lived but it accomplished two things: it succeeded in overthrowing an unpopular regime and it proved that in a moment of crisis the old antagonisms could be bridged.

The Gomulka regime, which for a brief time enjoyed the support of the masses, realized the tenuous nature of that support and sought a firmer power base. The peasants, mollified by the abandonment of collectivization and other reforms, were *de facto* once again neutralized, and the regime decided to turn against the intelligentsia, which it perceived as its main enemy. Ultimately it succeeded in driving a wedge between the intellectuals and students, on the one hand, and the workers, on the other, as manifested in March 1968, when Warsaw workers appeared strongly critical of the activities of students protesting against increasingly restrictive government policies.

One could argue that March 1968 represented the deepest chasm between the two crucial strata of Polish society, a gap that was not bridged for the next eight years. Thus, in December 1970, when the Baltic coast workers rose against the Gomulka regime, the intelligentsia and the students remained passive. Not until the summer of 1976, when the June riots, followed by mass arrests of Polish workers, gave birth to the formation of KOR was the gap closed again, with the formation of an alliance between the workers and the intelligentsia. Faced with this major change in the existing sociopolitical formula, the regime was caught by surprise and clearly did not know how to deal with the new situation.

The birth of Solidarity in August 1980 simply reaffirmed the strength of the alliance that continued in force until the imposition of martial law. The Communist regime tried very hard to cause divisiveness between the workers and their allies by focusing its ire particularly on the leaders of the Workers' Defense Committee who were among the first to be arrested in December 1981 and who remained in prison after the lifting of martial law and the release of most of the other internees.

The institutionalization of the worker-intellectual alliance reflected in the creation of Solidarity represented a new element in the Polish sociopolitical milieu. The October 1956 alliance proved fragile and broke down as soon as the Gomulka regime appeared to make some concessions, so much so that in both March 1968 and December 1970 workers, intellectuals, and students acted separately. The situation in 1976 was different, although initially it seemed as if the 1970 syndrome would repeat itself: in late 1975 and early 1976, intellectuals and students, largely in isolation, mounted a protest campaign against constitutional revisions decreed by the regime; this was followed by workers' riots ignited by a drastic increase in food prices in June 1976. The developments since 1980 strongly suggest that the united front of workers, students, and intellectuals has now become a permanent feature of the Polish political scene.

Historically, the intellectuals enjoyed a privileged status in Polish society and were traditionally viewed as its spiritual and cultural leaders. While the Polish people as a whole harbored deep mistrust of their political rulers, they tended to listen to and follow the prescriptions and messages of the writers, poets, and other members of the cultural and artistic elites. It must be said that although in general the behavior of Polish intellectuals during the Stalinist period was hardly inspiring, they contributed significantly to the process of national reawakening and liberalization in the mid-1950s and remained in the forefront of antigovernment opposition thereafter. This was true for both party and nonparty intellectuals, many of whom were accused of revisionism, severely punished, and eventually forced to leave the country.

Initially, their resentment of, and alienation from, the regime was mostly caused by the latter's threat of their own professional or group interests in areas such as censorship, contacts with the West, and other restrictive policies. However, in time, the intellectuals became increasingly politicized, and their fairly narrow, occasionally parochial requests transformed themselves into political demands for greater participation and autonomy and condemning government policies that tended to restrict them. The protest against constitutional amendments proposed by the Gierek regime in the winter of 1975–76 was a good illustration of the growing militancy of intellectuals and students. While to an outside observer the proposed changes in the Stalinist constitution passed in 1952 appeared relatively marginal, the fact that the changes were decreed by fiat without proper consultation and participation of the Polish citizenry was apparently seen as another example of high-handed government policy that had to be resisted. Although, in the final analysis, the regime had its way, some of the proposed amendments had to be modified under the pressure of the opposition; this concession could have been interpreted as at least a partial victory for the dissenters.

Perhaps encouraged by this success, the intellectual opposition not only took up the cause of the workers against the government in the summer of 1976, but also began to call for greater respect for human rights in general. This was no longer an *ad hoc* campaign focused on a single, specific issue, but a frontal attack on, and a challenge to, the existing system. The fact that for the first time in modern Polish history the intellectuals were no longer speaking only on their own behalf but also as members of a powerful alliance clearly presented a major problem for the regime, which thus far had proved unable or unwilling to handle it. There is little doubt that the intellectuals played a major role in the alliance in at least two ways: by giving it national and international exposure and visibility, and by raising its level of politicization by broadening the scope of its demands.

There is considerable evidence that, in comparison with the Soviet Union and the other East European countries, the dissident movement in Poland has been flourishing. In addition to the Workers' Defense Committee, there were other dissident groups active in the country in early 1978, representing separate political viewpoints. The Workers' Defense Committee—the oldest and best known of the dissident groups—was on the left of the political spectrum. Its programmatic goals appeared to be relatively modest, aimed primarily at achieving a gradual liberalization of the existing system. This was to be accomplished by working within and through the system, rather than by overthrowing it. The Committee's publications have made frequent references to the Polish constitution and various other legal provisions, which, in its eyes, could be utilized to gain and safeguard democratic rights and freedoms. Above all, the Committee's leadership was most anxious to avoid a major political crisis that could result in Soviet intervention *a la* Czechoslovakia. Consequently, the Committee's anti-Soviet pronouncements were relatively rare and muted, and they also tended to play down traditional Polish nationalist sentiments.

The other dissident groups have been much less known. Some were organized by defectors from the Workers' Defense Committee who were apparently dissatisfied with its relatively moderate program. Others went even further to the right and were strongly nationalistic and anti-Soviet. All of the dissident groups, including the Workers' Defense Committee, were pushed into the background by the emergence of Solidarity, which, for all practical purposes, became the sole political opposition movement, overshadowing even the Catholic church which until then had been perceived in the role of chief opposition spokesman. Some of the pronouncements made at the Solidarity Congress reflected the growing belief that both the leadership and the rank and file saw themselves becoming increasingly responsible for the future of the Polish state and nation.

In light of the above, it is not surprising that the second cultural variable to influence the popular attitude toward the present system has been nationalism, traditionally a powerful force in Polish politics. Although for a variety of reasons Poland never quite succeeded in developing its own brand of national communism, successive party leaders tried, with some measure of success, to utilize nationalist feelings for their own purposes by appearing as defenders of the country's national interest (as in the case of the Oder-Neisse line) or its ethnic purity (as in the case of the virulent anti-Semitic campaign of 1968). On the other hand, the Communist party did not come close to eradicating the traditional anti-Russian feeling that had permeated Polish society for generations and that attached indelible stigma to anything entering the country from the East. The initial popularity and semilegitimacy of Gomulka was based on his being identified above all as anti-Soviet rather than anti-Stalinist, and it was this (incorrect) perception that permitted him to enjoy a relatively lengthy honeymoon, certainly a longer one than he deserved.

The current military regime had no such credit to fall back on. With the West German threat to Polish western frontiers gone and the large majority of Polish Jews having left the country, the leadership has been in no position to mobilize nationalist sentiments against real or imaginary enemies, unless it were to be the Soviet Union. This the regime refused to do, at least until now. On the contrary, there is considerable evidence that, if anything, both Gierek and Jaruzelski have been more "pro-Soviet" than their predecessor, judging from their own pronouncements as well as from comments emanating from the Polish media in the past several years. To an average man in the street, the present leadership appeared to be more subservient to Moscow than necessary, and, rightly or wrongly, the Soviet Union continued to be blamed for Poland's recent difficulties. This mass perception did little to strengthen the regime's popularity and legitimacy, making it even more difficult for it to make and execute policy.

The final cultural component affecting political processes in the country in recent years was the continued attachment to certain traditional political and social institutions. One of the strongest manifestations of this traditionalism was the campaign against constitutional revisions decreed by the government, which mirrored an almost irrational attachment to a constitution passed at the height of Stalinism that was hardly ever respected or observed. To the question of why people protested, the standard response has been that the government had no right to tamper even with a basically undemocratic, quasitotalitarian constitution, which, after all, represented the most fundamental legal document in the land, one that could not be changed by party fiat. In line with this attitude, the recent campaign in defense of human rights tended to emphasize constitutional guarantees of individual freedoms. This also helps to explain the continuing frequent references by the opposition to the Gdansk and other agreements signed in the summer of 1980 that the military *junta* has broken by dissolving Solidarity and restricting the workers' right to strike.

More relevant for our discussion is the apparently strong attachment to such institutions as the Catholic church and the family farm. Space does not permit a full discussion of church-state relations in Communist Poland. Suffice it to say that after an earlier period of relative calm characterized by a *modus vivendi* between the pragmatic regime of Gierek and the essentially conservative church dominated by Cardinal Wyszynski, the most recent developments suggest that the official policy of the church has swung in favor of the worker-intellectual alliance, embodied in Solidarity. The effect of this switch should not be underestimated.

Conventional wisdom has long been that the Poles are strongly religious. This view is based on such evidence as crowded churches, a homogeneous population, and an increase in the numeric strength of the clergy. My own impression is that if indeed the church is still popular today, it is much less because of its religious or spiritual role, and infinitely more because of its function as the bastion of independence from Communist control. It could be shown that in the past the church enjoyed its greatest popularity at the height of governmental persecution and that it lost support when church-state relations improved. This relationship was eventually recognized by the Polish leadership, which in the past decade or so has tried to cultivate good relations with the church. For a while, this policy of accommodation seemed successful, as the essentially conservative clergy confined itself to the defense of its own interests, seldom venturing into the purely political arena. However, the deteriorating political and economic situation and the resulting growing reactionary character of the Gierek regime apparently persuaded the church hierarchy to abandon its semineutral stance and to add its opposition to that of the workers and the intellectuals, presenting the current regime with still another major challenge.

Although in 1980–81 the church generally supported Solidarity, that support appeared much stronger among the rank and file of the clergy than at the top of the hierarchy, which seemed at times to resent the fact that Solidarity preempted the church's traditional role as the sole bastion of anticommunist opposition. This ambivalent attitude became more pronounced after the death of Cardinal Wyszynski who had headed the Polish church for thirty-three years, and there is evidence that as a result the church's popularity among some segments of the population began to decline.

STRUCTURE

The concept of structure in this context includes "formal organizations through which the society makes authoritative decisions, such as political parties, legislatures, executives, and bureaucracies."[9]

In many respects the Polish Communist party in the early 1980s did not differ greatly from its counterparts in the other people's democracies. Its membership in mid-1981 stood at 2,691,000, which accounted for roughly 7 percent of the population.[10] This percentage had not changed greatly since the mid-1960s, when an intensive recruitment drive was undertaken by the Gomulka regime. In terms of social composition, the Polish party typified a highly bureaucratized structure, with 44.9 percent of its membership accounted for by government officials and white collar workers, 11.8 percent by peasants and farm workers, and only 43.3 percent by industrial workers.[11]

It may be argued that the situation in the middle echelons and in the rank and file of the party in the mid-1980s must have given little cause for joy to its leaders. The continuing dissatisfaction with the regime's performance, especially in the economic sphere, meant that the party, the vanguard of Polish society, whose task it was to lead the country to a better future, had not only failed to generate mass support for its policies but it had also allowed a serious challenge to the system's legitimacy to develop almost overnight.

As suggested earlier, the demands for greater intraparty democracy were successfully squelched in the wake of the Extraordinary Ninth Party Congress in July 1981. The fact that it was the military that seized power in December 1981 spoke for itself and testified to the near collapse of the ruling party. Apparently shortly after the imposition of martial law there was some discussion about dissolving the Polish United Workers' Party and replacing it with a new party, purged of both the conservative and revisionist wings, for which there was a precedent in Hungary following the 1956 revolt. For reasons that remain obscure it was decided to retain the old party, which continued to function courtesy of the military.

What were the reasons for the malaise within the ruling party? Perhaps the major one was the party's failure to penetrate and become an integral part of Polish society. Throughout most of its existence, quantity rather than quality was the chief determinant of recruitment into the party, with the result that little attention was paid to the caliber of the new entrants, most of whom were joining the party for opportunistic reasons. Periodic purges, in the guise of "verification campaigns" conducted in the name of ideological purity, succeeded only in eliminating the marginal elements of the rank and file, leaving the hard core or the "cadres" largely untouched. The emphasis on sheer numbers resulted in most of the new recruits coming out of the semieducated classes, who considered party membership a vehicle for rapid career advancement in the government or the economy. This, in turn, was responsible for the rather low intellectual and ideological level of the average party member, who was willing to pay lip service to the regime as long as he derived some tangible benefits from it.

The successive regimes, including the current one, never quite succeeded in defining the proper role for the ruling party. Periodically, especially following radical changes in the top leadership as in 1956, 1970, and 1980–81, there were calls for making the party a rather narrow, elitist organization whose main task was to provide overall guidance and leadership to Polish society, leaving the day-to-day administration and policy implementation to government bureaucrats and specialized groups, regardless of their political affiliation. This policy was usually tied to plans for a major overhaul of the economic system and debates about the importance of "scientific-technical revolution," both of which required major inputs from "experts" rather than from "reds." Usually, this "pragmatic" approach did not last very long, as the firmly entrenched party apparatus resented outside interference and the concurrent loss of power and influence. For all practical purposes, the regime never managed to make achievement rather than ascription the chief criterion of political recruitment, thus forfeiting its chance of making a real breakthrough on the road toward modernization.

In the mid-1980s party membership continued to be the prerequisite for political and socioeconomic advancement. As a result, the decision-making processes at various levels and in nearly all areas were monopolized by intellectual mediocrities who by and large tended to be ignorant of the real problems confronting the society at large. Periodic calls for the reestablishment of "links with the masses" remained largely unheeded, and the gap between the rulers and the ruled continued to widen. This lack of "contact with the masses" was clearly one of the major reasons for the series of blunders committed by both the Gomulka and the Gierek regimes, and the performance of the Jaruzelski government in this respect has not inspired much confidence.

Another reason for these seemingly irrational policies was the apparent inability of the party leadership to establish firm control over the middle-rank bureaucracy and the rank and file. It is well known that in all Communist parties it is relatively easier to purge the top-level leadership than either the middle-echelon apparatus or the membership at large, and the Polish party was no exception. After 1956 it took Gomulka several years to establish full control over the party, and the same was true, albeit to a lesser degree, for the Gierek regime after 1970. The result of this asymmetry between the top and the middle party echelons were frequent difficulties and delays in, and even sabotage of, new policies decreed by the top leadership and implemented by the middle, which, as a rule, tended to be more conservative than the oligarchy. The fact that the wholesale turnover at the very top of the party hierarchy in 1980–81 was not accompanied by a similar turnover in the Central Committee apparatus and internal security agencies meant that there was much greater continuity in the party than suggested by the apparent disarray on the surface and there is no doubt that this made it easier in December 1981 to impose martial law.

Little needs to be said about the remaining Polish political parties— the United Peasant Party (*Zjednoczone Stronnictwo Ludowe*) and the Democratic Party (*Stronnictwo Demokratyczne*). Despite the frequent elaborate show of consultations between the Communist party and its junior partners, for all practical purposes the latter amounted to little more than the traditional "transmission belts" linking the ruling party with the peasants and the intelligentsia. At times they acted as a kind of pressure group, but their influence on decision making has been minimal and they served mostly as a window dressing.

As suggested earlier, both the party and government bureaucracies resembled the traditional Communist stereotypes, characterized by inherent conservatism, fear and distrust of innovations, and determination to defend the *status quo*. Together with the great majority of the party's rank and file, the party apparatus tended to be opportunistic and careerist, and its level of intellectual and professional sophistication left much to be desired. Certainly there were sporadic attempts to improve the latter by the cooptation of better-educated individuals, but the overall success was meager. As a result, the standards of bureaucratic performance with respect to decision making and policy implementation were quite low.

Turning to the legislatures, here again, the early promises of greater parliamentary involvement in, and influence on, the political life of the country have not materialized. New party leaders started off by promising to make the Polish parliament—the *Sejm*—a focal point in the far-ranging discussions of major economic and social issues by making it more visible and by granting it a greater role in consultations and decision making. Although it seems that in recent years various parliamentary committees have been given more information that enabled them to discuss some specific problems in greater depth and to scrutinize policy implementation, the infrequent and brief plenary sessions of the *Sejm* continued to serve the ritualistic purpose of rubber-stamping governmental decrees and providing a forum for occasional major pronouncements by the party leaders.

To conclude, the political structures in Poland in the mid-1980s tended by and large to conform to the Soviet model emulated by all people's democracies. As such, they frequently acted as a major obstacle on the road to modernization and, thus far at least, periodic attempts to transform them in the direction of greater efficiency have failed in the face of bureaucratic resistance favoring the *status quo*.

GROUPS

Groups can be defined as "the social and economic formations, formal and informal, which participate in politics and make demands on the political structures."[12] It may be generalized that, in this respect, the Polish record has been much less impressive than that of Czechoslovakia and Hungary, in that the notion of pluralism, however broadly defined, has never been an integral part of Polish political culture. With few recent exceptions, the performance of formal groups has been rather dismal and there have been only a few examples of particular interest groups acquiring even a semi-legitimate status in the political system.

What were the reasons for this phenomenon? To a large extent, the emergence of functionally specific interest or pressure groups in Poland followed the same path as elsewhere in Eastern Europe, and was the by-product of rapid industrialization and growing complexity and differentiation of the socioeconomic system, which ultimately forced the ruling elite to seek advice from experts in various fields. In Poland, in contrast to some of the other countries in the region, however, only a few of these groups became institutionalized and were brought into the decision-making process. A good deal of the resistance to these groups was due to the character of the Polish Communist party, highly jealous of its prerogatives and resentful of the intrusion of outside specialists. Faced with the strong resistance of the party apparatus, the various groups either meekly surrendered or broke up, with individual members often coopted into the party establishment where they quickly adopted a conservative stance. Some groups never developed a corporatist elan or image of their own, and seemed content with playing the role of traditional "transmission belts."

The most prominent groups of this kind were the trade unions, which even during the relatively liberal periods in postwar Polish history never quite abandoned their role of obedient tools of the party. Throughout, their record of defending workers' interests has been most dismal and the fact that they played no part in the three major confrontations between the workers and the regime in December 1970, June 1976, and July–August 1980 speaks for itself. Hence it is hardly surprising that the chief demand of the workers striking on the Baltic coast in the summer of 1980 was the establishment of an independent labor union that would articulate workers' interests in an authentic fashion. It is also not surprising that the demands for restoration of outlawed Solidarity continue to be articulated by the opposition in the first half of the 1980s.

In the absence of empirical evidence, one can hypothesize that the failure of the Polish pressure groups until recently to assert themselves vis-a-vis the government was caused by, among other things, the general dislike of collectivism as a mode of human action. Reference has been made to the deeply rooted mistrust of authority and the attachment to individualism that characterized the traditional Polish political culture. It may be speculated that the idea of interest groups, which in the Communist context would not be truly representative or democratically organized, did not appeal greatly to many individuals who preferred to strike out on their own.

There were, of course, significant exceptions. One of the most articulate and visible groups represented the literary and artistic community, which for the past two decades has been rather deeply engaged in political activities, progressing from the defense of its professional and particularistic interests to demands for greater respect for human rights of all segments of the population. Many writers and artists were heavily involved in the crucial events of October 1956, March 1968, and the period after June 1976. Between these milestones in postwar Polish history, they maintained almost constant pressure on the ruling elite, reminding it of the constitutional guarantees for the freedom of expression. By and large, they proved remarkably effective, possibly because of their high national and international visibility, and there is no doubt that the relatively free Polish cultural and artistic climate owes much to their efforts.

The participation of students in challenging the legitimacy of the system was not surprising. Beginning in the mid-1950s, youth and student associations became a major thorn in the side of the successive regimes, which tried a number of times to mobilize both groups for their own purposes, without much success. There is considerable evidence pointing to a high degree of alienation and anomie among young people, caused by political, social, and economic factors such as the absence of channels for meaningful political participation, generational conflict, and reduced employment opportunities. Following the explosive events of March 1968, in the course of which the students suffered a major defeat at the hands of the police and conservative workers, they remained largely aloof from political activities for several years, only to return with a vengeance during the debate on constitutional revisions in late 1975. Since then they have been in the forefront of the opposition movement.

Two other groups—one formal and the other informal—deserve a comment. The formal, institutionalized pressure group is, of course, the Catholic church. As mentioned above, the church in recent years has moved away from defending its own institutional interests toward broader involvement in the country's political life. The reasons for this change of heart can only be guessed. It may have been due in part to a realization by the top church hierarchy that the *modus vivendi* with the regime that characterized church-state relations throughout most of the past twenty years was resulting in gradual erosion of support among many segments of Polish society, especially among the youth and the intelligentsia, who traditionally had viewed the church as the chief source of opposition to the system. In a sense, the church was playing into the hands of the government, which has carefully avoided direct confrontation with the Polish episcopate.

It may be speculated that the growing church militancy represented a shift caused by the entry of a new generation of clergy into leading positions within the hierarchy. The old generation, personified by Cardinal Wyszynski, was primarily concerned with sheer survival in the face of Stalinist pressures; later it became interested mostly in the maintenance of the *status quo* that granted the church a privileged and unique position in the system. However, in the mid-1980s there was no longer any question of the church's ability to survive and to retain its status, and it may be assumed that the new recruits at different levels of the hierarchy, as a rule much better educated and more sophisticated, were becoming impatient with their elders' benign neglect of major political and social issues plaguing the country. Judging from its pronouncements at the various Vatican Councils, the Polish church in the 1960s enjoyed a rather conservative reputation abroad, which at that time could have been justified by its situation at home. Nevertheless, some of the reforms decreed by the Councils, as much as they were initially resented by the church leadership, may have had an impact on the younger clergy, who gradually became politically and socially more conscious than in the past. The next logical step was greater engagement in political processes.

The overall result was that while the Gomulka regime was able to enlist the support of the church for many of its domestic and foreign policies, this was becoming increasingly harder for Gierek, despite his own conciliatory policy toward the church's top leadership. The climax came in 1976 when Cardinal Wyszynski, as well as individual members of the clergy, spoke out sharply against constitutional amendments and other social and economic policies. There was no longer any doubt that the regime has lost another potential and important ally.

The status and prestige of the church received a powerful boost in 1978 with the election of a Polish pope, John Paul II. The pope paid a long-delayed pontifical visit to his native land in the summer of 1979 which turned out to be an overwhelming success for the church and represented a crucial step in the gradual escalation of political opposition culminating in the birth of Solidarity only one year or so later.

As mentioned earlier, the church's relations with Solidarity were not always entirely cordial and smooth, and, according to some observers, certain church leaders became envious of the great success of Solidarity which tended to overshadow the traditional position of the church as the sole opposition leader. It could also be argued that, especially after the imposition of martial law, the leadership of the church became more concerned with the preservation of the *status quo* and of the church's ecclesiastical role than with the clergy's involvement in the country's politics.

What about the other, informal group—the peasantry? It is common-place to assert that, for a variety of reasons, peasants are hard to orga-nize and mobilize. Poland was no exception to this pattern. The ruling elite has traditionally viewed the peasants as class enemies. Through-out postwar history, Polish peasants had no formal representation in the political system. At the height of the collectivization campaign in the 1950s, the regime refused to allow the formation of an association representing the collective farmers. Until 1981, formally at least, the Polish peasants did not have an institutionalized representation defend-ing their interests against the government, unless one considers the United Peasant Party as a pressure group, which, as mentioned above, it was not. The establishment of Rural Solidarity was a major but short-lived effort by the peasants to institutionalize a genuine representation. It is estimated that prior to the December 1981 debacle it numbered some 3 million members.

Does this mean that the Polish peasantry did not play a major role in the country's affairs or exert pressure on the political system? The answer is clearly negative, yet it is also true that the peasants' influence has not been uniformly strong in the recent period. The first decade of Communist Poland saw the peasants as the major target of the Commu-nist political and economic offensive, starting with land reform and ending in the mass dissolution of the collective farms. The next fifteen years or so were devoted to regaining the peasants' confidence in the system and inducing them to expand production. In the early 1970s, the role of agriculture was greatly overshadowed by the drive for industrial modernization and a rapid rate of economic growth, and the farm sec-tor was almost forgotten. It was only in the aftermath of the food crisis of 1976 that the peasants reappeared as crucial political and economic actors.

Actually, the regime's relationship to individual farmers illustrates well the shortcomings of the Polish system. On the one hand, there is the top party leadership, which appears reconciled to the existence of the private farm sector for many years to come and is openly com-mitted to its support in the name of greater farm output and higher living standards. On the other hand, the peasants distrust the govern-ment and Polish agriculture has been beset by difficulties such as a continued exodus from the villages, the gradual aging of the farm popu-lation, and the fragmentation of individual holdings, making a substan-tial increase in output highly problematical without additional reforms and governmental aid.

To sum up, until 1980 the Polish regime, for various reasons, still refused to institutionalize a network of pressure groups, thus depriving itself of a potentially valuable ally and partner in decision making.

However, it could not prevent the emergence of formal and informal opposition groups that, by articulating increasingly political demands, have been contributing to the already serious problems faced by the system. What happened in 1980 is, of course, history and it is clear that since the establishment of Solidarity successive Polish regimes had to recognize, willy-nilly, the existence of interest groups that could not be ignored or excluded from participation in decision making with impunity.

LEADERSHIP

It is probably no exaggeration to say that postwar Poland has not been blessed with great political leaders—"the individuals in political institutions and groups who exercise more influence than others on the allocation of values."[13] Throughout its postwar existence, the country has been ruled by six individuals, and although all the evidence is not in, one may generalize that none of them exhibited the kinds of qualities that would have earned him the adjectives "great," "legitimate," or "charismatic."

Despite recent attempts to exonerate and rehabilitate him, Boleslaw Bierut, who ruled Poland during the Stalinist period, must go down in history as essentially a mediocre leader whose major achievement was that he managed to spare the country from the worst excesses of the mass political terror practiced in Bulgaria, Czechoslovakia, and Hungary. While this accomplishment was obviously not unimportant, it was largely offset by his crude policy towards the peasants and the intelligentsia. Bierut's successor, Edward Ochab, was an interim leader whose tenure lasted barely six months. His greatest achievement, in turn, was to pave the way for the return of Gomulka to power.

Wladyslaw Gomulka, who headed the Polish Communist party for roughly twenty years (1943–48 and 1956–70), was not a run-of-the-mill leader. For a brief period (1956–57) he was probably the only genuinely legitimate national leader in postwar Polish history. He was also a man of some principles, as illustrated by his behavior in the early postwar period when his convictions almost cost him his life. Yet, in hindsight, he was also a person of rather limited ability and narrow horizons, whose principles and convictions frequently became transformed into sheer obstinacy and irrational attachment to discredited concepts and ideas whose usefulness was long outlived. He represented a curious blend of pragmatic thinking—as illustrated by his revolutionary decision to dissolve the collective farms—and stubborn refusal to innovate—as reflected by his reluctance to reform and modernize the Polish economy. There is a good chance that he will be remembered chiefly as the leader who took almost fifteen years to squander the great reservoir of credit and confidence granted him by the Polish people in October 1956, and who ended up as a bitter and humiliated man.

By all counts, Gomulka's successor, Edward Gierek, appeared to be a man for all seasons. Unencumbered by ideological baggage from the past, untainted by participation in the factional struggles between the "Muscovites" and the "natives," possessing an impressive wartime resistance record in France, experienced as a party bureaucrat, and famed for his efficient administration of Silesia, economically the most important Polish province, he seemed the ideal choice to lead the country from inertia and stagnation toward a better future. Gierek was immediately hailed as a pragmatist, a technocrat, and a modernizer.

For a while, all the predictions appeared to have come true. In a relatively short time Gierek succeeded in mollifying the irate working class, granted major concessions to the peasants, improved relations with the church, and conciliated the intelligentsia. Yet, only a few years later, the same leader was forced to call off the drastic increase in food prices, thus rescinding a major policy decision within twenty-four hours in the face of massive resistance by the same workers who had brought him to power less than six years earlier. Although Gierek's role in the decision that triggered off the June 1976 riots is far from clear, he was commonly identified by the masses as being ultimately responsible for it. The laboriously constructed image of the pragmatic modernizer and efficient administrator became tarnished, and the whole system lost credibility overnight. One may hypothesize that the major reason that Gierek was not ousted was the lack of alternatives. No other member of the ruling oligarchy commanded sufficient support—both internal and external—to take over.

While Gierek's ouster in September 1980 was inevitable in light of the events of July and August, his replacement by Kania was not and again it reflected a dearth of suitable candidates. As it transpired, Kania did reasonably well in negotiation with both Solidarity and his own critics within the party. His leadership was reaffirmed at the Ninth Party Congress and his ouster in October 1981 was a surprise. In hindsight it was clear that Kania was viewed as too soft by the Kremlin, which wanted the Polish crisis ended and looked for someone willing to take extraordinary measures to do it.

Although Jaruzelski was clearly Moscow's choice, he also enjoyed considerable popularity in the country, if only as the first truly professional soldier commanding Poland's armed forces. His imposition of martial law in December 1981 can be interpreted as the result of a sincere belief that he and the military were saving the country from a catastrophe—whether in the form of a bloody confrontation with an invading Soviet army or in the shape of an equally bloody civil war. But it should not be forgotten that the repression of Solidarity was also the key demand of Moscow and in the Soviet interest, and that it served to save the PUWP from disintegration and loss of power. The coup was obviously long in preparation and was not a decision of the moment.

While it is too early in 1984 to pass judgment on Jaruzelski's performance in the past two years, it may be said that he has done as well as could be expected in clearly unfavorable circumstances. Although he did not hesitate to eliminate the political opposition, Jaruzelski's counterrevolution has been relatively mild. But so far he has failed to make any progress in achieving reconciliation with the society.

POLICIES

The last systematic component—policies—will be analyzed briefly, since many of them have already been discussed.

Prior to the summer of 1980 on the domestic scene, by far the most important policy decision made by the Gierek regime concerned the new model of Poland's economic development to be based on an extensive modernization of the country's industrial structure with the aid of Western credits and technology. Although the new strategy proved highly successful in stimulating rapid economic growth, it also overheated the economy and added to existing inflationary pressure. While real income and living standards undoubtedly rose in the early years of Gierek's rule, ultimately the output of consumer goods and foodstuffs could not keep up with increased demand fueled by higher wages, and serious shortages began to develop, causing growing dissatisfaction among consumers.

Another major reason for the mounting shortages was that the price of certain key foodstuffs such as meat had been kept frozen since the second half of the 1960s, making Poland probably the only country in the world where food prices remained constant for almost a decade, despite global inflationary pressures. It appeared that Gierek had learned a lesson from the fate of his predecessor and intended to acquire and maintain popular support by keeping food prices frozen. While politically justified in the short run, this decision proved disastrous in the long run, illustrating the vagaries of decision making, even within a supposedly enlightened and pragmatic Communist system.

Other policies initiated after December 1970 also appeared to make considerable sense and testified to Gierek's political acumen. A comprehensive reform of the educational system was clearly needed in light of the rapid socioeconomic transformation of the country. A new approach toward agriculture attempted once again to reassure the peasants about the survival of individual farms while at the same time encouraging them to expand output. Two successive reforms of local government, although politically inspired and aimed at diluting the power of provincial party secretaries vis-a-vis the center, were not devoid of rationality. The conciliatory policy toward the intelligentsia and the church also made good political sense. Thus, on the whole, the initial record appeared most impressive even though, as mentioned above, the implementation of the various measures left much to be desired.

In view of these early successes, it is even more difficult to explain the rationale behind the two highly controversial decisions that ultimately represented a serious defeat for the regime. The constitutional revisions instituted at the end of 1975 were a part of a synchronized pattern affecting all bloc members, but the opposition they evoked was damaging. While the decisions to raise food prices in June 1976 and July 1980 were eminently rational, both the preparations and the timing were faulty, suggesting the leadership's far-reaching ignorance of popular attitudes, rather striking in view of its earlier concern to gain legitimacy and acceptance.

Insofar as Poland's foreign policy was concerned, Gierek's greatest accomplishment lay in the area of economic policy. By rapidly expanding Poland's economic relations with the West, Gierek quickly succeeded in making Poland one of the fastest-growing countries in the world in the first half of the 1970s. He was also fortunate that his accession to power coincided with the emergence of the East-West detente. But the ultimate cost of the economic breakthrough proved prohibitive, as Poland's balance of payments deficit at the beginning of the 1980s soared to unprecedented heights.

The latter was also due to a combination of factors over which Poland exercised only partial control. Global inflation, caused by the rapidly growing cost of energy and fuel, together with the lasting economic recession in the West, resulted in an increased cost of Polish imports and a reduced value of the country's exports. The poor performance of Poland's agriculture, caused partly by an irrational policy of the government, was also responsible for the need to import large quantities of grain and for the decrease in the exports of agricultural commodities, which in the past had accounted for a large share of the country's foreign receipts. The difficult situation in the farm sector was, of course, also related to the scarcity of some of the foodstuffs and the necessity of raising their prices. This, in turn, threatened the stability of the political system, which found itself attacked by irate citizens.

Poland's relations with the Soviet Union and its smaller East European partners also seemed to develop smoothly in the early part of the 1970s. There is considerable evidence suggesting that the December 1970 crisis had serious repercussions throughout the bloc and that the members of the Warsaw alliance welcomed the replacement of Gomulka by Gierek, who was seen as a better guarantor of political stability. The fact that Brezhnev refused to intervene in the Polish succession crisis was a good indication of Moscow's disillusionment with Gomulka, despite the latter's apparent close relationship with the Soviet leadership.

Following his assumption of power, Gierek quickly replaced Gomulka as the Kremlin's favorite East European leader. The Polish attitude toward the Soviet Union, as mirrored in official statements and in the mass media, once again assumed a sycophantic character, almost reminiscent of the Stalinist era. In the international arena, the Soviet lead was followed unswervingly with regard to both the West and the East. Altogether, it may be assumed that Poland's behavior as a junior ally caused little worry to Moscow, at least in the early years of Gierek's rule.

There is little doubt that the June 1976 crisis gave considerable concern to the Soviet leadership, whose memories of the December 1970 Polish workers' riots must still have been quite fresh. It was the mark of growing Soviet sophistication as the leader of a multinational alliance that Moscow refused to intervene. Most likely, in the absence of credible alternatives, it still viewed Gierek as the leader with the greatest chance to restore stability in the country. A major political crisis in Poland that would reverberate throughout the region was probably the last thing the Soviet leaders desired at the time that the specter of Eurocommunism was beginning to threaten Communist unity. Subsequently, the Kremlin went so far as to bail out the Gierek regime in November 1976, when the deteriorating economic situation made the latter's position increasingly untenable. The major Soviet loan made at that time not only ensured a continuing supply of foodstuffs and essential raw materials for Polish industry, but also signified Soviet confidence in Gierek's ability to weather the crisis.

As indicated earlier, Moscow's initial support for Kania manifested its hope that the new leadership would be able to contain Solidarity. When Kania failed to do it, he was dropped in October 1981 and replaced by Jaruzelski who, as expected, received Moscow's warm imprimatur. His decision to impose martial law and his resolute deployment of security forces against the resisting workers were most likely strongly applauded by the Kremlin, even though the failure of the Polish Communist party to restore law and order and the need to call upon the military to do it, represented a serious challenge to the traditional Leninist notion of the leading role of the party.

Jaruzelski's unwillingness to apply neo-Stalinist methods to restore normalcy and his relatively mild treatment of the opposition clearly displeased the Soviet leadership and during 1983 there was growing talk about his being replaced soon by someone more obedient to Soviet wishes. Ultimately, however, Moscow must have realized that Jaruzelski and the military were the only force capable of holding Poland together and in the second half of 1983 there were signs that Jaruzelski was back in Soviet good graces.

CONCLUSION

The picture of Poland in the first half of the 1980s that emerges from the preceding discussion is of a country in disarray, if not in decay. Faced with a convergence of several crises, the political system appears unable to cope with the various challenges. As a result, the regime seems to have lost the purpose and sense of direction that had made it effective only a few years earlier.

Of the challenges described at the beginning of the chapter, the questioning of the system's legitimacy seemed most serious in the long run. The widespread protests against constitutional revisions in the winter of 1975–76, the workers' riots of June 1976, the growing societal and political involvement of the church, the establishment of an alliance between the workers and the intellectuals, reflected in the birth of Solidarity, the increasing restlessness of the students, and the human rights campaign all testified to the growing alienation of important social groups from the system, which in a relatively short time succeeded in losing most of its credibility and appeal.

The simultaneous appearance of the other challenges—those of distribution, participation, and penetration—further aggravated the already difficult situation. The economic crisis characterized by inflation and escalating shortages of foodstuffs and other consumer goods not only fueled antigovernment riots but also discredited the regime, bent on using "consumerism" as an instrument for acquiring legitimacy. The arbitrary decisions on all fronts taken without consulting interested segments of the population underscored the continued absence of channels for meaningful participation. Finally, the growing malaise and instability reflected the failure of the political system to penetrate and establish full control over Polish society. The birth of Solidarity and the subsequent crisis testified to the existence of a deep chasm that separated Polish society from its rulers.

It is clear that the first half of the 1980s was a difficult period for

Poland. The crisis of confidence in the system, combined with rising but unfulfilled expectations, resulted in a high degree of political instability. But is the country on the verge of a collapse which, ultimately, might force the Soviet Union to intervene after all in order to safeguard Communist rule? The answer is an emphatic no.

Historically, Communist systems have exhibited an impressive capacity for survival. Since the end of Stalinist rule, they have developed mechanisms for the absorption of internal and external shocks. There is little doubt that the ruling elite not only in Poland but also in the other East European countries has over the years become somewhat more pragmatic and sophisticated, better educated, and politically more sensitive. This meant that although the top Polish oligarchy did not hesitate to apply coercive measures when faced with a critical situation, it was more likely to try to solve the crisis in a pragmatic and nonviolent fashion before resorting to renewed repression. Illustrative is the so far relatively restrained reaction of the Jaruzelski regime to continuing political opposition.

There is no doubt that in the early 1980s it is still the intellectuals and the students who remain most unreconciled to, and alienated from, the regime. The latter clearly see the intellectuals as their major adversaries: in addition to keeping some of their leaders in jail even after the amnesty of July 1983, the Jaruzelski government dissolved several of the best-known professional and artistic associations, which *de facto* robbed the intellectuals and students of any meaningful representation and left them entirely at the mercy of the regime.

Insofar as the workers are concerned, it may be argued that until 1980 the single major source of their discontent had been economic rather than political. If, with luck, the harvests in the next few years prove successful, resulting in a significant improvement in food supply, one may speculate that much of the dissatisfaction will disappear. If, moreover, the government is willing to make some political concessions to the workers—for example, in the area of expanded and more genuine workers' self-government—there is a good chance that this would serve to defuse the current discontent and weaken the opposition.

The same is largely true for the peasants. If the government succeeds in dealing with some of the burning issues confronting Polish agriculture—social security for aging peasants; transfer of privately owned land to the state; and increased availability of inputs into the farm sector—it may be assumed that the peasants' response would be positive, resulting in an expanded farm output. On the political front, maintaining the *modus vivendi* with the church might also help to reduce the distrust of the peasantry.

The immediate question facing the present Polish leadership is what is to be done to restore its credibility and regain popular confidence in the system. In essence, the Jaruzelski regime is faced with three possible courses of action. One choice would be to adopt the "Czechoslovak model," which would imply a total suppression of the political opposition and maintenance of centralized controls over the economy and society at large. In the present configuration of domestic and international forces, the probability of this taking place is not very high. An alternate solution would be the adoption of the "Hungarian model," which would mean far-reaching economic reforms. It can be argued that as long as the economic power centers remain controlled by conservatives—which seemed to be the case in early 1980s—the likelihood of broadly gauged changes in the economy is not very great. The final option is the continuation of the present "model," which may be described as muddling through and hoping for the best. In the present circumstances, this solution seems most likely to be adopted, at least in the foreseeable future.

NOTES

Research for this article was conducted in Poland in 1976 and 1982 under the auspices of the International Research and Exchanges Board and UCLA Academic Senate Committee on Research, whose assistance is gratefully acknowledged.

1. Gabriel A. Almond and G. Bingham Powell, Jr., *Comparative Politics* (Boston: Little, Brown, 1966), pp. 35–37, 306–310.

2. Gabriel A. Almond, "Toward A Comparative Politics of Eastern Europe," *Studies in Comparative Communism,* 4, no. 2 (1971), p. 74.

3. Samuel P. Huntington, "The Change to Change: Modernization, Development and Politics," *Comparative Politics,* 3, no. 3 (1971), p. 320.

4. Ibid., p. 316.

5. Zbigniew Brzezinski, *The Soviet Bloc,* revised and enlarged edition (Cambridge: Harvard University Press, 1967), pp. 8–9.

6. Ibid, pp. 200 and 205–206.

7. Samuel P. Huntington, *Political Order in Changing Societies* (New Haven and London: Yale University Press, 1968), p. 55.

8. Huntington, "The Change to Change," p. 316.

9. Ibid.

10. *Rocznik Statystyczny 1982* (Warsaw, 1982), pp. 26, 32.

11. Ibid., p. 28. The breakdown refers to 1978.

12. Huntington, "The Change to Change," p. 316.

13. Ibid.

BIBLIOGRAPHY

Ascherson, Neal. *The Polish August.* New York: The Viking Press, 1983.

Bethell, Nicholas. *Gomulka.* Harmondsworth, England: Pelican, 1962.

Bromke, Adam. *Poland's Politics: Idealism vs. Realism.* Cambridge, Mass.: Harvard University Press, 1967.

Bromke, Adam, and Strong, John W., eds. *Gierek's Poland.* New York: Praeger Publishers, 1973.

Brumberg, Abraham, ed. *Poland: Genesis of a Revolution.* New York: Random House, 1983.

Brzeski, Andrzej. "Poland as a Catalyst of Change in the Communist Economic System." *The Polish Review,* vol. 16, no. 2 (spring 1970), pp. 3–24.

de Weydenthal, Jan B. *The Communists of Poland.* Stanford, Calif.: Hoover Institution Press, 1978.

Dziewanowski, M. K. *The Communist Party of Poland.* 2nd ed. Cambridge, Mass.: Harvard University Press, 1976.

Fallenbuchl, Zbigniew M. "The Polish Economy in the 1970s." In *East European Economies Post-Helsinki,* A Compendium of Papers Submitted to the Joint Economic Committee, 95th Congress, 1st Session (Washington, D.C.: U.S. Government Printing Office, 1977), pp. 816–864.

Fiszman, Joseph. *Revolution and Tradition in People's Poland.* Princeton, N.J.: Princeton University Press, 1972.

Kanet, Roger E., and Simon, Maurice D., eds. *Background to Crisis: Policy and Politics in Gierek's Poland.* Boulder, Colo.: Westview Press, 1981.

Korbonski, Andrzej. *Politics of Socialist Agriculture in Poland, 1945–1960.* New York: Columbia University Press, 1965.

Lane, David, and Kolankiewicz, George, eds. *Social Groups in Polish Society.* New York: Columbia University Press, 1973.

Lewis, Flora. *A Case History of Hope.* Garden City, N.Y.: Doubleday, 1958.

Milosz, Czeslaw. *The Captive Mind.* New York: Alfred A. Knopf, 1953.

Raina, Peter. *Independent Social Movements in Poland.* London: London School of Economics and Political Science, 1981.

Stehle, Hansjakob. *The Independent Satellite.* New York: Praeger, 1965.

Szczepanski, Jan. *Polish Society.* New York: Random House, 1964.

Zielinski, J. G. *Economic Reform in Polish Industry.* London: Oxford University Press, 1973.

Hungary

Bennett Kovrig

TACTICS OF TAKEOVER, 1945–49

The Communist party that entered the Hungarian political stage in late 1944 and proceeded to acquire a monopoly of power over the next five years had the historical distinction of being the first to emulate Lenin's Bolshevik coup in Russia. The military and political collapse of the Austro-Hungarian Empire in the final days of World War I made way in Hungary for a potentially liberal democratic regime under Count Mihaly Karolyi, but Karolyi's regime could not survive the demands of the victorious allies for a drastic dismemberment of Hungary—including the loss of Magyar-inhabited territories—to the benefit of the surrounding successor states. The political vacuum created by the government's resignation was filled on March 21, 1919, by an impromptu socialist-communist dictatorship, a self-styled "republic of councils," in which effective power lay in the hands of Bela Kun and a small band of Communists.[1] Most of its members, like Kun, were former prisoners of war whose socialist sympathies had been converted into fanatical allegiance to Lenin's Bolshevik party, from which they received guidance and financial assistance.

Kun's regime lasted four months. It made ambitious plans for a sweeping social and economic revolution but was hampered by the hostility of the advancing allies and by a state of near-anarchy on its diminishing territory. What popular support Kun attracted was due mainly to his Red Army's initial successes against the Allies. His repressive measures contributed to the rapid alienation of most social classes, notably the peasantry, but the direct cause of his downfall was military defeat. Kun and many of his fellow Communists fled into exile. In Hungary, under the regency of Admiral Miklos Horthy, there followed a succession of governments that paid lip service to multiparty-democracy but which were fundamentally authoritarian and conservative. Their appeal rested in large measure on popular revulsion at the Bolshevik experiment and at the territorial truncation administered by the Treaty of Trianon.

The Communist emigres tried to revive the party in exile, in Vienna and Moscow, and to foster some minimal level of activity in Hungary. They also performed a wide range of functions elsewhere as agents of the Comintern. Bitter ideological squabbles and efficient persecution by the Hungarian authorities left the domestic party in disarray throughout the interwar period. Kun and many of his associates fell victim to Stalin's purges in the late 1930s, while the vestigial party at home and abroad wallowed ineffectually behind the tactical shifts from popular front to submergence in the wake of the Nazi-Soviet Pact.

As the inevitability of Allied victory and Soviet occupation of Hungary became evident, the party's Muscovite branch, whose leading figures were Matyas Rakosi, Erno Gero, and Jozsef Revai, began under Russian tutelage to formulate its postwar strategy. Given its limited power base in Hungary and the uncertainties of future Allied cooperation, it envisaged a gradual "people's democratic revolution," initially in the governing structure and in land tenure, promoted through a multiparty antifascist front.[2] The emigres also dispatched a few partisan groups, whose low number and marginal military significance could not produce the resistance record that was so crucial an element in the Yugoslav Communists' rise to power. Meanwhile, the indigenous Communists, including Laszlo Rajk, Janos Kadar, and Gyula Kallai, existed as a largely ineffectual, dispersed, and beleaguered underground movement, making repeated attempts to join forces with an emerging Independence Front of opposition politicians. These initiatives, as well as the government's desperate efforts to secure a separate peace, were curtailed when in October 1944 the Germans imposed a Nazi-style regime headed by the Hungarian Arrow Cross leader, Ferenc Szalasi.

Upon their return to the liberated territories, the Muscovite Communists proceeded to rebuild the party and to promote the creation of a new government devoted to their initial minimal program. Under the aegis of the Soviet High Command a provisional government came into being in Debrecen in December 1944. Under the premiership of General Bela Miklos, who had crossed lines late in the war, the government included a minority of Communists as well as representatives of the Smallholder, Social Democratic, and National Peasant parties. The government's first major measure, urged by the Communists in the hope of gaining the allegiance of the landless peasant masses, was a sweeping redistribution of land. This and efforts to seize the initiative in economic reconstruction reflected only one aspect of the quest for power by the Hungarian Communist party (*Magyar Kommunista Part* or HCP). The promotion of Communist-influenced national and workers' committees, the prosecution of real and alleged fascists and war criminals by "people's courts," the purge and infiltration of the civil service, the police, and the army, and total control over the political police were other immediate objectives. The Soviet occupiers gave invaluable support in the form of political pressure, advisers, and NKVD agents, and released part of the vast quantities of confiscated foodstuffs for the relief effort engineered by the Communist Zoltan Vas on behalf of the starving population of Budapest. Rapine and pillage by the Red Army, on the other hand, reinforced the Hungarians' historical hatred of Russia and bolshevism.

The HCP's tactics were to wage a battle for power both from above, within the new governing structure, and from below, by mobilizing mass pressures for radical reforms. The party attempted both to seduce the old established Social Democratic party and to weaken its hold over the industrial workers by penetrating the trade unions. Communist sympathizers worked within the SDP, the less important National Peasant party, and even in the Smallholder party. The Smallholder party rapidly became the political umbrella for a broad spectrum of non-Marxist forces.

By the time the HCP held its first national conference in Budapest on May 20–21, 1945, membership had risen from around 2,000 in 1944 to 150,000, and some 1,500 basic party cells were in existence. The Muscovite and indigenous leaderships had merged, with the former predominant under General Secretary Rakosi. The slogan of the day was the "battle for reconstruction." An overoptimistic Rakosi called for municipal elections in the industrial labor stronghold of Budapest, but the outcome on October 7 gave the Smallholders 50.54 percent of the vote, while the United Workers' Front of socialists and Communists gained only 42.76 percent. In the November general elections, with the broadest franchise in Hungarian history, the HCP received 17 percent of the vote; the SDP, now running independently, won 17.4 percent, while the Smallholders received an even clearer majority with 57 percent. All parties espoused the goals of reconstruction and, in varying degrees, of economic and social reform, but the Communists' ill-concealed radicalism and their Soviet connection were clearly repellent to most Hungarians.[3] The Soviet authorities had imposed an agreement to maintain the coalition whatever the election outcome, and such a government came into being under the premiership of the Smallholder Zoltan Tildy. When the republic was proclaimed in January 1946, Tildy became president and was replaced by another Smallholder, Ferenc Nagy.

With its professed ultimate goal an ambiguous "people's democracy" rather than an outright dictatorship of the proletariat, the HCP intensified its battle from above and below. It resorted to manipulated front organizations, street demonstrations, the prohibition of noncommunist youth organizations, the infamous "salami tactics" to weaken other parties by concerted attacks on their "reactionary" elements, attempts to forge a left-wing bloc with the internally divided SDP and NPP, and the acquisition of key administrative offices, beginning with the Interior Ministry. While the Soviet Union imposed huge reparations and joint stock companies and obstructed Western aid, the HCP began to press for greater state control of the economy, starting with the effective nationalization of the coal mines. A Communist-Soviet financial stabilization program was inaugurated on August 1, 1946. Apart from preaching Hungarian-Soviet friendship, the HCP maintained a low profile in foreign policy, aware that Hungary's territorial-ethnic interests in Slovakia and Transylvania (partially satisfied in the Vienna awards of 1938 and 1940) would receive little support in Allied councils, as was confirmed by the Paris Peace Treaty of 1946.[4]

The next step on the road to a "people's democracy," outlined at the HCP's Third Congress in September 1946, was the progressive elimination of the capitalist economy and of its Western-oriented defenders in the government. The discovery by Interior Minister Rajk's operatives of an alleged antistate conspiracy provided the pretext for an offensive against the Smallholder party, and in April 1947 one of the party's leaders, Bela Kovacs, was seized by the Soviet secret police. Prime Minister Ferenc Nagy, who had tried to pursue a policy of compromise in the hope of outlasting Soviet occupation, was forced to resign, and he chose exile. The United States and Great Britain, junior partners to the Soviet Union in the Allied Control Commission, issued impotent protests at these outrages.

In Hungarian Communist historiography the period from early 1947 to mid-1948 is known as the "year of the turning point." This period encompassed the liquidation of the "conspiracy," the launching of the three-year plan, the national elections of August 31, 1947, the failure of the SDP's right wing to regain control of the party, the progressive nationalization of the banks and other large enterprises, and the unification of the two major left-wing parties in June 1948. The emasculation of the leading anticommunist party, the Smallholders, soon led to the emergence of several extra-coalition parties. Against a splintered opposition, and aided by massive disenfranchisement and balloting fraud, the HCP emerged from the August 31 election as the strongest single party, with an officially reported 22.3 percent of the vote. The coalition as a whole won 60.8 percent, with the more or less Marxist parties within it (HCP, SDP, NPP) getting 45.4 percent.[5]

With Stalin pulling the strings, a conference of Communist parties in

Poland in September 1947 adopted as a new revolutionary strategy the creation of "single-party popular fronts" on the Yugoslav model. This meeting, leading to the foundation of the Cominform, marked the beginning of the final phase of consolidation of the Soviet sphere, a process that was both a cause and an effect of the cold war. There ensued in Hungary an accelerated drive to neutralize the new opposition parties, drive their anticommunist leaders into exile, and engineer a power grab in the SDP by its left wing. This drive set the stage for the fusion in June 1948 of the SDP and the HCP into the Hungarian Workers' Party (*Magyar Dolgozok Partja* or HWP), with a combined membership of 1,128,130. During the following year the regime overcame the opposition of the Roman Catholic church by bringing Cardinal Mindszenty to trial on fabricated charges, nationalized the school system, launched the collectivization of agriculture, and eliminated the last remnants of free enterprise. The remaining noncommunist parties were absorbed into a new political umbrella organization, the People's Independence Front, along with the National Council of Trade Unions and other mass organizations. In the May 1949 elections the Front received 95.6 percent of the votes. On August 20, 1949, the constitution of the Hungarian People's Republic was adopted, legitimizing the revolutionary political transformation of Hungary. Aided and abetted by the Soviet Union, and through skillful destruction of the opposition forces, a handful of Communists had succeeded in acquiring dictatorial power.

FROM MOBILIZATION TO MODERNIZATION, 1950–70

The new dictatorship of the proletariat, ostensibly based on Marxism-Leninism, was simply a replica of its Stalinist prototype. The power and collective interests of the "working class" were represented by its vanguard, the party, and implemented through the legislative, administrative, and judicial organs of the state. The latter, together with mass organizations of workers, youth, and women, served as agents of enforcement and mobilization in support of goals formulated by the party leadership. The hierarchical organization of the party followed the Soviet pattern, with the pyramid rising from local through regional committees to the Central Committee and the Politburo. The reality of power was Stalinist, with General Secretary Rakosi enjoying unlimited authority and what subsequently came to be denounced as the "cult of personality." His closest lieutenants were Gero, Revai, and Mihaly Farkas, in charge, respectively, of the economy, culture and agitprop, and defense. A triennial party congress was formally charged with developing long-term policy and ratifying the Central Committee's decisions. In practice, the principle of democratic centralism meant unquestioning obedience to directives from above.

Table 1 Membership in Hungarian Communist Party

January 1919	10,000	January 1952	945,606
November 1924	120[a]	January 1956	859,037
December 1929	1,000[a]	December 1, 1956	37,818
February 1945	30,000	January 1957 (HSWP)	125,088
July 1945	226,577	December 1957	394,910
January 1946	608,728	December 1961	498,644
January 1947	670,476	December 1967	601,917[b]
July 1948 (HCP)	887,472	November 1970	662,000
July 1948 (HWP)	1,128,130	January 1975	754,353
January 1950	828,695	January 1980	811,833

[a] In Hungary only.
[b] Until 1966 the numbers include candidate members, a category abolished at the Ninth Congress.
Sources: Magyar Szocialista Munkaspart, *Legyozhetetlen Ero,* 2nd ed. (Budapest: Kossuth, 1974), pp. 22, 63, 82, 162, 169, 175, 179, 185, 193, 204, 224, 236, 250, 257, 285; *A Magyar Szocialista Munkaspart X. Kongresszusanak jegyzokonyve* (Budapest: Kossuth, 1971), p. 102; *A Magyar Szocialista Munkaspart XI. Kongresszusa* (Budapest: Kossuth, 1975), p. 6; *A Magyar Szocialista Munkaspart XII. Kongresszusa* (Budapest: Kossuth, 1980), p. 8.

The estrangement of Tito and Stalin in 1948, together with the growing cold war tensions, led to the imposition by the Soviet Union of even greater orthodoxy and uniformity in the East European satellites. Rakosi participated with exemplary vigor in the ensuing area-wide campaign against alleged Titoists. From 1949 to 1953 more Communists were executed than under the Horthy regime.[6] The major show trial was that of Laszlo Rajk, who was tortured and persuaded to confess to false charges before being executed. Many other Communists, including Kadar (who had participated in Rajk's elimination), were imprisoned. Rakosi's preferred targets in these purges were veterans of the 1919 commune (in which he himself had played a minor role), indigenous (as opposed to Muscovite) Communists, and left-wing socialists. By 1950 party membership had fallen below 830,000 (see Table 1). Over the life of the Hungarian Workers' Party, from 1948 to 1956, more than 350,000 members were expelled from the party.[7] These purges were only one aspect of the police-state terror that affected not only "class enemies" but also the population at large.

The period from 1949 to 1953 was truly totalitarian in the scope of state control over all aspects of life. The official version of Marxism-Leninism, Soviet models, and the glorification of Rakosi pervaded education and culture. In 1949 all enterprises employing more than ten workers and all rental housing were nationalized. State control was imposed on labor mobility and discipline. Coming on top of the ravages of war, Soviet exploitation and the rejection of Western aid by the Communists severely inhibited Hungary's economic reconstruction.

The inefficiencies and dogmatic application of the new command economy and the forced reorientation of Hungarian trade toward the Soviet bloc exacerbated the situation. The first five-year plan gave priority to intensive development of heavy industry and to the collectivization of agriculture. In both cases dogmatic insistence on replicating the Soviet model had disastrous consequences. Most of the raw materials necessary to turn Hungary into a "country of iron and steel" had to be imported. Forced industrialization brought a massive influx of new workers to urban areas, where the already critical housing shortage was alleviated by the deportation of "class enemies" to the countryside. The brutal collectivization campaign and increasingly heavy levies on farmers only alienated the peasantry, leading to declining productivity and even spontaneous demonstrations in the spring of 1953. Along with an apparently favorable growth rate in the national income and a state of full employment, the government's economic policies brought about a negative balance of trade in 1949 and 1952, an 18 percent drop in the real incomes of workers and employees between 1949 and 1952, and a general neglect of consumer needs.[8] Political participation by the masses was compulsory and ritualistic, and the system's popular legitimacy was abysmally low.

The tensions induced by political oppression and economic hardship were at a peak when in March 1953 Stalin's death ushered in a Soviet interregnum more sensitive to the stresses in the system. Summoned to Moscow, Rakosi was berated for his dogmatism and mismanagement of the economy and ordered to relinquish the premiership (which he had held along with the party's leadership) to Imre Nagy. A veteran Communist and Muscovite, Nagy had supervised the 1945 land reform but subsequently had become critical of the party's economic policies and had fallen into disgrace.[9] There followed a prolonged tug of war between Rakosi and Nagy, whose "New Course" aimed at abandoning forced collectivization and industrialization, laid greater stress on the satisfaction of personal consumption and welfare needs, and sought to mitigate the more repressive and arbitrary features of the totalitarian system. Collective farm membership fell by nearly 40 percent, investments were redirected to light and consumer industries, the first signs of cultural pluralism appeared, and most Communist political prisoners (including Kadar) were released. An unrepentant Rakosi continued to intrigue against his rival, and as the Moscow political climate evolved, Nagy came to be charged with "right-wing opportunist deviation." In April 1955 he was ousted from the premiership and, seven months later, expelled from the party. Khrushchev reportedly explained the reversal by saying, "I have to keep Rakosi in Hungary, because in Hungary the whole structure will collapse if he goes."[10]

The new Khrushchevian line was a blend of economic neo-Stalinism, modest relaxation of Stalinist terror, "peaceful coexistence" with the West, and reconciliation with Tito. Only the first of these components suited Rakosi. He abhorred detente with Tito, who in turn denounced Rakosi. Rakosi reassigned top priority to heavy industry, but his recapture of absolute power was challenged by an emerging alliance of rehabilitated Communists and of establishment intellectuals who began to relinquish their earlier slavish orthodoxy.[11] Of the liberated party members some, like Kadar, dutifully returned to loyal service; others adopted a more revisionist stance and looked for leadership to Imre Nagy. Khrushchev's anti-Stalin speech at the Twentieth CPSU congress emboldened revisionists and reformers, particularly writers, who began to voice open criticism of Rakosi's totalitarian system.

What began as an intraparty debate rapidly spilled over into the public sphere. One important catalyst was the Petofi circle, a debating forum established under the aegis of the Federation of Working Youth (*Dolgozo Ifjusag Szovetsege*). By July 1956 Gero was describing the Petofi circle as the "second leading center" in the country, a rival to the party.[12] Rakosi made plans for drastic suppression of dissent, but on July 18 he was stripped of office on Moscow's orders. His replacement as first secretary was Erno Gero, an unhappy compromise since the latter was as much a doctrinaire Stalinist as his predecessor. The reformist wave was strengthened by the apparent triumph of the Gomulka revisionists in Poland and by concessions such as the posthumous rehabilitation of Rajk and his ceremonial reinterment on October 6. While Gero traveled to Belgrade in quest of a belated accommodation with Tito, agitation by students and intellectuals took the form of manifestos demanding reinstatement of Nagy to the government, expulsion of Rakosi from the party, public trial for Farkas and others implicated in the Stalinist outrages, publication of foreign trade agreements including Soviet exploitation of Hungarian uranium, freedom of expression in literature, and finally, the evacuation of Soviet troops.

A demonstration before the Budapest radio studios, one of several mass meetings on October 23, was met with gunfire and launched the thirteen-day revolution.[13] There followed the appointment of Nagy as premier and Kadar as first secretary, clashes between the rebels and the party's last line of defense, the secret police, and a limited intervention by Soviet forces. Revolutionary councils sprang up nationwide and pressed Nagy for far-reaching reforms. In summary, the goal of the revolution was a pluralistic democratic system, encompassing retention of some central planning and nationalization (perhaps with workers' self-management) within a mixed economy; aid to independent farmers and free choice in the formation of agricultural cooperatives;

elimination of police terror; economic and political sovereignty and state neutrality; and such basic rights as free unions, the right to strike, and cultural and religious freedom. Unfettered multiparty contests would determine government policy, and the influence of a reformed national Communist party would be proportional to its electoral appeal.

The wave of nationalism and reformism drove Nagy to bring representatives of other former parties into his government. The Soviet Union issued a conciliatory declaration but also dispatched military reinforcements.[14] In the face of this threat, Nagy on November 1 proclaimed Hungary's neutrality and withdrawal from the Warsaw Pact, and appealed for U.N. support. Initially, the remnant of the disintegrating HWP had endorsed Nagy's reformist line, but now Kadar and a few associates were persuaded by the Soviet authorities to leave Hungary secretly.[15] While Soviet forces launched a massive air and land offensive in the early hours of November 4, a broadcast from the Soviet Union announced the formation of a "Revolutionary Worker-Peasant Government" by Kadar and Ferenc Munnich and called upon the Red Army to smash the "sinister forces of reaction."

Entirely dependent on Soviet military might amidst a passionately hostile population, the new regime initially held out the promise of major reforms. Kadar spoke of free elections and voluntary collectivization and held discussions with representatives of other parties and of the revolutionary workers' councils. Committees of economists brought in recommendations for radical change. However, the priority task of rebuilding the party, intraparty factionalism, the revival of Soviet-Yugoslav antagonism and of Moscow's position that revisionism was the principal enemy, all conspired to make the restoration of Communist power a painful and near-totalitarian exercise. Kadar personally eschewed Rakosi's despotic style, but the restoration of order demanded executions, deportations, imprisonment, and other repressive measures. Over two hundred thousand Hungarians sought refuge abroad. Nagy himself was kidnapped by the Russians and later executed. The party's cultural policy, momentarily impelled by Revai's dogmatic intolerance, turned repressive in the face of a writers' strike. Party membership had fallen from a prerevolutionary 860,000 to under 40,000. Thanks to an aggressive recruiting campaign, by the end of 1957 membership in the renamed Hungarian Socialist Workers' Party (*Magyar Szocialista Munkaspart* or HSWP) approached 400,000.

Industrialization remained the primary task of the regime, but Kadar pursued it in the context of his long-term goals of improving the standard of living and legitimizing the party in the eyes of the workers. Another immediate task, required by Soviet orthodoxy and the

worker-peasant alliance, was the "socialist transformation of the countryside." After the revolution only 11 percent of arable land remained
in the state and collectivized sector. In 1959 a new collectivization
campaign was launched, initially with much intimidation and compul-
sion. The chief culprit in these excesses, agriculture minister Imre
Dogei, was dismissed the following year, and other leading dogmatists
(i.e., opponents of Kadar's moderate line) were expelled from the leadership in 1962. By that time the collectivization drive had been essentially completed by less severe persuasion, and 92.5 percent of arable
land lay in the socialist sector.

The Kadar moderates thus overcame, without entirely eliminating,
internal opposition to their pragmatic pursuit of modernization and
legitimacy. In December 1961 (following Khrushchev's victory over
the "antiparty group" and renewal of de-Stalinization) Kadar forcefully
restated his alliance policy. Admitting that the task of modernization
could not be fulfilled by the party alone, he called on loyal extra-party
Hungarians to assume positions of responsibility and devote their talents to the common goal. To demonstrate his good faith, he gave the
green light to literary criticism of the Rakosi regime (as long as there
was no implication that the current system bore any resemblance or
responsibility). "Those who are not against us are with us"—the con-
verse of the Rakosi axiom—became the conciliatory slogan of the alliance policy. In ideological terms the Kadar line was defined as
centrism, or the struggle on two fronts against both the old sectarian-
dogmatic mistakes and right-wing revisionist deviations.

The HSWP's Eighth Congress in November 1962 declared that with
the completion of collectivization the foundations of socialism had
been laid and that Hungary was beginning the construction of a fully
socialist society. Socialist democracy would be expanded by a decentralization of authority and a division of labor. Although the party
would retain monopoly over ideological questions, definitions of national interest, and major policy decisions, other institutions and
groups would be given greater autonomy. The internal class struggle
was declared essentially concluded, while the former monolithic view
of society was amended to recognize not only collective and individual,
but also group interests. One tangible outcome was the abandonment
of class discrimination in higher education. There also followed an
amnesty for most political prisoners, the end of internment and internal
exile, and the attenuation of secret police activity, all in the spirit of
"socialist legality." Radio jamming was curtailed, foreign travel restrictions were eased, and cultural and religious activities came under more
tolerant control.

Khrushchev's fall in October 1964 and concurrent economic

difficulties in Hungary emboldened the more dogmatic elements in the party, but Kadar held fast to his centrist line and succeeded in persuading the Brezhnev leadership of his unimpeachable loyalty to the Soviet Union and of the compatibility of his policies with both Soviet and Hungarian interests. The next major step was to be a reform of the entire economic management structure, a "New Economic Mechanism." Its development, strongly supported by Kadar and promoted by a young former social democrat, Rezso Nyers, was approved at the May 1966 Central Committee meeting by only a narrow margin, over the opposition of advocates of the old command model. Launched in 1968, the NEM introduced some elements of a market economy, with pricing and investment techniques that decentralized planning and placed a premium on managerial expertise, productivity, and competitiveness in the world market.

By implementing his alliance policy, Kadar managed to overshadow the brutal imposition of his regime and reach an accommodation with the Hungarian people. His rule did not enjoy democratic legitimacy in the Western sense, but it gradually earned a degree of pragmatic popular endorsement that was uncommon in Eastern Europe.

CURRENT PARTY STRUCTURE AND DYNAMICS

In May 1972, celebrating his sixtieth birthday, Janos Kadar reflected with some candor upon the Hungarian revolution:

> In 1956, a very serious and critical situation presented itself which is called, scientifically, the counterrevolution. We are aware that this is the scientific definition of what took place in 1956. But there is also another concept which we all might accept: it was a national tragedy. A tragedy for the party, for the working class, for the people, and for the individual. We lost our way, and the result was tragedy. And if we have overcome this now—which we can state with confidence—this is a very big thing.[16]

Three years later, at the conclusion of the HSWP's Eleventh Congress in 1975, Kadar delivered an extemporaneous address in which he tried to dismiss fearful speculation that the party was veering toward a more rigid and dictatorial position. The dictatorship of the proletariat would remain in force, he said, but eighteen years' experience had shown that "it was not such a bad dictatorship after all. One can live under it, create freely, and gain honor."[17] There were no longer any antagonistic classes, only class allies, and the remaining differences were not about the desirability of socialism but about the rate of development of the socialist revolution. The role of the party was to lead and to persuade.

The implementation of the alliance policy and of the NEM had in fact generated persistent opposition among the party's more dogmatic elements. The latter were concerned about an alleged erosion of the preeminence of the party and the industrial proletariat, and at the November 1972 Central Committee meeting Kadar had forcefully to defend his policies, while conceding that liberalization had led to undersirable side effects. Problems in investments, trade, income ratios, and ideology were attributed to the inadequate implementation of earlier party resolutions. Denying the emergence of a "new class," he nevertheless admitted to the existence of arrogance, bureaucratism, and acquisitiveness among party members.[18] A tax on movable property was added to earlier measures to restrict excessive incomes from moonlighting and speculation. A more significant concession was a special "corrective" wage increase for 1.3 million workers in large state and construction industries, followed a year later by another special increase for certain other categories of workers. In an attempt to end debate, Bela Biszku warned that further argument would be incompatible with the Leninist norms of party life and democratic centralism.[19] There followed a campaign to revitalize the party's proletarian image, to curtail ideological and cultural deviations (prompting the investigation and expulsion of some "new left" intellectual critics), and to remedy some shortcomings of the NEM by a reassertion of central planning and control.

At the HSWP's Eleventh Congress in March 1975, Kadar appealed for ideological unity and stressed the need to expand worker participation in decision making.[20] There followed the introduction of a new system of economic regulators, but speculation that continuing economic difficulties would be met by a major recentralization was dispelled by a Central Committee resolution in April 1978; it confirmed the NEM and stressed productivity, managerial efficiency, technological modernization, and the gradual reduction of subsidies and price supports to make the economy more competitive in the world market. By the time of the Twelfth Congress, in March 1980, economic conditions had worsened considerably, but the basic principles of the NEM were reaffirmed.

With regard to internal party affairs, the composition of the membership has been profoundly altered by the passage of time and by social change. Some three-quarters of the members joined after 1956. Accepting the logic of the alliance policy, growing numbers of managers and supervisors, intellectuals and white-collar workers made the pragmatic choice to adhere to the party. The proportion of these groups in the membership rose to 48 percent in 1980. The leadership, meanwhile, periodically professes concern over the insufficient number of industrial and agricultural workers in the HSWP.

Although a number of organizational reforms since 1962 have aimed at enhancing intraparty democracy, and while the membership is continually exhorted to exemplary behavior, the diffusion of authority and the stress on secular expertise have induced a measure of alienation and apathy. As one party analyst noted, "The decline in the political content of party life, . . . the ebbing of the critical spirit, the fading away of responsibility, hinder the operation of democratic centralism, the basic rule of party life. Inevitably, this gives rise to liberalism and arbitrary interpretations in the implementation of party decisions."[21] One remedial measure was the 1976 party card exchange.[22] Partly as a result of this, between the party congresses of 1975 and 1980 6.4 percent of the membership resigned or was expelled, leaving the HSWP in 1980 with 811,833 members (representing 7.6 percent of the population).[23] Ideological deviants are no longer expeditiously liquidated. Rakosi died in the Soviet Union, while Gero and other deeply implicated survivors of the Stalinist phase were simply expelled from the party.

Despite the spread of ideological relativism even among the rank and file, the party remains politically supreme. The revised 1972 state constitution proclaims that the "Marxist-Leninist party of the working class is the leading force in society." At the base of the party's pyramidal structure lie 23,933 primary organizations, of which 7,426 are active in industry and construction, 3,750 in agriculture, 1,383 in transportation, and 1,596 in commerce. At the next level there are 76 district party committees and 117 city and Budapest district party committees. County party committees, together with the Budapest Party Committee, number 24. Lower units elect delegates to the next higher level, and conferences of county delegates elect participants in the quinquennial party congress, which is the ultimate legislative body. The 764 delegates to the Twelfth Party Congress elected the 127-member Central Committee. The Central Committee, in turn, elects the Politburo, the Secretaries and Secretariat department heads, and the Agitprop and other key committees. Over the last decade organizational reforms have enhanced the rank-and-file's participation at lower levels with the introduction of secret ballots, procedures for complaints and accountability of leaders, and broader participation in the drafting of congressional guidelines. Elections to the leading organs, however, generally take the form of ratification of Politburo nominations.

The Central Committee meets three or four times a year, normally for two days; it is charged with monitoring the implementation of congressional resolutions and seldom presents a challenge to the policies of the leadership. It routinely hears reports on international affairs and on two or three other current policy issues, and its resolutions are briefly summarized in the media. A preponderant number of current Central Committee members hold key positions of power elsewhere, including 30 in government and in state and local administration, 37 in party organizations, and 14 in trade union and other mass organizations; the Central Committee also includes a few token fulltime workers and intellectuals.

The top party leadership appears more collegial than in Rakosi's day, but its recruitment and deliberations are cloaked in secrecy. The Politburo, the party's executive, has 13 members. They currently include the prime minister, the head of state, the president of the National Council of Trade Unions, and the secretary-general of the Patriotic People's Front. A partly overlapping circle of power encompasses the 7 secretaries of the Central Committee, in charge of the Secretariat's departments. The latter cover all major policy areas and serve in effect as a parallel, but superior, government. Many officers of the Secretariat also hold related government posts, and individuals are frequently shifted from one sphere of authority to the other. All-important inter-party relations and liaison with Soviet authorities are conducted by the Secretariat.

The key leader in this political system, Kadar, is both first secretary and a member of the Politburo, but he holds no state office. He has shown consummate skill in preserving his centrist program by trimming the leadership to exclude both reformist and dogmatist critics. Rezso Nyers was dropped from the Secretariat and Politburo in 1974–75 because of his overly enthusiastic promotion of the NEM. At the other end of the spectrum, personnel changes in the Secretariat include the dismissal in 1976 of the conservative Arpad Pullai and, in April 1978, of Bela Biszku, Kadar's tough deputy, who had controlled the party apparatus as well as the army and security forces. Kadar's style of rule is to limit the personal power of his associates, leave the management of reforms to experts, and redeploy periodically the leading figures both within and between the party and the government.

Although party control is less obtrusive than it was in Rakosi's day, it still pervades the Hungarian political system. Senior party members hold all significant positions in government and mass mobilizing organizations, and the party retains full cadre authority (nomenklatura) and a generally respected advisory right over many thousands of lesser leadership posts. The party's authoritarian nature is reflected in the fact that party membership is the general rule in the Workers' Militia (an auxiliary security force), the border guards, and most officer ranks in the police and the armed forces. In contrast, only a minority of parliamentary deputies and local and municipal council members belongs to the HSWP. Local party units send confidential, weekly "atmosphere reports" to the HWSP's massive headquarters near the parliament. Few among the rank and file act out of profound ideological conviction; most serve as mere agents of the dominant power rather than as advocates of the public interest.

GOVERNMENT AND MASS ORGANIZATIONS

While the party reigns supreme, the promotion of socialist democracy and efficient administration has brought about changes in the nature of governmental authority. The main thrust of these changes has been to give greater scope to elected bodies and to recruit expert talent into administrative service regardless of party membership (though the political education of cadres has received renewed emphasis).

When the 1949 constitution was amended in 1972, the revision was presented less as a political program than as a reflection of achievements. A final version awaits the day when Hungary can be proclaimed a "socialist republic"; the 1972 constitution states that Hungary is a "people's republic." The preamble still pays tribute to the Soviet liberators but now also takes a longer historical perspective, referring to a "millennium" of the people's struggle. The earlier discrimination between "working people" and "citizens" has been abandoned, and all citizens are entitled to participate in public affairs. In addition to the party, the role of mass movements and trade unions in the building of socialism is acknowledged. The equal ranking of state and cooperative ownership is asserted, and private producers are recognized, though they "must not violate collective interests."

The national assembly is described by the constitution as the "supreme representative organ of the people," but it meets only for some ten days each year, and most rules take the form of presidential and ministerial decrees. Since 1966 the electoral law provides for single-member parliamentary constituencies and permits multiple candidacies. In practice, the party, through the Patriot People's Front (PPF), controls the electoral process. Despite a 1971 law that removed the PPF's exclusive screening power, candidacies opposed to the PPF program are unthinkable, and voters are reminded that they are choosing not between policies but between the personal qualities of candidates. The handful of multiple candidacies that have materialized in the last 4 general elections (9 in 1967, 49 in 1971, 34 in 1975, and 15 out of

352 in 1980) hardly represents a pluralistic revolution. In the 1980 election 0.7 percent of valid votes were cast against the PPF.[24]

The leadership of party and government was split in 1958, reunited in 1961, and separated again since 1965, with each prime minister being also a member of the Politburo. The initiative for appointment and dismissal of government leaders, formally vested in the Presidential Council, lies with the party. Of the current 18-member Council of Ministers, 3 are Politburo members and 11 are on the Central Committee.

Like other Communist state organs, the judiciary has traditionally been a servant of the ruling party's political goals, and it reached a nadir of subjection and arbitrariness in the purge trials and open class discrimination of the Stalinist period. While it has inevitably remained a defender of the established order, the reformulation of "socialist legality" in the direction of a more consensual, codified, and impartial code of law led in 1972 to a procedural and jurisdictional reorganization of the judicial system.[25] Particularly since 1970 greater administrative constraints have been imposed on the secret police, largely eliminating its old practice of summary justice and reducing its fearsome prominence in the lives of ordinary citizens. All this did not alter its basic political control function, but it is exercised with greater prudence and reliance on quiet persuasion. The very low incidence of reported political crimes can be attributed both to the effectiveness of this deterrence and to the positive socializing impact of Kadar's reforms.

The broadest umbrella for political mobilization is the Patriotic People's Front, whose tasks are defined in the programmatic statement adopted at its Sixth Congress in September 1976:

> The Patriotic People's Front is the most comprehensive framework of the alliance policy of the Hungarian Socialist Workers' Party. . . . It is our task to urge, in the name of this policy, the gathering together of our country's creative forces—party members and nonmembers, materialists and believers, people following different ideologies—and their conscious cooperation in the shaping and execution of this policy.[26]

The PPF works through some 4,000 committees with 100,000 members. Its specific tasks are to organize elections, to stimulate social awareness of public problems (e.g., environmental protection), and to mobilize individuals and groups in support of state and council measures (e.g., the promotion of unpaid "social work"). A related agency is the National Peace Council, with international responsibilities.

Under the alliance policy, the various mass organizations and

officially recognized interest groups have emerged as valid interpreters
and gatherers of opinion, but only within their narrow technical compe-
tence and in accordance with the overall objective of building socialism. The original function of the trade unions as downward
transmission belts has been expanded to allow them to serve the
"legitimate interests of a smaller community," and the 1967 Labor
Code provides for various rights, including that of veto over certain
management decisions (but not the right to strike).[27] More recently, the
party has instituted new procedures for worker participation in enterprise management. Enterprises and agricultural collectives have
benefited most directly from the decentralizing impact of the NEM,
and such organizations as the Hungarian Chamber of Commerce and
the National Council of Agricultural Cooperatives serve as advocates
of sectoral interests. While all this does not amount to political pluralism in the sense of liberty to contest fundamental principles, the
mobilization of organized interest groups as active participants in the
development of issue-oriented policies is a significant advance over
their erstwhile ritualistic role.

The Communist Youth League has a current membership of over
870,000. A majority of high school and college students, but only a
minority of working youths, belong to the League. At the CYL's Ninth
Congress in May 1976, First Secretary Laszlo Marothy called for better ideological education while recognizing the impossibility of "in-
oculating our youth against petit-bourgeois and bourgeois ideologies
and against an idealist world outlook."[28] The fundamental task of the
CYL is the preparation of members for admission to the HSWP, and
the membership profile suggests that being a member of the CYL facilitates access to higher education and career advancement, but most
young people join for nonpolitical reasons and remain largely indiffer-
ent to indoctrination.[29] Other active mobilizing organizations include
the National Council of Hungarian Women and the Hungarian-Soviet
Friendship Society.

SOCIOECONOMIC AND CULTURAL TRENDS

The key component in Kadar's reform program has been the New
Economic Mechanism, introduced in 1968. The general theory behind
the NEM is that the party sets political targets; government agencies
and local councils translate these targets into concrete economic programs; and enterprises carry out their assigned tasks with a "proper
degree of independence."[30] A differentiated pricing system provides for
fixed, limited-range, and floating prices for different categories of
goods. The state subsidizes essential consumer goods and remains the

sole source of credit and the determinant of major investment priorities. Nevertheless, the NEM represents a radical departure from the former command model in its relative decentralization of authority and its stress on incentives for productivity and on competitiveness.

The early record of the NEM was one of substantial improvement in national income, consumption, and productivity (see Table 2), but a number of problem areas soon materialized, prompting continuous tinkering with the mechanism. A disproportionate growth in incompleted investments (accounting for 80 percent of annual investments in 1971) brought stricter guidelines and credit controls in 1972. Growth in private and industrial consumption of imported goods from the West had an unfavorable impact on the balance of trade in the nonsocialist sector. Such shortcomings were blamed on the greater autonomy given to often unskilled enterprise managers. Meanwhile, wage differentiation and the expansion of a relatively affluent middle class provoked an egalitarian backlash on the part of some workers, party dogmatists, and a few new-left intellectuals. The modernization of agriculture has been pursued with some success through mergers of collective farms and the use of Western technology. Peasant incomes have risen more rapidly than industrial wages, and the regime continues to encourage private plot production, which accounts for roughly half of horticultural and livestock output. The initially rapid expansion of agricultural cooperatives into ancillary industrial activities drew manpower away from the state sector, and in 1971 the regime took steps to constrain such diversification. Alarmed by the rapidity of change, party conservatives thus managed in the early 1970s to halt and even reverse some of the reforms. However, as was noted earlier, the proponents of the NEM ultimately prevailed.

The Soviet Union's decision in 1975 to bring progressively its energy and raw material prices up to world market levels caused a dramatic deterioration in Hungary's terms of trade. The regime responded with a new system of economic regulators, designed in part to stimulate productivity and to bring prices into line with production costs. It also borrowed heavily in the West to finance the modernization of export-oriented industries. The worldwide recession of the early 1980s only aggravated Hungary's economic problems, and the government had to resort to severe deflationary measures and vigorous export promotion. In the midst of this crisis, experimentation with the economic mechanism continued, mostly in the direction of decentralization and privatization. The latter is designed to allow greater autonomy, through leasing and subcontracting, to retail and service units and even to production units within industrial enterprises, all in the interest of spurring productivity and reducing the vast "second economy."

Table 2 Key Economic Indicators in Hungary

	1938	1950	1955	1960	1965	1970	1975	1980
Population (at the beginning of the year), thousands	9,138	9,293	9,767	9,961	10,140	10,322	10,509	10,709
Natural increase per 1,000 population	5.7	9.5	11.4	4.5	2.4	3.1	6.0	0.3
Index of the National income, 1950 = 100	80	100	132	177	216	300	406	476
National Income by origin, percentage								
Industry	20	26	33	36	42	43	46	48
Construction	5	9	9	11	11	12	12	12
Agriculture	58	43	42	29	23	23	19	17
Other	17	17	16	24	24	22	22	22
Index of industrial production, 1950 = 100	63	100	186	267	386	523	712	840
Index of agricultural production, 1950 = 100	113	100	118	120	127	146	183	207
Index of external trade, 1950 = 100	—	100	179	287	470	748	1,503	2,003
Index of real wages per wage-earner, 1950 = 100	—	100	105	154	168	199	234	243
Per capita consumption of the population, 1950 = 100	93	100	115	152	176	228	281	316
Employment by socioeconomic sector, percentage		(1949)						(1982)
Nonagricultural manual workers		28.5	—	42.5	—	52.3	—	52.6
State agricultural manual workers		9.1	—	7.0	—	2.2	—	2.4
Shop-level production supervisors		1.2	—	1.5	—	2.0	—	1.9
Peasants in cooperatives		0.3	—	12.0	—	17.6	—	13.9
Intellectual (white-collar)		8.3	—	16.0	—	22.6	—	25.7
Artisans and merchants		50.7	—	21.1	—	3.3	—	3.5
Capitalists, landowners		1.9	—	0.1	—	—	—	—

Sources: Hungary, Central Statistical Office, *Statistical Yearbook 1981* (Budapest, 1982) and *Magyar Statisztikai Zsebkonyv 1981* (Budapest, 1982)

Between 1970 and 1980 the gross domestic product registered an average annual increase of 5.4 percent, and at the end of the decade Hungary's GNP per capita ($4,180) ranked fourth in the Soviet block and thirty-first in the world. By 1982, however, the economy was stagnant, and the party secretary in charge of economic policy, Ferenc Havasi, had to acknowledge that the living standard of one-third of the population had declined.[31]

Thanks to planned wage differentiation and unplanned second income disparities, the ratio of highest to lowest income in Hungary is at least 5 to 1, and conspicuous consumption coexists with widespread poverty. The period of rapid growth in the early 1970s was also marked by government efforts to improve other welfare functions, such as pensions and child care. Social restratification is evident in educational institutions, where children of the well-educated middle classes are overrepresented. Housing shortages remain a perennial problem in urban areas despite large-scale state construction programs and measures to encourage private ownership and construction.[32] Housing problems and other social stresses contribute to Hungary's very high divorce, abortion, and suicide rates. The low birth rate and a consequently aging population have negative implications for economic growth, and as a response the regime has restricted abortions and improved maternity benefits. Hungary has a population approaching 10,700,000, of which approximately 3 percent belong to German, South Slav, and Romanian minority groups.

Church-state relations have become progressively more normal in the Kadar era. Accord with the Roman Catholic church (which claims at least the nominal membership of 60 percent of Hungarians) was facilitated for both the regime and the Vatican by Cardinal Mindszenty's departure into exile in 1971 from the U.S. Embassy, where he had found haven after the defeat of the 1956 revolution. Mindszenty died in Vienna in 1975, and his successor to the archbishopric of Esztergom, Laszlo Lekai, was installed and named cardinal the following year. The churches receive modest state subsidies (Budapest has the only rabbinical school in the Soviet bloc), but their educational activities are severely restricted. Party policy is to acknowledge the persistence of religious faith and the necessity of tolerating a reduced level of church activity while maintaining the ideological struggle against religion. Said Kadar in 1976: "Without exception the churches are loyal to our system. . . . Is it possible that by doing this the churches may be prolonging their existence? It may be so. . . . It could be said that this is a compromise. . . . But we learn from Lenin that any compromise which advances our revolutionary course is acceptable."[33]

A notable feature of Kadar's alliance policy has been the liberalization in the area of culture. The guidelines developed in 1966 distinguish between works that deserve support and subsidy, those that are merely tolerated, and those that are prohibited. Most writers and academics resignedly exercise self-censorship and avoid critical comment concerning the Soviet Union and the Communist political system. The HSWP, for its part, insists on preserving the "hegemony" and not the "monopoly" of Marxism in Hungarian culture. In the late 1960s a few prominent sociologists (Andras Hegedus, Maria Markus) and philosophers (Janos Kis, Mihaly Vajda) ventured into forbidden territory with Marxian analyses of society and politics that departed from Soviet orthodoxy. Expulsion from the party, loss of employment, and induced emigration are the most common official reprisals for such transgressions.

By the late 1970s, a much more heterodox "democratic opposition" was making its voice heard. Ranging in ideology from Marxist utopian to Christian democrat, these dissident intellectuals have issued statements of solidarity with "Charter 77" and with Polish opposition groups, agitated on behalf of the neighboring Hungarian minorities' rights, mounted programs to aid indigent Hungarians, and published a variety of *samizdat* works and journals criticizing the regime's policies and even questioning its legitimacy. The Helsinki Final Act and the rise of Solidarity in Poland emboldened these critics; conversely, the crushing of Solidarity and the hard line taken by Brezhnev's successor, Yuri Andropov, had a negative effect. In December 1982 the Hungarian authorities took steps to curtail the unauthorized reproduction and dissemination of material by dissidents (notably by the son of the late Laszlo Rajk). The HSWP's relatively liberal ideologist, Politburo member Gyorgy Aczel, warned subsequently: "There is no room in our alliance policy for those who want to change its well-known slogan into that of 'he who is against us is also with us'."[34]

The popular legitimacy of the current political system does not bear easy assessment.[35] Older Hungarians who remember worse times are disposed to regard Kadar as the astute architect of a tolerable *modus vivendi* with the imperial power. The young are less ready to accept unquestioningly the constraints and contradictions of Communist rule and Soviet domination, and their alienation from the political system is the source of much official concern.[36] Overtly deviant behavior, or what the regime calls political crime, is marginal and rare. Instead, one finds a pervasive cynicism or, at best, disinterest regarding the party and its ideology. The pursuit of material wealth and deep-rooted patriotism are the more prevalent popular values, conditioned by a certain acceptance of socialist-collectivist principles.[37]

Lip service to popular participation notwithstanding, the Kadar regime has exploited this depoliticization and has sought to build the system's legitimacy on the satisfaction of material needs. The unspoken but universally understood fact that all change in Hungary is subject to Soviet restraint, and general appreciation that within these limits Kadar has skillfully served Hungarian interests, indicate the nature of the regime's legitimacy. Kadar's pragmatism is rewarded by an ideologically neutral public acceptance that is equally pragmatic. Shortly before his death in 1971, the eminent Marxist philosopher Gyorgy Lukacs expressed deep pessimism regarding the prospects for genuine socialist democracy within the bureaucratic-authoritarian systems of the Soviet bloc.[38] The secrecy of political decision making and leadership selection, pervasive propaganda and limited cultural freedom, an authoritarian and petty bureaucratism inherited from earlier times but aggravated by party norms, a standard of living that, despite improvement, remains well behind that of the affluent West, are all negative features of the system. One can debate the accuracy of a survey by Radio Free Europe in 1976–77 which suggested that in hypothetical free elections barely 5 percent of Hungarians would vote for a Communist party, but there is no doubt that the popular legitimacy of the official ideology, of one-party rule, and above all of Soviet hegemony is far from consensual.[39]

FOREIGN ECONOMIC RELATIONS AND FOREIGN POLICY

The dominant factors in Hungary's foreign economic relations are its membership in CMEA (the Council for Mutual Economic Assistance), its limited resources in raw materials and energy, and its dependence on foreign trade for 40 percent of the national income. Principal domestic raw materials are bauxite, low-grade coal, uranium (exported to the Soviet Union and not reported in trade statistics), and lesser amounts of oil and natural gas. The more important industrial products are pharmaceuticals, electrical and communications equipment, and commercial vehicles. Raw materials and semi-finished products accounted for 29.5 percent of 1981 exports; machinery and other capital goods for 25.3 percent; industrial consumer goods for 15.9 percent; and food products for 25.2 percent. In 1981, the socialist countries accounted for 51.5 percent of Hungary's imports and 58.2 percent of her exports (the Soviet Union alone for 28.6 percent and 33.4 percent). The industrial nonsocialist countries provided 40.2 percent of Hungary's imports and took 30.2 percent of her exports (the German Federal Republic taking the biggest share at 11.9 percent and 8.7 percent). The developing countries' share of imports was 8.3 percent, of exports 11.6 percent.

In recent years the major problems have been a negative balance of trade with the West and the rapid rise in raw material prices. CMEA traditionally served both as an assured supplier of raw materials and as a protected market for Hungary's relatively inefficient industries. With the introduction of the NEM, industrial modernization gained new impetus, but increased purchases of Western technology could not be matched by exports partly because of the European Economic Community's restrictions on food imports and the U.S. government's reluctance until late 1977 to grant Hungary most-favored-nation status. The surpluses accumulated in the socialist sector in the early 1970s could not alleviate the imbalance in Western trade, for the CMEA currencies are not freely convertible. Hungary became a member of GATT in 1973 and has pursued joint ventures with Western firms. In consequence of the general economic slump and the unfavorable terms of trade, Hungary's net debt to Western banks and governments rose by 1983 to over $8 billion (the highest per capita among CMEA countries). Hungary was admitted to membership in the International Monetary Fund and the World Bank in 1982 and committed herself to the deflationary route to economic recovery as the price of further loans.

The Soviet Union supplies approximately 90 percent of Hungary's requirements for oil (through the Friendship pipeline), iron ore, and timber, and a high proportion of other raw materials. The renegotiation of intra-CMEA prices worked to Hungary's detriment, for because of the commodity structure of Hungarian trade in that sector, the average increase in import prices was nearly double that of export prices. Along with the other East Europeans, Hungary has to share in the cost of developing new Soviet resources, notably the building of the Orenburg pipeline for Siberian gas. (Hungary also has a share in the new Adria pipeline, destined to be fed with OPEC oil.) A single Soviet-designed nuclear power station has been under construction for many years. Foreseeably, Hungary's ability to buy Western technology will decline and her economic dependence on CMEA will increase in the years to come.

Hungary's foreign and interparty policies in the Kadar era have remained firmly aligned with those of the Soviet Union. Apart from the party, the principal formal links with the Soviet Union and the other East European states are the Warsaw Treaty, CMEA, and bilateral treaties of friendship, cooperation, and mutual assistance. In the 1968 Czechoslovakian crisis Kadar initially played a mediating role, then assented to Hungarian participation in the Warsaw Pact intervention. The official media reported with commendable objectivity on the rise of Solidarity, and the popular reaction was one of sympathy tinged with concern about the side effects of yet another Soviet intervention. The increasingly apprehensive HSWP leadership welcomed General Jaruzelski's coup and offered various forms of aid.

Kadar had cultivated good relations with Khrushchev, Brezhnev, and their East European counterparts. Andropov's appointment was greeted with some optimism in Budapest. Although the former KGB head had been instrumental in crushing the revolution of 1956 (when he was ambassador to Budapest), he reportedly favored the Hungarian economic reforms. These reforms are regarded with some suspicion by the East Germans and other more orthodox regimes, but there are no major disharmonies between Hungary and the rest of the Soviet bloc. One exception is Romania, which harbors close to two million ethnic Hungarians in Transylvania and has employed brutal measures of dispersal, discrimination, and cultural assimilation.[40] The fate of the Hungarian minority in Romania is of passionate concern to most Hungarians, and as a result relations between the two regimes have been noticeably cool. There are smaller Hungarian minorities in Slovakia and in the Voivodina region of Yugoslavia, but more tolerant treatment, particularly in Yugoslavia, has attenuated historical animosities. Relations with Yugoslavia have signally improved since the tense period following the invasion of Czechoslovakia.

It is in the objective as well as the propagandistic interest of a small and vulnerable country like Hungary to support international initiatives for disarmament, peaceful settlement of disputes, and economic and cultural cooperation. One setback, perhaps of little lasting consequence, was Hungary's relegation to observer status at the mutual force reduction talks that began in Vienna in 1973. At Soviet insistence, Italy's nonparticipation was matched by that of Hungary, thereby excluding from the negotiations Hungary's armed forces (106,000 troops plus 15,000 border guards) as well as the Soviet forces (65,000 men in two tank and two motorized rifle divisions, plus tactical air force units) stationed on Hungarian territory. In endorsing the 1975 Helsinki Final Act, Kadar noted that it did not mean mutual ideological acceptance and intimated that Hungary's policies were already consistent with the act's prescriptions.

In Communist party relations, Kadar normally gives a muted echo to the Soviet line. Communist China is regularly denounced for its anti-Sovietism and rapprochement with the West. In the schismatic debate over Eurocommunism, Kadar tried to profess moderation, rejecting Western criticism of the East European model, while suggesting that other paths to socialism are conceivable as long as the experience of the Soviet party is kept in view.[41] The Hungarian party has adopted the Soviet model of detente in its pursuit of trade expansion and domestic ideological retrenchment. Full diplomatic relations with West Germany were restored in 1973, and diplomatic and commercial contacts with the West have multiplied. It was a measure of Kadar's success that in 1977 he not only was awarded the Lenin Peace Prize but also secured the return of the ancient crown of St. Stephen from the United States, where it had been held in safekeeping since the end of World War II. Third World contacts are nurtured both to show solidarity against colonialism and imperialism and to pursue commercial objectives. In sum, Kadar's foreign policy has been to normalize relations with all states subject to the limitations of Soviet interests. Meanwhile, through tourism and unjammed radio broadcasts (and Austrian television in western Hungary), Hungarians are uncommonly exposed to external influences that reinforce a historical Western cultural orientation whose ideological content the regime has great difficulty in counteracting.

PROBLEMS AND PROSPECTS

The Hungarian regime's pursuit of economic modernization and socialist democracy leads inevitably to a dilemma: as one Western analyst put it, "How to achieve democratic legitimacy (a Western concept) without destroying the leading role or supremacy of the Party (a Communist concept) in Hungarian society."[42] The regime needs the cooperation of a large, well-educated middle class that is no longer inhibited by past affiliations and that lays claim to material rewards, cultural freedom, and a role in decision making. The regime must also placate the demands of the industrial working class, not only for the sake of higher productivity but also to authenticate the ideologically preordained leading role of that class. In the absence of a free contest of political interests, the party alone must choose among priorities, persuade the public of the wisdom and inevitability of that choice, and forestall any independent challenge to its decision. As memories of the 1956 revolution's tragic repression fade, the task of mobilizing a politically apathetic younger generation to support actively a monolithic system that tolerates no pluralism becomes pressing but is also fraught with risks.

While the current Hungarian version of proletarian dictatorship bears no resemblance to the pluralistic political system that was anticipated in the 1956 revolution, it is also far removed in its day-to-day operation from Rakosi's totalitarianism. With the obvious exception of agricultural collectivization, the Kadar system owes much to the original orientation of the New Course. Even in agriculture, reforms have facilitated both economies of scale and a fruitful degree of privatization. Thus the Hungarian system is differentiated in some respects from the rest of the Soviet bloc. Compared to the Soviet and other East European versions, it manifests a more rational and flexible economic mechanism, fewer cultural constraints, and an unusual official sensitivity to popular opinion.

By 1983, however, the prospects for sustained economic growth had dimmed, while the Polish events had once again dashed hopes for peaceful democratization of the East European systems. At a national *agitprop* conference, both Aczel and the reformer Nyers suggested that the nation's political institutions needed to democratize their style of work;[43] but the Soviet bloc's ideological retrenchment probably allows Hungary little latitude to compensate for economic austerity by political liberalization. Meanwhile, the absence of credible constitutional guarantees, the ever-present shadow of the Kremlin, and the imminent necessity of finding a successor to Kadar (born 1912) inspire popular apprehension even about the permanence of the current alliance policy. "I believe," said Bela Biszku in 1969, "that the supreme guarantee has already been given—namely the Party itself, which has never forgotten the lessons of 1956 and which, in its inner life, incessantly fosters democracy. We are doing everything to prevent any group from ever again monopolizing the party and the socialist system and abusing power."[44] The circumstantial legitimacy of the Kadar regime rests on such promises, on the tangible benefits of the alliance policy, and on the fear of worse dictatorships.

NOTES

1. See Rudolf L. Tokes, *Bela Kun and the Hungarian Soviet Republic* (New York: Praeger, 1967). For a brief historical overview, see Bennett Kovrig, *The Hungarian People's Republic* (Baltimore: Johns Hopkins Press, 1970). A more comprehensive history of the Hungarian party can be found in Kovrig, *Communism in Hungary from Kun to Kadar* (Stanford: Hoover Institution Press, 1979).

2. Balint Szabo, *Nepi demokracia es forradalomelmelet* (Budapest: Kossuth, 1970), pp. 77–106.

3. Cf., Charles Gati, "Hungary: The Dynamics of Revolutionary Transformation," in Charles Gati, ed., *The Politics of Modernization in Eastern Europe* (New York: Praeger, 1974), pp. 51–84.

4. On Allied policy regarding Hungary, see Bennett Kovrig, *The Myth of Liberation* (Baltimore: Johns Hopkins Press, 1973), pp. 30, 52, 64–71.

5. Sandor Balogh, *Parlamenti es partharcok Magyarorszagon, 1945–1947* (Budapest: Kossuth, 1975), p. 525.

6. Paul Ignotus, "The First Two Communist Takeovers of Hungary: 1919 and 1948," in Thomas T. Hammond, ed. *The Anatomy of Communist Takeovers* (New Haven: Yale University Press, 1975), p. 398.

7. Magyar Szocialista Munkaspart, *Legyozhetetlen ero*, 2nd ed. (Budapest: Kossuth, 1974), p. 224.

8. See Bela A. Balassa, *The Hungarian Experience in Economic Planning* (New Haven: Yale University Press, 1959), pp. 31–35, 216ff; cf., Ivan T. Berend, *A szocialista gazdasag fejlodese Magyarorszagon, 1945–1968* (Budapest: Kossuth, 1974) pp. 86–93

9. Wrote Nagy: "The 'left-wing' deviationists, primarily Rakosi and Gero, in the years 1949 to 1953 brought the socialist reorganization of agriculture to a dead end, bankrupted agricultural production, destroyed the worker-peasant alliance, undermined the power of the People's Democracy, trampled upon the rule of law, debased the people's living standards, established a rift between the masses and the Party and government—in other words swept the country towards catastrophe" (Imre Nagy, *On Communism: In Defence of the New Course* [New York: Praeger, 1957], p. 194).

10. Quoted in George Mikes, *The Hungarian Revolution* (London: Deutsch, 1957), p. 61.

11. See Tamas Aczel and Tibor Meray, *The Revolt of the Mind* (New York: Praeger, 1960).

12. Paul E. Zinner, *Revolution in Hungary* (New York: Columbia University Press, 1962), p. 195.

13. Among the numerous accounts of the Hungarian revolution, two of the best are Ferenc A. Vali, *Rift and Revolt in Hungary* (Cambridge: Harvard University Press, 1961), and Miklos Molnar, *Budapest 1956* (London: Allen & Unwin, 1971).

14. See "Principles of Development and Further Strengthening of Friendship and Cooperation Between the Soviet Union and Other Socialist States," in Paul E. Zinner, ed., *National Communism and Popular Revolt in Eastern Europe* (New York: Columbia University Press, 1956), pp. 487–89. For the Western response to the revolution see Kovrig, *The Myth of Liberation*, ch. 5.

15. See William Shawcross, *Crime and Compromise* (New York: Dutton, 1974), pp. 82–85.

16. *Tarsadalmi Szemle*, June 1972, p. 9.

17. Radio Free Europe Research, Situation Report, March 22, 1975.

18. *Partelet*, December 1972.

19. *Nepszabadsag*, December 24, 1972.

20. *A Magyar Szocialista Munkaspart XI. kongresszusa* (Budapest: Kossuth, 1975), pp. 70–124.

21. Laszlo Rozsa, "Aktivitas, kiallas, demokracia," *Tarsadalmi Szemle*, May 1976, p. 29.

22. *Nepszabadsag*, October 24, 1975.

23. *A Magyar Szocialista Munkaspart XII. kongresszusa* (Budapest: Kossuth, 1980), p. 10.

24. For analysis of the composition of the 1975 national assembly, see Peter A. Toma and Ivan Volgyes, *Politics in Hungary* (San Francisco: Freeman, 1977), pp. 57–62.

25. See Toma and Volgyes, pp. 74–82.

26. *Nepszabadsag*, September 20, 1976.

27. *Nepszabadsag*, January 16, 1971.

28. *Nepszabadsag*, May 11, 1976.

29. Toma and Volgyes, pp. 96–98.

30. *Partelet*, September 1973. An excellent analysis of the development and implementation of the NEM can be found in William F. Robinson, *The Pattern of Reform in Hungary* (New York: Praeger, 1973), chs. 2–6.

31. *Nepszabadsag*, September 14, 1982.

32. Social welfare programs are outlined in Toma and Volgyes, ch. 10.

33. *Tarsadalmi Szemle*, March 1976, p. 18.

34. Radio Free Europe Research, Situation Report, January 24, 1983. Earlier cultural policies and problems are examined in Robinson, ch. 9.

35. On socialization, the media, and the political culture, see Toma and Volgyes, chs. 8, 9, and 11.

36. See *Tarsadalomtudomanyi Kozlemenyek*, No. 4, 1982.

37. Observed the president of the Patriotic People's Front, Gyula Kallai: "We must take into account that a significant part of the masses . . . is still not unified in its world outlook. This is linked to the fact that there remain traces of the old system's ideology, and indeed in certain political and economic circumstances this harmful inheritance may and does reemerge. We must confront calmly but determinedly the fact that the philosophy of individualism and egotism is, under the ostensible veneer of socialism, spreading through not negligible strata of our society" (*Nepszabadsag,* June 27, 1976).

38. Interview with Yvon Bourdet in *L'Homme et la societe*, April–June 1971, pp. 3–12.

39. Radio Free Europe, Audience and Public Opinion Research Department, "Political Orientation and Listening to Western Radio in East Europe," July 1977.

40. See Robert R. King, *Minorities under Communism* (Cambridge: Harvard University Press, 1973), chs. 8 and 9.

41. *Beke es Szocializmus*, January 1977.

42. Toma and Volgyes, p. 63.

43. Radio Free Europe Research, Situation Report, January 24, 1983.

44. Quoted in Robinson, pp. 263–264.

BIBLIOGRAPHY

Aczel, Tamas, ed. *Ten Years After*. New York: Holt, Rinehart & Winston, 1967.

Aczel, Tamas, and Meray, Tibor. *The Revolt of the Mind*. New York: Praeger, 1960.

Hare, Paul et al., eds. *Hungary: A Decade of Economic Reform*. London: Allen & Unwin, 1981.

Hungarian Socialist Workers Party, Party History Institute. *History of the Revolutionary Workers Movement in Hungary, 1944–1962*. Budapest: Corvina, 1973.

Ignotus, Pal. *Hungary*. New York: Praeger, 1972.

Kecskemeti, Paul. *The Unexpected Revolution*. Stanford: Stanford University Press, 1961.

King, Robert R. *Minorities Under Communism*. Cambridge, Mass.: Harvard University Press, 1973.

Kovrig, Bennett. *The Hungarian People's Republic*. Baltimore: Johns Hopkins Press, 1973.

———*Communism in Hungary from Kun to Kadar*. Stanford: Hoover Institution Press, 1979.

Laszlo, Ervin. *The Communist Ideology in Hungary*. Dordrecht: Reidel, 1966.

Nagy, Imre. *On Communism: In Defense of the New Course*. London: Thames & Hudson, 1957.

Radvanyi, Janos. *Hungary and the Superpowers*. Stanford: Hoover Institution, 1972.

Robinson, William F. *The Pattern of Reform in Hungary*. New York: Praeger, 1973.

Shawcross, William. *Crime and Compromise: Janos Kadar and the Politics of Hungary Since Revolution*. New York: Dutton, 1974.

Sinor, Denis, ed. *Modern Hungary: Readings from* The New Hungarian Quarterly. Bloomington: Indiana University Press, 1977.

Toma, Peter A., and Ivan Volgyes. *Politics in Hungary*. San Francisco: Freeman, 1977.

Vali, Ferenc A. *Rift and Revolt in Hungary*. Cambridge, Mass.: Harvard University Press, 1961.

Volgyes, Ivan. *Hungary: A Nation of Contradictions*. Boulder, Colo.: Westview, 1982.

Volgyes, Ivan, ed. *Political Socialization in Eastern Europe*. New York: Praeger, 1975.

Zinner, Paul E. *Revolution in Hungary*. New York: Columbia University Press, 1962.

4   Czechoslovakia

Otto Ulc

TACTICS OF TAKEOVER

With an area of only 50,000 square miles (the approximate size of North Carolina) and a population of 15 million, Czechoslovakia is not a large country, but it is strategically located in the geographic center of the European continent. When the Czechoslovak Republic was founded in 1918, it inherited the largest part of the industry of the dismantled Austro-Hungarian monarchy. The advanced level of economic development and the numerical strength of the working class thus provided an auspicious setting for testing Marxist visions of social transformation.

In 1945 when World War II ended, of all the European lands east of the Elbe, Czechoslovakia was in the most fortunate position. It had not suffered substantial war destruction (as had occurred especially in Poland and Yugoslavia) and it was not treated as a defeated enemy (as were Hungary, Romania, and Bulgaria) or burdened by reparations and foreign occupation. Czechoslovakia was regarded as an ally by the victorious powers. In a rare exception to the pattern in the other countries it occupied, the Red Army left Czechoslovakia before the end of 1945. The government-in-exile of President Eduard Benes in London was allowed to return to the Soviet-bound part of Europe, at least as a symbol of statehood and preservation of its continuity. However, symptomatic of things to come was the return route taken by the Benes government: it traveled to Prague via Moscow, where Benes, who had little faith in the West and few options left to him, signed a pact of friendship with Stalin.

There is enough evidence available to argue that Communist rule was *not* imposed upon Czechoslovakia from the outside. This particular Communist takeover was not a foregone conclusion, and the main credit for the outcome belongs not to the Kremlin in general or to Stalin in particular but to domestic forces—especially to the effort of the Communist Party of Czechoslovakia (hereafter CPCS). In contrast to neighboring Poland and Hungary, Czechoslovakia did not harbor anti-Russian sentiment. The CPCS had been a fairly strong legal party in the prewar years, with its leaders sitting in parliament and not in jail. The total prewar CPCS membership was 80,000. The Munich Pact had left a legacy of betrayal. Bitterness toward the West was enhanced by gratitude to the Soviet Union for its role in crushing Hitler. The war polarized and radicalized the country, and by 1945 the CPCS membership exceeded one million. Membership included not only prewar Bolsheviks but also nostalgic Slavophiles, ardent anti-German patriots, ex-collaborators, and opportunists of all types.

Under Nazi rule some suffered and others collaborated. As in other East European lands, Communist party membership was an effective protection for the collaborationists after 1945. Political involvement also provided an opportunity to settle accounts with personal enemies. Three million Sudeten Germans—i.e., one-fifth of Czechoslovakia's total population—were expelled from the country, leaving behind considerable property: houses, villas, shops, factories, fields, and farms. A CPCS official was invariably in charge of distributing ex-German property. Not surprisingly, the electoral success of the CPCS was greatest in these Sudeten counties.

The first governmental program was signed in April 1945 in the East Slovak town of Kosice. It called for a National Front government, state control of large industries, land reform, punishment of wartime collaborators, and the expulsion of Germans and Hungarians from the country. "National Front" denoted a coalition government without, however, any provision for an eventual parliamentary opposition. All conservative and rightist parties were banned. The most notable casualty was the Republican (Agrarian) party, powerful in the prewar years.

In the Czech lands, i.e., in Bohemia and Moravia, four political parties—the Communists, the Social Democrats, the Czech Socialists, and the Catholics—and in Slovakia two parties—the Communists and the Democrats—shared power. In accordance with the pattern of sovietization in other countries, the first prime minister, the left-wing Social Democrat Zdenek Fierlinger, was not an overt Communist but a fellow traveler. The chairman of the Communist party, Klement Gottwald, was one of his four deputies. In the coalition government the Communists obtained the key ministries: interior, information, agriculture, education, and social welfare. Thus they were put in control of land distribution, propaganda, the police, and the administration of social welfare benefits.

The Communists followed the usual blueprint of takeover:

infiltrating and gaining control of mass organizations (notably the trade unions and the youth movement); splitting the noncommunist parties by encouraging the formation of left wings; and attacking anticommunists with charges of a fascist past or fascist intentions.

Under Gottwald's leadership the Communist party espoused the allegedly Czechoslovak road to socialism. In May 1946 parliamentary elections were held, and in a free contest with other parties the CPCS was a winner, receiving 38 percent of the votes (43 percent in the Czech lands) and 114 of 300 parliamentary seats. Gottwald became prime minister.

A two-year plan of postwar reconstruction was introduced. At the same time the political mood in the country, affected by the fading postwar euphoria, started to hurt the CPCS—which was engaged in a drive to obtain a 51 percent majority of public support. The CPCS conducted a public opinion survey only to find that not more than 28 percent of the Czechoslovak electorate was expected to vote the Communist ticket in the elections scheduled for May 1948. With this prospect of an electoral loss, the CPCS leadership resolved to seize power. In February 1948 a governmental crisis was staged and skillfully exploited. The Communist minister of interior, Vaclav Nosek, refused to comply with a cabinet decision to reinstitute the dismissed noncommunist police commissioners. Twelve noncommunist ministers resigned as a result, causing the fall of the government. Their alleged plan was that President Benes would call for an immediate election, the Communists would be defeated, and the country would become a pluralistic democracy.

Though loyal to his agreement with the Soviet Union, President Benes did not want to sever ties to the West. He conceived of Czechoslovakia as a bridge between East and West. However, after six critical days, a visit from the Soviet ambassador Valerian Zorin, and Communist threats of violence, Benes succumbed; instead of calling for free elections that might have neutralized the CPCS, he issued a virtual mandate for one-party rule. Events followed swiftly: several noncommunist leaders fled to the West; others were arrested; the popular Jan Masaryk, minister of foreign affairs and son of T. G. Masaryk, the founder of the Republic, was found dead (officially a suicide, unofficially the victim of a political murder). President Benes refused to sign the new constitution in May 1948, resigned his office in June, and died in September of the same year. Within less than six months Czechoslovakia and its leadership had completely changed.

Gottwald, as head of the Communist party, became president, while Rudolf Slansky remained secretary general of the CPCS. (Slansky was hanged as an "enemy of the people" in 1952.) Antonin Zapotocky became prime minister in 1948 and succeeded Gottwald in the presidency after the latter's death in March 1953.

The National Front now became a vehicle for one-party rule. Noncommunist members of the National Front included only a few puppet parties and mass organizations. In May 1948, a single slate of candidates allegedly received 86.6 percent of the votes cast. A new constitution was promulgated in the same month. Although its form was democratic, its contents were not.

THE MAIN LINES OF POLITICAL DEVELOPMENT

Czechoslovak political institutions and processes, as they have evolved since 1948, have closely emulated the Soviet model. Accordingly, inherited precommunist structures were either abolished entirely (e.g., the administrative courts—a citizen's avenue of redress against bureaucratic decisions) or retained in form, though not in content (e.g., the independent judiciary was converted into an instrument of "class justice"). Other institutions of purely Soviet inspiration were introduced (e.g., the *Prokuratura,* an institution that is part public prosecutor, part watchdog, and part ombudsman).

For reasons of geography alone, the Czechoslovak copy could not be an exact replica of the Soviet master design. The imitation of all things Soviet that the Prague leadership obstinately pursued was often counterproductive. For example, an attempt to convert Czech fields to corn, in imitation of Khrushchev's infatuation with planting corn, resulted in considerable economic loss.

The postwar course followed by the Warsaw Pact countries may generally be characterized as Stalinism, superseded by de-Stalinization, inaugurated by Khrushchev in 1956. The Czechoslovak version of Stalinism was particularly durable and virulent. In the post-Stalin period Antonin Novotny, who was first secretary of the CPCS from 1953 to 1968 and president of Czechoslovakia from 1957 to 1968, maneuvered to extricate his regime and himself personally from responsibility for the Stalinist terror.

Novotny's strategy of whitewash retarded de-Stalinization for several years. This delay deepened the social crisis, until it erupted in the Prague Spring of 1968. At that time the scope of liberalization dwarfed all other reformist efforts in Eastern Europe, those of Yugoslavia included. Significantly, the impetus toward change was not directed against Communist party rule (as was the short-lived revolt in Hungary in 1956) but was led by Communist reformers themselves.

In August 1968, however, the Soviet Union, enforcing the Brezhnev doctrine of limited sovereignty, suppressed with arms the Czechoslovak challenge to the status quo. The few months of euphoric emancipation, with civil liberties restored and censorship abolished, were followed by a period officially termed "normalization." With the possible exception of Albania, Prague became the foremost European center of neo-Stalinism.

It has been argued that the probable success of the Stalinist model of socialist construction is in inverse proportion to the general advancement of the country in which the model is to be tested. The Stalinist variant, designed for backward, rural, autocratic Russia, was more likely to be successful when applied to backward, rural, and autocratic Bulgaria than to industrially advanced Czechoslovakia, with a tradition of pluralistic democracy. The imposition of a crash program of heavy industrialization and the building of steel mills in industrialized but iron-ore poor Czechoslovakia was designed to satisfy an alien doctrine and not domestic needs. Not surprisingly, in comparing the economic advancement of the East European countries, Czechoslovakia's record has been the least distinguished.

Economic activities down to the street-corner ice-cream vendor were nationalized, all agricultural land was collectivized, and the first five-year plan went into force in 1949. These changes were accompanied by a thorough personnel turnover. Political loyalty was declared the supreme recruitment criterion for any job. A special category of "proletarian executives" emerged. Persecution of "class enemies," e.g., cuts in social security benefits for orphans from bourgeois families, became the rule. The damage to the economic structure and to personnel has been felt ever since.

For reasons that have never been satisfactorily explained, Gottwald's leadership departed from the Leninist principle of elitist recruitement into the party ranks. Instead of strict admission requirements for the select few, the CPCS gates were open to mass enrollment. The Communist party, 1.59 million strong in March 1946, swelled to 2.5 million by March 1948. One in every three adults became a Communist. A subsequent purge reduced the CPCS ranks to some 1.5 million, a figure that has remained fairly constant to the present.

Another difficult issue of the Stalinist period was the nationality question and the sharing of power. In Czechoslovakia there are twice as many Czechs (inhabiting Bohemia and Moravia) as Slovaks (in Slovakia). The two nations have similar languages but a very dissimilar past, socioeconomic development, and political culture. In the postwar years the Slovak demands for federation were not met; instead, an unsatisfactory compromise, called "asymmetry," was introduced. This arrangement provided the Slovaks with a restricted autonomy, later to be diminished even further. Slovak grievances were to contribute significantly to the collapse of Novotny's regime in 1968.

Czechoslovak Stalinism was characterized also by political trials and executions of the innocent. Among the victims was Milada Horakova, a member of the parliament and a survivor of a Nazi concentration camp, one of the few women in postwar Europe to be tried and executed for a political crime. The main wave of political arrests took place in 1951 and affected one of the most prominent terror-makers, the secretary general of the CPCS Rudolf Slansky. He, along with thirteen codefendants, most of them Jewish, were found guilty; eleven were executed, and their ashes were scattered on a road south of Prague. In 1954 Gustav Husak, the leading Slovak Communist, was sentenced to life imprisonment for being a bourgeois nationalist. He was later released and in 1969 he became the first secretary of the CPCS, a post that he still holds. In the early 1950s a new generation of political prisoners, estimated at well over 100,000 languished in 422 jails and concentration camps.

Even after the deaths of Stalin and of Gottwald in March 1953 the Czechoslovak phase of Stalinism was not yet over. Antonin Novotny, the colorless new leader, continued Stalinist policies. More political trials were staged, and on May 1, 1955, an eighteen-thousand-ton statue of Stalin, allegedly the largest in the world, was unveiled in Prague.

In February 1956 Khrushchev denounced Stalin in his secret speech at the Twentieth Party Congress; Poland rebelled in the summer of 1956 and Hungary erupted in a revolution in the autumn. The dramatic challenge to Communist rule in Budapest generated in Prague an atmosphere of nervous vindictiveness and intensified intolerance. It was in this period of renewed call for class struggle and Bolshevik vigilance that the forced collectivization drive reached its peak.

A new constitution was adopted in 1960, officially terminating the transitional period of "people's democracy" which had lasted twelve years, and heralding the arrival of socialism. This bold self-assessment put Czechoslovakia next only to the Soviet Union: no other country had attained the distinction of having achieved "scientific socialism;" Accordingly, the Czechoslovak Republic (*Ceskoslovenska republika*— CSR) was renamed the Czechoslovak Socialist Republic (*Ceskoslovenska socialisticka republika*—CSSR). The new Czechoslovak constitution even surpassed its Soviet model by declaring Marxism-Leninism the state ideology and anchoring the leading role of the Communist party in this basic law of the land. To cover up the political past,

Novotny chose a complex road of procrastination, whitewash, and salami tactics of rehabilitation, which lasted a decade. As a gesture toward de-Stalinization several commissions of inquiry were established after 1956, each reporting a different version of the Czechoslovak emulation of the Stalinist terror. One commission found nothing irregular or inappropriate with regard to the trials; a second commission held that minor technicalities were in error; a third detected major deficiencies. Finally, in 1963, under the impact of Khrushchev's renewed attack on Stalin at the Twenty-second Party Congress in 1961, the last commission pointed to some of the guilty parties and their crimes, although not to Novotny. The greatest cadre change since the purges of the fifties ensued: the old guard, including the premier, Viliam Siroky, was retired. Siroky's place was taken by a Slovak party bureaucrat, Jozef Lenart. Some of the executed party members who had been rehabilitated were posthumously readmitted to the party.

Novotny's last five years in power were crisis-ridden and culminated in the fall of his increasingly ineffectual regime in January 1968. The troubled state of the economy, the Slovak question, and general social malaise characterized the eclipse of Novotny's rule.

After 1961 the rate of production growth slowed significantly, and in 1963 Czechoslovakia experienced a decline in its gross national product. The five-year plan for 1959–63 had to be abandoned. Economists began to attack openly the "cult of planning" as an awkward, ineffective system. The economy was in urgent need of rational criteria for recruitment, management, decentralization, and production. Yet, the CPCS apparatus feared that giving more autonomy to economic units would threaten its own monopoly of power, and would lead to gradual loss of control over the state and over society. The need for a New Economic Model (NEM) was recognized, but political considerations prevented its genuine implementation. The realization had been growing within the top CPCS leadership that a successful economic reform could not be carried out without a change in the political system, that the economy would not prosper as long as the CPCS retained its monopoly of power. After three years of preparation, a compromise policy was adopted, but it satisfied neither the reformers nor the conservatives.

Criticism of the economic system along with the rehabilitation of the victims of Stalinism were signs of a more relaxed political climate. Franz Kafka was rehabilitated in 1963; censors became more tolerant; good literature was published; and Czechoslovak artistic creativity, especially in the film industry, became well known abroad. Czechoslovak citizens were issued passports and were allowed to travel abroad in increasing numbers. Class discrimination subsided, academic degrees were restored, and even some objectivity prevailed in the official assessment of Czechoslovakia's precommunist past.

The protracted crisis of Novotny's rule had many causes, of which the Slovak issue was perhaps the most formidable. The marriage of the Slovaks with the twice-as-numerous Czechs had been, at best, a marriage of convenience, with the inconvenient aspects of the liaison increasingly visible. Except for linguistic and geographical proximity, these two nations had little in common. During World War II the Czechoslovak state was destroyed, the Czech lands were occupied by the Germans, and the Slovaks became semi-independent in a pro-German alliance. After the war the Czechs voted for the Communists, while the Slovaks sided with the anticommunists. Again, the Slovak aspirations for a federal solution were not realized. Prague, the Czech center, ran the affairs of the entire state. The 1960 constitution further curtailed the powers of the authorities in the Slovak capital of Bratislava, thus adding to the credibility and vigor of the Slovak complaints.

The Stalinist purges of the fifties had affected the Slovak elites with particular harshness and, indeed, the very concept of Slovak nationhood was condemned as bourgeois nationalism. Thus, the rehabilitation of the victims of Stalinism in the 1960s was seen also as a rehabilitation of Slovak national identity. It was in Bratislava, and not in Prague, that the first attacks on Novotny's regime were launched.

In 1967, the year preceding the Prague Spring, the Czechoslovak leadership came under increasing criticism. Two political events of importance to Czechoslovaks occurred in June: the Six Day War in the Middle East and the Fourth Congress of Czech Writers in Prague. Israel, which enjoys popular support in Czechoslovakia, demolished its Arab adversaries, the friends and allies of the Soviet Union. Soviet weapons were defeated. At the writers' congress in Prague, thoughtful and eloquent indictments of the Communist establishment and its rule were articulated: the narrowmindedness of the bureaucracy, the vulgarity of the censorship, and the subversion of socialist principles in general. The congress was highlighted by a masterful speech by the novelist and CPCS member Ludvik Vaculik, who accused the regime of having failed in its twenty years of unlimited rule to solve a single one of the problems facing Czechoslovak society.

The leadership, under attack, reacted with repressions: expulsions from the party, prohibition of publications, and the like. But Novotny's regime was losing ground. In December 1967 the Central Committee of the CPCS convened. The intraparty struggle came to an end in January 1968, when Slovak bureaucrat and compromise candidate Alexander

Dubcek was chosen to replace Novotny as the new leader of the ruling Communist party.

THE 1968 DEVIATION FROM THE SOVIET MODEL

The appointment of Dubcek marked the beginning of the eight months known as the Prague Spring. The events of 1968 catapulted Prague into the role of a challenger of the Soviet monopoly over applied Marxism. The aim of Czechoslovak reformers was to combine socialism with democracy and economic security with civil liberties—and to eliminate Leninism as a crippling distortion of Marxism. In this ambitious quest, sacrosanct and hitherto unchallenged articles of faith were attacked and eventually rejected.

Hundreds of books have been written about the Prague Spring.[1] Here we can mention only the most fundamental observations relating to this experiment in "socialism with a human face." For one, it was an interrupted process. Soviet intervention prevented full implementation of the experiment. From the Soviet viewpoint Dubcek's cardinal error was weakening the leading role of the Communist party. Such heresies were enunciated in the Action Program of April 1968. This document, drawn up by the CPCS, in some respects resembles Western Eurocommunist pronouncements of the 1970s, but in other respects it was a compromise, eclectic and quite general. Bold promises were muted by qualifying clauses. In this "first step toward a new democratic model of socialist society" little was said about the leading role of the Communist party, but the CPCS had nonetheless issued the Action Program without consulting the minor parties, other components of the National Front, or the nation at large.

The abolition of censorship significantly enhanced the political role of the mass media. The press, radio, and television became "schools of democracy." They discussed quite openly the darker aspects of the previous twenty years of socialist construction: the purges, tortures, show trials, concentration camps, and the like. The airing of these previously taboo subjects served as an effective socialization program, and after a few months the Soviet type of one-party rule was thoroughly discredited. Public opinion surveys confirmed the overwhelming popularity of the new course: Dubcek's team received some 90 percent of popular support.

In June 1968 a rehabilitation law was passed. The law submitted to review the punitive record of the state over the preceding two decades. Any person convicted of a political crime in the state period was entitled to a retrial. Retrials could be initiated by a relative or heir. An overwhelming majority of those who chose this avenue of belated redress were rehabilitated.

The Soviet leadership may have misunderstood and misinterpreted Czechoslovak developments in 1968, but only in part. Whereas Prague did not plan to secede from the socialist camp and join the capitalist West, loyalty in foreign affairs was not matched by similar loyalty in domestic matters. The trend toward broader political participation, though short of pluralistic democracy, did indeed weaken the leading role of the Communist party and was substantially alien to the Soviet understanding of socialism. Moscow feared that such a course would undermine the Czechoslovak regime and would endanger stability in other parts of the socialist camp, notably Poland and East Germany. Soviet efforts to stop the heretics escalated from consultations and warnings through reprimands, threats, intrigues, and military maneuvers, finally to military intervention.

The Soviet invasion of August 21, 1968, was a textbook example of military efficiency and political ineptitude. The armies of the more dogmatic members of the Warsaw Pact moved into Czechoslovakia in response to an invitation that never arrived. The Czechoslovak populace did not greet with sympathy those rendering "fraternal assistance in defense of socialism." Indeed, the Soviet invasion caused the most profound shift in the Czechoslovak political outlook since World War II: people who had been divided in 1948 became united in 1968. The rift between the Communists and the anticommunists, between the supporters and the opponents of the regime, disappeared; wounds were healed by acute patriotism and anti-Sovietism. However, this unity was soon shattered by an alienated but compliant population that placed private interests, such as career and family, ahead of patriotic fervor and declarations of political faith.

THE PROCESS OF "NORMALIZATION"

In the first period of one-party rule, when Communist power was achieved and consolidated after 1945, the leadership consisted mainly of veteran Czechoslovak Bolsheviks of the prewar era—Gottwald, Slansky, Kopecky, Dolansky, and Siroky. By the 1970s, all of these leaders were dead.

The old Bolshevik generation was augmented by postwar CPCS recruits, by former left-wing Social Democrats, and by opportunists of various types. Since 1968, the leadership has been dominated by the beneficiaries rather than by the co-architects of Communist rule. Changes in personnel after the 1968 invasion, culminating in a massive party purge in 1970, provided numerous vacancies that were filled with

individuals with often manifestly inferior qualifications, with career-
ists, and with a disproportionate number of persons of Slovak nationality.

At the top of the hierarchy is Gustav Husak, the first postwar ruler of
Slovakia, who had been sentenced to life imprisonment after being
convicted of alleged demonstrations of "bourgeois nationalism," a
treacherous Titoist deviation. Rehabilitated during the 1960s, he returned to the political arena in 1968, a supporter of liberal reforms, yet
an autocrat; a supporter of Dubcek, yet after the invasion his denoun-
cer. Like the Hungarian leader Janos Kadar, Husak had been arrested
and tortured by his own comrades. However, in other respects Husak's
background and record are quite different from those of the leaders of
the other Warsaw Pact countries. Husak is a university-educated intellectual and a member of the Slovak ethnic minority; his dubious wartime record as a resistance fighter was tainted by collaboration with the
Slovak pro-Nazi regime. After twenty years of exclusion from public
office, he became head of the CPCS in 1969 and head of state in 1975,
positions to which he was reelected unanimously in 1980.

Husak was expected to emulate Kadar's policies in Hungary after
1956: a relatively brief course of repression to be followed by a program of national reconciliation, characterized by tolerance and by
modernization efforts within the confines of Moscow's hegemony.
However, whereas Kadar followed a centrist course opposing both the
left and the right wings of the party, Husak steered a dogmatic course,
attacking only the progressive reformers and his former supporters. As
a result, he became identified with the policies of the CPCS conservatives.

The "progressive" versus "conservative" dichotomy is inappropriate
for the political leadership in postinvasion Czechoslovakia. Rather the
distinction is between conservative and hard-line factions. Husak, the
main representative of the conservative wing, has projected the image
of the lesser evil. The leader of the hard-liners is Vasil Bil'ak, an ethnic
Ruthenian and a consistent Stalinist who in the 1960s was among those
opposed to the rehabilitation of Husak. Whether the Czechoslovak
leaders are of pragmatic or dogmatic orientation, they are beneficiaries
of the invasion and their careers depend on Soviet tutelage.

The imposed process of "normalization" led to the annulment of the
innovations of 1968. Rehabilitated victims of Stalinism were "de-
rehabilitated," economic reforms were blocked, censorship reinstated,
and the policy of class struggle reintroduced with such a degree of
intolerant fury as to prompt the French Communist poet Louis Aragon
to label Czechoslovakia "the Biafra of the soul."

In the postinvasion purge of 1970, a full one-third of the total

1,500,000 Communist party membership was removed from the ranks. While the post-1948 purge had weeded out opportunists and bourgeois elements, in 1970 committed Communists, among them prewar party veterans, were purged. The measure affected the Czechs (constituting 90 percent of all casualties) more than the Slovaks, and singled out individuals with higher education, party seniority, and positions of responsibility. Some 75 percent were assigned to manual labor. As a rule, party membership means lifetime involvement. Except for serious illness or advanced age, there is no way for a Communist to retire but in disgrace. Expelled Communists are the current pariahs of Czechoslovak society, replacing the traditional class enemies: capitalists, big landowners, and other prominent pillars of the destroyed bourgeois order. The new pariahs are victimized and ostracized, and their children are barred, by governmental ordinances, from access to higher education.

The CPCS has regained its numerical strength. As of April 1981, 1,550,000 Czechoslovak citizens, one in seven adults, were card-carrying Communists. The statisticians stress the youth and the working-class background of the majority of the new recruits. Opportunism, not mentioned, is a predominant motive for joining. Party membership is a prerequisite to holding managerial positions even in eminently nonpolitical fields. The so-called *nomenklatura* appointments, which require the consent of the party Secretariat (of the district, regional, or central committee, depending on the importance of the position), amount to over 100,000.

Husak has adhered very closely to the Soviet model in substance and even in form. A Czechoslovak party congress has been invariably scheduled just after each Soviet party congress. The CPCS structure and functions are similar to the Soviet model: the Politburo initiates policies and supervises their implementation, which is left in the hands of the executive branch of the government, including the cabinet, various ministries, and other offices of a ministerial rank. The Secretariat of the Central Committee of the CPCS is the nerve center of the party bureaucracy, and the first secretary is the most powerful person in the country. The country is divided into provinces and the provinces into districts. Each unit is headed by a party bureaucrat of appropriate rank.

Federalization, a sharing of power by Prague and Bratislava, is the only innovation of 1968 that has survived, albeit in a modified form. It should be recalled that Slovak national aspirations were instrumental in the fall of the Novotny regime. On October 28, 1968, the day of the fiftieth anniversary of the foundation of the Czechoslovak Republic by T. G. Masaryk, a Constitutional Law on Federation was promulgated.

In response to demands for maximum autonomy, separate institutions, such as the Slovak Ministry of Justice, were set up, and even dual citizenship was established: one could become a citizen of the Czechoslovak Socialist Republic (CSSR) and of either the Czech Socialist Republic (CSR) or the Slovak Socialist Republic (SSR).

The nationalistic euphoria was bound to subside. Dual citizenship, about as practical as dual citizenship in the United States and, say, North Dakota, was found too cumbersome and was abolished, as were some other innovations of decentralization. An element of the original 1948 asymmetry has remained. The state was federalized, but the Communist party was not. No *Czech* Communist party, as opposed to the Slovak Communist party, has ever been brought into existence.

Since 1948 the Czechoslovak electoral system has followed the Soviet system of a single slate of candidates. Since the Soviet invasion in 1968, two general elections have been held. In 1976, Czechoslovak voters allegedly broke records of electoral loyalty by casting 99.97 percent of their votes for the candidates of the regime.

The political leadership in postinvasion Czechoslovakia is characterized by both stability and insecurity. The Politburo that came to power in 1969 remains largely unchanged. In contrast to the genuinely popular leaders of 1968, however, those placed in power by the invading Soviet forces evoke neither affection nor respect. Their tenure depends on continued Kremlin sponsorship. Leading roles in political and economic institutions, in culture, and in academia have often been filled by individuals lacking talent and ability. Awareness of their precarious status and of the absence of public support serves to unite these insecure power holders.

Developments at the Fifteenth CPCS Congress, held in Prague in April 1976, illustrate the cohesion between the conservatives and the hard-liners. At issue was a proposed amnesty, blanket or partial, for the purged Communists, who, if readmitted to the party, undoubtedly would challenge numerous incumbents for their jobs. Husak alone spoke in favor of reconciliation, and only a token amnesty was adopted. The danger to present officeholders was thus thwarted, and the policy of wasting talents, injurious to the state and economy, was reconfirmed.

Even if the passage of time does not endow the rulers with the desired aura of legitimacy, it does to some extent desensitize the populace. However, the rationality of the policy makers is not unrelated to the legitimacy of their mandate. Public acceptance of the imposed status quo might be withdrawn if the rulers' behavior were to become too arbitrary and their boasts too implausible. When Czechoslovak intellectuals were assigned to be dishwashers, such a manpower allocation measure might well have been viewed as innovative, and perhaps modernizing, but hardly rational. Thus, while time has enhanced public acceptance and even genuine preference for a noncapitalist system—notably, for socialized medical care, other facets of socioeconomic security, and state ownership of the key means of production—the Soviet-imposed ruling group remains in low esteem, matching in prestige, some critics claim, the wartime puppet regime.

Insecurity begets intolerance. "I would not hesitate to fire even Albert Einstein,"[2] is a symptomatic declaration by an official of the Academy of Sciences in Prague. Among the costs of normalization are the 280,000 individuals who lost their jobs for political reasons, and the 150,000 who went into exile—a mini-diaspora of mainly the young, the skilled, and the well-educated. Thousands of scientists were dismissed as were 900 university professors. Two-thirds of the members of the Union of Czech Writers were expelled and their works banned, twenty-one scientific institutes were closed, and several scholarly disciplines, such as history, were decimated. An estimated one million citizens in a country of fifteen million have become casualties of "normalization." Economic hardship (above all, prohibition of employment in one's field) is the most commonly applied measure. For example, Bedrich Placak, professor of medicine and the first Czechoslovak to perform open-heart surgery, was reassigned to manual labor as a member of a subway construction crew because of his "immature" political views.

The 1975 spirit of Helsinki bore its best fruit in "Charter 77," characterized by the Yugoslav dissenter Milovan Djilas as "the most mature and accomplished program produced by Eastern Europe from the war up to today."[3] "Charter 77," issued in January 1977 in Prague and signed by several hundred Czechoslovaks from all walks of life, is an appeal to the government to obey its own laws. It cites the provisions of valid Czechoslovak statutes and ratified international conventions and stresses the necessity of living up to these commitments. The signatories of the charter emphasize that they do not challenge the government nor do they form an opposition.

Beginning with the main party daily, *Rude pravo,* on January 12, 1977, all the Czechoslovak mass media have vilified the signatories of the charter, declaring it a hostile, antistate pamphlet, a product of CIA-inspired anticommunist hysteria. While not a single sentence of it has appeared in any Czechoslovak publication, thousands of citizens have been forced to append their signatures to the condemnation of the charter, which they have not been permitted to read. Refusal to sign poses the threat of employment termination for the individual and implies ruin for the entire family.

"Charter 77" has issued position papers on such topics as living standards, destruction of the environment, treatment of the Gypsy minority, and the stationing of Soviet troops on Czechoslovak territory. The statements and actions of "Charter 77" are carefully framed to thwart accusations of subversive intentions. An open letter to Husak argued: "We know of no humane state in which a publicly declared intention to abide by the constitution is taken a priori to be an intention to overthrow the system."[4] Still, "Charter 77" has failed to generate any dialogue with the authorities, who have not refrained from accusing it of subversive political acts.

In 1980–81 spokesmen for "Charter 77" established working ties with Solidarity. Drawing parallels between the Polish crisis and the situation in Czechoslovakia, the Prague regime concluded that despite all the differences, the objectives of the antisocialist forces in both countries were the same. Subsequent arrests in Czechoslovakia and Poland and the declaration of martial law in Poland dealt a powerful blow to the progressive forces in those countries. Despite their courage and resourcefulness, Czechoslovak human rights activists remain under close police scrutiny and are isolated from the nation at large.

The Prague regime faces a more formidable task in trying to control widespread religious belief, especially among young people, who ordinarily would be unlikely church advocates. Religious belief is a cause for dismissal and purge and for further punishment of the offender's family. CPCS authorities do not consider religious persecution a violation of constitutional guarantees of civil liberties. In the words of the party daily newspaper, "We have no intention of making room for a reactionary political clericalism revived under any kind of pretext and especially under the slogans of religious freedom."[5]

"REAL SOCIALISM" AND THE SOCIAL CONTRACT

The Czechoslovak political system, as it exists in Husak's era, is officially labeled *realny socialismus,* a term as awkward in English as in Czech: socialism that is real, realistic, fatalistic, and resigned to the facts of life.

As in Hungary in 1956, the Soviet leadership opted to pacify the Czechoslovak populace with an improved supply of consumer goods. "Normalization" thus involved a certain depoliticization of the people, transforming them from unruly citizens to consumers devoting their energies to the laborious acquisition of goods constituting the socialist petit-bourgeois ideal: an automobile, a country house, modern household appliances, a vacation abroad. Since the desired goods are seldom available and their prices high, the citizen is often forced to take a second job. Whatever time remains is spent chasing after items in short supply. The results attest to remarkable public ingenuity: enterprising citizens try to obtain medication available only in the West, drive obsolete cars for which no spare parts are available, and build luxurious mansions from officially unobtainable materials. In a country of full employment the bars are full at any hour of the day. Advocates of what appears to be old-fashioned austerity are occasionally heard rejecting consumerism as a kind of bourgeoisification, a sell-out goulash Communism—ostentatious, status-conscious consumption.

The Soviet invasion in August 1968, the largest military undertaking in Europe since World War II, convinced Czechoslovak society that the price of any emancipatory initiative was prohibitive. Instead, an implicit social contract was formulated: rulers would rule and citizens would be rewarded with a relatively high standard of living and the opportunity to attend to their private affairs in exchange for not meddling in public affairs. Preoccupation with the pleasures of the consumer society has become a caricature of the heralded new socialist morality. While this social contract does not produce socialists, neither does it produce challengers of the system.

Those who reached adulthood in and around 1968 represent the most alienated generation in the country. Witnesses of exuberant hopes and national humiliation, they draw parallels between the Munich betrayal of 1938 and the Moscow betrayal of 1968, and ultimately they question the reason for Czechoslovakia's existence as an independent state.

Fortunately, the impact of repressive measures is blunted by widespread corruption. This relatively new phenomenon penetrates all spheres of life and reaches into high political office, the Secretariat of the Central Committee included. It is not considered abnormal or immoral to offer and accept bribes. The ethical implications of the issue aside, a word must be said in favor of corruption: it facilitates otherwise impossible achievements and blunts the impact of harsh political demands. A corruptible school official may ultimately be the only hope for a young person seeking access to higher education who comes from a politically questionable family.

Husak's policy of normalization has not been without its successes. The political activism exhibited by Czechoslovaks in the late 1960s has turned into political apathy. Standards of living have risen, and riots of the Polish type are not in sight.

Aside from the obvious beneficiaries of the political system such as party and governmental bureaucrats, the police, and political appointees of all stripes, the most satisfied social stratum seems to be the farmers. After the trauma of enforced collectivization during the 1950s, farming villages became oases beyond the total control of the state. In agriculture individual initiative has not been completely stultified by administrative fiat. The rural population is oriented toward consumerist values, and its aspirations are thoroughly apolitical. In consequence, the village has become the regime's pillar of stability.

Less-developed Slovakia benefited from postinvasion investment policies considerably more than did the historical provinces of Bohemia and Moravia. An impressive growth of private-home construction transformed the Slovakian countryside. Slovakia's increased prosperity, however, has contributed to the growing rift between the Czechs and the Slovaks. In the opinion of some observers, this split has developed into the most serious nationality conflict in the history of the country. Though the responsibility for this destructive development lies largely with Husak's leadership, the origins of the present rift may be traced back to the Prague Spring. When the armies of several Warsaw Pact countries invaded Czechoslovakia, the tanks were aimed at the Czech rather than the Slovak heretics. It was a punitive expedition against the Czech nation, evidenced, *inter alia,* by the results of the 1970 purge of the Communist party; of the half million members purged, 90 percent were Czechs. Nine out of ten subsequent political trials were Czech affairs. Whereas in Slovakia the assignment of an intellectual expelled from the CPCS to manual labor is an exception, in the Czech lands such an assignment is the general rule. Many vacancies in prominent positions are filled by outsiders from Slovakia and the Slovak representation in the federal offices in Prague is (in Czech pubic opinion) disproportionately high. The Czechs, twice as numerous as the Slovaks, also resent the preferential treatment of Slovakia with respect to the allocation of investment resources. This type of affirmative action to redress the imbalances of Slovak history is not at all appreciated by the Czechs. Such grievances, perhaps more imaginary than real, do pose a danger to the cohesiveness of the republic and are being exploited by some Politburo members (such as Alois Indra and Antonin Kapek) for their own political ends.

ECONOMIC REALITIES

The years 1971–75 were economically the most successful in the history of socialist Czechoslovakia. By 1975, however, the situation had changed substantially as a result of the cumulative impact of party policies and external causes. Energies expended in pursuit of private, often illicit material satisfactions had a detrimental effect on the public good. Once political criteria became the key priority in postinvasion recruitment policy, management of the economy by mediocre but politically unobjectionable cadres was destined to yield undesirable results.

The waste in manpower allocation has been exacerbated by irrational investments on the part of central planners. A society starved for desired goods is being inundated with unwanted products. By the end of 1980, some 30,000 industrial building sites stood unfinished.[6] In Czechoslovakia, as in Poland, the policy makers made their country heavily dependent on items that could not be put to efficient use. Iron-poor Czechoslovakia, for example, remains the world's third largest per capita producer of steel, an uneconomic but ideologically desirable product.[7]

Furthermore, the country has to cope with industrial obsolescence. Czechoslovakia emerged from World War II relatively unscathed, and in 1945 it had at its disposal the best industrial plant in Central Europe. Several decades later, the advantage has turned into a substantial handicap. An estimated 70 percent of the country's industrial property is antiquated. In contrast to Poland's excessive borrowing from the West, Czechoslovakia chose economic isolation and remained cut off from modern Western technology. Lubomir Strougal, the relatively pragmatic Czechoslovak prime minister, is credited with saying: "If things go on this way, we'll have to put up signs on the frontier, 'Entering Czechoslovakia, the Museum of an Industrial Society'."[8]

Because of obsolescence, energy consumption is up to 50 percent higher than in Western industrialized countries. Because of outdated factory equipment and technological procedures, Czechoslovakia ceased to be competitive on world markets. In 1980, Vasil Bilak, second to Husak in the Politburo, acknowledged that only 2 percent of exported products met world standards.[9] Instead of technologically sophisticated products, the country exports consumer goods (to the detriment of the domestic consumer), food, and raw materials such as timber. This situation, most unusual for an industrially advanced country, prompted the perhaps whimsical observation that Czechoslovakia was on its way to becoming an underdeveloped country.[10]

The main reason for this depressed situation has been the chronically unfavorable trade balance. Balance-of-payment difficulties have spread from Western trading partners to the Warsaw Pact allies, the Soviet Union included. During the 1960s Czechoslovakia was the banker for the less-developed socialist allies. For example, in 1966 Czechoslovakia granted a $500 million loan to the USSR to modernize and expand its oil fields in Western Siberia. However, since 1974, Czechoslovakia has experienced a trading deficit in dealing with its socialist partners. In 1973, the year of OPEC's onslaught on the world economy, Czechoslovakia encouraged the oil-producing countries to raise crude oil prices, expecting that such a step would injure the capitalist orbit—which it did—and *eo ipso* benefit the socialist orbit— which it did not. The Soviet Union, too, raised the price of its oil and natural gas to its East European customers. The export of weapons has been a success in an otherwise gloomy picture. In the 1976–80 period Czechoslovakia exported arms to the value of $3.7 billion ($2.7 billion to other Warsaw Pact members and $975 million to the Third World).

Josef Boruvka, the liberal minister of agriculture in 1968, was fond of saying, "Wherever socialism steps in, the grass ceases to grow." Neglect of environmental protection, violation of pollution standards (e.g., radioactivity generated by lignite power stations two hundred times greater than that of atomic plants), and excessive use of pesticides and chemical fertilizers contribute to the devastation of the physical environment. In order to cope with the energy crisis, the government in Prague placed its bets on nuclear energy. Construction of eight reactors is under way. Opponents of atomic energy, in neighboring Austria in particular, follow the development with considerable apprehension.

In the 1980s, the failure of government to live up to its part of the social contract has become all too evident. Because of the rising prices of Soviet crude—the world oil glut notwithstanding—bus transportation in Czechoslovakia was reduced by half, and civilian domestic air transport was almost totally eliminated. Average living standards leaped backward to the level of the early 1960s. The CPCS found itself debating the phenomenon of socialist unemployment.

Svatopluk Potac, deputy prime minister in charge of overall planning, acknowledged that economic conditions were "substantially more difficult" than in the 1970s. For both domestic and external reasons, the prognosis was not encouraging, and the current five-year plan, the seventh, is likely to be the last. According to Potac, "Each year has its specific characteristics. The era of long-term continuity of economic development and the fundamental stability of five-year plans is over."[11]

With the economy in decline, the party turned to ideology in justification of its rule. Its message was militant and intolerant, and the tone was shrill. In contrast to previous assurances about the unassailability of the socialist system and its immunity to pernicious Western influences, party pronouncements now blamed the capitalist West for Czechoslovakia's economic malaise. *Rude pravo,* on March 12, 1983, put it thus: "Our Communist party and socialist society are undergoing a hard and complex economic and political struggle. . . . We in socialist Czechoslovakia are in the front line of this struggle. We have to smash

the barricades erected by the enemy . . . we are at war." The vocabulary employed has not been heard since the 1950s. Jan Fojtik, a secretary of the CPCS Central Committee, for example, condemned
President Reagan for his "insane pronouncements in this era of excep-
tionally rapacious American imperialism".[12]

The intensified ideological fire produced a predictable sterility and
decay in the arts and sciences. For example, American historian Barbara Tuchman's Pulitzer-prize-winning book, *The Guns of August,*
translated and published in Poland and Romania, was condemned in
Czechoslovakia as a work glorifying Nazism.[13] The educational system, politicized and militarized, was further enriched by a Police University to educate doctors of police sciences. In addition to heightened
ideological militancy, in 1983 the party launched a campaign emulating
Andropov's drive against sloth and corruption in the Soviet Union.
Hard work, labor discipline, honesty, and modesty were the key demands propounded by the media.

PROSPECTS

The transformation of the pluralistic political system of prewar
Czechoslovakia into a Stalinist, and subsequently a neo-Stalinist, system may be viewed as a "great leap backward." Nothing of substance
materialized from Gottwald's postwar pledge to embark on a Czechoslovak road to socialism. In subsequent years the political system
under Novotny's leadership reached the point of immobility. The aim
of the reformers in 1968 was to undo the main damage caused by the
exaggerated emulation of all things Soviet. This modernization measure precipitated the formulation and application of Brezhnev's doctrine of limited sovereignty. After the Soviet invasion of
Czechoslovakia, the principle of limited sovereignty was incorporated
into a new Soviet-Czechoslovak friendship treaty of May 1970, the
status quo ante was restored, and the reforms were rescinded.

Under the facade of consensual leadership, political life is not conflict free. Hard-line ideologues represented by Vasil Bilak are opposed
by those who favor a more rational approach to problem solving. The
federal prime minister, Lubomir Strougal, is counted among the latter.
President and First Party Secretary Husak performs the role of a consensus preserver and perpetuator of conservative politics as it has
evolved in the postinvasion era.

Self-interest commands the Czechoslovak political elite to preserve
a state of limited sovereignty. Awareness of the alienation, if not outright hostility, of the population promotes a unity of convenience and
indeed of necessity within the leadership. Under these circumstances

the ruling pattern is bound to be noninnovative. Exhortation and tightening of discipline are no substitute for substantive reforms of the economic political systems. The Politburo fears that any innovation may contribute to the destabilization of its rule. In time, however, a timid, static system is apt to exhibit signs of aging and decrepitude. Personal compatibility between the Soviet and individual East European rulers is certainly an advantage but it is an insufficient guarantee of a lasting relationship. All East European leaders are judged first of all on their capacity to govern. If this capacity is lost, so is Soviet support.

NOTES

1. Among the more recent works is H. Gordon Skilling, *Czechoslovakia's Interrupted Revolution,* (Princeton: Princeton University Press, 1976).
2. *Die Zeit* (Hamburg), cited by *Listy* (Rome), August 1973, pp. 18–19.
3. *New York Times,* April 14, 1977.
4. *Czechoslovak Newsletter* (New York), February 1979, p. 1.
5. *Pravda* (Bratislava), July 10, 1980.
6. Ibid., July 11, 1981.
7. See V. V. Kusin, "Husak's Czechoslovakia and Economic Stagnation," *Problems of Communism,* May–June 1982, pp. 24–37.
8. David Binder, "Czechoslovakia, the East's New Economic Disaster," *New York Times,* November 8, 1981, p. 21.
9. *Nove Slovo* (Bratislava), May 22, 1980.
10. "When Will Czechoslovakia Become a Developing Country?" *Listy* (Rome), December 1976, pp. 19–21.
11. Svatopluk Potac, *Nova Mysl,* January 1983, p. 27.
12. Jan Fojtik, *Tvorba,* April 21, 1982, p. 3.
13. *Halo Sobota,* weekend supplement of *Rude pravo,* February 5, 1983, p. 3.

BIBLIOGRAPHY

Bradley, J. F. N. *Politics in Czechoslovakia, 1945–1977.* Washington, D.C.: University Press of America, 1981.
Dubcek, Alexander. *Czechoslovakia's Blueprint for Freedom.* Edited by Paul Ello. Washington, D.C.: Acropolis, 1968.
Golan, Galia. *The Czechoslovak Reform Movement.* Cambridge: Cambridge University Press, 1971.
———. *Reform Rule in Czechoslovakia: The Dubcek Era, 1968–1969.* Cambridge: Cambridge University Press, 1973.
Jancar, Barbara W. *Czechoslovakia and the Absolute Monopoly of Power.* New York: Praeger, 1971.

Korbel, Josef. *Twentieth Century Czechoslovakia: The Meaning of Its History.* New York: Columbia University Press, 1977.

Krejci, J. *Social Change and Stratification in Postwar Czechoslovakia.* London, 1972.

Kusin, Vladimir V. *The Czechoslovak Reform Movement.* Santa Barbara: ABC-Clio, 1973.

―――. *The Intellectual Origins of the Prague Spring: The Development of Reformist Ideas in Czechoslovakia, 1958–1967.* Cambridge: Cambridge University Press, 1971.

―――. *From Dubcek to Charter 77.* New York: St. Martins, 1978.

Mlynar, Zdenek. *Nightfrost in Prague.* New York: Karz, 1980.

Oxley, A. et al. *Czechoslovakia: The Party and the People.* London: St. Martins, 1973.

Paul, D. W. *The Cultural Limits of Revolutionary Politics.* New York: Columbia University Press, 1979.

―――. *Czechoslovakia.* Boulder, Colo.: Westview Press, 1981.

Remington, Robin A., ed. *Winter in Prague: Documents on Czechoslovak Communism in Crisis.* Cambridge, Mass.: MIT Press, 1969.

Riese, Hans P., ed. *Since the Prague Spring.* New York: Vintage, 1979.

Selucky, R. *Czechoslovakia: The Plan That Failed.* London, 1970.

Sik, Ota. *Czechoslovakia: The Bureaucratic Economy.* White Plains, N.Y.: International Arts and Sciences Press, 1972.

Skilling, H. Gordon. *Czechoslovakia's Interrupted Revolution.* Princeton: Princeton University Press, 1976.

Suda, Zdenek. *The Czechoslovak Socialist Republic.* Baltimore: Johns Hopkins University Press, 1969.

―――. *Zealots and Rebels.* Stanford: Hoover Press, 1980.

Svitak, Ivan. *The Czechoslovak Experiment, 1968–1969.* New York: Columbia University Press, 1971.

Taborsky, Edward.*Communism in Czechoslovakia, 1948–1960.* Princeton: Princeton University Press, 1961.

Ulc, Otto. *Politics in Czechoslovakia.* San Francisco: W. H. Freeman, 1974.

Zinner, Paul E. *Communist Strategy and Tactics in Czechoslovakia, 1918–1948.* London: Pall Mall, 1963.

The German Democratic Republic

5

Arthur M. Hanhardt, Jr.

The German Delmocratic Republic (GDR) steers a hazardous course among the integrative demands made by the Soviet Union, recent Polish events, the pressures of the world economy, and internal problems. The ability of Erich Honecker, general secretary of the ruling Socialist Unity Party (SED), to deal with these problems is hindered by the fact that his options are limited by the Soviet leadership and by the domestic situation in the GDR. Thus, the GDR's leaders have little room for effective maneuver in dealing with rising domestic expectations that conflict with the demands of the international economy and other events beyond their control. Why does the GDR find itself in this predicament?

The Soviet Union is the principal trading partner of the GDR. Ever since the East German "economic miracle" of the early 1960s, which in some ways rivaled the rapid development of the West German economy in the early 1950s, the GDR and the Soviet Union have become increasingly intertwined economically. The interrelationship between the economies is especially important since it has approached the level of integration. That is, the GDR supplies the USSR with finished goods, while, in return, the Soviets send raw materials, including over 87 percent of the GDR's oil requirements. This trade structure has bound the GDR very closely to the Soviet Union, and the Soviet leadership has exploited its advantage systematically, although in the late 1960s the terms of trade showed a trend favoring the GDR.

The rise of Solidarity in neighboring Poland caused the GDR leadership to be concerned lest the "Polish disease" spread. After first ignoring Polish developments, the GDR joined the Soviet Union and hardline states in criticizing and condemning Solidarity. The Jaruzelski regime was greeted with enthusiasm and relief in December 1981. As had been the case in Prague in the spring of 1968, the GDR had survived the shock waves of threatened change.

In the 1970s, and particularly since the 1973–74 OPEC boycott, the economic position of the GDR deteriorated. The economic decline has had two aspects. First, within the framework of greater integration within the Council for Mutual Economic Assistance (CMEA), the GDR and other East European states have had to help finance the development of Soviet natural resources. This has added a substantial, but unknown, amount to the GDR's financial burden. Second, and more important, the Soviets have gradually raised the prices of delivered raw materials while insisting that the prices it pays the GDR for finished goods remain unchanged. Finally, the level of exports of raw materials from the Soviet Union to the GDR has begun to decline in the 1980s. This has put the GDR in an uncomfortable squeeze.

The economic discomfort of the GDR has several sources. The relationship with the USSR is one; another is the GDR leaders' commitment to keep domestic prices stable. According to official pronouncements the inflation affecting the capitalist world will not affect socialist economies. The SED leadership has responded by exhorting the work force to achieve greater productivity in order to hold off price increases.

Another source of GDR economic problems is its relationship to the world economy. If productivity is to rise to pay for more expensive raw materials and to subsidize domestic prices, then relief must be sought in Western markets. The GDR had great expectations in this respect in the mid-1970s, when increased international recognition ended GDR political isolation from the West. In 1974 the United States finally recognized the GDR, and East Germany became a full member of the United Nations.

Access to international markets was seen as a means by which the GDR could modernize and expand its economy. The industrial skill of the GDR, particularly in specialized areas of manufacture such as precision instruments, would gain the recognition and rewards that had previously been denied to a country that before its partition had shown up on nearly every list of the world's "top ten" industrial nations. Expanded Western trade had an unspoken political aspect as well. Trade flexibility might give the GDR some leverage vis-a-vis the Soviet Union: benefits denied by the Soviets might be obtained elsewhere.[1]

Diplomatic recognition and participation in international commerce came hard on the heels of the oil boycott and consequent economic problems in the West. Trade figures rose but so did prices; the GDR was becoming increasingly indebted as a result of its expanded Western trade. The best estimate for 1980 indicates that about 27 percent of GDR foreign trade went to the West. Still, exports were insufficient to cover the cost of Western imports. In 1982 the U.S. dollar indebtedness of the GDR rose to 13 billion.[2] Exact figures are difficult to obtain but it is clear from the trends that the GDR has not escaped the effects of world trade conditions.

Among the internal problems causing trouble for the SED regime is an unofficial peace movement based in the churches of the GDR and popular among young people. Under the motto "Swords into Plowshares," the movement has links to antinuclear organizations active in the Federal Republic. As with any other movement not directly controlled by the official organs of state, the SED has dealt harshly with participants in unsanctioned peace demonstrations.[3]

Despite such problems, the SED is firmly in control and ostentatiously loyal to the Soviet Union. This loyalty was clearly demonstrated in the 1975 GDR-USSR Friendship Treaty, at the conference of European Communist Parties in 1976, and more recently at the Tenth Congress of the SED, held in April 1981, where Erich Honecker, in his closing remarks, stated that "Our party, the SED, is linked forever with the party of Lenin, the CPSU."

The theme of Soviet-GDR loyalty has been so repetitious that it has become too much for some East Germans to bear.[4] Indeed one researcher found that in the October 1977 issues of the official SED newspaper, *Neues Deutschland,* coverage of "the sixtieth anniversary of the Bolshevik Revolution . . . was accorded roughly six times as much space as was devoted to the observation of the founding of the GDR (October 7)."[5]

In the GDR today lack of popular enthusiasm for the bond with the USSR is a significant source of tension. Indeed, some segments of public opinion think that the industrially advanced GDR, with its high standard of living (by Soviet bloc measures), should not slavishly follow the Soviet lead on the road to socialism, and that German conditions, German experience, and German leadership should modify Soviet models.

Manifestations of tension take a variety of forms, ranging from the punk phenomenon to support for the kind of reform communism espoused by Rudolf Bahro.[6] While anomic manifestations are easily dealt with by the state security apparatus, the ideas generated by Bahro and other dissident intellectuals—mostly writers—who have challenged SED orthodoxy are more difficult for the state and the party to handle. The most common means of dealing with internal dissent has been to exile the dissenters. Bahro, for example, continues his work in West Germany, where he is active in the Green movement. There have been several occasions when oppositional groupings have challenged the

dominant authority, first of Walter Ulbricht, who led the SED from
1949 to 1971, and then of his successor, Erich Honecker, who has had
to cope with critical voices since mid-1976.

In comparing the political system of the GDR with that of the East
European states, it must be remembered that the GDR has had a
unique pattern of emergence and growth. In a generation, East Germany has been transformed from a vanquished and hated foe to an
accepted and integral member of the Soviet bloc.

THE SOVIET ZONE OF GERMANY:
A HISTORICAL FRAMEWORK

The Communist system in the GDR owes its origins to the complex
and interrelated events that accompanied the end of World War II in
Europe and led to the division of what remained of the German Reich
into three—later four—Allied zones of occupation. Although the Allied
Control Council was meant to be an administrative agency for all of the
zones, its formal capacities as a central administration were few. This
meant that as time passed and as the wartime alliance all too quickly
degenerated into competition and conflict, the commitment at Potsdam
to treat Germany as a whole faded. Compounding this growing fragmentation was the addition of France as the fourth occupying power.
France had not been present at Yalta and Potsdam and refused to be
bound by any notion of a unified approach to a future Germany.

The "Ulbricht group," German Communists sent to Soviet-occupied
Germany from Moscow in April 1945, carried instructions reflecting
Soviet intentions of treating postwar Germany as a single unit.[7] Ulbricht and his colleagues from the Communist party of Germany
(KPD), all of whom had spent much of their time during the 1930s and
the war years in the Soviet Union, were under orders to go slowly in
the reconstitution of the KPD, concentrating instead on placing "their"
people in important administrative posts in close cooperation with the
Soviet Military Administration in Germany (SMAD).

The Soviet Union's initially cautious approach was motivated by the
ideas that Soviet influence could be maximized throughout postwar
Germany by a low profile presence, emphasizing cooperation among
democratic, antifascist forces. This strategy met with some success.
There was considerable feeling among German survivors on both the
Left and the Right that only broadly based cooperation among political
forces could lead to policies that would prevent a recurrence of nazism
in Germany.

It soon became apparent that the all-German approach had limitations from the Soviet point of view. Inter-Allied cooperation had revealed severe problems, and the SMAD was aware that its influence was going to be insignificant beyond the Soviet Zone. Consequently the SMAD issued Order No. 2 on June 10, 1945 authorizing creation of antifascist democratic parties and labor unions.

The day after Order No. 2 was issued, the KPD was formally organized. Three other parties were also founded in the Soviet Zone: the Social Democratic Party of Germany (SPD), the Christian Democratic Union (CDU), and the Liberal Democratic Party of Germany (LDPD). All four parties were joined in August 1945 in an Antifascist Democratic Bloc. With the establishment of this bloc the first period in the history of the Soviet Zone/GDR, known as the Antifascist Democratic Order, began.

The Antifascist Democratic Order is the name given to developments in Soviet Zone politics from 1945 to the foundation of the GDR in October 1949. These four years brought massive changes in the political system, economy, and social structure in the area under Soviet control.

Changes in political life in the Soviet Zone came swiftly once political parties had been organized. From the beginning the SPD moved toward unification of the socialist forces. However, the idea was coolly received by the KPD, which preferred to build on its special relationship with the Soviet Military Administration and to consolidate its own position vis-a-vis the public. Early elections held in Berlin in the fall of 1945 indicated considerable support for an independent SPD in the Western sectors of that divided city. These election results plus strong opposition to unification from the Western zones led to a changing of the fronts. Now the Communists were pressing for unity with the support of the SMAD. In April 1946 the Socialist Otto Grotewohl and the Communist Wilhelm Pieck clasped hands, symbolically uniting the two socialist movements in the Socialist Unity Party (SED). Initial parity between Social Democrats and Communists in the SED leadership yielded to dominance by the latter. Increasingly the SED became the mixed cadre and mass party that it has remained ever since.

The Christian Democratic Union represented unification of another kind. Conflict between Catholics and Protestants had been seen as a factor contributing to the rise of nazism in prewar Germany. A union of Protestants and Catholics would tie them together in a political force that would forward the cause of democratic politics and Christian values. Although its first programs took liberal social positions, including public ownership of major industries, the CDU came increasingly into conflict with the occupation authorities and the SED over religious and political issues. One leader after another was forced out of the party and subsequently left for the West. By 1949 the Christian Democrats had accepted SED leadership.

German liberalism, represented by the Liberal Democrats, was the fourth political tradition to be represented in the new party structure. This organization articulated the needs of the bourgeoisie and private business. The importance of the Liberal Democrats has diminished as the private sector has declined, but it remains as a symbolic base of support for the Socialist Unity Party. The presence of several political parties in the GDR indicates the need to bind the groups that those parties "represent" (e.g., the middle class, the religious believers) to the leadership of the SED. While similar parties were banned elsewhere in Eastern Europe, the GDR remains in a state of transition to one-party rule, which may yet take years to achieve.

The CDU and LDPD were joined by other parties and mass organizations to complement the work of the SED. The Democratic Farmers' Party of Germany and the National Democratic Party of Germany were established in 1948. The Farmers' Party was designated to aid the SED in organizing the agricultural sector. The National Democrats were founded following an amnesty of former Nazis and military officers. Many of its members had become associated with the "National Committee 'Free Germany'" while in Soviet captivity. They represented a source of support for the newly emerging system and were organized toward that end.

In addition to the parties, several mass organizations helped to transform the political scene in the 1945–49 period as part of what became the "National Front of Democratic Germany." The Free German Trade Union Federation was founded shortly after the Soviet Military Administration's Order No. 2. Originally the Trade Union Federation was the vehicle used by the Socialists in an effort to build their strength in competition with the Communists. As the Trade Union Federation came under the increasing influence of the Socialist Unity Party, it was integrated into the economic changes sweeping the Soviet Zone.

Three further mass organizations were gathered into the National Front. The Free German Youth was based on earlier German models and the Soviet Komsomol. Especially important in the formation of new cadres as the SED consolidated its position, the youth organization has produced many of the current GDR leaders, including SED General Secretary Erich Honecker.[8] The Democratic Women's Association of Germany and the Cultural Association were the other mass organizations of the National Front.

These organizations and parties have provided a symbolic pluralism in the political system of the GDR. During the early years they frequently articulated vital interests, some of which clashed with the program of the SED. The SED prevailed. In the 1945–49 period, many activists, particularly those associated with the Social Democrats, the Christian Democrats, and the Liberals, left the Soviet Zone.

Changes in the economy of the Soviet Zone were manifold. Among them was the Soviet reparations program. Originally Soviet reparations were to come from its own zone plus a percentage of the production of the other zones. In exchange the Soviets were to supply food to the West. This arrangement broke down and the Soviets stepped up their reparations program, dismantling and carrying off over 1,000 factories and converting over 200 industrial operations into Soviet stock corporations. Production from these corporations was taken by the Soviets. Other changes resulted from Soviet policies aimed at nationalizing banks, large industrial enterprises, Nazi holdings, and the property of people who had fled from the Soviet Zone. Nationalization and socialization further hindered the productivity of an already truncated economy.

The social and economic policies of the Soviet Military Administration and the SED also had far-ranging effects in agriculture. The large landed estates were converted into state farms. All holdings of over 100 hectares were expropriated. The land seized was distributed to landless farmers, agricultural laborers, and German expellees from Eastern Europe. Thus the conditions for later collectivization were established. The Farmers' Party played a significant role in this "revolution on the land" by helping the SED bridge the ideological gap between the urban and rural elements of the working class. Thus the countryside was transformed, while those who could not accept the change left for the West.

The large-scale migration to the West had an impact on the social structure of the Soviet Zone that was as profound as changes in the political system and economy of the early postwar years. There was a considerable leveling of the "heights" of German society in the Soviet Zone. Dispossessed landholders were joined in the West by many leaders of political organizations and economic enterprises who saw the policies of the Soviets and the SED severely restricting their freedoms. This migration had two implications. First, it meant that the social structure was adapting to the Soviet model of a workers' and peasants' state. Secondly, potential opponents of political and social change were leaving the field to those who either accepted the new order or had made their peace with the emerging socialist system. Although this did not mean an end to opposition from within, it did simplify matters.

By 1949, when the two German states were officially established, the antifascist era was drawing to a close, and the SED felt secure enough to make significant changes, which were announced at two key SED meetings: the Third Party Congress (1950) and the Second Party Conference (1952). The Third Party Congress transformed the SED into a Leninist party fully recognizing the disciplines of democratic centralism and Soviet leadership. The Second Party Conference called for the coordination of GDR development with the Soviet Union in a process that continues to this day. In addition the SED called for increasingly intense class conflict to assure the triumph of the workers and peasants. Together, these pronouncements launched the GDR on a road that led from Soviet occupation in 1945–49 to its status as the always reliable "junior partner" of the Soviet Union in the 1980s.

POLITICAL DEVELOPMENTS, 1949–71

The following discussion of the main lines of political development in the GDR from 1949 through 1971 will follow the chronological periods defined by the SED itself. These periods are the construction of socialism from 1949 through 1958; the completion of socialist production relations from 1958 through 1963; and the comprehensive construction of socialism from 1963 to the Eighth SED Party Congress (1971), which ended the "Ulbricht era."

The period of the construction of socialism in the GDR was characterized by several significant developments. Politically, the dominance of the SED was established. In the economy the expansion of the socialist sector was accelerated. And the social system moved toward an idealized socialist model.

The predominance of the SED had been apparent in the 1945–49 period. In fact the National Front, which fielded a single list of candidates in the first election to the People's Chamber (parliament) in 1949, clearly showed the superiority of the SED that has continued ever since. The SED held 100 seats, while the Christian Democrats and Liberals had 60 each. The National Democrats and the Farmers' Party each had 30 seats, the Trade Union Federation had 40, and the other mass organizations a total of 80 parliamentary seats. Since many of the members of the Trade Union Federation and mass organizations were also SED members, SED preeminence was assured.

SED influence quickly spread through the state apparatus as well. At the national level the ministries were dominated by the SED and the decisions of the SED Politburo were made binding on the government apparatus. Central control over state governments was assured in 1952 with the transformation of the traditional *Laender* (states) into 14 administrative districts.

While the SED was establishing its dominance over the framework of government, its leadership had to overcome challenges from within its own ranks and from the people. A major challenge from within came in the wake of the revolt of June 1953, the first of the massive uprisings in the Soviet bloc. Insecurity following the death of Stalin in march 1953, combined with a distressed economy, led the SED to announce a "New Course" that aimed unsuccessfully at reducing popular dissatisfaction. The intraparty debate on which path to follow in the light of uncertain developments in the Soviet Union resulted in the formation of a group opposed to Ulbricht, led by the minister of state security, Wilhelm Zaisser, and the editor of the party newspaper *Neues Deutschland,* Rudolf Herrnstadt.

Following the revolt, the Soviet leadership felt compelled to support Ulbricht, opting to preserve continuity while attending to its own problems. Since Ulbricht's opposition had connections with the defeated Beria faction in Moscow, it was possible for him to strike back and reassert his leadership in a purge of Zaisser, Herrnstadt, and their sympathizers.

A severe challenge to the SED came in June 1953, when German workers rioted in East Berlin and elsewhere in the GDR, as a result of economic pressures generated by the expansion of the socialist sector of the economy. While the socialist sector grew rapidly during the first five-year plan (1951–55)—first as a result of nationalization and later with the return of the Soviet stock corporations—the infrastructure, in terms of plant, equipment, and investment, was inadequate. High work expectations, unrealistic plan goals, lack of trained personnel, and agricultural collectivization together created unbearable pressures. The New Course sought to relieve rising dissatisfaction by slowing the tempo of socialization, but the attempt failed. Driven to higher productivity without higher wages, workers went on a rampage in East Berlin and at 271 other locations in the GDR on June 17. Soviet troops and tanks were used to quell the worst riots.[9]

The revolt made clear that socialist consciousness had not penetrated the GDR citizenry sufficiently to sustain the pace of the first five-year plan. Consequently the plan was revised downward several times, while allowing for progress toward building the energy and industrial base for future development. The revised plan was also coordinated with the newly established CMEA, in which the GDR was to play an increasingly important role.

The next challenge from within the SED came after the Twentieth Party Congress of the CPSU in 1956. De-Stalinization and the discussion of a "third (socialist) path" between the Soviet model and capitalism led to a lively debate among party philosophers and economists in 1956–57. The debate clashed sharply with Ulbricht's orthodoxy. Again the course of events, this time in Poland and Hungary, turned a rising oppositional tide in Ulbricht's favor. Not willing to risk a repeat of the 1953 riots in the GDR, the Soviet leadership backed Ulbricht in a purge of Wolfgang Harich and others associated with ideological and economic revisionism. This was to be the last major intraparty threat to Ulbricht's leadership until his ouster.[10]

The second five-year plan (1956–60) encountered so many problems that it was discarded in 1958 in favor of a seven-year plan designed to harmonize with the rhythm and demands of Soviet plans. The seven-year plan assured the increasing dependence of the GDR on the economy of the Soviet Union. All of the plans favored the development of heavy industry and required increased imports of raw materials, since the GDR has few resources besides lignite ("brown coal"), salts (for chemicals), and uranium (exported to the Soviet Union).

While the events of 1953 had shown that socialist goals and socialist reality were still far apart, it was clear that the construction of a socialist society was progressing. During the period from 1953–58, efforts were undertaken to collectivize the land parceled out in the postwar land reform. Although the pace was slow, the SED delegated party workers to assume leadership roles in rural areas and to run collectives. In the cities, the middle-class and private businesses were systematically undercut. Middle-class children had difficulty obtaining access to higher education. Private businesses faced problems with finance and supplies. At the same time thousands of workers were enrolled in the Workers' and Peasants' Faculties, where they could attain university matriculation standards and gain career advantages on graduation. These policies had long-range effects on the social structure of the GDR and cultivated its image as a workers' and peasants' state progressing toward socialism.

The second period proclaimed the completion of socialist relations in production. Beginning with the Fifth SED Party Congress in 1958 and ending with the Sixth Party Congress in 1963, the period was characterized by mobilization and consolidation. Mobilization took several forms, ranging from the proclamation of "ten commandments of socialist morality," through educational reforms and the propagandistic goal of surpassing the Federal Republic of Germany in important areas of consumption, to the comprehensive collectivization of agriculture. These acts of mobilization caused a flood of emigration. In turn, this massive movement to the West led to an act of consolidation: construction of the Berlin Wall in 1961.

By 1958 Walter Ulbricht, strengthened by his survival of the challenges of 1953 and 1956–57, issued a socialist version of the ten commandments (e.g., "Thou shalt protect and multiply the people's property"). Ulbricht's proclamation was part of a concerted action to expand socialist consciousness and to propagate the socialist personality through secular parallels to religious institutions such as socialist marriage and socialist communion, the latter a ritual for youth initiation.

More effective than socialist rites in mobilizing youth was the transformation of the educational system. A mandatory ten-year polytechnical curriculum was introduced in 1958–59. The aim of educational reforms was to give students strong preparation in the sciences and technical fields along with thorough training in the disciplines of labor (a weekly "day of practical work") and of Marxism-Leninism. Advanced education was made available on a broad basis through evening and correspondence curricula as well as at expanded universities and technological institutes. Massive efforts were undertaken to encourage working-class people to advance through education. The educational system has become a source of considerable and justified pride in the GDR. And there is evidence that the political socialization that is taking place throughout the educational system is having a positive impact in inculcating the values and beliefs of socialism. Students who have passed through the system owe their place and status in good measure to training provided by the state.[11]

The GDR economy was relatively strong in 1958–59, and perhaps as a consequence Walter Ulbricht promised that the GDR would surpass the Federal Republic of Germany (FRG) in per capita consumption of important foodstuffs and consumer products. This goal was unrealistic. Other goals also proved to be unrealistic, in part because they relied on unachievably high rates of productivity. The need to produce more without increasing investments, costs, and labor has been a constant theme in GDR economic development. Failure to improve productivity led to the scrapping of the seven-year plan begun in 1958.

The seven-year plan was supposed to bring the GDR economy in line with that of the Soviet Union, but a combination of impossible goals (e.g., 84 percent increase in productivity, 110 percent increase in machine construction, and 85 percent increase in production of consumer goods), the agrarian collectivization drive, and the construction of the Berlin Wall led to cancellation of the plan in 1962. The gap between promise and performance was too wide to bridge, even with the good start of 1958–59.

The full collectivization of agriculture, that is, the transformation of all farms into agricultural cooperatives, by 1960 was a goal ratified by the Fifth SED Party Congress. This goal was achieved, albeit at considerable cost. While collectivization had been pursued since 1952, the pace had been slow. By 1956 there were roughly 6,300 agricultural cooperatives. By mid-1960 this figure had jumped to over 19,000 with half of the increase coming after 1958. Collectivization met with considerable resistance, which in turn was met by massive SED intervention in the rural areas. Factory workers were assigned to the countryside. Endless debates and discussions were undertaken to convince farmers to give up their independence and join a cooperative. Eighty-four percent of the arable land of the GDR was under the control of cooperatives by 1961. For all practical purposes the goal of full socialization of agriculture had been achieved. The costs came in lowered productivity (at least in the short run) and the massive emigration of farmers to the FRG.

Farmers were not the only ones leaving the GDR in 1960 and 1961. The intensity of the collectivization campaign led Germans employed in other sectors of the economy to question their prospects in the GDR. Also contributing to massive emigration was the positive attraction of the "good life" in the FRG, with its availability of consumer goods and other rewards. While the greatest number of emigrants had been registered in the turbulent year 1953 (over 300,000), nearly 200,000 arrived in the FRG in 1960, and in the first eight months of 1961 over 150,000 people had left the GDR.

This population drain, a total of over 2.5 million in the twelve years between 1949 and 1961, could not be tolerated by the GDR leadership, especially since the great majority of those leaving were in their productive years and represented skilled crafts and professions. The SED response was the construction of the Berlin Wall on August 13, 1961.

Although widely interpreted as an act of desperation, which it was, the sealing of the Berlin sector boundary and the enhanced fortification of the East-West demarcation line also meant that, for the first time since 1949, the GDR leadership could begin to consolidate its regime within its own borders. The population of the GDR now had either to oppose or to accept the system without the alternative of leaving. The lack of large-scale overt opposition since August 1961 would indicate that most GDR citizens—either actively or passively—have accommodated themselves to the post-1961 realities.

In the last phase of the Ulbricht era—that of the comprehensive construction of socialism (1963–71)—dynamic elements emanating from economic reforms guided the lines of political development. At the Sixth SED Party Congress (1963), a "New Economic System" was proclaimed, modifying important aspects of the central planning system, which had deteriorated into chaos in the early 1960s. The New Economic System was accompanied by changes in party organization, the emergence of a "state consciousness" among the East German population, and strained relations with the Soviet Union leading to Ulbricht's ouster in May 1971.

The planned economy of the GDR was having considerable difficulty fulfilling the demands of an expanding socialist industrial sector while attempting to provide more and better consumer goods. Clearly the way out lay in the direction of decentralized management and a system of economic incentives. Both paths were taken in the New Economic System. Associations of nationally owned enterprises created rationalized industrial complexes. Although managers were given responsibilities within a planned framework, they and their work were judged by standards of profitability, turnover, and cost effectiveness. This was in accord with the theories of the Soviet economist Yevsei Liberman, who also suggested material incentives for both managers and workers. Ideology was toned down while the "economic levers" of profitability and personal rewards were emphasized.

In tandem with the New Economic System was a shift to party organization according to the production principle, then favored by Khrushchev for the Soviet party. By organizing the SED along the lines of activities in construction, agriculture, industry, and ideology, party organization could parallel the economic organization. This reorganization led to an infusion of young and technically competent party members at the middle level of responsibility. Their intrusion threatened older party cadres to the extent that the production principle was abandoned in 1966 in favor of a return to the territorial principle of state and local party organization, which had never been completely abandoned. Again this shift was in line with changes in the Soviet Union, where the territorial principle was restored shortly after Khrushchev's political demise in 1964. In spite of the failure of the production principle, the dynamic influence of the new cadres was felt in the SED as well as the economy.[12]

An emphasis on youth and education during this period, along with continuing improvement in the standard of living, led to the emergence of what West German analysts have called a "state consciousness" in the GDR. Cut off from the West, citizens of the GDR began to take pride in what was becoming their own "economic miracle." Western observers noted increasing identification of citizens with a state that was providing comprehensive social security and an increasingly better life.[13]

In the second half of the 1960s there was considerable stress on the role of technology in the overall construction of socialism. The success of the economy and of the SED was seen in the expansion of the economy through technological sophistication, in what was termed a "scientific-technical revolution." Industries such as instrumentation, electronics, and chemicals received special attention and investment funds. Training in these fields was also emphasized and led to rapid growth on a relatively weak infrastructure. This weakness led to economic difficulties in 1970, when the economy could no longer maintain the pace. The New Economic System, which had undergone modification, was finally abandoned in 1970.[14]

To Walter Ulbricht, the scientific-technical revolution was an important means by which the GDR could assert itself within CMEA and also show the West what socialism was capable of producing. Because of his seniority among Communist leaders, Ulbricht began formulating the theory that a technologically based and developed socialist society was a special stage on the way to full communism with its own laws. The transition to a communist society, according to this interpretation, would be a long process. Increasingly—and irritatingly—Ulbricht began to lecture other Communist leaders, including the Soviets, and to pose as the "father" of the GDR.

Tensions grew between Ulbricht and the Soviet leadership under Brezhnev. Not only did there seem to be a clash of personalities based on Ulbricht's "more-Communist-than-thou" attitude, there were also substantive differences between East Berlin and Moscow over detente and policy toward the FRG. Ulbricht was very uncomfortable with Brezhnev's approach to the West. After all, his political career had been saved by the East-West conflict in 1953 and 1956–57, and a "frontline" mentality was good propaganda. The Soviet Union was also promoting the normalization of relations between the two Germanys and cultivating Soviet-FRG trade. Both policies were anathema to Ulbricht. Improved relations with the FRG threatened an intolerable influx of Western influence. Ulbricht viewed Soviet trade with the FRG as a diminution of GDR influence.

By the spring of 1971 it was time to replace the uppity and footdragging Ulbricht. Ulbricht was ousted between his appearance at the Twenty-fourth Congress of the CPSU in the spring of 1971 (where he spoke of his personal acquaintance with Lenin) and the Eighth SED Party Congress in June 1971. In contrast to the experiences of other East European countries and the USSR, the transition was smooth as Erich Honecker, former leader of the Free German Youth, took over the party reins. Ulbricht went into honorable retirement as titular SED chairman and died in 1973 at the age of 80. He left behind a stabilized social and political system, which was on the verge of receiving the international recognition that Ulbricht had so urgently desired. The economy had been stabilized as well, although a weak infrastructure and dependence on imported raw materials hampered access to the heights of achievement and world markets.

THE HONECKER LEADERSHIP

The SED claims that the GDR is presently a "developed socialist system" in the process of making the transition to communism under the leadership of Erich Honecker. Honecker made significant changes in the SED's political line at its Eighth Party Congress. While not easing up on the need for scientific-technical development in the GDR, he emphasized that the party must return to the basic principles of Marxism-Leninism. That is to say, the welfare of the workers and peasants must have first priority in a socialist state.

A return to ideological basics was swiftly reflected in the economy with the conversion of the remaining private sector into nationally owned enterprises. Also nationalized were enterprises with mixed private and state ownership (borrowed from Chinese practice of the 1950s). Over 100,000 enterprises were affected by this move, which effectively eliminated any significant private production.

A new line was also evident in Honecker's emphasis on the GDR's ties to other socialist countries and to the Soviet Union. Gone was the notion that the GDR was somehow different from the other socialist countries. This shift was reflected in the constitutional changes adopted in 1974. The revised constitution no longer referred to a German nation divided into two states. The GDR was now defined as a "socialist workers' and peasants' state . . . forever and irrevocably allied with the Soviet Union."

In fact the course set by Erich Honecker in 1971 has been steadfastly followed, bringing the GDR into closer alignment with the Soviet Union both in economic and in political affairs. This course was confirmed by the GDR-Soviet Friendship Treaty of October 1975 and at the Ninth SED Party Congress in 1976, which adopted a new party program and statute. The new statute made Honecker general secretary of the party in line with the current Soviet usage. In 1981 the party numbered about 2,172,110 members and candidates, or about 13 percent of the GDR population of about 16,740,000. This percentage translates into a ratio over twice that of CPSU members and candidates to the Soviet population. Rather than an exclusively elite party, the SED functions as a mass and cadre (elite) party. Indeed the SED is an instrument of mobilization and leadership. That there is concern over the relative size of the SED was articulated by Honecker in his report of the Central Committee to the Ninth Congress, wherein he urged that Leninist principles be used in the selection of new members and announced that there would be no increase in total membership.

The National Front of the GDR (formerly the National Front of Democratic Germany) continues to serve as an umbrella for the parties and mass organizations. Overall the importance of the minor parties has decreased. In spite of the fact that the Christian Democratic Union has experienced a slight growth in membership, its relative position has declined. Traditionally first among the fraternal National Front parties, it has recently yielded its place to the Democratic Farmers' Party, signaling the relative importance of the agricultural sector. Although the multiparty system is a "deviant" and perhaps declining feature of the GDR political system, it shows no immediate signs of being phased out.

The mass organizations represented in the National Front continue to serve the SED. The trade union, youth, and women's organizations are of particular importance in this respect. The women's association deserves special mention because of the key role that women play in the GDR economy, which suffers chronically from an acute labor shortage. Just over 50 percent of the labor force is female and over 87 percent of the women of working age are either employed or under apprenticeship. The World Congress of Women was held in East Berlin in 1975, and much is made of the legal equality of women in the GDR, which was firmly established by the Family Law Code of 1965. The economic importance of women is not reflected, however, in the political leadership of the SED or the other mass organizations. As of 1980, about one-third of the SED members and candidates were women and less than one-third of the trade union association presidium were female. There is no evidence that this situation is the source of any active protest by East German women.

The varying composition and character of the top level of political leadership reveal much about change in the GDR. The Ulbricht group, charged with restoring political life in the Soviet occupation zone in cooperation with the Soviet Military Administration, formed the nucleus of the elite that guided the fortunes of the GDR in its early years. These top functionaries, who had been in exile in the Soviet Union, asserted themselves in the crises of 1953 and 1956–57. Not only did members of the Ulbricht group have strong Soviet backing, they were also extremely effective at political infighting and were able gradually to coopt loyal new members into the SED inner circle.

The post-1961 consolidation along with the emphasis on economic and technological development required the recruitment and advancement of a new type of elite member, one who was technically trained and competent as well as politically loyal to the SED.[15] Many of the dissatisfied had left the GDR before 1961. Those who remained owed their advancement and education to the system. It is symbolic that Ulbricht's successor had been the first chairman of the Free German Youth in 1946. Indeed since Honecker replaced Ulbricht, more and more former youth organization leaders have been coopted into the top ranks of the SED apparatus, replacing the Ulbricht group as its members have grown old, retired, and died.

Honecker himself has consolidated his leading position. In addition to being SED general secretary and chairman of the National Defense Council, he was made chairman of the Council of State in October 1976, thus combining all major roles in the GDR leadership, much as Brezhnev did in the Soviet Union. Earlier in 1976 Konrad Nauman and Werner Felfe had joined the SED Politburo. Both men had been colleagues of Honecker in the Free German Youth. It is interesting to note as well that the SED inner circle, again following recent Soviet practice, includes the ministers of state security and national defense.

Honecker's promise to improve the lot of the workers and peasants was implemented by a series of measures aimed at raising wages at the low end of the income scale and providing better housing and increased benefits in terms of vacations, pensions, and working conditions. Honecker also promised stable prices. In recent years, the worldwide inflationary trend has placed enormous pressure on the GDR's economy, which is dependent on imported raw materials. Economic pressures are compounded by the SED's commitment to a comprehensive system of welfare and public services.

The SED has responded to these problems with a program of "socialist rationalization," aimed at raising labor productivity. At the same time, prices of imports from East and West continue to rise, while export prices are not keeping pace. With the Polish specter constantly in mind, the SED leadership has responded by bringing back to power the technocrats who had been successful in the mid-1960s. The urgency of the situation is reflected in virtually every edition of the party newspaper, *Neues Deutschland*. The goal of the rationalization campaign is a 28 to 30 percent increase in labor productivity by 1986 through improvement of production organization and modernization to a higher level of production processes by means of more efficient utilization of materials and increased automation.

The 1981–85 Economic Plan promulgated at the Tenth Congress indicates how the GDR intends to cope with its economic problems. First priority is accorded to heightened productivity. This has been a constant theme in the GDR political economy since before the workers' revolt of June 1953, caused by the prospect of working longer for less compensation in order to achieve plan goals. Industrial productivity in the GDR improved steadily in the 1970s. From a 1955 base of 100, industrial productivity rose to an index level of 253 in 1970 and 407 in 1980. Figures for 1981 claim a five percent productivity increase. There is considerable doubt that this trend can continue without increasing investment beyond affordable levels. Repeatedly Honecker has warned that investment funds are virtually unavailable. The 1981 plan called for no growth in investment.

A second high priority is allocated to robotics and automated production processes in GDR industry. In 1980 the GDR employed 220 robots and fewer than 400 in 1981. By 1985 the plan calls for the use of 40,000 to 45,000 industrial robots. In spite of beginning its own robotics industry in 1980 (production: 40), this is an unlikely goal, especially given the shortage of investment money. In addition there is a semantic problem here because the GDR literature applies the term "robot" to a wide range of automated production elements that fall short of the robotic standards of reprogramability, multi-axis deployability, and universality generally demanded by the term in the United States, Western Europe, and Japan.

A third plan priority is aimed at aiding the economy through effective energy use. GDR economists hope to improve the utilization of imported petroleum in industrial production, while accelerating the exploitation of native lignite resources. Lignite will be used increasingly for thermal energy, while the petroleum thereby saved will feed the petrochemical industry now unable to rely on the previously increasing, but now stable, level of imports from the Soviet Union.

Finally the SED has exhorted the population to continue making sacrifices. The political risks of these exhortations are apparent because measures supporting continued improvements in living standards must be bought in part with hard currency and/or investment funds, both of which are in desperately short supply. The people of the GDR have become accustomed to consumer consumption and are now looking beyond dishwashers, TVs, and refrigerators toward big-ticket durable consumables, notably autos.

Socioeconomic difficulties have been accompanied by problems related to cultural policy. While a feeling of state consciousness may have broadened the SED's base of support, intellectuals—particularly writers—have been a source of grave concern to the SED. This concern has been heightened because much of the literature and art to which the SED objects has been "socialist"–inspired. The East German cultural community took seriously Honecker's statement at the Eighth SED Party Congress that if one proceeded from a firm socialist basis, there could be no taboos in art and literature. The expectations of cultural liberalism that this statement aroused were quelled by subsequent policies and actions.

Two incidents in 1976 demonstrated the limits of what the cultural policy of the GDR would tolerate. Wolf Biermann, a popular poet and balladeer, had emigrated to the GDR from West Germany in 1953 for ideological reasons, attracted by the communist promise in the East. His songs, while condemning Western capitalism, also criticized socialist bureaucracy in the GDR. His uncompromising communism brought him into conflict with the SED, which banned his public appearances in 1964. Following a semipublic concert in an East Berlin church in the fall of 1976, Biermann was given permission to undertake a concert tour in the FRG. Once Biermann was out of the country, his GDR citizenship was revoked. Biermann's exile caused a wave of protest among East German artists and writers. The protesters were, in turn, subjected to reprisals, forcing some to withdraw their public support for Biermann.

In a related case, Rainer Kunze, who published his novel *The Wonderful Years* in West Germany, was expelled from the GDR Writers' Association in November 1976. Kunze's stories were apparently not sufficiently "positive" in character and the Writers' Association accused him of "revisionism."

The Biermann and Kunze cases underline the difficulty the SED has had bringing cultural life into line with the demands of socialist realism. During the earlier years of the GDR, efforts to encourage worker-writers and to create proletarian art forms failed. East German writers have produced some outstanding literary works—the writings of Volker Braun, Anna Seghers, Christa Wolf, and others—but the relationship between the requirements of artistic excellence and the demands of the cultural bureaucracy has often been unsatisfactory.

INTERNATIONAL RELATIONS

The political development of the GDR must be seen against the background of international politics.[16] This background has three essential elements: GDR interactions with the Soviet Union and Eastern Europe; GDR-West German relations; and the relationship between the Soviet Union and the United States.

Beginning with the occupation, ties between the Soviet Zone/GDR and the Soviet Union have had ranking importance. When prospects for reunification did not materialize, the interests of the SED leadership lay in the closest possible relationship with CMEA and the Soviet Union. Indeed, the economic development of the GDR is closely related to its development as a "junior partner" of the Soviets. This relationship has enhanced the GDR's prestige in Eastern Europe, where since 1963 it has enjoyed the highest standard of living of the East European countries. On the cost side, the GDR has had to pay dearly in terms of unfavorable trade relations with the Soviet Union. The Soviets supply the GDR with all of its natural gas, 87 percent of its petroleum and 60–70 percent of its nonferrous metals. Raw material prices have gone up, while income from GDR exports have only been able to recoup about two-thirds of the increases.

Relations with the Soviet Union, somewhat strained late in the Ulbricht era, have been restored to the inseparability confirmed by the mutual Friendship Treaty and the revised GDR constitution. East German support for the Soviet positions on Poland and nuclear arms provide more recent examples of the GDR bond with the old and new Soviet leadership.

Even though no hint of an independent labor movement is evident in the GDR, the fear that something similar to Solidarity might turn up at home led the SED to react cautiously to Polish events in August 1980. After initial hesitation the SED adopted the Soviet line as its own. By exploiting anti-Polish prejudices, the SED cleverly masked the price it had to pay in lost raw materials and economic aid because of Poland. The official SED party organ, *Neues Deutschland,* enthusiastically greeted the Jaruzelski regime and promised to support its battle against the "internal and external counterrevolution."[17]

The SED is prominent in support of the Soviet propaganda offensive against NATO theater nuclear force modernization via the "two-track" decision, which sought to deploy Pershing II and cruise missiles in Europe while simultaneously negotiating arms reductions with the Soviet Union. The SED supports the peace movement in the FRG, while suppressing the domestic unofficial peace campaign by claiming that the government's is the only peace movement needed in the GDR.

Such loyalty has had a mixed reaction in Eastern Europe. Wartime memories linger. The wealth of the GDR promotes jealousies. Nonetheless the key military importance of the superbly equipped National People's Army within the Warsaw Treaty Organization has been accepted. The cultural orthodoxy, political conservatism, and identification with the Soviet Union have not enhanced the GDR's popularity in Eastern Europe.

GDR policy toward the Federal Republic of Germany is aimed at *Abgrenzung,* or the barring of West German influence. Throughout its history, the GDR has had to deal with influences from West Germany and West Berlin, which exert a strong attraction on the East German population. Western TV is available in most of the GDR and, since the normalization of relations between East and West Germany in 1972, there has been a huge influx of visitors from the Federal Republic and West Berlin. The SED feared this influx and has waged a continuous campaign against West German influence, in spite of its commitment to peaceful coexistence and the Helsinki Accords. Border incidents, visa charges, financial arrangements, the status of West Berlin, and particularly emigration are points of constant friction between the two Germanys.

Abgrenzung was emphasized in 1980, when, shortly after Helmut Schmidt's reelection, Erich Honecker doubled the amount of money Western visitors are required to exchange for East German currency. This unilateral change in policy had the desired effect of reducing the number of visitors to the GDR and East Berlin, while not radically affecting East German hard currency income.[18] In fact FRG-GDR relations were at a virtual standstill from the Schmidt-Honecker summit of December 1981 until after the federal election held in the FRG in March 1983. The summit took place at the same time that General Jaruzelski proclaimed martial law in Poland, thus scotching any meaningful East-West initiatives. In October 1982, Schmidt's government fell to a conservative-liberal coalition headed by a Christian Democrat, Helmut Kohl. Kohl's government could undertake little until it had been confirmed in the 1983 election, opening the way to substantial loans to the GDR in exchange for some adjustments in the death traps on the GDR side of the border with the FRG.

GDR foreign policy within the relationship between the United States and the Soviet Union is also at a near standstill. As the GDR moves toward greater socialist integration, capacity to trade with the West declines. Economic resources cannot be stretched far enough to reap maximum benefit from East-West trade, which is becoming increasingly expensive to the GDR. Moreover, as confrontation has replaced detente in U.S.-Soviet relations, the likelihood of the GDR obtaining U.S. most-favored-nation status has disappeared.

On the political front, relations with the West are tempered by the fact that the Four Powers still have responsibility for Berlin, as determined by the Quadripartite Agreement on Berlin of 1971. This arrangement sets limits to what can be done in Berlin without endangering relations between the Soviet Union and the United States. Berlin remains a touchstone for East-West relations, and the GDR leadership must keep this in mind as it continues pursuing *Abgrenzung*.

Until U.S.-USSR relations are improved, the range of movement for GDR foreign policy will be mostly limited to approved initiatives in the Third World. In developing countries, the GDR is showing its expertise in internal security matters, intelligence operations, and military training. Some 2,700 military advisers were stationed in seven African countries in 1980.[19]

Common to all three elements of the international picture is the common theme of the GDR-Soviet connection. This relationship is crucial to the future of the GDR. Yet there is a residue of anti-Soviet feeling in the GDR that more than thirty years has not expunged. No matter how far socialist integration progresses in theory, it remains to be seen to what extent and for how long it will be accepted by the East Germans. At this point they have no alternatives. Not even the dissidents provide a viable competing perspective. Meanwhile, profound economic troubles in the West are prompting many to consider themselves quite fortunate in the relative security that the GDR system provides.

CONCLUSION AND PROSPECTS

The GDR, among the East European communist regimes, is economically successful and politically orthodox. The position of the GDR party and state leadership is to a great extent dependent on the support of the Soviet Union, support that is reciprocated by absolute loyalty. The SED consistently subjects its and the nation's interests to those of the Soviet Union.

The subject relationship of the GDR has not yet brought on any great or protracted public dissatisfaction beyond that expressed by dissidents who come principally from the cultural sector and who have, for the most part, been successfully neutralized, silenced, or exiled. Broader public dissatisfaction has tended to concentrate on the failings of the consumer economy in the GDR. Recently this kind of dissatisfaction has been muted by the economic problems evident in the West. A decade ago, East Germans looked longingly toward the consumer paradise in the FRG. Now the GDR citizen tends to count his or her blessings in an economy that has a labor shortage, little inflation in basic commodities, and a comprehensive welfare state. While this comparison has not led to a reversal of population movements between East and West Germany, it perhaps makes life in the GDR more bearable.

In reviewing the state of the GDR, what may be an early warning of prospective change is inherent in the growing unofficial peace movement in the GDR. Rudolf Bahro, in a provocative article, suggests that the youth of both Germanys are rebelling at political and social structures and values that can no longer meet the imperatives of no-growth, postindustrial political economies in a nuclear age.[20] Bahro finds youth dissatisfaction expressing itself in the peace and ecology movements.

In the East and West these movements also include sentiments for a neutralized, disarmed, and reunified Germany that could return to its national roots free of American *and* Soviet influences.

Bahro's analysis and prediction are idealistic and naively unrealistic, but cannot be ignored when thinking about prospective futures in the GDR. The youth and peace movements may prove to exert pressures that the formidable powers of the GDR establishment will have great difficulty in resisting. Indeed, when the Soviets answered the November 1983 deployment of NATO missiles with more nuclear missiles of their own in Czechoslovakia and the GDR, the unofficial GDR peace movement—Women for Peace and Swords into Plowshares—received a notable impetus. That this impetus was met with repression in the arrest and jailing of the Women for Peace leader Baerbel Bohley only underscores the seriousness with which the SED treats this growing form of dissent.

For the immediate future, the prospects of the GDR are controlled as much from Washington and Moscow as they are from East Berlin. Through its ups and downs, the relationship between the United States and the USSR helps to regulate the balance in Central Europe. As long as neither side is willing to accept or impose a change at the point where East and West meet, ways will be found to keep the GDR political and economic systems going.

The twin traumas of inflation and unemployment are still keenly felt in both Germanys. If the worst effects of both can be contained and controlled in the GDR, then the general line of development will continue. In 1968 I concluded a survey of the GDR with the following speculation about its future:

> The prospects, then, are for a continuation on course, even if Ulbricht is no longer at the helm. This is even more the case when Ulbricht's possible successors are taken into account. There is no one among the hopefuls who has the qualities of leadership and authority to move the German Democratic Republic from its present place in the formation of the communist party state system.[21]

If Honecker were substituted for Ulbricht, the same could be said today. Firmly at the side of the USSR, the GDR leadership has little room to maneuver, no matter who may be at the helm.

NOTES

I would like to thank Dennis Emerson, University of Oregon Library, and Marianne Strenger, Inter Nationes, Bonn, and Barbara Keen, Battelle-Seattle, for assistance and documentation for this revision.

1. The GDR already had access to the European Economic Community through its special relationship with the Federal Republic of Germany. Trade between the two Germanys is considered intra-German trade under the terms of the Treaty of Rome.

2. *Der Tagesspiegel,* (West Berlin) November 2, 1982.

3. Wolfgang Buescher et al. (eds.), *Friedensbewegung in der DDR* (Hattingen: edition transit, 1982).

4. At a celebration of the founding of the GDR on October 7, 1977 in East Berlin the audience got out of hand when a rock band was replaced by a Russian balalaika ensemble. The ensuing scuffle had strong anti-Soviet overtones.

5. C. Bradley Scharf, *East German Accommodation to Soviet Foreign Policy Requirements,* unpublished paper presented at the Western Slavic Association meeting, Reno, Nevada, February 1978, p. 18.

6. "Ihr koennt wenigstens aua bruellen," *Der Spiegel,* vol. 37, no. 1 (3 January 1983), pp. 42–46 and Rudolf Bahro, *Die Alternative* (Frankfurt a/M: Europeaeische Verlagsanstalt, 1977).

7. Wolfgang Leonhard, *Child of the Revolution* (Chicago: Regnery, 1958). This remains one of the best "inside" accounts of the Moscow sojourn and postwar return of KPD leaders.

8. See Heinz Lippmann, *Honecker* (New York: Macmillan, 1972).

9. For a treatment of the 1953 revolt see Stefan Brant, *The East German Rising of 17th June 1953* (London: Thames and Hudson, 1955).

10. Intra-SED struggles are covered in Carola Stern, *Ulbricht: A Political Biography* (New York: Praeger, 1965).

11. For a discussion of political socialization see A. M. Hanhardt, Jr., "East Germany: From Goals to Realities," in Ivan Volgyes, ed., *Political Socialization in Eastern Europe* (New York: Praeger, 1975), pp. 66–91.

12. Thomas A. Baylis, *The Technical Intelligentsia and the East German Elite* (Berkeley: University of California Press, 1974).

13. Gebhard Schweigler, *National Consciousness in Divided Germany* (Beverly Hills: Sage, 1975).

14. Michael Keren, "The Rise and Fall of the New Economic System," in Lyman H. Legters, ed., *The German Democratic Republic: A Developed Socialist Society* (Boulder, Colo.: Westview Press, 1978), pp. 61–84.

15. Peter C. Ludz, *The Changing Elite in East Germany* (Cambridge, Mass.: MIT Press, 1972).

16. For a more detailed discussion see Melvin Croan, *East Germany: The Soviet Connection* (Beverly Hills: Sage, 1976), also Hans-Adolf Jacobsen (et al.), *Drei Jahrzehnte Aussenpolitik der DDR* (Munich: Oldenbourg, 1979).

17. Werner Micke, "Bilanz 1981," in *Neues Deutschland,* 29 December 1981, p. 1.

18. "Deutsch-Deutscher Reise Verkehr 1981," *Deutschland Archiv*, vol. 15, no. 3 (March 1982), p. 237.

19. "Wir Haben Euch Waffen und Brot Geschickt," *Der Spiegel*, vol. 34, no. 10 (March 3, 1980), pp. 42–61.

20. Rudolf Bahro, "Ein Netz von erheblicher Spannkraft," in *Der Spiegel*, vol. 36, no. 50 (December 13, 1982), pp. 58–67.

21. Arthur M. Hanhardt, Jr., *The German Democratic Republic* (Baltimore: Johns Hopkins Press, 1968), p. 113.

BIBLIOGRAPHY

Baylis, Thomas. *The Technical Intelligentsia and the East German Elite.* Berkeley: University of California Press, 1974.

Brant, Stefan. *The East German Rising 17th June 1953.* London: Thames and Hudson, 1955.

Croan, Melvin. *East Germany: The Soviet Connection.* Beverly Hills: Sage, 1976.

Hangen, Welles. *The Muted Revolution.* New York: Alfred A. Knopf, 1966.

Hanhardt, Arthur M., Jr. *The German Democratic Republic.* Baltimore: Johns Hopkins Press, 1968.

Herspring, Dale. *East German Civil-Military Relations.* New York: Praeger, 1973.

Keefe, Eugene K. (ed.). *East Germany: A Country Study.* Washington, D.C.: U.S. Government Printing Office, 1982.

Lippmann, Heinz. *Honecker.* New York: Macmillan, 1974.

Ludz, Peter C. *The Changing Elite in East Germany.* Cambridge: MIT Press, 1972.

Schweigler, Gebhard. *National Consciousness in Divided Germany.* Beverly Hills: Sage, 1975.

Smith, Jean Edward. *Germany Beyond the Wall.* Boston: Little, Brown, 1969.

Starrels, John, and Anita Malinckrodt. *Politics in the German Democratic Republic.* New York: Praeger, 1975.

Stern, Carola. *Ulbricht: A Political Biography.* New York: Praeger, 1965.

6   Romania

Walter M. Bacon, Jr.

To the uninitiated, socialist Romania is a country of paradox. No bloc state as stridently defends its national priorities and so openly rejects Soviet domination. Yet, no bloc state is as uncompromisingly Stalinist in its economic and social policies and methods. The anomaly is real enough but the paradox is superficial. It is Romania's very orthodoxy that determines its resistance to Soviet hegemony. Romania is a nationalist Communist party state precisely because it is a Stalinist party state.

The West, which has bankrolled much of Romania's defiance of Soviet control, misjudged the cause and direction of Romanian autonomy from its inception in the early 1960s. Western "logic" assumed that a successful, even if only partial, escape from Soviet tutelage would lead to managed pluralism and its concomitant socioeconomic decompression. Instead, in the 1970s and 1980s, the West became increasingly disillusioned as the regime of Romanian Communist party (RCP) General Secretary Nicolae Ceausescu relentlessly suppressed the few dissidents who dared question the validity of a personality cult of ludicrous proportions or challenge the authority of the omnipresent bureaucracy of coercion.

The Soviets, for their part, while undeniably annoyed by the RCP's refusal to conform, have refrained from the kinds of intervention they employed to crush other East European deviations in 1956, 1968, and 1981. The cause of Soviet restraint lies both in the certainty of Romanian armed resistance to "fraternal assistance" and in the realization that there is no prospect of creeping democracy endangering RCP control. Ceausescu's Romania is neither Dubcek's Czechoslovakia nor Kania's Poland. From their own experience, the Soviets appreciate that Stalinism itself breeds nationalism and manipulates that source of popular legitimacy without undermining—perhaps even facilitating— the party's monopoly of political power.

The Stalinist evocation and exploitation of nationalism also helps to

explain the apparent paradox of the Romanian people's toleration of
the RCP's iron-fisted control. Why have they not risen up and challenged the regime as the Hungarians, Poles, and Czechs and Slovaks
did under far less onerous circumstances? Romania's essentially peasant culture has produced sporadic, if intensely violent, mass uprisings
but those that have occurred were triggered as often by ethnic hatreds
as by popular demands for change. Ethnic antagonisms are endemic in
modern Romania where, even after the post-World War II territorial
adjustments and emigrations, substantial numbers of Hungarians, Germans, Serbs, Ukrainians, Bulgarians, Turks, Jews, and Gypsies remain
and serve as abrasive reminders of Romania's former political subservience. Romania only ephemerally experienced participatory democracy as it exists in the West. Those movements for reform that
infrequently arose originated with disenchanted, often intellectual elements of the ruling elite. Precommunist political stability was a function of popular passivity, patrimonial political culture, and successive
regimes' astute exploitation of a pervasive Romanian nationalism, nurtured by centuries of foreign domination. Even if the RCP regime is
comparatively oppressive and the privations visited on the Romanian
people would be intolerable in most other East European states, at
least those who are doing the oppressing and depriving are stridently
Romanian—not Russian, Hungarian, or Bulgarian. Even the most severe critics of the Ceausescu regime are disarmed by this logic that
prefers Romanian oppressors to foreign liberators.

It would be unrealistic to suggest that the Romanian Stalinists seren-
dipitously discovered that their evocation of nationalism could elicit a
popular legitimacy undeserved and unobtainable through the ordinary
processes of attaining normative commitment. It would be equally unrealistic to assert that cynical exploitation of the emotions of a guileless
populace was the exclusive rationale for the RCP's pursuit of its national course. There are thus two interdependent explanations of contemporary Romanian nationalism, the one socioeconomic, the other
political. An examination of the historical roots of the Romanian deviation may help to clarify the relative importance of each.

HISTORICAL BACKGROUND

The history of modern Romania is one of a nationalism that, while it
permeated all strata of society, was cynically used by successive conservative ruling elites to avoid genuine social, economic, and political
reforms. It is also a history of the elites' opportunistic but exception-
ally skillful exploitation of favorable international circumstances to
enhance Romania's national power and interest.

The Danubian principalities of Wallachia and Moldavia dealt with the effects of the Ottoman advance into Europe by first resisting but then accommodating to Turkish rule. The Romanians in Habsburg-ruled Transylvania preserved their Latin identity, as did those in Russian-ruled Bessarabia. The Danubian Romanians had to tolerate both the corrupt rule (on Turkish behalf) of Phanariot Greeks and the frequent Russian-Turkish confrontations that took place mostly on their soil. An anti-Phanariot revolt (1821) and the Ottoman defeat in the Russo-Turkish war of 1828–29 opened the principalities to Russian influence while still nominally under Turkish rule, and Romania's young aristocrats who went to Western Europe became infected there with liberal and romantic nationalist ideas. They provided a spark for the 1848 revolutions that, although suppressed, defined the political program for the next generation of Romanian leaders: to unite Wallachia and Moldavia under a single representative (though not quite democratic) national government.

Inspired and encouraged by the French, these Romanian nationalists took advantage of Russia's defeat in the Crimean War and of the Congress of Paris's indecision to elect Alexander Ion Cuza, a Moldavian boyar, prince of the United Principalities of Wallachia and Moldavia. Cuza emancipated the peasants (1864) and introduced numerous other westernizing reforms. This was resented by the landed oligarchs who succeeded in replacing Cuza with Prince Karl (Carol) of Hohenzollern-Sigmaringen (1866), a move they justified by the desire to enhance the chances for international recognition of Romania's independence. In fact the new prince was able to extract such a recognition in exchange for Romania's participation in the Russo-Turkish war of 1877–78. In 1881 Carol was proclaimed king of Romania.

Cuza's agrarian reforms were diluted under the new rule and the "peasant problem" continued to plague the fledgling kingdom. Local "jacqueries" in 1888, 1889, 1894, and 1904 were forerunners of the bloody peasant revolt of 1907 in which perhaps 10,000 Romanians perished. The old kingdom's political system, which never approached the democratic ideals of its 1866 Belgian-model constitution, remained ineffective in addressing the explosive problems of land hunger, rural overpopulation, and gross socioeconomic inequalities. The Conservative and Liberal parties, which alternated in office with numbing predictability, differed only in rhetoric. Drawing upon the aspirations of westernized urban elites, the Liberals acknowledged the agrarian crisis but placed a higher priority on the realization of a Greater Romania that would unify the Danubian Romanians with their brethren in Hungarian-ruled Transylvania, Austrian-ruled Bukovina, and Russian-ruled Bessarabia. The Conservatives, who represented intransigent landed interests, were blamed for the intensifying agrarian problems and, because of their Germanophilism, for the failure to unify all Romanians in a unitary nation-state. Both were able to postpone meaningful reform before World War I by manipulating the irredentist cause that gained widespread support because of policies of Magyarization and Russification pursued, respectively, in Transylvania and Bessarabia.

In World War I Romania was initially neutral, adroitly playing off entente and central powers' offers of territorial compensation in return for belligerency. Eventually, the Russian offensive of 1916 and the promise of Transylvania and Bukovina tipped the scales in favor of the entente (August 1916), but the ensuing war was an unmitigated disaster with Bucharest occupied by a German army in December of the same year. Fearful that the revolutionary tide that swept through allied Russia would engulf his demoralized peasant army, King Ferdinand promised electoral and land reforms in April 1917. The cession of significant parcels of land to Hungary and Bulgaria in the dictated Treaty of Bucharest (May 1918) was partially offset by the union of Bessarabia with Danubian Romania. Fate, however, was on Romania's side. When the central powers collapsed and the Habsburg domains split into their constituent ethnic parts, the Romanians of Transylvania and Bukovina rallied to the national cause. With Romania's last minute rejoining of the entente's war effort and the collapse of the Romanov and Habsburg Empires, the dream of the nationalists, a unitary nation-state, including the territories of Transylvania and Bessarabia, was realized.

With the irredenta at last satisfied, the pressing agrarian problems again came to the fore. In 1921 a second land reform was promulgated that, while it included large-scale expropriations, only temporarily suppressed the peasants' land hunger. The oligarchy avoided more radical reforms by exploiting the popular fear of Bolshevism and of Hungarian, Soviet, and Bulgarian territorial revisionism. Again, a lasting solution of the agrarian problem was sacrificed to the purported needs of Greater Romania. The few reforms that were implemented were the necessary minimum needed to stop further erosion of the oligarchy's privileged socioeconomic and political status.

Beset by omnipresent corruption and frequent dynastic crises, interwar Romania was only superficially democratic. Through a thoroughly politicized Ministry of Internal Affairs, the party in power could manipulate elections to procure lopsided majorities in parliament. The National Liberal party, which dominated governments prior to 1938, was an essentially conservative amalgam representing urban and rural elites. It espoused an autarkic policy of extensive industrialization in which agricultural exports and suppressed rates of consumption would finance Romania's modernization. The National Peasant party, which briefly held power following Romania's only free national elections in 1928, advocated an agrarian-based modernization with genuine reforms. Because of their moderation and the depression's catastrophic effects, the National Peasants lost some of their largely rural support to the racist extreme right and to more radical peasantist groups, such as the Ploughman's Front. The Social Democratic Party's support was never great and was limited to urban intellectuals and the nascent labor movement.

With few exceptions interwar Romania's mediocre political leaders were unwilling to rectify the system's myriad shortcomings, instead blaming them on foreigners, including the Jews and other ethnic minorities who were "surely" in league with Romania's numerous external enemies. In this atmosphere the resurgence of chauvinistic nationalism was all but inevitable. Extremist groups, such as the right-wing Iron Guard, gained popularity. To forestall the Iron Guard's bid for power, King Carol II established a cryptofascist royal dictatorship in 1938 that lasted until the outbreak of World War II. Assisted by the Axis, the Soviet Union, Hungary, and Bulgaria reclaimed most of the territories Romania had acquired in 1913–18. Carol II was forced to abdicate in favor of his son, Michael, when General, later Marshal, Ion Antonescu and the Iron Guard seized power in September 1940. Romania participated in the German invasion of the Soviet Union and its forces retreated with those of its allies until the advancing Red Army had retaken Bessarabia and was poised to invade Moldavia. On August 23, 1944, King Michael, in league with the leaderships of the armed forces and the National Peasant, Liberal, Social Democratic, and Communist parties ousted Antonescu and declared war on Germany.

Romania's history from 1859 to 1944 may be interpreted as the balancing of the competing priorities of nation building and socioeconomic modernization. The former was achieved by appealing to the patriotism and self-sacrifice of the masses but the latter proved impossible because the basic reforms it required would have undermined the interests of the ruling oligarchy. While it is patently inaccurate to assert that no progressive reforms ever took place prior to the Communist assumption of power, those few that were implemented were cosmetic and ineffective. The ruling elite excused its failure to alleviate rural suffering and its alienation of ethnic minorities and westernized intellectuals by conjuring up the spectre of a nation besieged by external and internal enemies bent on nothing less than the destruction of Greater Romania. Thus, the ruling elite selfishly manipulated the deep-seated nationalism of the masses at the calculated expense of those reforms that might have provided the regime with other forms of legitimacy.

Of the interwar political parties only the Romanian Communist party rejected the priority of maintaining the territorial integrity of Greater Romania. Founded in May 1921 and effectively outlawed in April 1924, the RCP both supported the USSR's revisionist claim to Bessarabia and endorsed Comintern's call for the national self-determination of Romania's ethnic minorities. Both the Social Democratic and the National Peasant parties enjoyed broader support among workers because the Communists' antinational policies alienated ethnic Romanians of all social classes. The RCP leadership was dominated by ethnic minorities and was popularly associated with the nation's historical enemies. As a result RCP membership was very small, numbering perhaps 1,000 on the eve of the August 1944 coup.

THE COMMUNIST TAKEOVER

Utilizing Hugh Seton–Watson's periodization of the "East European Revolution,"[1] in Romania the period of August 23, 1944 to March 6, 1945 was that of a "genuine coalition." The Romanian government headed by Generals Constantin Sanatescu and Nicolae Radescu included members of the four parties that had participated in the coup of August 23. Among the important RCP participants were Lucretiu Patrascanu as minister of justice, party first secretary Gheorghe Gheorghiu-Dej as minister of transportation, and Teohari Georgescu as under secretary of the Ministry of the Interior. The latter, who had systematically ignored Radescu's orders, provoked the crisis of February 1945, during which the prime minister imprudently, but accurately, condemned the Muscovite RCP leaders Ana Pauker and Vasile Luca as foreign agents. Andrei Vyshinsky, Soviet deputy minister of foreign affairs, appeared in Bucharest to inform the king that the "fascist" Radescu government had to be replaced by one of the National Democratic Front (NDF), a radical coalition formed in October 1944. The NDF included the RCP, the Social Democrats, leftist intellectuals under the name of the Union of Patriots, and the Ploughman's Front, the latter led by Moscow's choice for prime minister, Petru Groza. The new government, dominated by Communists and Groza's followers, was installed on March 6, 1945 signaling the beginning of the "bogus coalition" period.

The traditional parties were included in Groza's government but their representatives were designated by the Soviets rather than by the parties themselves. Eventually the Liberal and National Peasant parties went into opposition where their power was sapped by the harassment of their members, the suppression of their newspaper and, finally, the arrest and imprisonment of their leaders. The king, who after August 1945 had refused to recognize the legitimacy of the Groza government, and the traditional parties had unrealistically expected Western support. But, internally, Groza's position was strengthened by the Soviets' return of northern Transylvania to Romanian control and by his promulgation of sweeping agrarian reforms. Unlike their unperceptive former leaders, hundreds of thousands of Romanians recognized the permanence of Soviet domination and rushed to join the RCP, which by December 1948 numbered more than 800,000 members.

In November 1946 "elections" were held that returned a huge NDF majority (347 of the 383 parliamentary seats). With the signing of the Paris Peace Treaty in February 1947, the pace of Sovietization quickened. In July the National Peasant party was outlawed and in November its leadership was tried for collusion with the West. The fellow-traveling dissident Liberals were eliminated from their government posts that same month, and the RCP "Muscovite" faction, Pauker, Luca, and Emil Bodnaras, took over the portfolios of Foreign Affairs, Finance, and War, respectively. King Michael was forced to abdicate in December and a people's republic was proclaimed, thus ushering in the period of "total control."

If the coup of August 23, 1944 was an attempt to salvage the traditional political culture of Romania, it succeeded only in postponing "Stalinization" and "satellitization." Once in undisputed control, the RCP ruthlessly set about to change the Romanian polity. Three concurrent processes were evident.

The first of these was the elimination of alternative sources of authoritative values, the necessary prerequisite for what Kenneth Jowitt has called the "breaking through" process.[2] In February 1948, the RCP absorbed the remainder of the Social Democratic party and established the Romanian Workers' party (RWP). The fellow-traveling rumps of the pre-1945 parties were altogether eliminated by 1953 when Groza's Ploughman's Front dissolved itself. The churches, another source of systemically dysfunctional values, were either coopted by the state, as in the case of the traditionally subservient Romanian Orthodox church, eliminated, as accomplished in the forced merger of the Uniates with the Orthodox, or persecuted as agents of "imperialism." Culture, always a source of national consciousness, was Sovietized with the establishment of state censorship and the imposition of "socialist realism" by the party-controlled artists' unions. Education was laicized and centralized in August 1948, and the mass media were reorganized under strict party control in May 1949. Those who ventured criticism were silenced. By 1955, Jowitt contends, the "breaking through" process had been completed, leaving the RCP as the single source of authoritative values for Romanian society.

The second process was the socialist transformation of the economy, closely imitating the Soviet precedent. In June 1948, the manufacturing, mining, banking, insurance, and transportation industries were nationalized and in July a State Planning Commission was established that produced the goals of the first five-year plan for 1951–55. The collectivization of agriculture in the overwhelmingly agrarian society was initiated with the establishment of machine tractor stations in late 1948. The first "artelization" (collectivization) drive began in 1949. The peasants, whose land hunger was unassuaged by the land reform of 1945, resisted and coercion was applied, especially against Romanian "kulaks." The pace of collectivization diminished somewhat in the mid-1950s to be rigorously reinitiated in the latter part of the decade. In 1962 Gheorghiu-Dej announced that collectivization had been completed. The economic priorities of the first decade of RCP rule were typically Stalinist: rapid multilateral industrialization with an emphasis on basic industries; draconian rates of capital accumulation; and exploitation of labor, both rural and urban.

The third process was "satellitization" in which Romanian state and national interests were systematically subordinated to Soviet priorities. First, the party had to be reliable. The presence of Ana Pauker, Vasile Luca (ethnically Jewish and Ruthenian, respectively) and their Muscovite associates in the higher echelons of the RWP was an initially adequate guarantee of the party's subservience. The party's ethnic Romanian proletarian component, led by Gheorghiu-Dej was equally subservient to Stalinist political and economic priorities. The party had purged and arrested its "potential Tito," Lucretiu Patrascanu, even before the Soviet-Yugoslav dispute had become public.

A verification campaign completed in 1950 had rid the party of roughly 30 percent of its members, "opportunists" who had joined between 1944 and 1950 and whose loyalty to the Soviet Union was problematic at best. But the apparent harmony between the Muscovites and native Communists camouflaged an intense internal tug-of-war that pitted Pauker and Luca against Gheorghiu-Dej. Flaunting their Moscow connections, Pauker and Luca had carved out semi-autonomous fiefdoms within the party. However Gheorghiu-Dej proved the more supple politican, both convincing Moscow of his reliability and adeptly exploiting Stalin's anti-Semitism. In May 1952, Gheorghiu-Dej purged Pauker, Luca, and Georgescu, blaming them for the recruitment scandals revealed during the verification campaign. The fact that Moscow acquiesced in Gheorghiu-Dej's triumph was an adequate testimony to his dedication to the cause of "satellitization."

Total RWP subservience to its Soviet animators was the prerequisite for the political and economic satellitization of Romania. Political subordination, manifested in Bucharest's obedient parroting of the Moscow line in international and interparty affairs, was symbolized in the signing of the Soviet-Romanian twenty-year treaty of friendship, collaboration, and mutual assistance (February 1948). Romania also signed the treaty establishing the Council of Mutual Economic Assistance (CMEA) of January 1949, and the Warsaw Pact of May 1955. As early as 1945 theoretically jointly owned "Sovrom" companies had been incorporated that legalized the Soviet exploitation of Romanian natural resources and industries while, at the same time, Romania strained to pay its huge reparations debt to the USSR. In effect, Romania had become a political and economic dependency of the Soviet Union.

But the danger of Romanian nationalism, with its traditionally Russophobic component, had to be contained as well. Romanian culture was russified. The orthography of the Romanian language was slavicized, obscuring its latinity. Geographical names, from counties to streets, were changed to deemphasize their historical origins and were replaced by names evoking the new relationship between Romania and its Soviet "liberators." Russian language became a required course in Romanian schools despite the dearth of adequately prepared teachers. History was rewritten, obliterating any suggestion of past conflicting Russian and Romanian national interests. Any manifestation of Romanian national consciousness was suppressed with the predictable result of creating a wellspring of nationalist resentment and frustration.

The death of Joseph Stalin was not welcomed by Gheorghe Gheorghiu-Dej, the former's most fawning satellite imitator. Still less welcome was Moscow's instruction to its East European dependencies to adopt an emulative reformist "new course." Having only recently rid the RWP leadership of its Muscovites, Gheorghiu-Dej was now under fire by the party's intellectuals, led by Miron Constantinescu and Iosif Chisinevski, who deplored the excesses of the general secretary's Stalinism. Once again Gheorghiu-Dej proved to be the superior politician. First (August 1953), he moderated some of the harshest economic consequences of his Stalinism. Then (April 1954), he relinquished the RWP first secretaryship while retaining the prime ministry *a la russe.* Concurrently, however, he purged a further 17 percent of the RWP membership and packed the Secretariat with his own men, among whom was the then thirty-six-year-old Nicolae Ceausescu. By October 1955 he was strong enough to reclaim the position of RWP first secretary, installing Chivu Stoica, a staunch supporter, as prime minister. In

December, at the Second Congress of the RWP, he reiterated his determination to impose a Stalinist transformation on Romania although he carefully couched his program in "new course" phraseology. When Constantinescu and Chisinevski attempted to manipulate Khrushchev's "secret speech" at the Twentieth CPSU Congress against the RWP Stalinists, Gheorghiu-Dej cleverly turned the tables on them. While Khrushchev was defeating the Stalinist "antiparty group" in the Soviet Union, Gheorghiu-Dej purged the RWP's "Khrushchevites."

In a spectacular *tour de force* Gheorghiu-Dej, who, in the early 1950s held the party's leadership on the basis of his Stalinism, was able to retain leadership in the late 1950s despite his Stalinism.

THE ROAD TO SELF-ASSERTION

While there is disagreement over when, exactly, the RWP leadership began to assert its autonomy, there is a consensus that the conflicting economic priorities of the Romanian and Soviet parties played a large part in the overt split. The Stalinist economic model imposed on the satellites during the first few years of Communist rule suited the relatively undeveloped Balkans better than the more advanced economies of the northern tier. Thus, the latter welcomed the "new course" adopted by Stalin's successors, while two of the bloc's less-developed members, Romania and Albania, did not. In Romania the Stalinist transformation of the economy began to bear fruit in the mid-1950s as manifested in rapid rates of economic growth, urbanization, proletarianization, and social modernization. The RWP leadership, thus justified in its preference for the Stalinist model, was loath to change course just when positive results were becoming apparent. Gheorghiu-Dej resisted de-Stalinization as well as Moscow's new policy of economic integration and the division of labor that would have left Romania as the bloc's source of raw materials. Instead the RWP continued on a course of rapid multilateral (extensive) development. In his successful defiance of Soviet priorities, Gheorghiu-Dej was assisted both by the Stalinist legacy of a vertically integrated economy and by exogenous bloc events.

In the late 1960s the Soviets lost a number of their capabilities to bring the RWP leadership to heel. The Hungarian revolution had, in part, exonerated the RWP's orthodox line and had demonstrated the consequences of too rapid a decompression from Stalinist control. The onerous Sovroms had been liquidated in 1954 and the Red Army occupation was terminated in 1958. It was, however, the incipient Sino-Soviet split that provided Gheorghiu-Dej with the room to maneuver. Khrushchev's concessions to the Chinese, especially the legitimization of their independent course in the November 1957 sixty-four party declaration, enabled the RWP to claim autonomy and to refuse to participate in the integrative "socialist division of labor" advocated by the Czechs, East Germans, and Soviets. Such a subjugation to bloc-wide economic planning, the Romanians correctly reasoned, would largely negate the progress already achieved and would condemn Romania to perpetual relative underdevelopment.

Repeated visits by high-ranking Soviet and bloc delegations failed to break the Romanian's resolve, and Stalinist economic goals were again clearly articulated at the Third RWP Congress in June 1960. Concurrently, both because of the principle of nonintervention and because of the obvious political advantages, the RWP refused to take sides in the increasingly vituperative debate between their Chinese and Soviet comrades, even attempting, somewhat disingenuously, to mediate the dispute in 1964.

Gheorghiu-Dej's adept exploitation of existing conditions had at least two consequences that further strengthened his position vis-a-vis the Soviet leadership. Encouraged by Romania's growing defiance, the West had offered an alternative source of the economic and technolog-ical assistance on which the Soviets had reneged because of the Roma-nians' insistence on extensive industrialization. The opening-up of Western credit and markets both created alternative outlets for Roma-nian goods and decreased Romania's dependence on the bloc.

Second, the RWP's defiance of the hated Russians gave the regime a measure of legitimacy it had theretofore lacked. The popular support, however, was not without its drawbacks as Gheorghiu-Dej realized that it was based on the nationalist remnants of a political culture whose values were inherently inimical to his Stalinist designs. His efforts to supplant "bourgeois nationalist" sentiments with "socialist patriotic" ones, through a program of intensive political socialization headed by his secret police chief, Alexandru Draghici, were largely unsuccessful. Still, the burgeoning support elicited by the RWP's autonomous course facilitated the party's decision to ease Stalinist control. Amnesties in 1963 and 1964 liberated all remaining political prisoners who flocked to the national cause almost as soon as they were released from prison.

In April 1964 the RWP felt strong enough, both domestically and internationally, to declare its independence from Soviet tutelage. In a "Statement on the Stand of the Romanian Workers' Party Concerning the Problems of the International Communist and Working Class Movement," an enlarged RWP Central Committee Plenum declared its steadfast intention to pursue its own road to socialism:

> There does not and cannot exist a "parent" party and a "son" party or "superior" parties and "subordinate" parties, but there exists the great fam-

ily of Communist and workers' parties, which have equal rights. No party has or can have a privileged place, or can impose its line and opinions on other parties. . . .[3]

ROMANIA'S OWN ROAD TO SOCIALISM

Of the three types of revolutionary processes noted above—the intolerance for and elimination of alternative sources of authoritative values, the socialist transformation of the economy, and satellitization—only the third was renounced by the Romanian Stalinists. That reassertion of the priority of national interests over Soviet or bloc interests had both internal and external consequences, not the least of which was Romania's much-vaunted "independent" foreign policy.

In domestic policies the RCP, which in 1965 had reclaimed its historical name, embarked on a variety of programs designed to reduce Soviet penetration of the Romanian polity. Soviet counselors in the security services, the backbone of any Stalinist regime, had been eliminated in the early 1960s. While intelligence-gathering cooperation with the KGB and GRU continued when Romanian and Soviet interests converged, subordination of Bucharest's services to Moscow's was categorically terminated. Romania loosened her ties with the Warsaw Pact without renouncing her membership in the alliance. In military matters Romania negotiated the withdrawal of Soviet forces in 1958, and since 1962 the regime has refused to allow Pact ground exercises on Romanian territory. Since 1969 Romania has sent only token contingents to joint exercises elsewhere in the bloc. Gradually Romania has found nonbloc sources of armaments and has established her own arms industry. Especially in the 1970s older, Russian-trained command personnel have been retired and replaced with reliable nationally trained officers. After 1968 Romanian military doctrine rejected Pact norms and adopted a purely defensive Yugoslav-like people's war strategy. The derussification of the instruments of state coercion has all but eliminated the most potentially dangerous source of Soviet penetration in the Romanian polity. Consequently, the Soviet Embassy in Bucharest became less a viceroyalty and more a diplomatic mission, albeit one where, one suspects, antiregime intrigue is a major preoccupation.

Culture was renationalized; the language purged of its recent slavicization. A rich history, in which Bessarabia figured prominently, was reclaimed; Russian language was dropped as a required course in the schools and almost immediately disappeared from most curricula; geographical names reverted to their original Romanian forms; and the giants of "bourgeois" Romanian letters, arts, and sciences were restored to their rightful place of honor. The often maltreated intelligentsia was recognized as the guardian of the nation's cultural identity and, with the party's encouragement, pushed aside the sovietophile impostors in the faculties, museums, artists' unions, and research institutes. Once again Romania acknowledged her cultural ties with the West.

FOREIGN POLICY

The Socialist Republic of Romania (SRR), having undergone another symbolic name change in 1965, developed economic ties with the West at the expense of established ties with other CMEA members. The CMEA's proportion of the SRR's external commerce fell from two-thirds of the total in 1960 to barely one-third of the total in 1974. Increased commerce with the West was initially the result of the USSR's refusal to support the extensive development plans of the Romanian Stalinists. However, once the Western sources of credit and technology had been tapped, the SRR, like other developing economies, acquired an insatiable appetite for Western investments and machines, piling up huge hard-currency debts, a problem exacerbated by the oil price shocks and petrodollar surpluses of the 1970s. By 1982 the SRR's hard-currency indebtedness amounted to more than $10 billion and the government was unable to meet interest and principle payments, despite frenzied attempts to reduce hard-currency imports, renegotiation of the debt, and substantial assistance from the International Monetary Fund.

In its effort to escape dependence on bloc sources of trade and investments and in its unwillingness to compromise its ambitious development plans, the RCP leadership had unwittingly undermined both its long-term Stalinist quest for autarky and its mid-term aspiration for diffusion of inducements for normative commitment. In the first instance, the Romanian economy had become too integrated into the world economy, its hard-currency-earning petroleum-refining industries suffering from the worldwide oil glut and the reduced marketability of its goods during the Western recession. These impediments to exporting were complemented by the rapid rise of interest rates and successive shortfalls in production targets caused by both systemic failures and natural disasters. Second, by the early 1980s the government was forced to renounce further reliance on Western credit and to shift the burden of relatively high rates of capital accumulation to the long-suffering Romanian citizen whose standard of living declined drastically, thus eliminating any immediate possibility of generating legitimacy on the basis of greater material abundance. The new austerity was reflected in the reintroduction of rationing of basic foodstuffs and electric power and in spot shortages of both consumable and durable goods in 1981–83.

Romania's goal of achieving functional autonomy within the Soviet bloc was also manifested in a number of well-publicized deviations from bloc foreign and interparty policies. Bucharest has continued to steer a neutral course in the Sino-Soviet dispute. The Chinese and Romanian leaderships continue to use support of each other to define their relationships with the USSR. In 1964, 1971, 1978, and 1982 Ceausescu made official visits to the People's Republic of China and Chinese leaders returned those visits in 1966, 1978, and 1983. While each side realizes the limits of the other's support, exchanges of visits and intensified economic, cultural, and military interactions serve to distinguish Romania's relations with Beijing from those of other Warsaw Pact states. Romania, alone among the Warsaw Pact states, maintains full diplomatic relations with Albania and has sided with the Chinese-supported anti-Vietnamese Kampuchean forces led by Prince Norodom Sihanouk.

In 1967 Romania established diplomatic relations with the Federal Republic of Germany, a state with whom only the USSR among the bloc states had formal relations. Romanian-West German economic exchanges were second in value only to Romanian-Soviet trade in the early 1980s. In the 1960s Romania also established friendly relations with de Gaulle's France and with the United States, profiting from their economic and diplomatic support. Ceausescu grandly received Richard Nixon and Gerald Ford in Bucharest and was the guest of President Carter in Washington. The European Economic Community and the United States have extended preferential tariff status to Romanian goods and the West has symbolically supported Ceausescu's rejection of Soviet dominance. While other bloc countries eventually, albeit more timidly, established better relations with the West once Moscow had fully endorsed detente, Romania's "Westpolitik" anticipated that of its allies.

In the oil-rich Middle East as well, Romania has steered a course divergent from that of its allies. It did not sever relations with Israel in 1967 after the Six-Day War, but it has steadfastly supported the recommendations of U.N. Security Council Resolution 242. In 1977 Ceausescu was instrumental in convincing Anwar Sadat to make his historic visit to Jerusalem. He did not condemn the subsequent Camp David Accords but has continued to urge the necessity of an overall regional settlement. The SRR established and retains diplomatic ties with the PLO and has lent its support to the priority of an independent Palestinian state. Bucharest has frequently sent its diplomatic troubleshooters to the Middle East and played a positive role in the Lebanese crisis of 1982–83. While the importance of the region as a supplier of crude oil for Romania's refining and petrochemical industries certainly accounts for some of the regime's interest in Middle Eastern affairs, one may also attribute Bucharest's measured and effective diplomacy to the fear that a superpower confrontation there would demand greater bloc cohesion, especially in the Warsaw Pact's southern tier.

Romania condemned the Warsaw Pact invasion of Czechoslovakia, an action in which no Romanian forces took part. In fact, the RCP both consistently supported the Dubcek leadership's right to determine its own course and roundly condemned the invasion and the Brezhnev doctrine that sought to justify it. While gradual normalization has evolved since 1968, Romanian-Soviet relations are sporadically worsened by the Pact's or CMEA's policies which are perceived as reasserting the USSR's military, political, or economic hegemony. Romania has consistently called for the dismantling of both the Warsaw Pact and NATO; it has taken non-, but not necessarily anti-, Soviet positions concerning the MBFR, INF, and CSCE negotiations; it has opted out of Soviet attempts to further unify pact forces and to integrate CMEA member-states' economies; and it has intensified its varied relationships with the bloc's putative adversaries.

In the 1970s Romania began to identify itself with Third World causes, in keeping with its reidentification as a "socialist developing country." Bucharest has supported calls for a New International Economic Order; has joined the "Group of 77" and has acquired "invited guest" status at the nonaligned conferences; has significantly increased its aid commitments to and trade with Third World countries; and has generally associated itself with Third World priorities in international organizations. As high-level diplomatic contacts with bloc states and the West have declined, President Ceausescu has visited an impressive number of Third World states and has grandly received their heads of state on reciprocal visits.

In interparty relations the RCP has upheld the principles of the 1964 declaration that asserted each party's right to determine policy in accord with local conditions. Both state and party relations with Yugoslavia and the LCY remain warm. Together with the Yugoslavs, the RCP manipulated the conditions prior to the 1976 Berlin conference of European parties to ensure a Eurocommunist victory at the expense of the Soviet party. The RCP has maintained particularly warm relations with the Italian and Spanish parties, which have been frequent targets of Soviet attacks. The RCP has scuttled Soviet attempts to condemn any party at interparty conferences.

The net effect of Romania's desatellitization has been the lowest levels of intrabloc (i.e., Soviet) dependence of any of the European member-states of the Warsaw Pact and CMEA.[4] The pursuit of divergent policies has produced a number of benefits for a regime that is otherwise unattractive both for its own citizens and for alternative sources of foreign economic and political support. Internally, it has enabled a harsh regime to acquire the popular support necessary for mobilization and achievement of at least some of its ambitious economic goals. Until recently, the anti-Russian overtones of desatellitization, coupled with the foreign credits that enabled the economy to achieve the highest growth rates in Europe, were sufficient to mute demands for both economic and social de-Stalinization. Romania's considerable international prestige and Ceausescu's disproportionate role in international affairs were a source of pride for a fiercely nationalistic people.

But the very success of Romania's integration into an increasingly interdependent world system rendered its fragile economy, and thus the rising material expectations of its citizenry, all the more vulnerable to international economic and political crises. In the early 1980s international recession triggered economic retrenchment that undercut much of the popular legitimacy gained by the Ceausescu regime. In turn, faced with the failure of normative commitment producing political socialization campaigns, the regime has resorted to coercive measures that are distasteful to the international community.

Romania's maverick foreign policy was initially enthusiastically supported by the West, which perceived in the Romanian deviation the opportunity, by example, to wean bloc countries away from total obeisance to the Soviet Union. Hand-in-hand with the geostrategic and profit motives, the West also believed that desatellitization would somehow permit or encourage domestic de-Stalinization, a hope seemingly realized in the liberalization of 1964–71. Western banks and governments overinvested on the basis of these unrealistic expectations. As a result, after having fully understood that Romanian autonomy was founded on Stalinism, the West was trapped between the need to continue support for reasons purely of power politics and the need to distance itself from the most oppressive regime in Eastern Europe. The recession and interest-rate inflation of the 1980s have provided a partial economic escape for both Romania and the West without undermining the instrumentalities established for mutual diplomatic support.

Given the Soviet reactions to bloc deviations in 1956, 1968, and 1981, why has Moscow allowed Romania to desatellitize? If one hypothesizes that the potential loss of the Communist party's monopoly of political power in Hungary, Czechoslovakia, and Poland was the prime stimulus for the intervention, then the response is obvious. There is no other bloc state in which party control is more complete than in Romania. Dissent is rapidly and effectively suppressed. There are no viable competing sources of authoritative values. The state and party are highly centralized. In short, Romania is functionally as orthodox a Communist party-state as one could expect. If, on the other hand, one were to hypothesize that geostrategic considerations, triggered by a potential weakening of the Warsaw Pact, were the foremost rationale in the Soviets' decisions to intervene, then the response is equally obvious. First, while gradually withdrawing from most military aspects of the pact, Romania remains a member. Second, Romanian military self-reliance is not a threat to Soviet European strategy. Third, as long as Central Europe remains the most likely battlefield, Romania is the European pact state with the least geostrategic importance. Fourth, and most importantly, Ceausescu has ably exploited the international environment and has carefully calculated just how far he can deviate without eliciting more than rhetorical abuse by the Soviets. In short, Ceausescu has astutely perceived potential costs to the Soviets of intervention and has never made it worth their while. The costs would have been greatest during the heyday of detente and the Romanian deviation was most assertive at precisely that time. With the waning of detente, Bucharest has muted its dissent. Many of Ceausescu's recent peace efforts thus reflect his concern over loss of maneuverability in foreign affairs and his ability to build domestic legitimacy at the expense of his allies.

DOMESTIC PATTERNS

Romania's assertion of autonomy in international and interparty affairs has always been intimately linked to domestic economic, social, and political developments. As already mentioned, Gheorghiu-Dej's initiation of the national course was motivated by his commitment to Stalinist socioeconomic goals. Even after the need for coercive control had diminished with the rise of nationalist support for the regime, the Romanian leader maintained a massive bureaucracy of coercion. Despite the amnesties of 1963 and 1964, the recruitment of the once maligned intelligentsia in the national cause, and the growing legitimacy of the regime, the secret police, the dreaded "Securitate," remained a potent symbol of the logic of citizen apathy and alienation and of the regime's insecurity. So powerful was the apparatus of terror that its chief, Alexandru Draghici, challenged Ceausescu for supreme political power following Gheorghiu-Dej's death. It is a tribute to Ceausescu's political agility and confidence that he was able both to purge Draghici and to launch a brief period of liberalization during the second half of the 1960s. A new constitution, promulgated in 1965, abandoned the principle of the dictatorship of the proletariat and included a list of civil rights comparable to those in constitutional instruments of Romania's de-Stalinized allies. Draghici's former fiefdom was split in two and its authority diminished. In June 1967, an RCP Central Committee plenum declared the opening of a new era of state-citizen relationships based on the vague notion of "socialist legality" and history was adroitly reinterpreted to lay the primary responsibility for past abuses on the Soviet Union.

This Romanian version of the "hundred flowers" resulted in a veritable blossoming of culture for the first time since 1945. Between 1968 and 1971 the artistic and academic communities reclaimed traditional inspirations and liberties. By the early 1970s liberalization was developing a momentum beyond party control and was generating un-Stalinist expectations among the professional classes. Returning from a visit to a China still in the throes of Mao's "great proletarian cultural revolution," Ceausescu moved decisively to stifle cultural pluralism for which there was no place in his Romania. Manifestations of "bourgeois decadence" (i.e., Western influence) were suppressed. The RCP exercised its preemptive right to define the limits of artistic license. Culture could be, indeed should be, patriotic (i.e., nationalist), but it could not be "normalist" or "obscurantist." Ceausescu formulated his cultural policy at the first Congress of Political Education and Socialist Culture in 1976: culture was subordinated to political education whose purpose was the formation of the new Romanian socialist man. An annual "Hymn to Romania" festival propagating nationalism, essential to the regime's legitimacy, was instituted and a joint party and state council was established to oversee all cultural activities. Consequently Romania's cultural life has stagnated and expressions of artistic individualism have been submerged in a flood of idolatrous quasiculture that has forced the most talented Romanians into exile or apathetic mediocrity.

Romania's economy was a Stalinist success until the late 1970s. Even if one suspects the reliability of government statistics, the country's economic growth rate was among the highest in Europe from 1965 to 1979, averaging between 6.1 percent and 9.2 percent annually.[5] From 1965 to 1975 industry's proportion of national income climbed from 48.6 percent to 57.1 percent and industry's proportional employment of the work force from 19.2 percent to 30.6 percent.[6] Transportation and construction grew at similarly spectacular rates.[7] These significant accomplishments were the result of investment rates averaging close to 30 percent of national income and the wholesale transformation of an agricultural into an industrial work force. The RCP's industrialization policies diversified and modernized an essentially agrarian economy and promised a multilaterally developed socialist economy by 1990. By the early 1980s however, the spectacular growth had all but disappeared, labor shortages had cropped up, productivity had sagged, and shortages of practically everything had appeared. The Romanian economic miracle had come to a screeching halt.

While natural disasters and worldwide recession certainly played significant roles in deepening the economic crisis in Romania, its roots lay in the very success of the economy. Extensive industrialization and labor transfers had reached a point of diminishing return. Better, not more, goods were demanded by both individual and corporate consumers. Neither workers nor managers had incentives to increase productivity or quality in the highly centralized system in which they were only passive participants. The New Economic Mechanism, bearing some resemblance to Soviet and East German reforms of the 1960s, was introduced with great fanfare in March 1978. Innovations included partial devolution of decision making to industrial administrations and individual enterprises; replacement of gross output with a vaguely defined "net profit" as the authoritative indicator of success; and profit sharing and worker self-management. Planners scaled down overly ambitious production and investment targets. The reforms were, however, superficial.

In fact, the RCP leadership was confronting the inevitable shift from extensive to intensive development and discovering that both domestic and foreign sources for the required productivity-enhancing technologies were lacking. In keeping with Romanian tradition, the regime wrapped itself in Stalinist inertia and appealed for nationalistic sacrifice rather than implementing genuine decentralizing reforms. Romanian workers have become restive, relying more and more on unofficial sources of income and consumer goods. Corruption has become endemic and managerial incompetence widespread. Given the grim humor with which the Romanian has long comforted himself, he is likely to say that this year is an average one: worse than last year, better than next.

While the Romanian leadership remains inflexibly orthodox in its definition of goals and institutional patterns, some structural peculiarities distinguish the SRR from other bloc states. While the unicameral Grand National Assembly of 369 deputies (1983) and the State Council, which is the interim and more important legislative body, bear close resemblance to national state structures of other bloc states, at the county and communal levels the positions of party secretary and state executive are merged. At the national level too, there are joint party-state bodies such as the National Defense Council and the Supreme Council on Socioeconomic Development, but there is an explicit recognition of the party's primacy in decision making and the state's purely managerial function. Political executives, whatever role they happen to be playing at a given time, are encouraged to be generalists ("Renaissance reds"). The party has adopted a deliberate policy of cadre rotation in which only a few highly specialized individuals hold the same position for more than two or three years. Such a policy makes for inefficiency in a modernizing society, but there are two good explanations for it. First, Ceausescu guards his authority so jealously that he institutionalized a system that prevents a potential rival from establishing a bureaucratic power base from which to launch a challenge. Second, by disassociating administrators from specific bureaucratic interests, he diffuses the impact of disruptive bureaucratic group politics. For whatever reason, the policy of cadre rotation has served to make political executives more dependent on Ceausescu and, it is rumored, on his wife, Elena, who directs the RCP's cadre policy *(nomenklatura)*.

The RCP itself is proportionally the largest East European party—its 3.15 million members constitute about 14 percent of Romania's population of about 22.5 million. The size of the party reflects the RCP's rejection of the Soviet "vanguard" model and underscores "the unity of the party and the people theme" constantly sounded in RCP ideological pronouncements. That ideology itself is Marxism-Leninism-Ceausescuism. Ceausescu has turned traditional Communist ideology on its head, arguing that Marxism-Leninism is valid first in its national manifestations and only then, cumulatively, in its universal form:

> . . . the role of the Nation does not diminish and even less does the Nation disappear after the victory of the socialist revolution; on the contrary, during the whole period of socialist construction and of the transition to communism, the Nation and the national state will have a mission of paramount importance. . . . the consolidation of the nation, the development of each socialist country, leads to the strengthening of the solidarity of all those countries, to the development of collaboration, [to] new relations based on full equality among states. . . . To ignore the vital interests of the people and their will to shape their destiny freely, without any interference from the outside, to tolerate the encroachment of the sacred sovereignty of the people would mean to denounce the principles of Marxism-Leninism, to fall into the positions of national nihilism and cosmopolitanism, greatly harmful to the cause of socialism and peace.[8]

He has made Marx, and, if one can follow the distorted logic, even Lenin, the advocates of Romanian nationalism.

Structurally also, the RCP is somewhat different. It has a relatively large Political Executive Committee of forty members, fourteen of whom are members of a core Standing Committee; there is a comparatively small Secretariat of seven secretaries; and a large Central Committee of 425 full and candidate members.

Mass organizations are, as in other Soviet model countries, transmission belts. The existence of Councils of Working People of Co-inhabiting Nationalities testifies both to the deleterious effects of Romanian nationalism on the ten percent of the population who are not ethnic Romanians and to the regime's justified fears that the Soviet Union might try to manipulate ethnic minority dissatisfaction to undermine Ceausescu's authority. Ideologically Ceausescu has tried to redefine nationality in a manner that deemphasizes ethnicity but the sizable Hungarian minority (roughly 8.5 percent of the population), in particular, has resisted the general secretary's semantic slight-of-hand.

Perhaps the most curious aspect of contemporary Romania is the personality cult surrounding Nicolae Ceausescu and, more recently, his wife. Romania rivals North Korea as the most personalist Communist party-state. Nicolae Ceausescu's party and state titles seem endless: president of the Republic, general secretary of the RCP, supreme commander of the Armed Forces, president of the State Council, chairman of the Council on Socioeconomic Development, chairman of the Socialist Unity Front (the electoral front), honorary chairman of the Academy of Social and Political Sciences, etcetera. Poetry, art, and music portray him as an original Marxist-Leninist theorist, a man of the people, a competent administrator, and a devoted patriot. They praise his intelligence, his energy, his courage, and his selflessness and commitment. They identify him as the most recent incarnation of a long line of Romanian national heroes—Burebista, Decebal, Stephen the Great, Michael the Brave, Alexander Ion Cuza, et al. His rule is justified by his genius and by destiny, and its legitimacy is at once secular and mystical. He is one with the nation and with Romania's Communist future. He is both a Bolshevik and a Bourbon.

Explanations of the cult range from a practical need to focus popular nationalism on a single symbol to a predictable outcome of Stalinist centralism and egomaniacal paranoia. Many intellectuals, to whom the cult is alternately distasteful and amusing, believe that Romania's essentially peasant and Orthodox culture facilitates its existence. The impartial observer must also credit Ceausescu with being an able leader and a canny politician. Few contemporary leaders are such astute analysts of Soviet intentions and international opportunities; few Communist bosses so adroitly manipulate personnel; few politicians exhibit such an acute sense of timing, knowing precisely when and how to play on popular emotions. Ceausescu is a tireless "campaigner" with a schedule of visits, meetings, inspections, and speeches that would tax the energies of a man half his sixty-five years (1983). If the front pages of the RCP daily, *Scinteia,* are to be believed, he is everywhere at once, judiciously making practically all domestic and foreign policy decisions.

In the latter 1970s and early 1980s the personality cult has expanded to include Elena Ceausescu and their son, Nicu. Elena Ceausescu is clearly the second most powerful person in the country, extolled in verse and song as the very personification of Romanian womanhood. Her official responsibilities include control of science, technology, and RCP cadre policy and—through her numerous female proteges—a number of mass cultural organizations. The press calls her Romania's "first comrade." Nicu Ceausescu, a secretary of the Union of Communist Youth, has also delved into cultural and foreign policies. As many as three dozen other members of the Ceausescu clan occupy high posts in the party and government. While culturally consistent, the Ceausescu nepotism calls into question the regime's state goal of creating a socialist meritocracy. Instead, as one Bucharest wit quipped, it appears to be "socialism in one family."

PROSPECTS

The Socialist Republic of Romania is an anomaly among the East European party-states. While it exercises the autonomy characteristic of Yugoslavia and Albania, it remains a member of the Warsaw Pact and the Council of Mutual Economic Assistance, earning it the label of a "partially aligned" state.[9] It is both a developing state and a European socialist state. Its Communist party leadership clings tenaciously to anachronistic Stalinist objectives and methods that its nominal allies have rationally abandoned. It is a Marxist-Leninist regime that has coopted the country's rich history and made it a basis for its rule. In the context of immediate policies it rejects "proletarian internationalism" in favor of national priorities. It maintains certain manifestations of traditional political culture clearly in conflict with ideological expectations and norms. It is a political system so closely identified with a single individual that Ceausescu's disappearance could not but substantially alter the very basis of the marginal legitimacy the regime now enjoys based on an increasingly inflated currency of nationalism.

With or without Ceausescu, socialist Romania faces an uncertain future. Material privations demoralize the entire population but dysfunctionally affect particularly those very elites essential for overcoming centuries of socioeconomic retardation. Yet, the Stalinist system seems incapable of implementing changes that might generate the means for meeting the rising expectations of a modernizing society. Labor unrest, such as that which broke out among miners in 1977, is a distinct possibility despite the continued use of methods of coercive control incompatible with the development of normative commitment to the regime. The final paradox of contemporary Romania is that any dramatic departure from domestic Stalinism leading to a more multifaceted legitimacy might lead either to the Soviet intervention that orthodoxy has thus far prevented or to the logical reintegration of Romania into the bloc, resulting in the loss of the nationalist legitimacy that has served the regime so well.

NOTES

1. Hugh Seton-Watson, *The East European Revolution,* 3rd ed. (New York: Praeger, 1956), pp. 167–171.

2. Kenneth Jowitt, *Revolutionary Breakthroughs and National Development: The Case of Romania, 1944–1965.* (Berkeley and Los Angeles: University of California Press, 1971), pp. 1 and 92–149.

3. As translated in William E. Griffith, *Sino-Soviet Relations 1964–1965* (Cambridge, Mass.: MIT Press, 1967), p. 293.

4. William Zimmerman, "Dependency Theory and the Soviet-East European Hierarchical Regional System: Initial Tests," *Slavic Review, XXXVII,* 4 (December 1978), pp. 604–623.

5. Marvin R. Jackson, "Perspectives on Romania's Economic Development in the 1980s" in Daniel N. Nelson (ed.), *Romania in the 1980s* (Boulder, Colo.: Westview Press, 1981), pp. 262–263. Different statistical methods lead to different growth rate calculations.

6. William F. Robinson, "Selected Demographic and Economic Data on Eastern Europe," Radio Free Europe Research, RAD Background Report/19, (Eastern Europe), 29 April 1977, pp. 13 and 15.

7. Andreas C. Tsantis and Roy Pepper, *Romania: The Industrialization of an Agrarian Economy under Socialist Planning* (Washington, D.C.: The World Bank, 1979), pp. 672–673.

8. Nicolae Ceausescu, *Romania on the Way of Building Up the Multilaterally Developed Socialist Society,* vol. 13 (Bucharest: Meridiane Publishing House, 1978), p. 71; speech of June 2, 1976.

9. Robert L. Farlow, "Romania and the Policy of Partial Alignment" in James A. Kuhlman (ed.), *The Foreign Policies of Eastern Europe: Domestic and International Determinants* (Leyden: A. W. Sijthoff, 1978), pp. 191–207.

BIBLIOGRAPHY

Braun, Aurel. *Romanian Foreign Policy Since 1965: The Political and Military Limits of Autonomy.* New York: Praeger, 1978.

Cretzianu, Alexandre, ed. *Captive Rumania: A Decade of Soviet Rule.* New York: Praeger, 1956.

Fischer-Galati, Stephen. *The New Rumania: From People's Democracy to*

Socialist Republic. Cambridge, Mass.: MIT Press, 1967.

———. *Romania.* New York: Praeger, 1957.

Gilberg, Trond. *Modernization in Romania Since World War II.* New York: Praeger, 1975.

Graham, Laurence S. *Romania: A Developing Socialist State.* Boulder, Colo.: Westview Press, 1982.

Ionescu, Ghita. *Communism in Rumania 1944–1962.* London: Oxford University Press, 1964.

Jowitt, Kenneth. *Revolutionary Breakthroughs and National Development: The Case of Romania, 1944–1965.* Berkeley and Los Angeles: University of California Press, 1971.

King, Robert R. *A History of the Romanian Communist Party.* Stanford: Hoover Institution Press, 1980.

Montias, John Michael. *Economic Development in Communist Rumania.* Cambridge, Mass.: MIT Press, 1967.

Nelson, Daniel N., ed. *Romania in the 1980s.* Boulder, Colo.: Westview Press, 1981.

Roberts, Henry L. *Rumania: Political Problems of an Agrarian State.* New Haven: Yale University Press, 1951. [Reprinted, Hamden, Conn.: Archon Books, 1969.]

Seton-Watson, Robert William. *A History of the Roumanians: From Roman Times to the Completion of Unity.* Cambridge: Cambridge University Press, 1934. [Reprinted, Hamden, Conn.: Archon Books, 1963.]

Tsantis, Andreas C. and Pepper, Roy. *Romania: The Industrialization of an Agrarian State under Socialist Planning.* Washington, D.C.: The World Bank, 1979.

7   Bulgaria

Patrick Moore

Compared to most other East European countries, Communist Bulgaria is often regarded as a sleepy Balkan backwater that has seemingly been bypassed by the more striking processes at work in the region. It has not witnessed the political turmoil that has existed in the GDR, Poland, Hungary, or Czechoslovakia, the intellectual ferment and ideological innovations of the "Yugoslav road" or Czechoslovakia's Prague Spring. Bulgaria has not been subject to the economic reforms of Yugoslavia, Czechoslovakia, or Hungary, nor to the foreign policy adventures of its Balkan neighbors Yugoslavia, Romania, or Albania. Furthermore, although Todor Zhivkov acquired his party's highest office in 1954, that is, well before any other current leader in the Warsaw Pact, he remains probably the least-well-known abroad. This situation mirrors his country's general image. The contrast is most glaring with Poland, which has known no fewer than six party chiefs during the same period, only two of whom, namely Edward Ochab and Stanislaw Kania, have made less of an impression on the foreign public, and that only because of their relatively brief tenures.

This overall impression may seem justified if one treats Communist countries on a superficial, comparative level, as though they began in 1945 as clean slates; but the picture appears otherwise if one carefully examines Bulgaria's political culture and Communist period in the context of Bulgarian history. To do so it is necessary to trace the main developments in the country's evolution and examine the primary political, economic, and social trends.

BULGARIAN POLITICAL CULTURE
IN ITS HISTORICAL FRAMEWORK

Although art treasures from ancient times are proudly displayed at home and abroad by the current Bulgarian leadership, the first development of political significance for modern times—i.e., the

nineteenth and twentieth centuries—were the medieval "empires."
These so-called empires were actually personal achievements of powerful rulers rather than of nations in the modern sense and their frontiers consequently fluctuated greatly over the course of decades. Such
states have nonetheless left an important twofold legacy in the development of the modern Bulgarian self-image and nationalist doctrine,
following a pattern common throughout Eastern Europe. First comes
the idea of past greatness, which serves to reawaken, bolster, and
sustain patriotic pride in difficult times with the implicit corollary that
earlier glories may some day return. The second aspect is a wealth of
historical arguments that can be used to justify at least in part subsequent territorial claims; in other words, the frontiers of one or another
Bulgarian medieval state are cited "evidence" that those lands should
be part of a nineteenth- or twentieth-century Bulgarian polity. In practice all this meant that writings on the Bulgarian past, starting with
Father Paisii's *Slaveno-Bulgarian History* (1762), inspired the Bulgarian national awakening and revival of national consciousness, which,
in turn, were the necessary ideological preconditions for the eventual
struggle for independence. Then, as the establishment of a Bulgarian
state came closer to realization, medieval precedent was marshaled
along with other arguments to stake out its frontiers, especially in
Macedonia and Thrace.

Between the medieval and modern states, however, came a period all
Balkan peoples like to regard as the nadir in their respective histories
and the source of present-day backwardness vis-a-vis Western Europe,
namely that of Ottoman rule. Modern Western scholarship rejects the
idea that Turkish rule brought only negative results, and holds instead
that it was not the Ottoman system itself that was bad, but rather that it
was the abuses and alterations of it setting in with the Empire's decline
that led to a worsening of conditions for the Bulgarian peasant. In the
case of Bulgaria the Ottoman era may be dated from the fall of the
Vidin kingdom in 1396 to the establishment of the new Bulgarian state
in 1878, a period of almost 500 years. The politically important aspects
of this period are chiefly changes that took place in Bulgarian society.

The first and most essential transformation stemming from the Ottoman period was the elimination of the native aristocracy. Socially, this
meant that the Bulgaria of the nineteenth-century national awakening
would be fundamentally a peasant society, with the Orthodox clergy,
village notables [*chorbadzhii*], merchants, and secular intelligentsia
having roots in that milieu. Politically it served to impart a strongly
egalitarian climate in which peasant and/or even socialist movements
could, at least theoretically, thrive. This was all the more true as the
leading elements under Ottoman rule, the higher clergy and the nota-

bles, became identified with that alien system and lost their influence in the course of the nineteenth century.

A second aspect of the Turkish legacy was the virtual removal of the Orthodox church as a political force in modern times. Although that institution served as the preserver of Bulgarian cultural identity and provided a tangible link with the medieval past during the five centuries of foreign rule, it also acquired a variety of administrative functions. While this could be positively regarded as a surrogate Bulgarian state, the Orthodox church nonetheless was part of, and had decayed with, the Ottoman system. Furthermore, it became intellectually ossified and had little to offer the restless writers, teachers, and revolutionaries of the nineteenth century who were attracted to modern European ideas (even if through a Russian filter), which all the more served to reduce the church's influence. Finally, the church acquired a dual role vis-a-vis the national movement. As part of the Ottoman framework, and following its direct subordination to the Greek patriarchate in 1767, with Greeks in its highest offices, it was regarded by Bulgarian patriots with more than just suspicion. On the other hand, once the fight for a separate Bulgarian church, or Exarchate, had begun in 1860, the struggle for its administrative boundaries, especially in Macedonia, was tantamount to the fight for the frontiers of a Bulgarian state and hence became a matter of top patriotic concern. As to the clerics themselves, individual priests played active roles not only for the Exarchate in Macedonia but also in the national awakening and revolutionary movement; it was, in fact, a cleric, Father Paisii, whose *Slaveno-Bulgarian History* (1762) marked the beginning of the awakening in an attempt to rediscover a glorious past. The clergy's position was nonetheless secondary, and leadership of the Bulgarian national movement was largely in the hands of secularly minded intellectuals who looked to modern Europe as their model for Bulgaria's future. Once independence had been achieved, the church's role as an institution was clearly subordinated to the state.

The third point worth noting is that the declining Ottoman Empire bequeathed to all its successor states a variety of negative phenomena that were ill-suited to the development of modern, industrial societies based on the rule of law and with well-functioning democratic institutions according to the Western pattern. Learning and culture had stagnated, and the first task of the zealous and nationally minded teachers, who were the forces behind the national awakening, was to spread basic literacy as well as useful knowledge. Although the country did enjoy increased prosperity as a provider of supplies to Constantinople and the army after 1830, and although landlords increasingly sold unprofitable estates to peasants, who now had at least some land, precious little had been done to encourage industry or improve communications. The general state of political disintegration leading to the arbitrary rule of local authorities for years had put the peasant at the mercy of the Turkish landlord and roaming armed bands, with predictable results for agriculture. The political culture bore the stamp of what is generally known in the West as the "Balkan mentality": mistrust of the city and government; a tendency to look out for one's own narrow interest with a corresponding absence of civic responsibility; and a personal and paternalistic style of rule with a large degree of patronage and corruption.

The effects of this legacy are evident from the history of the Bulgarian monarchy, which for practical purposes can be dated from the Treaties of San Stefano and Berlin in 1878 and the establishment of a Bulgarian state to the Communist coup in September 1944. First, however, it is necessary to turn to two principal issues in foreign affairs with major domestic repercussions, namely relations with Russia and later the USSR, and the Macedonian question.

Throughout the decades preceding independence the Bulgarian attitude toward the largest Slavic nation was ambivalent.[1] On one hand, there was admiration for Russian achievements and hope that "grandfather Ivan" would liberate Bulgaria from the Turks. On the other, there was pride in Bulgaria's own accomplishments, including having had both Christianity and an alphabet before the Russians did, together with the realization that St. Petersburg's wars with Constantinople were bringing their country only Turkish reprisals and dashed hopes. When liberation finally did come at the end of Russian bayonets it did not mean that Bulgarians at once became masters in their own house; on the contrary, the role and behavior of Russian officers and officials in meddling in Bulgaria's internal affairs was such that many Bulgarians felt that they had exchanged one foreign occupier for another. The tsar's insistence on having the upper hand in Bulgaria's political life led to such tensions that the two countries did not even have diplomatic relations between 1886 and 1896. The difference between them was clear: great power Russia sought to use small power Bulgaria to further its own interests, while the Bulgarians wanted to defend their independence and pursue their national territorial goals. This is not to say that Russophobia became widespread. On the contrary, the pro-Russian sentiments in the population at large were such that Bulgaria's participation in both world wars on Germany's side scarcely enjoyed unqualified domestic support, and precisely on account of generally Russophile attitudes in World War II the country did not formally

declare war on the USSR but only on the Western Allies. The main
reason, however, for Sofia's alliances with Berlin both times is the
second main theme in Bulgarian external affairs, Macedonia.

For at least most of the past hundred years, the region encompassed
by Macedonia has been contested by Sofia, Belgrade, and Athens,
since the possessor would thereby become the dominant Balkan
power. The uncertain ethnic character of the majority Slavic population—they are variously regarded as Bulgarians, Serbs, or a separate
Macedonian nationality—has underlain the dispute between Sofia and
Belgrade, which is the chief dimension of the tangled Macedonian
question that affects post-1944 Bulgaria and hence this study. The bulk
of the disputed area had been assigned to Bulgaria in March 1878 by the
Treaty of San Stefano, only to be returned to Turkey just four months
later by the Treaty of Berlin. The San Stefano boundaries nonetheless
remain for most patriotically minded Bulgarians the country's legitimate ethnic and historic frontiers; in the twentieth century Bulgaria has
gone to war once against Turkey and three times against Serbia or its
successor Yugoslavia primarily over Macedonia. Each time it has felt
disappointed and cheated, being left in each final peace treaty since
1913 with only a tiny corner known as "Pirin Macedonia," which is
much smaller than Belgrade's "Vardar Macedonia."

As was suggested above, Sofia sided with Berlin in both world wars
since the Germans offered it more Macedonian territory than could the
Allies, who were linked to Belgrade. This has been Bulgaria's main
irredenta, and the repeated failures to acquire it permanently have led
to bitterness, frustration, and an inferiority complex in the national
body politic.[2] Large numbers of pro-Bulgarian Macedonians fled to
Bulgaria, at first after failed uprisings against the Turks, and after 1912–
13, when much of their land was assigned to Belgrade. Well-armed and
well-organized, they became a force to be reckoned with in domestic
politics; one astute observer described them already in 1913 as "something between a nation, a party, and a profession."[3]

In terms of internal developments and the legacy of the monarchy,
the main feature of political life was the wide discrepancy between the
Western, liberal, democratic, constitutional model and actual practice
in a Balkan country, onto which a system that had evolved over centuries in a different type of society was suddenly grafted. Since Bulgaria lacked a large educated middle class to provide a base for stable,
program- and issue-oriented political parties, the groupings that
emerged tended to center on charismatic or powerful leaders and be
linked through patronage rather than ideology, despite their often
Western-sounding names and programs. This political vacuum stemming from the weak social base for a Western constitutional system

was filled by other institutions: the monarchy, often short-lived authoritarian governments, the military, and the principal Macedonian organization known as the IMRO. The climate of political violence in Sofia in the 1920s has, moreover, been likened to the Wild West, with IMRO factions especially conducting their vendettas openly in the streets. Among those killed by the IMRO was Peasant Union leader and Prime Minister Alexandar Stambolisky in 1923. His rule had marked a bold if somewhat chaotic attempt to put the interests of the peasant majority first, even to the point of seeking accommodation with Belgrade over Macedonia. In so doing he wanted to be able to devote full time to domestic issues and to promote South Slav solidarity, but he thereby antagonized the monarchy, the military, the IMRO, and the urban classes. The two principal monarchs during this period, Prince and later Tsar Ferdinand (1886–1918) and Tsar Boris III (1918–43), were primary actors on the political stage, helping to make and unmake governments. As for the military, suffice it to say that one of its coups brought down Stambolisky in 1923, and another in 1934 put an end to IMRO as a force and sought to develop the country along rational lines until the coup leaders were politically outmaneuvered by Boris in 1935.

If the balance sheet of royal Bulgaria did not bode well for a stable political future based on rule of law and smoothly functioning democratic institutions, a few positive points should nonetheless be noted. First, although a Turkish and Slav Moslem minority existed and today is almost 10 percent of the total population, compared to multinational states like Yugoslavia or interwar Poland, Bulgaria enjoyed relative freedom from the internecine and minority squabble that plagued the political life of many of its neighbors. Secondly, comparative social as well as ethnic homogeneity and a fairly egalitarian distribution of land, together with advanced social security, cooperative, and credit systems, spared the country the social cleavages of, for example, Poland or Hungary. Widespread free and accessible public education, harking back to the emphasis on education and use of reading rooms—a unique Bulgarian institution that combined the functions of a library and political club—in the national awakening, also boded well for the development of a modern society. As a result, interwar Bulgaria achieved the highest literacy rates in the Balkans at that time.[4] Despite this and a strong attachment to the work ethic among national cultural values, the country was nonetheless too poor and the peasants too attached to their old techniques and inefficient land holding patterns to permit the development of a flourishing West European-type of commercial agriculture or an industrial revolution of the kind needed to produce real structural changes in what was still a peasant society. It should be noted that much of the industrial development that took place was linked to complementing agriculture and promoting the food industry rather than costly "prestige" industries ill-suited to Bulgaria's resources, and that Bulgarian agriculture became more specialized and devoted to profitable garden and industrial crops.

What then, was the place and evolution of the Bulgarian Communist Party in this environment? From the preceding discussion it should be clear that a number of factors existed that could work in the party's favor. First, a series of wartime defeats that were regarded as national disasters led to a climate of radicalization and accompanying political violence, in which the Communists could look forward to at least protest votes. Second, their links to the Soviet Union could serve them well among a Russophile population, which might not always make a sharp distinction between old Russia and the USSR. Third, the Orthodox church was hardly a strong competitor in ideology and too weak as an institution to be the kind of opponent that the Polish Communists would have to face in their Roman Catholic church. Fourth, parliamentary democracy was not sufficiently healthy in and of itself to consign a conspiratorial party to the fuzzy fringes of political life as in West Germany or bring it into the system to the extent that this has happened to the Italian Communists since World War II. Finally, given the opportunistic nature of most parties and politicians, the Communists could appeal with their ideology and generally uncompromising behavior to idealists of the Left.

On the other side of the ledger, there is also a variety of points. First, and perhaps most obvious, is the numeric weakness of the classic base of a Marxist party, namely the workers, although this problem did not prevent the Russian, Yugoslav, Albanian, and Chinese parties, among others, from coming to power, albeit under revolutionary conditions. Appeals to the Bulgarian peasant population were of limited success because the great majority of these people tended to identify with Stambolisky's party, not the Communists. Most BCP members nonetheless had to be drawn from the peasantry and the intelligentsia, although the party's best-known leader, Georgi Dimitrov, was a printer by trade. Second, even if neither the church nor democratic institutions could pose much of an obstacle, there were forces afoot that certainly did, chiefly the monarchy, its authoritarian governments, and the military. The BCP was suppressed intermittently, particularly after an ill-fated attempted uprising in 1923 and an assassination plot in 1925 in Sofia's Sveta Nedelia Cathedral. For most of the interwar years the Communist party remained insignificant, despite a flirtation with the IMRO in 1924 and its brief use in 1931–32 of a forerunner of the popular front tactic.

The Communists, moreover, made difficulties for themselves in addition to those already present in the Bulgarian political landscape. First, they proved dogmatic in ideology and their political tactics. This stemmed from their origins in the radical revolutionary or "narrow" (as opposed to the reformist "broad") wing of the Bulgarian Marxist (Social Democratic) Party that had been founded in 1891 and split into the two wings in 1903. The BCP was formed in 1919, the first Balkan Communist party, as part of the Third International. Its leaders, "grandfather" Dimitar Blagoev, Vasil Kolarov, and Georgi Dimitrov, longtime (1924–44) head of the Comintern, enabled the BCP to project an international profile far beyond the scope of its role within its own country, where they proved unwilling and unable to form an alliance with the other major force on the Left, the Peasant Union.

A second problem of the Communists' own doing was their failure to capitalize on sources of national discontent. In the wake of the defeat in World War I, they managed to poll in the 1920 election over 20 percent of the largely discontented population, but were never subsequently regarded as a special standard-bearer of national interests. It should be noted, however, that its representatives in the Comintern succeeded in securing that body's approval for a formula of an autonomous Macedonia within a Balkan federation, assuming that cultural and historic links would hold such a unit close to Bulgaria. Furthermore, in World War II the BCP held the attitude that Vardar Macedonia fell within its sphere of authority since the Bulgarian army was in occupation there, even though it formally had to submit to the Comintern's ruling in 1941 that the area came under the jurisdiction of Tito's Yugoslav Communist party.

Finally, it should be pointed out that the Bulgarian party, unlike its Yugoslav, Albanian, or Greek counterparts, failed to use the turbulence of World War II to launch an effective partisan movement or, like Tito or Enver Hoxha, to seize power on its own. One should not be too critical of the Communists on this score, since Bulgaria was not an occupied country, and its alliance with the Axis had brought it important territorial gains, including occupation rights in Vardar Macedonia. What partisan activities the BCP did launch were highly modest by Yugoslav standards and the party actually preferred the tactic of infiltrating the Bulgarian army instead. Nonetheless two crucial facts remain in the balance. First, the BCP came to power in a September 1944 coup thanks first and foremost to the advance of the Red Army following Moscow's politically motivated last-minute declaration of war on Bulgaria, and it was to the Soviets that the BCP ultimately owed its power. Unlike the Yugoslav Communists, it could not rely on a strong indigenous popular base. Second, vis-a-vis Tito, the BCP was unable to overcome the stigma of being the new master of what was in the last analysis a defeated Axis power. In negotiations over Macedonia or a projected Balkan federation, as will be shown below, the Yugoslavs held the political cards. All that the BCP and even its prestigious leader Georgi Dimitrov could do was to buy time and hope to hold out for a federal arrangement that would enable Macedonia to drift toward its supposedly natural Bulgarian moorings.

TURBULENT YEARS IN POLITICS, 1944–57

The Bulgarian Communists were certainly aware of their weakness and sought to compensate for it by a particularly ruthless and bloody consolidation of power, which most observers agree was the most brutal in postwar Eastern Europe. The September 9, 1944 coup did not bring them alone to the top, but rather the Fatherland Front, comprised of a number of democratically minded parties and politicians, including various shades of Agrarians, Stambolisky's nominal heirs. The Communists held only two ministries in the new cabinet of sixteen, but they were Justice and the Interior, which gave them control of the courts and police, respectively. When Bulgaria switched sides and joined the Allies, moreover, the army left the country to participate in the joint onslaught against the retreating Nazi armies and their remaining satellites, thereby leaving armed power within the country in the hands of the Soviet military occupation authorities and the Communist-controlled militia. There were thus few impediments to a determined Communist drive for power.

The general outline of the Bulgarian pattern is similar to that of the "salami tactics" applied throughout Eastern Europe at the time, with the main difference lying in the intensity and scope of political violence. A network of Communist-dominated Fatherland Front committees were set up under the war-horse Tsola Dragoycheva to create a mechanism of control and administration. The intent was to bypass the existing local government system subordinated to the government in Sofia, which the BCP did not yet have totally in its hands. At higher levels, wartime and other leaders assumed to be hostile to the new regime were shot or imprisoned, and then independent-minded members of the Fatherland Front were turned upon. A "plebiscite" in September 1946 eliminated the monarchy headed by the minor Simeon II, who went into exile, a "people's republic" was declared, and "elections" were held. Nonetheless, what remained of an opposition managed to obtain 30 percent of the votes despite the Communists' monopoly of and willingness to use the means of coercion. All pretense of maintaining a democratic facade was dropped in June 1947, however, once the U.S. Senate ratified the Paris Peace Treaty with Bulgaria. The treaty had been concluded the previous February and conferred international legitimacy on the Fatherland Front Bulgaria. The following day the principal Agrarian leader, Nikola Petkov, was arrested and eventually put on "trial" and executed. By the end of 1948 the BCP had eliminated any institutionalized opposition; as well as the BCP and the Fatherland Front there remained only the Bulgarian Agrarian Union (BAU), now nothing more than a front organization and a lobotomized version of its former self.

If the demise of Petkov marked the effective silencing of the non-communist opposition, the next major event was the "trial" and execution in 1949 of Communist leader Traicho Kostov for the alleged heresy of "Titoism," which was a general catchword in the bloc for allegedly promoting national interests at the expense of one's "internationalist duty" to the USSR. In reality the issue was a power struggle between Communists who had spent their political lives by and large in Bulgaria and those who had passed long years in the USSR; and the occasion prompting action was the need for a successor to Dimitrov and Kolarov, both of whom were in poor health and who died in 1949 and 1950, respectively.

The new leader who emerged as Bulgaria's "little Stalin" was Valko Chervenkov, who had gone into Soviet exile following the 1925 Sveta Nedelia plot and who after his return to Bulgaria experienced a rapid rise up the ladder to power. His ascendancy stemmed perhaps from his aptitude, political shrewdness, and marriage to Dimitrov's sister, but probably chiefly from Stalin's confidence in him. By 1950 he held the top offices in the government and the party, namely prime minister and secretary-general. He had managed to outmaneuver the leading remaining home Communists, primarily Anton Yugov, who lost the key post of minister of the interior in 1948, and even some notable "Muscovites" like the plucky Dragoycheva, who was ousted from the Politburo in 1948. Chervenkov sought personally to control virtually all aspects of politics, the economy, and culture. He became the object of a lavish personality cult that was as grotesque and laughable as its counterparts elsewhere. One specifically Bulgarian manifestation was a contrived "folk song" written in the traditional Slavic antithesis form, performed by the leading Philip Kouteff ensemble, stating that there are "not two nightingales singing in the garden" but "two true friends, the very good Stalin and comrade Chervenkov," who "spoke only one word," namely, "peace."

Chervenkov's days of glory were numbered, however, and on his protector's death on March 5, 1953 he and his supporters had every reason to feel ill at ease. It went without saying that the ensuing power struggle in Moscow would have repercussions throughout Eastern Europe. The gradual changes, known broadly as the New Course, that appeared in the USSR were mirrored in Bulgaria. There the exposure to Stalinism had been more brief than in the Soviet Union and the system's economic policies (see below) were highly disagreeable to a people not used to such ruthless and brutal rule. The first outbreak after Stalin's death of anti-Stalinist violence in Eastern Europe took place, in fact, in Plovdiv in May 1953 when tobacco workers protested a new policy of, in effect, less pay for more work.

Briefly stated, the New Course adopted chiefly cosmetic forms. The most important and meaningful were the easing of police terror and a reduction of compulsory deliveries of agricultural products to the state. The more atmospheric measures stressed less arbitrary rule, care for the well-being of the population, release from prison of some "trial" victims, etcetera. But two fundamentals went unchanged: basically the same individuals remained in power, and they and the BCP held control through coercion.

One Soviet-inspired change that did, however, lead eventually to concrete results was the division of party and state offices. Cherven-kov chose to relinquish his party post and to hold onto the prime ministership, just as Malenkov in the USSR became head of the government. The new BCP leader was the apparently unimpressive Todor Zhivkov; as in the Soviet Union where Nikita Khrushchev now headed the CPSU, it was the seemingly innocuous party figure who won out in the struggle for power. In both cases this was achieved by controlling the vital network of patronage, or *nomenklatura,* and as a result of various internal and external developments. The key factors favoring Zhivkov over Chervenkov were: the reemergence under the new circumstances of political figures who had been down but not out such as Yugov; a shift in Soviet support to Zhivkov thanks to a Soviet-Yugoslav rapprochement in 1955 (Chervenkov had been pointedly associated with the anti-Tito campaign that had begun in 1948 and Belgrade wanted to settle old accounts); and simply Khrushchev's desire to have men in power throughout Eastern Europe who owed their ascension to him, and not to Stalin.

Although Chervenkov's political demise did not come at once, and he held on as deputy prime minister until 1961, the real watershed in his career came at the BCP Central Committee's April 1956 "de-Stalinizing" plenum, held in the wake of the famous CPSU Twentieth Congress where Khrushchev denounced Stalin in his "secret speech." The main legacies of the plenum were its resolution that attacked Chervenkov's style of rule; a subsequent speech by Zhivkov showing that there was nonetheless reluctance in the party to break completely with

Stalin; the replacement of Chervenkov as prime minister with his enemy Yugov; and, in general, a more confident and open mood in society and the press. Within the BCP, critical and self-critical discussion became the order of the day, the Fatherland Front's newspaper *Otechestven Front* acted as a voice for reform, and a relaxation that first appeared after Stalin's death continued to be evident in literature.

The new atmosphere was not to last long, however. Some older party leaders never accepted the "April line"; many who did were soon uncomfortable with the sharpness of the subsequent discussions, especially those concerning the country's close relationship to the USSR and the lack of a real multiparty political structure. The Hungarian revolution in the fall of 1956 underscored their fears, even though the pressures generated by Stalinism in politics, the economy, and society did not produce such a sharp reaction in Bulgaria as in non-Balkan, more industrial, and complex countries such as Hungary or Poland. The cooling of relations between Moscow and Belgrade in the wake of the Hungarian events, moreover, relieved the BCP of earlier Soviet pressure to be more accommodating to the Yugoslavs, who had scores to settle with the Bulgarian leadership. In a temporary but striking reversal of roles, it was none other than Chervenkov who was charged with restoring orthodoxy in intellectual and cultural life. A purge of both reform-oriented individuals and Stalinists was effected, thereby conveniently enabling Zhivkov to check any possible threat from either camp.

In conclusion, the pattern of the BCP's first fourteen years in power, during which Soviet control or influence was particularly marked, closely followed that of developments in the USSR and the other East European countries where a similar relationship to Moscow obtained. In the following years the respective countries were, however, to display increasingly individual profiles more in keeping with their traditional political cultures. It is to that period that this chapter now comes.

THE ZHIVKOV ERA, 1958–84

The next stage in postwar Bulgarian political history runs from the aftermath of the events of 1956 to the BCP's Eighth Congress in November 1962. The main trends were the further strengthening and consolidation of Todor Zhivkov's power, owing chiefly to Khrushchev's support and running parallel, especially in and after 1961, to the Soviet leader's renewed efforts toward de-Stalinization, and a corresponding decline in the fortunes of Bulgaria's conservative elements led by Chervenkov and by Yugov. This was a time of widespread factionalism, with at least one key Muscovite and three major domestic groups vying for power. There is ample room for speculation as to Yugoslav involvement with particular reform-minded elements, and as to Chinese links to the diehard Stalinists epitomized by Chervenkov. However the salient point is that Khrushchev's success in revitalizing the de-Stalinization campaign at the CPSU's Twenty-second Congress in October 1961 and his subsequent backing of Zhivkov proved decisive.

The first milestone in Bulgaria in this period was the plenum of the BCP Central Committee held on November 28–29, 1961. Although the "Leninist" Dimitrov's image was untarnished despite his years of association with Stalin, the clear message for Sofia from the previous month's CPSU gathering was that Chervenkov, the living symbol of Bulgarian Stalinism, would have to meet his political demise once and for all. That he had not been completely turned out of high office earlier is indirect evidence of his continued support from and the strength of Stalinist elements in the party, testimony to the survival in Communist ranks of the Bulgarian penchant for political extremism. Now, however, he lost his posts in the Politburo, in the Central Committee, and as deputy prime minister amid sharp criticism from Zhivkov as being doctrinaire and preoccupied with centralization.

Purges continued at lower levels but the next important move at the top came in the form of Khrushchev's visit to Bulgaria in May 1962. During this visit Khrushchev showed clearly that Zhivkov had his blessing over Yugov, and he encouraged the former over conservative rivals in pursuing rapprochement with Yugoslavia in line with Moscow's own policy toward Belgrade. These trends came to fruition at the Eighth Congress in November, which witnessed a massive purge, including Yugov's removal from the prime ministership and Chervenkov's expulsion from the BCP. Yugov was attacked for a variety of Stalinist sins including "violations of socialist legality," factionalism, and ambition. Again, his longevity in office despite such a past serves witness to the depth of the divisions within the party. Nevertheless, the Congress ended with a clear majority for Zhivkov in the Politburo, if only for the first time, as well as with the ouster of the Interior Minister Georgi Tsankov.

The next development of political significance in postwar Bulgaria is also one of the elements most shrouded in mystery, namely the attempted *coup d'etat* of April 1965, the first such event in Soviet-dominated Eastern Europe. Very little is known about this plot,[5] except that it seems to have been led by one Ivan Todorov-Gorunya and to have involved men with a background in the same World War II partisan detachment and links to the Vratsa district to the north of Sofia.

Although one can see foreign connections in a possible "inspiration" by the 1964 Soviet removal of Khrushchev or by the Chinese example of hard-line militancy, the main roots seem to have been indigenously Bulgarian and recall that country's traditions of military involvement in politics and national revolutionary romanticism. The complex motives appear to have involved resentment over the politicians' continued role in army affairs, and personal frustrations. In particular the coup's engineers resented the slow pace of replacing Soviet-trained military leaders with partisans in a parallel move to the ascendency of domestic Communists over the Muscovites; the failure, in fact, to rehabilitate many partisans persecuted during the Chervenkov era.

Once the conspiracy was uncovered no death sentences were handed out, but the Interior Ministry was reorganized under Zhivkov's supervision and divided into two parts. A CPSU delegation led by head ideologist Mikhail Suslov arrived, a series of meetings was held with officers, and an extensive shakeup of party officials took place in Vratsa and other districts.

Subsequent to the attempted coup and its aftermath the attention of Bulgaria-watchers has not been drawn so much to developments at the top of the political pyramid as to manifestations of nationalism— including signs of discontent with the Soviet connection—to trends in economic reform, and to long-term changes in society. Suffice it to say that the overall appearance has been one of stability, with older or less competent leaders being periodically retired or replaced, and younger, well-educated people being brought up in their stead. As will be shown below, while Zhivkov's rule has hardly been free of the traditional Balkan proclivity to nepotism, it has also been marked by a tendency to select and promote relatively young, talented individuals. Such a policy is in sharp contrast to either Ceausescu's socialism-in-one-family or the CPSU's gerontocracy. Zhivkov has also removed potential rivals whom he had come to regard as too powerful, the most noteworthy case being the demise of Boris Velchev in 1977. Otherwise his leadership seems to have involved a far greater degree of stability than that found in contemporary Romania or Poland, let alone pre-1962 Communist Bulgaria, together with a greater infusion of new blood than had been the case with the CPSU.

THE BULGARIAN POLITICAL SYSTEM

When analyzing power relationships within Communist polities it is important to distinguish between theory and practice, between appearance and reality, and the Bulgarian case affords no exception. First, the Bulgarian constitution describes the BCP's role as "leading" and, in a practice that is at least rare in most noncommunist states' constitutions, mentions by name another country, the Soviet Union, and formally sanctions close links to it. The document does not, however, specify how these principles are to be put into practice, let alone hint at the magnitude that they actually have assumed as the basic facts of Bulgarian political life. This is to say that, in internal affairs, the 825,876-strong party (of whom only 42.7 percent are workers) is in effective control and all other bodies that would appear politically important on paper—the 4,388,000-member Fatherland Front,[6] the 120,000-member and nominal heir of Stambolisky's BAU,[7] the labor unions, women's and youth organizations, etcetera—are in reality the BCP's "transmission belts" to various segments of society. As such, they should in no way, at least on the basis of their actual performance to date, be regarded as "pluralistic" political forces representing special interests vis-a-vis the party. The Fatherland Front is the umbrella political organization that organizes governmental elections and on whose ticket all candidates are elected. The BAU serves as a formal link to the country's largest historical left-of-center party which generally had had the support of the country's peasant majority. Today the BAU is truly a "transmission belt" along the lines of the East German ODU or LDPD, which appear in that country in the guise of traditional Christian Democrat or Liberal parties, respectively.

In a similar vein to these mass organizations, the state bodies that on paper resemble their Western counterparts have quite different roles in practice. In theory the most important governmental body is the *Narodno Sabranie* or National Assembly, which contains 400 members, of whom about three-fourths are BCP and the rest BAU members. By its name it carries on the country's precommunist parliamentary tradition and supposedly represents the embodiment of popular authority; in reality, however, it meets only for a few short sessions each year at which it hears speakers not debate but rather present policies previously decided by the top party leadership, and at which it rubber-stamps a variety of legal measures.

Governmental authority rests in the hands of the 34-member Council of Ministers,[8] but this body too only serves to amplify and execute rather than formulate policy guide-lines predetermined by the BCP leadership (to which, it should be said, many of the ministers belong).

Just as power flows from the BCP outward and down through front and governmental bodies, authority within the party moves in one direction, namely from top to bottom as per the Soviet model. At the top of the structure[9] are the Politburo with 10 full and 3 candidate members, the Central Committee Secretariat with 10 secretaries, and the 197-strong CC itself. These constitute the real center of political power and the heart of Bulgaria's *nomenklatura* or ruling class. The individuals involved also enjoy various forms of privileges that can range from access to the most desirable vacation spots at home and abroad, to special rights in securing goods in short supply such as a nice apartment or a car, to virtually guaranteed admission for their children at prestigious educational institutions regardless of their objective qualifications; in sum, a combination of status symbols and practical gains that make membership in the *nomenklatura* both sought-after and jealously protected. This is not a system that is inherently conducive to change. Power and privilege are similarly extended proportionately down the ladder to lesser officials and to ordinary BCP members. The structure, which, it should go without saying, attracts all manner of opportunists, is lubricated by a network of influence and connections and would seem quite familiar to the *chorbadzhii,* even if its most recent source of inspiration is Soviet.[10]

What, though, of those at the top of this pyramid of power, pull, and privilege? The most important single individual is Todor Zhikov (born 1911), who has headed the BCP since 1954, served as prime minister between 1962 and 1971, and as State Council chairman, or head of state, since 1971. Of peasant stock, he rose through the party ranks in a career that required a great deal of political intuition and agility. Zhivkov is, however, in the last analysis a bureaucratic type and not a theoretician, nor a major revolutionary charismatic national leader, a star on the international Communist stage like Bulgaria's own Dimitrov or Kolarov, nor a brilliant orator. His formal education is limited, and he can scarcely be described as the type of technocrat-innovator for whom some Western observers have been waiting with Job-like patience. His years in office nonetheless testify to his skills as a political survivor. Todor Zhivkov should also be given credit for at least one additional point, namely surrounding himself with a group of relatively young and better-educated individuals.

Whereas dullness and gerontocracy have been the hallmarks of the Soviet leadership, Zhivkov's Bulgaria has witnessed some other trends. The only Politburo member over 75 is Tsola Dragoycheva (born 1898), whose role is clearly symbolic as a link with the BCP's past—as is that of Stefan Voitec in Romania. Dragoycheva's involvement in Macedonian polemics with the Yugoslavs has been such that to drop her from the Politburo would appear to symbolize a concession to Belgrade that Sofia would not want to make; hence she is kept on, even though others of her generation have been retired. Some younger leaders and current Politburo members who have come up under Zhivkov and who may eventually succeed him are profiled below. Grisha Filipov (born 1919) is the current prime minister and as of Brezhnev's death was clearly the man second only to Zhivkov. He is an economist with a government career and his Soviet ties have served him well. However, since it is to *whom* one is connected that is important, his political fate could be ultimately tied to the outcome of post-Brezhnev Kremlin power struggles. Furthermore, the fact that Filipov speaks Bulgarian with a heavy Russian accent is regarded as offensive by many Bulgarians in a national leader and could work against him if the post-Zhivkov political scenario were to call for someone with a more "patriotic" image. Petar Mladenov (born 1936) has been foreign minister since 1971 and has an impressive education and background in international relations. He reportedly enjoys a high standing in Moscow. Stanko Todorov (born 1920) left the prime ministership in 1981 to become chairman of the *Narodno Sabranie* in what then appeared as a demotion. It seems, though, that he has brought some of his former prestige to his new office, and he should not be ruled out as a dark horse in a succession struggle. Ognyan Doynov (born 1935) has an engineering and economic administrative background. His career has risen dramatically since 1974. Andrei Lukanov (born 1938) is only an alternate member of the Politburo but deserves mention because he possesses a number of qualities that may serve him well in the long run. A third-generation BCP leader from the Lukanov family, he has been educated in part in the West and is reportedly intelligent. After graduating from the Moscow Institute for International Relations he began a career in the Ministry of Foreign Affairs and that of Foreign Trade.

The Zhivkov leadership in Bulgaria would, therefore, appear to distinguish itself by longevity, stability, and elevation of younger people to high office. A few qualifications are in order. First, while Zhivkov has headed the BCP for about thirty years and has generally seemed to be in good health, there is no assurance that his luck will hold out indefinitely in obtaining and keeping the confidence of each new leader in the Kremlin. Any Soviet power change raises the specter of East European leaders backing the wrong horse and losing heavily. Secondly, at the end of 1982 Zhivkov disappeared from public view for weeks on end, and although he subsequently stated openly he had been ill, there was much speculation that his health could be even poorer than he had admitted or that his absence had been at least in part political.

Third, his rule has not been without its blemishes, including nepotism. If his performance in this respect pales besides that of Nicolae Ceausescu or of Enver Hoxha, it may well be because the Zhivkov clan is relatively small. In any event, his daughter Lyudmila's political and cultural career rose in a meteoric way, and by the time of her still unexplained death in 1981 at age 39 she was a full member of the

Politburo and undisputed master of Bulgarian cultural life. Lyudmila Zhivkova, it must be said, was a remarkable personality with a philosophy that owed more to traditional Bulgarian and Asian mysticism than to Marxism-Leninism.[11] She spoke more of "beauty" and "light" than of class struggle; among her last words were "think of me as fire." She also presided over an era in cultural life in which virtually any artist could count on at least being given a chance. It was an era in which great efforts were made for the celebration in 1981 of the 1300th anniversary of Bulgarian statehood—she died just weeks before the culmination of the festivities—and in which much attention was paid to promoting Bulgarian history and culture at home and abroad. Although she was generally respected and liked, the rapid rise of her career nonetheless tarnished her father's name with nepotism, an impression that was reinforced after her death by the sudden political emergence of her clearly less-able younger brother, Vladimir. On the other hand, if Zhivkov has shown a readiness to promote relatives, he has also displayed ruthlessness in demoting other people whom he had come to regard as rivals, the last such major case being Velchev's fall.

Finally, it should not be forgotten that the apparent stability of the Zhivkov years is an exception in modern Bulgarian history. They were preceded by a period of severe factionalism and instability, and even under Zhivkov there was an attempted military coup and some strange events surrounded the person and career of his daughter. One should not, therefore, assume that the country has broken with its turbulent past or that the calm surface really reflects what lies beneath.

POLITICS BY OTHER MEANS: THE COMMUNIST RECORD IN THE ECONOMY, SOCIETY, AND CULTURE

Since this is a survey chiefly of Bulgarian political life with no pretentions of being a comprehensive review of other aspects of modern Bulgaria, and since the Communists themselves generally give primacy to political considerations, treatment of other facets of postwar Bulgaria will center on their relationship to BCP policy and to politics in general.[12]

In economics, three main tasks stemming from ideological dictates faced the Communists, namely the institution of centralized planning, the collectivization of agriculture, and the development of heavy industry. Following some preliminary efforts, a two-year Reconstruction Plan was instituted for 1947–48, followed by the country's first five-year plan begun in 1949. It has become something of a truism that Communist central planning in theory is a highly rational approach but in practice contributes to confusion and anarchy since it cannot possibly provide for all eventualities and lacks the flexibility to adapt to new developments and challenges. The Bulgarian case has proven no exception, but at the heart of the problem of economic inefficiency is not just the planning system as such, but the assignment of priorities. Especially in the early years, heavy industry was favored, often in disregard for the country's resources, over the more traditional agriculture.

Industrialization, particularly iron and steel, was something of a Stalinist sacred cow and was eagerly promoted throughout Eastern Europe. Bulgaria had neither the natural resources, the skilled labor, nor the technology for it. But that did not prevent the establishment of, for example, the Kremikovtsi metallurgical plant, which from the outset required imports of ore, coke, electricity, and equipment, the latter of which generally came from the USSR and was scarcely of top international quality. Even after the work force was properly trained, the country had from the outset an expensive white elephant.

Other aspects of industrial development similarly followed Stalinist dicta at the outset, such as country-by-country autarky, although this was scrapped as part of the de-Stalinization program in favor of specialization within Comecon. Two areas in which Bulgaria has sought to make a name for itself are forklift trucks and industrial robots. Even here it, like other nonmarket economies, has had to face lowered quality, rising real prices, and lack of ability to keep up with technological innovation. Zhivkov himself has lambasted the quality of Bulgarian industrial production from machine-building to consumer goods, and on the latter score has admitted that Bulgarians prefer to buy foreign to domestic goods.[13]

A variety of attempts has been made over the years to promote or improve radically the Bulgarian economy, particularly industry. The most ambitious was the Great Leap Forward of 1958–60, which sought to achieve a five-year plan in three years. The plan failed to achieve its high targets, especially in agriculture; nonetheless growth rates were impressive despite the waste inherent in applying Stalinist shock techniques to something as sophisticated as industrial economic development. Politically the move is interesting not only for its obvious Chinese point of reference (a connection also rumored in the 1965 coup) but also because of its traditional Bulgarian qualities of radicalism, romanticism, and violence. Subsequent reform projects such as the New Economic System of the mid-1960s or the more recent New Economic Mechanism have sought to foster efficiency and reduce waste but have failed to produce any qualitative changes. For all the talk of financial accountability of each enterprise and reduction of bureaucratic interference in decision making, fundamental, basically political, facts of life remain.[14] These include the retention of centralized planning, ultimate BCP control over economic life, perhaps deliberate vagueness in spelling out exactly how the "reform" is to operate, and the continuance of essentially bureaucratic individuals in key posts. The primacy of political over economic considerations and the fundamentally timid nature of the Zhivkov leadership is further illustrated by the fact that the New Economic System was killed in practice after August 1968 out of fears that it, too, could lead to Czechoslovak-type political repercussions. At least, economic reform under Zhivkov can be described as administrative tinkering that has not altered the basics of the system.[15]

But what about the traditional mainstay of the Bulgarian economy, namely agriculture? Collectivization began slowly, took off at the height of Chervenkov's rule in 1950, and was completed by 1958. The reasons for this alpha-and-omega of Stalinist economic practice were not only to attain a "higher" and presumably more efficient form of agricultural organization and in the process to benefit industry by freezing surplus labor and generating surplus funds, but also to destroy the foundations of the old peasant society. On the last point it has succeeded, and urbanization has developed to the point that the BCP is now looking for ways to reduce the concentration of population, especially in Sofia, and to promote small and medium-sized towns while offering incentives for young couples in particular to stay in the villages. But the inefficiency of the collectivized system, in Bulgaria as elsewhere, is shown by the fact that, although private plots constitute only 12.5 percent of the total arable land, they account for 39.9 percent of meat production, 55.7 percent of eggs, and 28.5 percent of vegetables.[16]

This is not to say, however, that the spirit of administrative reform has not touched Bulgarian agriculture; on the contrary. Already in the 1950s experimentation with establishing large and professionally managed units had begun, and within Comecon's division of labor Bulgaria has given high priority to agriculture. The essential principle of the innovations in Bulgarian agriculture has been combining the farms themselves with the facilities of the food processing industry and with qualified, skilled administration in what has become known as agro-industrial complexes. They have developed in stages, shifting at first to ever greater and more recently back again to somewhat smaller units, and have been burdened by the same political and bureaucratic problems that have beset industrial reform. The performance of the private plots and even the productivity of Bulgarian agriculture as a whole relative to that of some other East European countries nonetheless testifies to the continuance of traditional Bulgarian farming skills reinforced by the *rabota* (work) ethic of the country's peasantry as well as the application of new techniques.

Although the country cannot be described as truly industrial in the Western sense, the agricultural population is now a minority. As of 1981 the population was 63.5 percent urban[17] and of the GNP 47.8 percent was generated by industry and only 18.6 percent by agriculture.[18] Sofia has grown from a market town and administrative center to a city of 1,155,600, while Plovdiv contains 464,950 inhabitants in a country of 8,905,580.[19] One traditional Bulgarian value highly beneficial to a modern society is the great degree of emphasis and prestige accorded to education, and the country enjoys one of the highest ratios in the world of students to the total population.

If political considerations have loomed large in the scope, direction, and limitations of Bulgarian economic development, the same can certainly be said of cultural life. Briefly, first came a Stalinist era, followed by a minor thaw that began in 1953 echoing the Soviet lead. Frightened by the Hungarian and Polish specters of 1956, in which intellectual and especially literary ferment were key components, the BCP retrenched and established Chervenkov as watchdog in this sphere; a release of cultural energies ensued in 1961 on his demise.

Susbsequent years witnessed an ebb and flow, but the real atmospheric change came under Lyudmila Zhivkova's leadership in the late 1970s. Artists, particularly young ones, could expect a chance to show their worth, and in the realm of scholarship immense attention was paid to Bulgarian history as the 1300th anniversary of Bulgarian statehood in 1981 approached. While basic ideological criteria were maintained and there has certainly not been the diversity and relative objectivity that has characterized Yugoslav scholarship, serious studies have appeared in, for example, social and diplomatic history. Many efforts were crowned by the Bulgarian Academy of Science's impressive 14-volume *History of Bulgaria*.

Since Lyudmila's death, attempts have been made to rewrite her legacy and portray her as an orthodox Communist and devoted friend of the USSR amid indications of a tightening up on the cultural scene. As will be shown shortly, however, many of the patriotic and historical aspects are continuing out of important domestic and foreign political considerations.

FOREIGN POLICY: THE SOVIET CONNECTION

Bulgaria's foreign policy line has in general so closely paralleled that of the Soviet Union that some have quipped that there is no such thing as a Bulgarian foreign policy. It is true that Sofia has followed Moscow's lead in East-West relations and its efforts at establishing special cultural and economic links to distant countries like Japan and Mexico should be seen in that overall context. In the developing countries it actively supports the USSR's friends such as Angola, South Yemen, and Nicaragua. The BCP appears to have a special role at the CPSU's behest vis-a-vis Arab Communist parties, judging by the prominent Communist Middle Eastern exiles who turn up in Bulgaria and incidents such as the Egyptian authorities' engineering a raid on the Bulgarian Embassy but on no other one in Cairo in 1978.

The main focus of Bulgarian foreign relations is still the traditional twofold one of Russia and the Balkans, especially with Yugoslavia over Macedonia. On the first count, the Bulgarian leadership and media have been and are ostentatious in describing the closeness of the country's ties "through the centuries" with Russia and the USSR, omitting, of course, the negative aspects, as is typical of the rewriting of history in Communist polities. Zhivkov himself makes statements that the USSR and Bulgaria "will act as a common organ that has common lungs and a common circulatory system."[20]

Reality, however, is more complex. It is true that Bulgaria can be seen as having benefited from its close ties to the Soviet Union in at least two respects. First, politically, Sofia has in the postwar period "solved" the traditional dilemma facing the Balkan states in modern times in view of their repeated failure to sink their differences and work together, namely to obtain the reliable backing of a great power. This ally may be more inclined to smother rather than just support; its motives in standing behind Bulgaria vis-a-vis Yugoslavia may be less than disinterested; and the degree to which Sofia may take foreign policy "initiatives" toward Yugoslavia without Moscow's clearance or even "suggestion" may be more than questionable, but a great-power protector the country certainly has.

The second advantage to Bulgaria has been economic. Despite the fact that Bulgaria, like Romania, was mercilessly exploited by the USSR immediately after World War II, and despite the assertion that "capitalist" Greece has made impressive economic advances since the war without Soviet "fraternal aid," it remains a fact that the Bulgarian economy has made great strides under a system that has stressed ever closer links to the Soviet Union. The line of argument, and it is one that in Eastern Europe is applied not only to Bulgaria, is that the USSR serves as a reliable supplier of raw materials and technology. It does so on more favorable terms for Bulgaria than the country would encounter on the free market, partly because it takes Bulgaria's less-than-international-quality goods in return. For political reasons, the Soviets cannot allow a loyal Bulgaria to encounter too great difficulties at home and so, the theory goes, have become since at least the 1970s more or less locked into an expensive relationship. Under the circumstances, the nominally client Balkan country, which for reasons of state is obliged to reach out to a powerful ally anyway, actually derives the principal economic benefits. Western economists might argue that both countries lose in such a relationship that is really a poor man's mutual aid club, but the politically important aspect is that an economic case *is* put forward to defend the Bulgarian-Soviet connection.

The negative balance sheet is much more straightforward. While making all due allowance for the country's Russophile traditions, it is argued that the degree of submissiveness displayed by the BCP in all aspects of public life to things Soviet is not in keeping with the national dignity of an independent country on which the Soviets imposed their system. It should be recalled that the Bulgarian attitude toward Russians has always been ambivalent, including a desire for recognition of Bulgaria's historical achievements while acknowledging the obvious successes of the much more numerous Russian people. There have been, moreover, signs that the Bulgarian leadership has recognized this and tried to deflect feelings of injured national pride away from the USSR and off in the direction of the traditional "Serb" enemy, i.e., Yugoslavia, over the Macedonian question.[21]

The postwar Macedonian imbroglio with Yugoslavia has gone through several stages. Between 1944 and 1948, when the Soviets expelled Tito from the bloc, there was much talk of a federation between the two ethnically related countries. But there were formidable obstacles in great power interests and involvement, the question of whether Bulgaria would become one of seven Yugoslav republics or a one-to-one partner with Yugoslavia as a whole, and the problem of the relationship of the Yugoslav and Bulgarian parts of Macedonia to each other and to the other components of the federation. With time Sofia has accused Belgrade of using the project as a scheme to gobble up Bulgaria and other Balkan territories; meanwhile the Yugoslavs claim that the Bulgarians, except perhaps Dimitrov, used the idea as a means of keeping a foot in the Macedonian door and of acting as a pro-Soviet check against Yugoslavia.

The next important stage began around 1958, when Soviet-Yugoslav relations had cooled again to the point that Sofia could enter into open polemics with Moscow's blessings, or at least without its opposition, and thereby make public the more forward policy possibly put through in party circles by the Macedonian-born Yugov in 1956. At that time relatively good Soviet-Yugoslav atmospherics had prevented the BCP from making known its "new" interpretation that the Macedonian Slavs and the areas they inhabit are historically, ethnically, and culturally Bulgarian. These points were increasingly brought out in historical articles. The effective denial was made of Yugoslavia's *de jure* claim to the area, namely the existence of a separate Macedonian Slav nationality, the home of which is within the Yugoslav federation and which defeated Bulgaria had formally recognized at least in the immediate postwar years. The denial took the form of the reduction in the number of ethnic Macedonians recorded in the Pirin area in the Bulgarian census from 187,729 in 1956 to 8,750 in 1965 to none at all in 1975, in that the last-named census omitted nationality categories altogether. The intensity of the polemics themselves has generally fluctuated with the state of Moscow-Belgrade relations of the moment. Sofia has also shown deference to the Soviets' Balkan interests by stressing bilateral over multilateral cooperation with other countries on the peninsula, since Moscow is presumed to mistrust regional groupings outside its control. Nonetheless, amid the increased promotion of the Bulgarian national past in the late 1970s, historical and ethnic claims became increasingly unambiguous. In 1982 and 1983, when Bulgaria's role in the First Balkan War of 1912–13 was extolled on a grand scale in the presence of the Bulgarian military and with the highest political imprimatur, some observers suggested that increasing resentment over the relationship to the USSR could be at the root of what was really an intensified campaign of "surrogate nationalism."[22] There must be some political fire as the cause of the nationalist smoke.

QUESTIONS FOR THE FUTURE

At this juncture it may be convenient to consider some issues for Bulgaria-watching in the coming years, matters that could point to change in a variety of fields. To continue from the preceding section, one question that arises is the Bulgarian-Soviet relationship and its domestic repercussions. The BCP leadership can be described as a client of the CPSU, to which it ultimately owes its power, and to which its professions of loyalty seem ingrained. There are, moreover, close institutional links between the two countries, notably between their respective military and security apparatuses. The close economic relationship develops apace, with the USSR accounting for 48.4 percent of Bulgaria's total exports and 54.7 percent of its total imports in 1981. The domestic strains, however, may also continue, especially if the perception grows that Moscow's and Sofia's interests do not coincide, as was the case with suspected Bulgarian involvement in the 1981 assassination attempt on Pope John Paul II, in which many Bulgarians felt their country was subjected to international shame and humiliation by doing the Soviets' dirty work. It will in any event be interesting to see if the Zhivkov leadership continues to feel the need to use the "surrogate nationalism" approach and if in so doing it can control the nationalist genie once let out of its bottle.

A second area of interest is leadership. The most obvious question deals with Zhivkov's successor but in turn is linked to numerous other issues, such as factions within the BCP, relationships of individuals to their Soviet protector and consequently the effects of Kremlin power struggles on Bulgaria, and the quality of persons who attain high office. The old traditions of instability and military involvement could easily reappear.

A much more complex matter is the relationship of the Soviet-inspired system to the efficient functioning of the economy as a whole. It has been argued that the reason Bulgaria has witnessed no Polish-, Czechoslovak-, or Hungarian-type upheavals and that the economy seems to function more smoothly than those of some other CMEA countries is that the Soviet system works up to a point in developing an originally overwhelming agricultural country like Bulgaria, but that it dysfunctions once the economy attains a certain level of industrialization. If this theory is correct, signs of real structural problems in the Bulgarian economy might appear in the coming years, despite the *rabota* ethic, perhaps accompanied by social unrest and ultimately the political challenges that have appeared elsewhere. Until now the Bulgarian population as a whole has scarcely been politically restive, but this could change, particularly if food and consumer good supplies become tighter and tighter as the system goes into decline. The Zhivkov era has generally presented a picture of stability, but such periods have been rare in Bulgarian history and the present one may well prove transitory.

NOTES

1. Michael B. Petrovich, "The Russian Image in Renascence Bulgaria, 1760–1878," *East European Quarterly*, no. 1, 1967.

2. J. F. Brown, *Bulgaria under Communist Rule* (New York: Praeger, 1970), pp. 266–269.

3. Leon Trotsky, *The War Correspondence of Leon Trotsky: The Balkan Wars, 1912–1913*, George Weissman and Duncan Williams, eds. (New York: Monad Press, 1980), p. 219.

4. Joseph Rothschild, *East Central Europe between the Two World Wars* (A History of East Central Europe, vol. 9) (Seattle: University of Washington Press, 1974), p. 332.

5. See Brown, pp. 173–187.

6. BCP membership figures are as of March and April 1981 and the Fatherland Front statistics are from June 1982.

7. BAU membership has been constant since 1957.

8. As of mid-1983.

9. As of mid-1983.

10. Michael Voslensky, *Nomenklatura: Die Herrschende Klasse der Sowjetunion* (Vienna: Molden, 1980).

11. Iordan Kerov, "Lyudmila Zhivkova, Fragments of a Portrait," RAD Background Report/*253* (Bulgaria), *Radio Free Europe Research,* 27 October 1980.

12. For specialized studies see the bibliography below.

13. *Rabotnickesko Delo,* 31 May 1983.

14. For a much more detailed discussion see the Dobrin work listed below and

15. Cam Hudson, "Bulgarian Economic Reforms: Between the Devil and the Deep Black Sea?" RAD/BR *142* (Bulgaria). *RFER,* 2 July 1982.

16. *Statisticheski Godishnik,* 1982, pp. 267, 281, 290, and 291.

17. Ibid., p. 31.

18. Ibid., p. 145.

19. Ibid., p. 473.

20. *Rabotnichesko Delo,* 20 September 1973.

21. For these issues in general see Patrick Moore, "Macedonia: Perennial Balkan Apple of Discord," *The World Today* (London), no. 10, 1979, pp. 420–428.

22. Patrick Moore, "The Bulgarian Military, Macedonia, and the 'Lyudmila Effect'," Bulgarian Situation Report/5, *RFER,* 18 April 1983, item 1.

BIBLIOGRAPHY

Brown, J. F. *Bulgaria Under Communist Rule.* New York: Praeger, 1970.

Dobrin, Bogoslav. *Bulgarian Economic Development Since World War II.* New York: Praeger, 1973.

Jelavich, Charles and Barbara. *The Establishment of the Balkan National States, 1804–1920* (A History of East-Central Europe, vol. 7). Seattle: University of Washington Press, 1977.

King, Robert R. *Minorities Under Communism: Nationalities as a Source of Tension among Balkan Communist States.* Cambridge, Mass.: Harvard University Press, 1973.

Miller, Marshall Lee. *Bulgaria During the Second World War.* Stanford, Calif.: Stanford University Press, 1975.

Oren, Nissan. *Bulgarian Communism: The Road to Power, 1934–1944.* New York: Columbia University Press, 1971.

———. *Revolution Administered: Agrarianism and Communism in Bulgaria.* Baltimore: Johns Hopkins University Press, 1973.

Pundeff, Marin V. "Bulgarian Nationalism," in Peter F. Sugar and Ivo J. Lederer, eds., *Nationalism in Eastern Europe.* Seattle: University of Washington Press, 1969.

Rothschild, Joseph. *The Communist Party of Bulgaria: Origins and De-
velopment, 1893–1935*. New York: Columbia University Press, 1959.
———. *East Central Europe between the Two World Wars* (A History of East-
Central Europe, vol. 9). Seattle: Washington University Press, 1974.
Todorov, Kosta. *Balkan Firebrand*. Chicago: Ziff-Davis, 1943.
Wolff, Robert Lee. *The Balkans in our Time*. New York: W. W. Norton, 1967.

8 Albania

Nicholas C. Pano

Although it is the smallest and least-developed of the East European Communist states, the People's Socialist Republic of Albania has at various times since 1945 enjoyed a prominence far out of proportion to its size and power. To a considerable degree Albania's notoriety has stemmed from the fact that its rulers have steadfastly pursued the goals they established for themselves on their advent to power in November 1944. These were to maintain and strengthen their hold on Albania, to preserve the country's independence and territorial integrity, to modernize its economy and society, and to build socialism in accordance with the Leninist-Stalinist Soviet model. Since the early 1970s the Albanians have attracted further notice as a consequence of the efforts of their leaders to establish themselves as arbiters of "Marxist-Leninist purity."

Albania's efforts to realize these objectives have brought it into conflict first with Yugoslavia in 1948, then with the Soviet Union and the greater part of the Communist world during the 1960s, and with its most recent patron and ally, China, in the 1970s. By the early 1980s, the People's Socialist Republic of Albania enjoyed the dubious distinction of being the most isolated and dogmatic of the East European party states.

The Albanians are considered to be the descendants of the Illyrians, among the earliest inhabitants of the Balkan Peninsula. In 167 B.C. the Romans conquered the Illyrians. Subsequently, the Albanians were overrun by the Goths, Bulgars, Slavs, Serbs, Normans, Byzantines, and Ottoman Turks. Except for the years 1443–68 when the Albanians temporarily freed themselves from Turkish control under the leadership of their national hero Skanderbeg, Albania remained under Ottoman rule until 1912.

Some 500,000 Albanians, however, who lived in what is today the Yugoslav autonomous province of Kosovo, remained outside the boundaries of the new Albanian state. After winning its independence, Albania experienced a period of political instability that lasted until 1925, when Ahmed Zogu, a northern tribal chief, seized power. In 1928 he proclaimed Albania a monarchy and ruled until 1939, when Italy invaded and occupied Albania.

Following the Italian invasion, Zog fled the country. Zog's departure and the failure of the World War II Allies to recognize his regime in exile set the stage for the power struggle between the wartime Communist and noncommunist resistance forces.

THE COMMUNIST TAKEOVER: 1941–46

Prior to 1941 communism had been only an inconsequential factor in Albanian political life. During the 1920s a handful of Albanian students, intellectuals, and young workers developed an interest in Marxism and sympathy for the new Soviet regime; about twenty-five of them went to the Soviet Union for ideological and political training after the fall from power in December 1924 of the short-lived Fan Noli government, which they had backed. The first Communist cell in Albania was formed in 1927, but the movement attracted little support during the 1930s. When Italy invaded and occupied Albania in April 1939, the Communists were few in number (about 200), lacked leadership and discipline, had little contact with the masses, and were divided into four contending factions.

Differences among these factions being apparently irreconcilable, a number of prominent Communists, among them Enver Hoxha, a thirty-three-year-old schoolteacher turned revolutionary, began to agitate for the dissolution of the existing Communist groups and the formation of a united Albanian Communist party. This plan was given impetus by the Nazi invasion of the USSR in June 1941 and assisted by the Yugoslav Communist party, which had maintained a loose liaison with the Albanian Communists since 1939. In November 1941, at a secret meeting in Tirana, representatives of three of the Albanian groups along with two Yugoslav advisers agreed to establish an Albanian Communist party and elected an eleven-member Central Committee with Hoxha as secretary. The entire party leadership and most of the 130 persons subsequently admitted to the party were relatively young Communists who had not been trained in the Soviet Union and who had no ties with the Comintern. Approximately two-thirds of the original party members were students or young intellectuals of upper- or middle-class backgrounds, and the rest were mostly laborers and artisans.

The most pressing problems confronting the newly formed party were to establish an organizational structure, expand its membership, improve its ties with the people, and gain control of the resistance movement. The realization of these tasks was facilitated by the disorganization of the prewar power elite. King Zog had gone into exile in the early hours of the Italian invasion, taking with him many political leaders; most of those who remained in Albania were collaborating with the Italians, and those who weren't were not yet ready to act. Taking advantage of this leadership vacuum and the organizational and military advice of their Yugoslav advisers, the Communists had made substantial progress, by the end of 1942, toward the realization of their objectives.

By January 1942 they had formed eight district party committees, which in turn established local party organizations to supervise the operations of the cells and other basic party units. As the district and local party organizations began to function, they recruited, on a highly selective basis, individuals who were actively opposing the Italians. The Communist Youth Organization, created in November 1942, also served to swell the ranks of Communist sympathizers among younger Albanians. Throughout the summer of 1942, Communist guerrilla units conducted military actions that they extensively publicized and that seem to have been well received by the people. Communist propaganda efforts were further enhanced when the party newspaper *Zeri i popullit* commenced publication in August.

With their numbers growing and their prestige rising, the Communists convened a meeting of representatives of all the Albanian resistance organizations at Peza in September 1942. The Peza Conference established the National Liberation Movement (NLM), a coalition of the majority of the active Albanian antifascist groups, and authorized the creation of popularly elected national liberation councils throughout Albania to conduct the war effort on the local level and to exercise political control when the occupation forces had been expelled. Better organized and more politically astute than the other groups comprising the NLM, the Communists easily dominated the organization. Thus, by the stratagem of an antifascist popular front, the Communists had assumed by the end of 1942 a leading, though not exclusive, role in the struggle to liberate Albania.

In November 1942 a number of prominent liberal and moderate politicians established a staunchly anticommunist organization, the National Front (NF), which advocated the formation of a republican regime in Albania after the war, and the preservation of the ethnic Albanian state created in 1941 by the Axis powers with the incorporation of the Yugoslav province of Kosovo-Metohija into Albania. During the first half of 1943 both the NLM and NF conducted military operations against the Italians and waged war with each other; the NF forces were larger, but the NLM appears to have been more active in fighting the enemy and more effective in publicizing its successes.

As a result of peacemaking efforts by patriotic noncollaborationist Albanian politicians and members of the British military mission, which had entered Albania in April, the NLM and the NF sought to resolve their differences on August 2, 1943, with the Mukaj Agreement. This pact provided for equal representation of both groups on a "Committee for the Salvation of Albania," designed to direct the war effort; the reorganization of the national liberation councils to ensure proportional representation for the NF; and the holding of a plebiscite in Kosovo after the war to determine the future of the region.

The Albanian Communist leadership refused to approve the agreement, however, fearing loss of NLM control to a coalition of NF and noncommunist elements, and their Yugoslav advisers objected to the proposed plebiscite on the grounds that Kosovo-Metohija was an integral part of Yugoslavia. The Communists then called for an all-out struggle against both the NF and the Germans, who had occupied Albania in September following the Italian surrender. Repudiation of the Mukaj Agreement and the resumption of warfare with the NF led to the resignation from the NLM of Abas Kupi, its last important noncommunist leader. Kupi, an ardent monarchist, now formed the Legality Organization, which favored the restoration of King Zog. As 1943 drew to a close, the NLM found itself opposed by the combined forces of the German Army, the pro-German Albanian puppet government, the NF, and the Legality Organization.

The winter of 1943–44 marked the turning point of the Albanian power struggle. Despite the best efforts of the formidable military forces of the opposition and the ravages of one of the bitterest winters in Albanian history, the NLM managed to survive and in turn launched a massive offensive against its enemies in the spring of 1944. Aware of the consequences of an NLM victory, the British military mission made repeated efforts to arrange a truce among the contending Albanian factions and to bring the noncommunist forces into the war against the Germans. But their efforts were unsuccessful, and as a result, during the final stages of the "national liberation war," the Communists had little difficulty in convincing most of the people that their opponents were "collaborationists," "traitors," and "war criminals."

When most of southern Albania had been freed from Nazi control, the NLM convened a congress on May 24 at Permet. At this meeting the NLM became the National Liberation Front (NLF), Hoxha was appointed supreme commander of the National Liberation Army, King Zog was forbidden to return to Albania, and all treaties concluded by the Albanian government prior to 1939 were declared null and void. In late October, when about three-fourths of Albania had been liberated, the NLF convoked a congress at Berat. The congress established a provisional government headed by Hoxha and dominated by Communists. The NLF pledged to hold free elections for a constituent assembly, and expressed its desire to maintain good relations "with the great allies, Great Britain, the Soviet Union, and the United States."

By late November 1944 the Germans evacuated their last position in Albania and the Communist-dominated provisional government was installed in Tirana, with the apparent support of the majority of the people and with the sympathy (because of the NLF contribution to the war effort) of the U.S. and British governments. Thus, even before the end of World War II in Europe, communism had triumphed in Albania, the only country in Eastern Europe except Yugoslavia where Communists had seized power without any Soviet assistance. The young, ambitious, nationalistic, indigenous Communist leadership that had emerged during the war now confronted the immediate task of consolidating and legitimatizing its authority.

During 1945–46 the Communists moved swiftly to strengthen their hold on the Albanian political system. After eliminating virtually all their active opponents by purges and "war crimes" trials, they renamed the NLF the Democratic Front (DF) and in its name ran a slate of Communists and their sympathizers for the constituent assembly convoked by the provisional government. On December 2, 1945, the DF slate polled 93 percent of the ballots cast, and on January 11, 1946 the newly elected constituent assembly formally abolished the monarchy and proclaimed Albania a "people's republic." On March 14 the new constitution of the People's Republic of Albania was promulgated. Thus, by the spring of 1946, the Communists had legitimized their position in Albania. Enver Hoxha, secretary general of the Albanian Communist party, was now also prime minister, foreign minister, defense minister, and commander-in-chief of the armed forces in the new government.

POLITICAL TRENDS, 1946–81

Between 1946 and 1956 Hoxha successfully withstood three major challenges to his leadership. The first came from Koci Xoxe, Hoxha's powerful deputy, who, representing the older, less well-educated proletarian faction of the party, favored an accelerated socialist revolution and exclusive ties with Yugoslavia and the Soviet Union. With the United States and Britain becoming increasingly hostile, Hoxha temporarily accepted the Xoxe program in 1946, but the Yugoslavs, unplacated, backed Xoxe in the spring of 1948 in an effort to overthrow Hoxha. Hoxha, however, exploited the Soviet-Yugoslav split, which occurred at this time, and succeeded in purging Xoxe and his followers at the First Congress of the Albanian Party of Labor (APL) in November 1948. After a public trial, Xoxe was executed in June 1949.

The next major challenge to Hoxha's leadership came in the early 1950s, when a segment of the Albanian leadership headed by Politburo members Bedri Spahiu and Tuk Jakova began to urge, among other things, a slowdown in the industrialization program, a delay in the collectivization of agriculture, a softer line toward religion, a "democratization" of the party, and, after 1953, the initiation of a program of de-Stalinization. Hoxha, who had during the late 1940s enthusiastically embraced the Stalinist line, strenuously opposed these positions as hindrances to the successful construction of socialism, and by June 1955 he had purged most of his principal antagonists, including Jakova and Spahiu.

The final challenge to Hoxha's leadership during the 1950s came on essentially the same issues at the Tirana city party conference in April 1956. His opposition this time came mainly from middle-ranking bureaucrats and military officers, but Hoxha again prevailed and definitively established his control over the APL at the Third Party Congress in May, when he filled the Politburo and Central Committee with his loyal followers. There were no further significant challenges to his leadership until the 1970s.

Hoxha's success was due not only to his superior political skills and personal popularity but also to the support of the Soviet Union. At the Albanian Third Party Congress, however, after perfunctorily endorsing the line proclaimed at the Soviet Twentieth Party Congress and promising to improve relations with Yugoslavia, Hoxha proceeded to defy the USSR by refusing to rehabilitate Xoxe and announcing his intention to collectivize agriculture rapidly and to accelerate the pace of industrialization.

In retrospect, it is clear that Hoxha's decisive victory over his domestic opposition in 1956 and his public defiance of the Soviet Union at the Third Party Congress represented a major turning point in Albania's postwar history. Developments both within and outside Albania during 1956 enhanced Hoxha's position and further unified the Albanian ruling elite. The experiences of Poland and Hungary convinced it that any serious deviation from the Stalinist model would lead to internal unrest and perhaps rebellions, which would, in turn, provide the Soviets and Yugoslavs with an excuse to intervene in Albania and impose a regime more to their liking. This world view united the Albanian leadership and profoundly influenced its policy decisions during the late 1950s and early 1960s.

Tirana's persistence in Stalinism along with its unwillingness to align its foreign and economic policies with those of the USSR culminated in the Soviet-Albanian ideological and diplomatic break in December 1961. Albania's successful defiance of the USSR on this occasion was made possible by support from China as well as by the solidarity of her own leaders, the only member of Hoxha's inner circle to question the party's stand toward the Soviet Union having been purged over a year before the split. Between 1961 and 1964, the most pressing concern of the Albanian regime was to prevent an economic collapse following the termination of all Soviet aid programs. By 1964, when the Chinese had filled this gap and the economic situation had been stabilized, Hoxha moved to implement his ideological and cultural revolution, whose main features he had outlined in 1961.

As conceived by Hoxha, the ideological and cultural revolution would, first, destroy those attitudes, traditions, and institutions that had up to this point impeded the regime's efforts to build a modern nation-state. Specifically, he aimed to eliminate the influence of religion, excessive family and sectional loyalties, prejudices toward women, "bourgeois" economic and social outlooks, poor labor discipline, and a general indifference toward political authority. Second, the movement sought to ensure that Albania, unlike the Soviet Union and the East European party states, would not fall into the revisionist heresy and would make the transition to communism in accordance with the principles of Marxism-Leninism, as interpreted by Tirana. Hoxha appears to have been influenced and encouraged by China's unfolding cultural revolution during the 1960s, and this common development served to strengthen the bonds between Tirana and Beijing at this time. But the Albanian cultural revolution, unlike the Chinese, did not mask a power struggle between rival factions in the leadership and was consequently better planned and controlled.

At its height, 1966–69, the Albanian cultural revolution took the form of a massive party attack on the military and state bureaucracies in an attempt to forestall the rise of an Albanian "new class" and to strengthen party supremacy in all areas of the nation's life. One of the most spectacular aspects of this movement, not yet duplicated in any of the East European socialist countries, was the destruction of the institutional church and the proclamation of Albania in 1967 as the world's first atheist state. Other noteworthy results of the cultural revolution were the achievement of the total collectivization of agriculture, the reduction in size of collective farmers' private plots, a women's emancipation campaign, and the reform of the educational system.

As China phased out its cultural revolution during 1969, there was apparently agitation by some party leaders as well as by intellectuals and young people for Albania to follow Beijing's example. Although the objectives of the ideological and cultural revolution had not been fully realized, Hoxha recognized that the Albanians were ready for a respite from the constant demands that had been made on them since 1966. Between 1970 and 1973 Albania thus enjoyed a period of somewhat relaxed party controls and, like China, opened its door a crack to tourists and other foreign influences.

Between 1973 and 1975, however, Hoxha reversed his course. In response to what he perceived to be dangerous developments and threats to his leadership, he cracked down, successively, on the youth and cultural sectors, the military, and the technocrats.

In March 1973 Hoxha became alarmed by reports of mounting school dropouts and academic failures at all levels of instruction; high rates of unauthorized absences from work by young people; a substantial increase in crimes committed by juveniles; the growing popularity of "western" dress, hair styles, and music among the country's younger generation; and the open repudiation of "socialist realism" by some writers and artists, who exhorted their colleagues to turn to the "West" for inspiration. Consequently, the Albanian party leader began to reinstitute strict party controls over youths and intellectuals, and major leadership changes took place in the League of Albanian Writers and Artists and the Union of Albanian Labor Youth. Todi Lubonja, Fadil Pacrami, and Agim Mero, the three Central Committee members who had apparently argued convincingly for the more moderate line toward youth and culture, were purged.

By 1974, aware of the military establishment's desire to decrease party influence in such areas as military training and discipline, to downgrade the importance of mass popular mobilization (Hoxha's concept of "people's war") in defense strategy, and to lessen Albanian dependence on China, Hoxha seems to have feared a military putsch. Accordingly, between July and December 1974, he deposed the entire top level of the military establishment, including Defense Minister and Politburo member Beqir Balluku, reputedly the fourth-ranking member of Albania's ruling hierarchy.

During 1975, when the differences between the technocrats and party leadership over planning priorities for the 1976–80 five-year plan and the desirability of Albania's seeking new sources of economic aid became acute, Hoxha launched a massive purge of the nation's economic and managerial elites. This move also provided him with scapegoats for the failure of the 1971–75 five-year plan to realize its goals.

Thus, by the mid-1970s, the internal stability and cohesive leadership that had characterized Albanian politics for two decades had broken down. At both the Seventh APL Congress (1976) and the Eighth Congress (1981) there were numerous changes in the composition of the Politburo and Central Committee. The cabinet shake-ups that began in the mid-1970s became a regular feature of Albanian political life during the late 1970s and early 1980s. It was against this background that Prime Minister Mehmet Shehu, the second-ranking member of the Albanian ruling elite, reportedly committed suicide in December 1981.

These extensive leadership changes appear to be attributable to three major factors. First, differences had obviously developed within the Albanian leadership over such issues as the Sino-Albanian relationship, the regime's hard-line cultural policies, and, above all, the definition of the respective roles of the party and the state bureaucracy in the economic and military sectors. Second, Hoxha found it necessary to remove from top positions individuals loyal to him when their failure to carry out their responsibilities posed a threat to his regime. Third, Albania's ruler began to lay the groundwork for the orderly transfer of power following his death by replacing some of his aging colleagues with younger, better-educated, militant Communists. It appeared that Hoxha also hoped to undercut his domestic opposition and to make his policies binding on his eventual successors by incorporating his views on key ideological and political issues into the new Albanian constitution promulgated in December 1976.

POLITICAL STRUCTURE

According to the 1976 constitution, the Albanian Party of Labor is "the vanguard of the working class and the sole leading political force of the state and society" (Article 3). As emphasized throughout this document, the party is dominant in all aspects of the nation's life.

In organization and structure the APL resembles its East European and Soviet counterparts. Theoretically, the party congress that meets every five years is the APL's highest organ, but in actuality it merely approves the leadership's policies and its nominees to the Central Committee. The APL Central Committee elected in 1981 consists of 119 members and generally meets twice a year. In reality the Politburo and Secretariat are the most important party organs. The Politburo is the locus of power in the APL and the nation's leading policy-making body. In 1983, it consisted of sixteen members (eleven voting members and five nonvoting candidates). The APL Secretariat, which supervises

Table 1 Composition of the Albanian Party of Labor, 1948–81
(In Percentage of Total Membership)

Year	Laborers	Peasants	White-Collar Workers	Others
1948	23	67	10	0
1952	12	31	55	2
1956	20	31	45	4
1961	29	27	42	2
1966	33	26	37	4
1971	36	30	34	0
1976	38	29	33	0
1981	38	29	33	0

Source: *Zeri i popullit,* November 11, 1948; April 1, 1952; May 26, 1956; February 14, 1961; November 2, 1966; November 2, 1971; November 2, 1976; November 2, 1981.

the work of the party bureaucracy, is headed by First Secretary Enver Hoxha and four other secretaries.

Below the national level there are party organizations at district, city, village, and ward levels. There were also in 1981 approximately 3,000 basic party organizations on farms and in factories, offices, and military units. Although about 64 percent of the Albanian population live in rural areas, a majority of the basic party organizations are in the cities. This discrepancy reflects the fact that the party, except during the late 1940s, has recruited its members mainly from among office workers and laborers. As Table 1 shows, white-collar workers comprised the largest social group in the party during the 1950s and 1960s. Since the onset of the ideological and cultural revolution, the leadership has sought to increase the representation of laborers to give the party a more strongly proletarian flavor. After holding steadily at about 10 percent between 1948 and 1961, the proportion of women party members rose to about 23 percent in 1971 and 30 percent in 1981 as a consequence of the women's emancipation campaign.

Since 1948 APL membership has averaged between 3 and 4 percent of the total population, the smallest ratio of party members to population in Eastern Europe. As Table 2 indicates, there was only a modest growth in APL membership between 1948 and 1961. This reflects the frequent purging of the party ranks that accompanied the leadership struggles between 1948 and 1956. But membership has more than doubled in the two decades since 1961.

Since only a small percentage of the population belongs to the party, various mass organizations serve as its auxiliaries. The most important of these is the Democratic Front (DF), the mass political organization open to all citizens of voting age (eighteen years and over). In theory the principal function of the DF is to nominate and campaign for candi-

Table 2 Growth of the Albanian Party of Labor, 1941–81

Year	Membership
1941	130
1944	2,800
1948	45,382
1952	44,418
1956	48,644
1961	53,659
1966	66,327
1971	86,985
1976	101,500
1981	122,600

Sources: *Rruga e Partise,* 6 (November 1959), p. 88; *History of the Party of Labor of Albania* (Tirana, 1971), pp. 327, 369, 411, 474, 572, *Zeri i popullit,* November 2, 1971; November 2, 1976; November 2, 1981.

dates for local and national elective posts. In practice it is the chief agency for the transmission of the party line to the masses and for the mobilization of popular support for the policies of the regime.

The Union of Albanian Labor Youth, comprised of young adults between fourteen and twenty-six, in addition to inculcating loyalty to the regime, serves as a recruiting agency for the party. The United Trade Union of Albania is charged with maintaining high worker morale and a high level of productivity among the nation's laborers. It also seeks to ensure that party and state economic directives are carried out. A major responsibility of the Union of Albanian Women is to raise the economic and social consciousness of the nation's females by encouraging women to enter the labor force and to become more actively involved in social and cultural activities. Since APL members hold key leadership and staff positions in the mass organizations, their activities are thus closely controlled by the party.

The structure of the Albanian government is similiar to that of other Communist states. According to the 1976 constitution, the 250-member People's Assembly, which is elected for a four-year term and meets twice a year in two- or three-day sessions, is the "supreme organ of state power." The constitution further stipulates that all actions taken by the Assembly must conform to "the general line and orientations of the Albanian Party of Labor" (Article 67). In practice the Assembly does little more than approve the legislative proposals submitted to it and ratify the actions taken by the government and the Assembly Presidium between legislative sessions. Although the Assembly elects its Presidium and the cabinet, the composition of both these bodies is determined by the party.

The fifteen-member Assembly Presidium, which is dominated by top-ranking party members, serves as the nation's legislature when the Assembly is not in session. In addition it awards decorations, ratifies treaties and international agreements, appoints and discharges diplomatic officials, and supervises the work of the district people's councils. The Presidium chairman is the Albanian head of state, an exclusively ceremonial position in the Hoxha regime.

Headed by the prime minister, the Council of Ministers is the government's leading executive and administrative authority. It serves as the instrument whereby APL policies and directives are transmitted to the state bureaucracy. With few exceptions, cabinet ministers have been members of either the Politburo or the Central Committee. The 1976 constitution created a Presidium of the Council of Ministers, chaired by the prime minister and comprised of all deputy prime ministers. This body's main function is to check on the implementation of cabinet decisions and directives.

Local government organs consist of people's councils at the district, city, and village levels. The authority of these bodies is exercised primarily through their executive boards. They have jurisdiction over administrative, economic, and sociocultural matters within their respective geographic areas. Their decisions, however, may be set aside by action of a higher-ranking people's council or the Assembly Presidium.

The Supreme Court, elected by the People's Assembly for a four-year term, is the highest judicial organ. A reform of the judiciary in 1968 abolished the district appeals courts. On the local level justice is dispensed by the people's courts, whose judges are elected by their constituents for four-year terms. Appeals—which have become rare in recent years—of decisions of the people's courts are heard directly by the Supreme Court. Rounding out the legal establishment is the Attorney General's Office, which represents the government in legal proceedings and verifies the constitutionality of legislation and ministerial decrees. With the explanation that the process of establishing the socialist legal system had been completed, the Ministry of Justice was abolished in September 1966.

Three constitutions have been promulgated in Albania under the Communist regime. According to party spokesmen, each of these reflects a specific stage of Albania's "uninterrupted revolution."

Since Albania was only in the initial stage of its socialist revolution, the March 1946 constitution made no mention of such matters as the special role of the Communist party, the collectivization of agriculture, the nationalization of trade, or other aspects of the socialist order. It was therefore necessary to frame a new constitution correcting these shortcomings in July 1950, as Albania embarked on her program of intensive socialist development. This document was essentially similar to those adopted by the East European "people's democracies" in the late 1940s and early 1950s.

At the Sixth APL Congress in November 1971, Enver Hoxha announced that Albania had entered "the stage of the complete construction of socialist society." In the light of this development and the experience of the ideological and cultural revolution, he claimed that the 1950 constitution had become obsolete. It was, however, only after he had squelched his domestic opposition that Hoxha gave a high priority to the drafting of a new constitution in October 1975. The tone and content of this document, which was drafted by a committee dominated by Hoxha and his associates, seem to have been influenced by the developments of the early 1970s in Albania. Although the 1976 constitution did not significantly alter the structure of the Albanian political system, it did change the name of the country to the People's Socialist Republic of Albania (Article 1). This latter gesture was intended to underscore Tirana's contention that Albania, alone among the European Communist states, was building socialism according to the tenets of Marxism-Leninism.

The constitution emphasizes the supremacy of the party in every sphere. In commenting on this underlying theme of the constitution, Albanian leaders have repeatedly stressed that they have no intention of limiting the party's role to that of a guide or teacher, as has allegedly occurred in some "revisionist" and "ex-socialist" countries. Rather, in Albania the party will continue to be deeply involved in the direction and control of every activity and institution. The constitution thus is intended to ensure there will be no retreat from the hard-line Stalinist domestic, military, and foreign policies that Albania has steadfastly pursued since the late 1940s, and which have come to distinguish it from the remainder of the East European socialist community.

Specifically, the constitution proclaims Marxism-Leninism as the nation's official ideology (Article 3); commits Albania to support "revolutionary" national and social liberation struggles (Article 15); abolishes private property except for wages, personal residences, and articles for personal or family use (Articles 16, 23); prohibits the granting of concessions to "bourgeois and revisionist capitalist monopolies and states," or obtaining credits from them (Article 28); forbids the practice of any religion and obliges the government to maintain a program of "atheistic propaganda" to develop a "scientific materialistic outlook in people" (Article 37); requires universal military service "for the defense of the socialist homeland" (Article 62); stipulates that the armed forces are led by the party and designates the first secretary of the

Albanian Party of Labor as commander-in-chief of the armed forces (Articles 88, 89); declares it an act of treason for anyone "to sign or approve . . . the surrender or occupation of the country" (Article 90); and bans the establishment of foreign military bases and the stationing of foreign troops on Albanian soil (Article 94).

LEADERSHIP AND CHANGING ELITE PATTERNS

Between 1956 and 1971, the Albanian leadership was among the most stable in Eastern Europe. During this time only one Politburo member, Liri Belishova, and five Central Committee members were removed from their posts for ideological or political errors. Enver Hoxha (born 1908) was the most important member of the ruling elite. His inner circle included Politburo members such as Prime Minister Mehmet Shehu (born 1913), Central Committee Secretary Hysni Kapo (born 1915), Defense Minister Beqir Balluku (born 1917), cultural specialist Manush Myftiu (born 1919), ideologist Ramiz Alia (born 1925), and economic trouble-shooter Spiro Koleka (born 1908).

Party leadership posts up to the mid-1970s were held almost exclusively by early converts to communism who had fought in the national liberation war. About half of the fifty-three members elected to the Central Committee at the Fourth APL Congress in 1961 were also related by blood or marriage. With few exceptions, those elected to the Central Committee and other important party posts between 1956 and 1971 were recruited from the ranks of the party and state bureaucracies headquartered in Tirana. The leadership was also relatively young. The average age of the Albanian Politburo up to the mid-1960s was less than fifty.

The unity of the Albanian leaders appears to have been strongest during the 1960s when there seems to have been a consensus on key domestic and international issues. Hoxha's associates also seem to have appreciated that they owed their positions to the powerful APL first secretary and that their fates were tied to his.

By the early 1970s, in the aftermath of the intensive phase of the ideological and cultural revolution, the solidarity of the APL leadership began to crumble as the cultural, military, and economic elites sought to assert a greater voice in decision making in their respective domains. At this point Hoxha responded to what he perceived as a threat to his regime by purging or disciplining the bulk of the first generation Albanian specialists in these areas. By this action the APL first secretary underscored his determination to prevent the emergence of powerful and potentially disruptive interest groups within the leadership and demonstrated that he would not hesitate to take harsh actions even against long-time colleagues and former friends. Of the thirty-five Central Committee members dropped from that body or demoted to candidate status between 1973 and 1976, three had been elected in 1948, two in 1952, eleven in 1956, seven in 1961, five in 1966, and seven in 1971.

As Hoxha began to rebuild the party and state leaderships during the 1970s and 1980s, he turned, in a marked departure from past practice, to the district party secretaries and to successful farm and factory managers for the new blood this task required. For the most part, the new Politburo and Central Committee members elected in 1976 and 1981 and the recent appointees to the cabinet were relatively young, in their forties and early fifties, with fairly extensive experience at the local level. Presumably, they are all staunch supporters of Hoxha's policies. It remains to be seen whether they have the requisite talents to deal with the problems they have inherited and whether they will find it any easier than their predecessors to live up to Hoxha's expectations.

In November 1976, Lenka Cuko, first secretary of the Lushnje district party organization, was elevated to the Politburo. This marked the first female representation in this body since 1960. Further underscoring the growing role of women in the APL, Cuko was appointed to the Central Committee Secretariat in 1983. Women also comprised about 20 percent of the Central Committee elected in 1981. At the local and district levels, the percentage of women holding party offices has increased, along with that of officials of proletarian background. The latter now comprise about 85 percent of local party officeholders. Although former laborers and individuals from working-class backgrounds reportedly held 40 percent of the administrative positions in the state bureaucracy in 1978, there are no data available concerning the representation of this group in the party central bureaucracy.

During the 1970s and 1980s there were significant changes within the top echelons of the Albanian leadership. As noted previously Beqir Balluku, the fourth-ranking member of the APL hierarchy was purged in 1974. Hysni Kapo, the third-ranking member of the ruling elite, who supervised the day-to-day operations of the APL for Hoxha, died in 1979 following a lengthy illness. Another long-time Hoxha confidant, Spiro Koleka, appears to have voluntarily retired from the Politburo in 1981 to set an example for other aging party cadres.

The most dramatic change within the leadership occurred in December 1981 when the Albanian press and radio announced that Prime Minister Mehmet Shehu, the second-ranking member of the party hierarchy and reputed favorite to succeed Hoxha, had committed suicide. Subsequently, Hoxha accused Shehu of having been a "traitor" and a "longtime foreign intelligence agent." In this connection, Shehu was alleged to have engaged in a conspiracy to assassinate Hoxha. While these charges seem to be groundless, it does appear that some differences over foreign and domestic policy issues had developed between Hoxha and Shehu. Perhaps, the most important of these disagreements concerned the impending political succession in Albania.

As he began to plan for the transfer of power following his passing, Hoxha seems to have concluded that Shehu, who had not enjoyed the best of health in recent years, was not the logical candidate to succeed him. In addition to his age and health, Shehu was unpopular with younger Albanians, including many party members and officials. Furthermore, Hoxha appears to have lacked confidence in Shehu's ability to oversee the administration of the nation's bureaucracy and the increasingly complex economy. Indeed, during the late 1970s and early 1980s, First Deputy Prime Minister Adil Carcani had been given a growing measure of responsibility for the management of the government. Relations between the two leaders deteriorated following Shehu's unsuccessful attempt to forestall a move by Hoxha to reduce further the power of the prime minister or possibly to remove him from office. Having incurred the displeasure of Hoxha and been confronted with the prospect of accepting a secondary role in the ruling elite, Shehu reportedly took his own life.

Adil Carcani became prime minister in January 1982. During 1982, there was an extensive purge of Shehu's proteges and supporters in the party and government. The regime also instituted a propaganda campaign to vilify Shehu.

Ramiz Alia appears to have emerged as the major victor from the political upheavals that engulfed Albania during the 1970s and early 1980s. A member of the APL Central Committee since 1948, and of the Secretariat and Politburo since 1960, Alia in 1983 was clearly the second-ranking member of the party leadership and the prime candidate to succeed Hoxha. In November 1982, he was appointed, in addition to his other duties, to the post of chairman of the Presidium of the People's Assembly to give him broader public exposure. Since his appointment to his new position, Alia has traveled extensively in Albania, defending the policies of Hoxha.

Despite the turmoil in the Albanian leadership, Enver Hoxha appeared to be firmly entrenched in power as 1983 drew to a close. With the death of Tito, Hoxha has become the senior, in length of service, of the Communist rulers of Eastern Europe. Barring any major leadership changes in Albania prior to the demise of Hoxha, it seems likely that Alia, Carcani, along with such recent Politburo appointees as Simon

Table 3 Sources of Albanian National Income by Sectors (In Percentages)

Sector	1938	1950	1960	1970	1978
Industry and construction	4.4	15.6	43.6	52.6	52.6
Agriculture	92.4	76.3	44.4	34.5	37.9
Transportation, trade, etc.	3.2	8.1	12.0	12.9	9.5

Sources: Harilla Papajorgji, *The Development of Socialist Industry and Its Prospects in the People's Republic of Albania* (Tirana, 1964), p. 137; *35 Years of Socialist Albania* (Tirana, 1981), p. 116.

Stefani, Muho Asllani, Lenka Cuko, and Foto Cami will assume significant roles in a post-Hoxha regime.

SOCIOECONOMIC AND CULTURAL TRENDS

In 1945 Albania was a war-devastated, underdeveloped agricultural nation. After devoting its initial efforts to repairing the damage Albania had suffered during World War II, the regime moved swiftly to nationalize industry and to set the stage for agricultural collectivization. The long-range economic objective of the Albanian leaders since the late 1940s has been to transform their homeland from a backward agrarian nation into a modern industrial-agricultural state. Although this ambition had not been fully realized by 1978, Albania had, as Table 3 demonstrates, made considerable progress toward this goal.

In the development of the economy, Albania's rulers have also, owing to the nation's pre- and post-World War II experiences, given a high priority to making their homeland virtually self-sufficient and thus largely immune from external economic coercion. Albania's persistence in this policy since the late 1940s contributed to the development of tensions in its relations with Belgrade and subsequently with Moscow. Both Yugoslavia and the Soviet Union regarded Albania's development strategy as unrealistic, uneconomic, and, above all, inimical to their own interests.

Albania embarked on its program of long-range economic planning in 1951. From the outset the leadership has given a high priority to the rapid development of industry as well as to the exploitation of the country's natural resources such as oil, chrome, copper, iron, and hydropower. As is evident from Table 4, the industrial sector registered relatively high growth rates during the first and second five-year plans because of Albania's minuscule industrial base. The dramatic falloff in industrial growth during 1961–65 reflects the halt in Soviet aid programs in 1961. Albania experienced a high level of growth between 1966 and 1970, owing to the assistance received from China and the

Table 4   Average Annual Growth Rate of Albanian National Income by Sector
(In Percentages)

	1st FYP 1951–55	2nd FYP 1956–60	3rd FYP 1961–65	4th FYP 1966–70	5th FYP 1971–75	6th FYP 1976–80
National Income	11.2	7.0	5.8	9.1	6.7	5.2
Industry	21.5	18.9	8.0	13.4	8.7	6.1
Agriculture	4.8	0.6	6.2	4.1	5.9	4.0
Construction	16.7	18.6	5.0	9.4	3.2	4.4
Transportation, trade, etc.	24.2	7.6	1.8	8.0	2.0	5.4

Source: *30 Vjet Shqiperi Socialiste* (Tirana, 1974), p. 187. *Zeri i popullit,* November 5, 1976; November 4, 1981.

strict discipline imposed on the labor force during the ideological and cultural revolution. The decline in industrial growth since 1970 stems from the breakdown of labor discipline in the early 1970s and the apparent inability of the Albanians to absorb the aid provided by China because of shortages of skilled labor and management deficiencies. These as yet unresolved problems as well as a reduction in the volume of Chinese aid for the 1976–80 period appear to have resulted in a cut of about 33 percent in the original industrial growth rate estimates for this period. Nevertheless, the Albanians by 1980 were able to produce domestically 90 percent of the nation's requirements for spare parts and about 85 percent of their consumer goods needs. The country's first steel mill had also commenced operations by that date.

As in other Communist-ruled nations, Albanian economic planners have been deeply concerned by the chronic problems plaguing the agricultural sector of the economy. After abandoning his initial collectivization drive in 1954 in response to a Soviet request, Hoxha launched a massive collectivization campaign in 1956. By 1960 approximately 86 percent of the nation's farm land was incorporated into the socialist sector. The collectivization drive, however, caused much resentment in the countryside and resulted in a temporary decline in farm output. Full collectivization was achieved in 1967, and since that time the size of farmers' private plots has been reduced to about a quarter to three-quarters of an acre. During the 1960s and early 1970s Albanian agriculture regularly achieved only about 50 percent of its assigned production targets. In 1976 the regime claimed the nation had achieved self-sufficiency in the production of bread grains and would meet virtually all its food needs from domestic production in 1980. To improve agricultural output, the government has expanded the output of chemical fertilizers and sought to increase the number of agricultural specialists.

Up to the late 1970s Albania has been able to develop and survive largely as a result of the outside economic and technical assistance it has received. In July 1978, as a consequence of the growing ideological rift between Beijing and Tirana, China, which had been Albania's chief foreign aid donor since the 1960s, abruptly terminated its economic and military assistance programs in Albania. This development resulted in Albania's failure to achieve its goal of near economic self-sufficiency in 1980 and, along with several natural disasters, assured that the targets set for the Sixth Five-Year Plan (1976–80) would not be realized.

Between 1944 and 1982 the Albanian population increased from 1,100,000 to 2,800,000. Approximately 65 percent of Albanians alive in 1982 have grown up in the period of Communist rule; because of Albania's policy of isolation, few have had any direct contacts with foreigners or the outside world. According to 1975 census data, peasants comprised about 50 percent of the population, laborers 36 percent, and white-collar workers 14 percent. Approximately 64 percent of the population still lived in rural areas.

Since 1945 Albania has had the highest birthrate of any European country and between 1971 and 1982 the population grew at an average of 2.2 percent annually. At the beginning of the 1980s Albania's population was predominantly young, with about 37 percent under age 15.

The ultimate social objective of the APL leadership has been to create the "new socialist person." In order to achieve this goal the regime has emphasized the need to wage unrelenting class war. Consequently there have been campaigns to eradicate "bourgeois" attitudes and outlooks, emancipate women, destroy religion, break down the distinction between physical and mental labor, and bridge the gulf between the urban and rural areas.

Although some progress has been registered in all these areas, it seems unlikely the Albanians will be any more successful in efforts to create their "new socialist person" than have their comrades in Eastern Europe and the Soviet Union. Despite the intensive regimentation of the ideological and cultural revolution and the post-1973 cultural crackdown, the Albanian press in 1983 still devoted much space to exposing the "social evils" that persisted in the country. The alacrity with which Albanian youth and intellectuals embraced "alien influences" during the relaxation of the early 1970s suggests that the regime's social doctrines command only a superficial allegiance. Furthermore, the government concedes it can do little to halt the transmission of "bourgeois ideas and values" into Albania by means of foreign radio and television broadcasts.

Although subjected to what are probably the most rigid ideological strictures among the European Communist states, Albanian culture, measured in terms of its output and breadth, has flourished under the

Communist regime. The rapid expansion of the educational system and the virtual elimination of illiteracy in the country have played major roles in this development.

In the early 1980s there were over 700,000 students enrolled in the school system. About one in four Albanians was attending an educational institution. The schools are one of the most important agencies of political socialization in Albania. A 1969 educational reform was designed to upgrade the ideological aspects of the instructional program. Under the reformed curriculum students spend six and a half months in academic study, two and a half months at physical labor, and one month in military training each year. To be eligible to attend an institution of higher education, a student must work for one year on a factory or farm.

With the growth of an educated and literate population, there has been a marked increase in literary and artistic output. Most works of fiction center around the themes of the war of national liberation and the building of socialism. By the early 1980s there were over 1200 books published annually in Albania. Music, drama, art, and the cinema have also developed in recent years. These, too, are closely bound by the canons of "socialist realism."

With the complete electrification of the country in 1970, radio and television have become increasingly important. Most significantly for the regime, they have brought the Albanian masses into contact with foreign cultures and ideologies. As of 1983 it did not appear as if Albania was jamming foreign broadcasts.

FOREIGN POLICY AND FOREIGN ECONOMIC RELATIONS

There have been four distinct phases in Albania's international relations since the end of World War II. Between 1944 and 1948 Albania was a Yugoslav dependency and its foreign policy was strongly influenced by Belgrade. During 1949–60 Albania was a Soviet satellite and its external policies were closely aligned with those of the other members of the Communist camp. From 1961 to 1969 Albania enjoyed a special relationship with China. During the 1970s, however, Chinese-Albanian relations steadily deteriorated as Beijing and Tirana differed over both domestic and foreign policy issues. Since the Sino-Albanian rupture in 1978, Tirana has followed an independent course in its international relations.

Immediately following the Communist seizure of power, Yugoslavia, with the apparent approval of Stalin, assumed a dominant role in Albania. Tito discouraged Albania from establishing diplomatic and economic ties with Western Europe and the United States and sought to bring Tirana's foreign policy into line with that of Yugoslavia. As a consequence of a series of agreements concluded in 1946, the Albanian and Yugoslav economies were closely integrated. At the same time, Belgrade, with the help of Koci Xoxe and the other pro-Yugoslav elements in the Albanian leadership, was paving the way for the transformation of Albania into one of the constituent republics of the Yugoslav Federation.

An indication of Albania's unique position in the Communist camp at this time was that the Albanian Communist party was the only ruling party not invited to participate in the Cominform. The Soviet-Yugoslav rupture in mid-1948 enabled the Albanians to end the special relationship with Yugoslavia that Belgrade had imposed on them.

Following the break with Yugoslavia, Albania drifted into the Soviet camp. Although there was still sentiment within the Albanian leadership for normalizing relations with the United States and Great Britain, Hoxha was angered by their refusal to recognize his regime, by their opposition to Albania's admission to the United Nations, and by their perceived support for Greek claims to parts of southern Albania. What finally confirmed Hoxha in his decision to align Albania totally with the Soviet Union and in his resolve to develop a Stalinist-type regime were the joint Anglo-American-sponsored clandestine operations to overthrow his government between 1949 and 1953. These ventures were betrayed and thwarted as a result of information supplied to the Soviets and the Albanians by the Russian agent H. A. R. (Kim) Philby.

As a full-fledged member of the socialist camp, Albania was admitted to CMEA in 1949 and was one of the signatories to the Warsaw Pact in 1955. During the 1950s approximately 90 percent of Albania's foreign trade was with the CMEA countries, and the USSR was Albania's major trading partner and source of foreign aid. The Albanians have acknowledged that the assistance they received from the Communist camp was crucial to the economic gains registered during the periods of the first and second five-year plans.

By the second half of the 1950s, however, serious differences had arisen between the USSR and Albania. Hoxha was unnerved by the Soviet-Yugoslav rapprochement of the mid-1950s. This, he feared, might be a prelude to a new Yugoslav move to annex Albania. The Albanian leaders also opposed wholesale de-Stalinization in their homeland on the grounds that it could lead to internal unrest, possible Soviet intervention, and their eventual removal from power. Tirana was further concerned about Soviet proposals to establish an "international socialist division of labor" among the CMEA countries. Under this arrangement Albania would have been restricted to supplying the CMEA community with foodstuffs and raw materials. This situation, it was believed, would keep Albania in a state of perpetual dependency and make its leaders more vulnerable to Soviet coercion.

These were the major considerations that led to the 1961 Soviet-Albanian break. Albania, however, could not have taken this drastic action without the assurance of Chinese support. As in 1948, it was a development within the Soviet camp—this time the Sino-Soviet rift—that made it possible for the Albanian leadership to remain in power and to continue to pursue its own line. Although Soviet-Albanian diplomatic and economic relations were severed in 1961, Tirana did maintain its ties in both these areas with the East European Communist states. Albania, however, ceased to participate in the Warsaw Pact and in CMEA, and in September 1968, in the aftermath of the Soviet invasion of Czechoslovakia, officially renounced its membership in the Warsaw Pact.

China's economic and military aid contributed significantly to Albania's survival following the Moscow-Tirana split. During the 1960s China and Albania developed a special relationship that became particularly close between 1966 and 1969 when both countries were in the throes of their respective cultural revolutions and when China was virtually isolated from the rest of the world.

The Sino-Albanian relationship underwent a transformation in 1969, as China phased out its cultural revolution and sought to strengthen its ties with the West, including the United States. Tirana was especially distressed that the developments in China were reinforcing the domestic agitation that brought about the brief period of relaxation in Albania during the early 1970s. The Albanian leaders also appear to have been disappointed with the nature of the support they received or were promised from Beijing following the Soviet invasion of Czechoslovakia, and by China's apparent decision to scale down the level of its economic aid to Albania following the conclusion of the fifth five-year plan.

Since the early 1970s Albania has responded to these developments by attempting to lessen its economic dependence on China. To this end it has sought to improve diplomatic and economic relations with Yugoslavia and Greece. By the mid-1970s, Yugoslavia had become, next to China, Albania's most important trading partner. Tirana has expressed interest in expanding its commercial and cultural ties with Third World countries and other nations with the notable exceptions of the United States, the Soviet Union, and Israel.

Sino-Albanian relations rapidly deteriorated following the death of Mao Tse-tung in September 1976 when China's new leaders opted for a moderate domestic course and continued to court the United States, the countries of Western Europe, and many Third World nations.

Tirana viewed these developments as a "betrayal" of both Marxism-Leninism and its own national interests. By early 1978, Albania had begun to take the Chinese to task for alleged delays in the delivery of promised economic assistance. The Albanians were also distressed by China's rapprochement with Yugoslavia as well as by what they termed Beijing's "imperialistic" policy toward Vietnam.

In July 1978, obviously angered by the continuous and escalating Albanian attacks on their policies and leaders, the Chinese responded by halting their economic and military assistance programs. This action marked the formal end of the Sino-Albanian alliance.

PROSPECTS AND PROBLEMS

At the onset of the 1980s, Albania finds itself at another crucial historical juncture. As Albania's post-World War II experiences have demonstrated, the country's fate has been profoundly influenced by developments in the Communist world. Within two years of Mao's death, the special relationship between Tirana and Beijing had been terminated and the two erstwhile allies were engaged in ideological warfare. Similarly, Albanian-Yugoslav relations, which had begun to improve during the 1970s, took a new turn for the worse following the death of Tito in 1980. The major irritant in the Albanian-Yugoslav relationship since 1981 has been Tirana's support of the demand of the ethnic Albanians of Kosovo that their province be granted republic status within the Yugoslav federation. Since its break with China in 1978, Albania has been able to survive without the backing of a major Communist or noncommunist power. It will be interesting to note how long Tirana is able and inclined to maintain this independence.

The Albanian economy will continue to be a major source of concern to the leadership. Although the split with China did not result in the crippling of the Albanian economy, it did force the regime to cut back somewhat its ambitious industrialization program. So long as Albania lacks an economic patron, it will find itself increasingly vulnerable to the vicissitudes of the international economy. Albania's most pressing economic problems, however, are domestic in nature. There is a shortage of skilled workers and well-trained managers in virtually every sector of the economy, labor productivity and discipline remain poor, and the country continues to be saddled with an inefficient, highly centralized planning and management system. These problems have also made it impossible for the regime to satisfy the rising economic expectations of the masses.

As the educational level of the Albanian people continues to rise and as radio and television ownership has become widespread, the country's rulers have found it increasingly difficult to insulate the population from outside influences. This situation has created pressures on the leadership to modify its austere Stalinist policies in the social and cultural sectors. While Hoxha has successfully resisted these pressures in recent years, it seems likely that his successors will find it more difficult to do so.

Finally, it appears that the Hoxha era will end during the 1980s. It remains to be seen whether Hoxha's passing will result in a repudiation of his policies as was the case in the Soviet Union after Stalin and in China following Mao or whether his successors will persevere in the hard-line course that has been the hallmark of the Hoxha regime. To a large extent, the stance of the new leadership will depend on the nature of the domestic and external problems they inherit and on the degree of loyalty they can command from the Albanian elites.

BIBLIOGRAPHY

Amery, Julian. *Sons of the Eagle: A Study in Guerilla War.* London: Macmillan, 1948.

Bardhoshi, Besim, and Kareco, Theodhor. *The Economic and Social Development of the People's Republic of Albania During Thirty Years of People's Power.* Tirana: "8 Nentori," 1974.

Biberaj, Elez. "Albanian-Yugoslav Relations and the Question of Kosovo," *East European Quarterly,* 16 (January 1983), pp. 485–510.

Fontana, Dorothy Grouse. "Recent Sino-Albanian Relations," *Survey,* 21 (autumn 1975), pp. 121–144.

Frasheri, Kristo. *The History of Albania: A Brief Survey.* Tirana: "Naim Frasheri," 1964.

Griffith, William E. *Albania and the Sino-Soviet Rift.* Cambridge: MIT Press, 1963.

Hamm, Harry. *Albania: China's Beachhead in Europe.* New York: Praeger, 1963.

History of the Party of Labor of Albania. Tirana: "Naim Frasheri," 1971.

Keefe, Eugene K. *Area Handbook for Albania.* Washington, D.C.: U.S. Government Printing Office, 1971.

Logoreci, Anton. *The Albanians: Europe's Forgotten Survivors.* London: Victor Gollancz Ltd., 1977.

Marmullaku, Ramadan. *Albania and the Albanians.* Hamden, Conn.: Archon Books, 1975.

Pano, Nicholas C. "Albania in the Era of Kosygin and Brezhnev," in *Nationalism in the USSR and Eastern Europe,* edited by George W. Simmonds. Detroit, Mich.: The University of Detroit Press, 1977, pp. 474–494.

———. "Albania in the Sixties," in *The Changing Face of Communism in Eastern Europe,* edited by Peter A. Toma. Tucson: University of Arizona Press, 1970, pp. 244–280.

──────. "Albania in the 1970s," *Problems of Communism*, 26 (November–December 1977), pp. 33–43.

──────. "Albania: The Last Bastion of Stalinism," in *East Central Europe: Yesterday, Today, Tomorrow*, edited by Milorad M. Drachkovitch. Stanford, Calif.: Hoover Institution Press, 1982, pp. 187–218.

──────. "The Albanian Cultural Revolution," *Problems of Communism*, 23 (July–August 1974), pp. 44–57.

──────. *The People's Republic of Albania.* Baltimore: Johns Hopkins Press, 1968.

Peters, Stephen. "Ingredients of the Communist Takeover in Albania," *Studies on the Soviet Union*, 11 (no. 4, 1971), pp. 244–263.

Pollo, Stefanaq, and Puto, Arben. *The History of Albania.* London and Boston: Routledge and Kegan Paul, 1981.

Prifti, Peter R. "Albania," in *The Communist States in Disarray, 1965–1971*, edited by Adam Bromke and Teresa Rakowska-Harmstone. Minneapolis, Minn.: University of Minnesota Press, 1972, pp. 198–220.

──────. "Albania and the Sino-Soviet Conflict," *Studies in Comparative Communism*, 6 (autumn 1973), pp. 241–279.

──────. *Socialist Albania Since 1944.* Cambridge: MIT Press, 1978.

Skendi, Stavro (ed.). *Albania.* New York: Praeger, 1956.

Thomas, John E. *Education for Communism: School and State in the People's Republic of Albania.* Stanford, Calif.: Hoover Institution Press, 1969.

Tretiak, Daniel. "The Founding of the Sino-Albanian Entente," *China Quarterly*, no. 10 (April–June 1962), pp. 123–143.

9   Yugoslavia

Robin Alison Remington

The Yugoslav state rose from the ashes of World War I in 1918 only to be dismembered with the approach of World War II. Out of the chaos and devastation of the Second World War, Yugoslavia was reunited under the leadership of the Communist Party of Yugoslavia (CPY). Unlike most of their East European comrades who rode to power on the coattails of the Soviet army, Yugoslav Communists fought an indigenous battle of national liberation. Led, sometimes driven, by the Croatian peasant turned locksmith, turned revolutionary, Josip Broz— who under the name of Tito was to become one of the most important statesmen of postwar Europe as well as its most controversial Communist leader—the party followed Chinese methods that had yet to succeed in China. There is evidence that the Yugoslavs were keenly aware of their model. Take the following statement by Mosa Pijade, veteran ideologue and Tito's instructor in Marxism during his prison days: " 'The people are water, a partisan is a fish; fish cannot live without water.' That principle of the Chinese partisans holds here too."[1]

Such a pattern of revolutionary takeover had the advantage of building a large, genuine constituency that looked to the party for leadership. The integrating myth of partisan solidarity became the foundation of a "revitalized belief system" in support of the second try at uniting the South Slavs into a common Yugoslav state.[2] As in the interwar years, and with considerably more success, the CPY attempted to become an effective, cross-ethnic, nationwide party. It is a continuing attempt, and one that must be understood in the context of Yugoslav political cultures and historic legacies. Otherwise present-day Yugoslavia makes no sense.

To grasp the impact of historic ethnic considerations on Yugoslav communism, Americans must shed a good deal of culture-bound intellectual baggage. Yugoslavia is the heart of the Balkans. In that part of the world a state is an internationally recognized entity with the formal attributes of territorial integrity, sovereignty, and control of its domestic affairs that conducts foreign policy on the basis of legal (if sometimes fictitious) equality with other such internationally recognized entities. A country is the piece of real estate occupied by the state. Neither a country nor a state is a "nation." Rather, a "nation" is a group of individuals united by common bonds of historical development, language, religion, and their self-perceived collective identity. A "nation" may or may not be recognized as such by the international system. It may be coterminous with a state, but in the Balkans it usually is not. Bluntly, there is no Yugoslav nation.

Yugoslavia is a state—a state perhaps in the process of becoming a nation. The official ideology of the League of Communists of Yugoslavia (LCY) is committed to nation-building and national (ethnic) integration. To what extent the commitment has been translated into reality is hotly debated. At a minimum one can identify the goal. A conservative estimate is that substantial work has been done on the foundations.

According to the 1981 census, the Yugoslav population is 22.4 million, including six official "nations" and a variety of nationalities. The nations are Serbs, 8.1 million (36.3%); Croats, 4.4 million (19.7%); Moslems, 1.9 million (8.9%); Slovenes, 1.75 million (7.8%); Macedonians, 1.3 million (5.9%); and Montenegrins, 577,000 (2.5%). The national minorities include Albanians, Hungarians, Turks, Slovaks, Bulgars, Romanians, Czechs, Italians, Germans, and Gypsies. The criterion for distinguishing between "nations" and "national minorities" is in part whether or not the group in question has another potential homeland. In short "nationalities" are members of nations whose "native countries border on Yugoslavia."[3]

The nations of Yugoslavia share a common, visceral knowledge of foreign domination. Trying to survive on a pivotal intersection between Europe and the Ottoman Empire, they knew only too well the running battles of international crossroads. The Slovenes were ruled by Charlemagne, then by the Germans (Austrians) until the end of World War I. The Croats, existing in a state of token autonomy under the Hungarians dating from 1102, lived on memories of an independent Croatia. From 1018 the Macedonians were ruled alternately by the Turks, Bulgarians, and Serbs. The Serbian empire that under the Nemanja dynasty in the fourteenth century included the territory of present-day Albania, Bulgaria, Macedonia, and much of Greece submitted to Turkish occupation after the battle of Kosovo in 1389. The Montenegrins, Serbs who reteated to the black mountains from which they took their name, held out for another hundred years before they too yielded to the Turkish yoke at the end of the fifteenth century.

For our purposes the salient consequences of this star-crossed South
Slav history are the following:

1. The two largest nations of Yugoslavia, the Serbs and the Croats,
survived hundreds of years of domination by feeding on heroic legends
of past empires. This historic consciousness solidified their sense of
"nationhood," i.e., separateness from each other. Such an attitude was
instrumental for national survival, but it became extremely dysfunctional when the Serbs and Croats attempted to unite in the Kingdom of
Serbs, Croats, and Slovenes in 1918.

2. The nations of Yugoslavia suffered under radically different im-
perialisms. Consequently they brought with them into the twentieth
century diverse legacies in terms of political culture, economic development, and religion; there were even two alphabets for Serbo-
Croatian. Under Austrian influence, the Slovenes and Croats were
ardent Catholics, western, European. For the Serbs, Macedonians,
and Montenegrins, the Turkish heritage meant much more than economic backwardness. Orthodox or Muslim, these nations were influenced by oriental politics and culture in ways that can be seen even
today.

These varied political experiences helped shape the future political
tactics of the South Slavs in dealing with one another. The Serbs,
whose nineteenth-century history reads like a serialized epic of repression and revolt led by simultaneously feuding families, tend toward
centralism and authoritarian military solutions.[4] Conversely, in their
attempt to carve out substantial home rule under the Hungarians, the
Croats became well versed in passive resistance and political obstruc-
tionism, with which the Serbs have had scant patience.

Mutual wartime atrocities sharply worsened interwar antagonisms.
Yugoslavs fought each other in a savage civil war that did nothing to
create the ethnic trust so essential for postwar national integration.
Ustashi massacres drove those Serbs living in Croatia lucky enough to
escape into the partisan army. Reinforced by Serb/Montenegrin military traditions, the resistance movement was heavily Serbian and disproportionately Montenegrin.[5] Given the exigencies of wartime
recruitment, the party itself reflected a similar ethnic composition.
Vows of brotherhood and equality notwithstanding, the resultant credibility gap has done much to determine the politics of Communist Yugoslavia.[6]

MAIN LINES OF POLITICAL DEVELOPMENT, 1948–70

By the end of World War II, the Yugoslav party had grown from an
estimated 12,000 members to 140,000. Most of these new members
were drawn from the ranks of the partisan army. They were young,

predominantly peasants, and dedicated more to Tito personally than to the dimly understood principles that he supported. In the euphoria of victory, party and army were almost dizzy with success. Not only had the country been liberated from the German invaders largely by its own efforts[7], but also a social revolution was underway. Everything seemed possible, and individuals were swept forward on a wave of political optimism that tended to hide harsh economic realities. Even before the occupation and civil war, Yugoslavia had struggled with the unenviable economic legacy of the Turks. At the end of the war, it was still a small, economically backward Balkan country with the added burden of having suffered almost unbelievable devastation. Some 1.7 million people, roughly one of every nine inhabitants, had died in battles, concentration camps, or as a result of ethnic-inspired atrocities. Another 3.5 million had been left homeless. Much of the manufacturing industry had been destroyed or seriously damaged. In these circumstances the first job of the new Communist government was to repair the damage, with the ideological imperative that the economy should be reorganized according to what were considered proper socialist principles.[8]

Yugoslav economists looked to the Soviet model. The efforts of the CPY to rebuild the economy were Stalinist in both goals and methods. Emphasis was on extensive, rapid industrialization starting with the most basic industrial infrastructure. Financing was at the expense of depressed agricultural prices, facilitated by unskilled labor moving from the countryside into the factories. Planning was centrally organized and based on an administered credit system with marked disregard for costs. This course lasted from 1945 to 1949, when the split with Moscow intervened.

The Soviet-Yugoslav differences that climaxed with Yugoslav expulsion from the Cominform in 1948 have been well documented elsewhere.[9] For our purposes, it is important to avoid the commonplace that Tito was expelled from interparty circles because he was a "national communist." True, the Yugoslav party was proud and not overly fond of accepting Soviet military advisers, advice, or the political-economic penetration that had become the norm in Soviet relations with the other East European regimes. Nonetheless, the difficulty from Moscow's perspective was not Yugoslav nationalism so much as Tito's revolutionary ambitions in the Balkans.

The Yugoslav leader aided the Greek guerrillas after Moscow had abandoned them for fear that the civil war in Greece would sabotage what was left of the wartime alliance. He demanded public Soviet support for a Yugoslav Trieste and pressed toward a Balkan federation despite Stalin's lack of enthusiasm for the project. In short, Yugoslav expansionism clashed with Soviet foreign policy priorities. At the same time, domestically, the Yugoslav party was more, not less, ideologically dogmatic than the other East European regimes, still cautiously attempting to establish the nature of "peoples democracies" as distinct from the Soviet model. While Stalin was mistaken to think he could shake his little finger and Tito would fall, he was correct that at bottom his problem with the Yugoslavs was "conceptions that are different from our own."

From 1948 until 1956 the Soviet-Yugoslav split became the fundamental fact of Yugoslav domestic and foreign policy. The Yugoslav leadership's number one problem was the nature of the party rank and file. How to explain the break to the young, for the most part ideologically immature and enthusiastic cadres that had been weaned politically on myths of Soviet infallibility and love of Stalin? How to cushion the personal pain and disillusionment of the core of seasoned Communists who had survived the purges of the 1930s and the war? The ideological self-image of the Yugoslav leadership plus the practical fear of demoralizing the party rank and file ruled out simply denouncing the Soviets and switching sides in the East-West struggle over the fate of Eastern Europe. To do so would have risked party disintegration as well as Soviet invasion. Moreover, even had these restraints not existed, there was no immediate political welcome waiting in the West. Rather, the first reaction to the split was disbelief. The Yugoslav policy of minimizing its expulsion from the Cominform as "a mistake" and continued expressions of loyalty to the Soviet Union and to Stalin personally, combined with an attempt to shore up Belgrade's socialist credentials by an intensified collectivization drive, did nothing to still such Western suspicions.

The initially cautious American and British reaction notwithstanding, the U.S. Embassy in Belgrade believed that the split was real and must have made a convincing case to the State Department, for in July 1948 the U.S. government agreed to unfreeze Yugoslav gold and other assets in the United States.[10] Meanwhile, Tito was denounced as a "tyrant, murderer, spy" by his former Cominform comrades. East European show trials of "Titoist" heretics increasingly ruled out all hope of reconciliation, while maneuvers on Yugoslavia's borders underlined the Balkan socialist maverick's precarious military position.

Both politically and economically, the Stalinist model had become patently inappropriate. The search for alternatives began. In 1952 the historic Sixth Congress announced that the "leading role" of the Communist party was to be confined to political and ideological education. The resolution called for open party meetings, decentralization of party organization, autonomy for local party organs, elimination of bureaucratism, and socialist democracy. The name of the CPY was changed to the League of Communists of Yugoslavia (LCY) to symbolize the new decentralized organizational structure; the Politburo became the Executive Committee to eliminate Stalinist terminology. In short, the Soviet model was publicly dumped on the rubbish heap of Yugoslav party history. The political consequence of this act was immense: it signaled the end of the official party monopoly of political life.

Workers' Self-Management

Having rejected the Soviet example, the Yugoslav leadership worked desperately to fill the political-economic vacuum with an ideologically acceptable alternative. Party theorists turned to such classics as Marx's analysis of the Paris Commune and Lenin's *State and Revolution* and to the thinking of British socialists such as G. D. H. Cole. The new system emphasized worker democracy—the truly radical assumption that factories belong to the workers. In principle, workers in each factory or enterprise became the trustees of socially owned property. As such they elected workers' councils, which in consultation with management boards decided what and how much to produce, at what prices, and for what wages. These decisions were expected to take into account demand (market), production costs, and general rules laid down by the government in the form of annual and medium-range social plans. The key changes in economic management are shown schematically below.[11]

	Stalinist model	*Self-management*
Goals:	1. Socialism by means of state power	1. Withering away of the state
	2. Equalization of the positions of the workers in relation to state-owned means of production	2. Worker management of social property
	3. A new social order for its own sake	3. Personal happiness of individuals
Agents:	Hierarchically organized state apparatus	Autonomous enterprise
Means:	1. State ownership	1. Social ownership
	2. Central planning	2. Social planning
	3. Administrative allocation of goods	3. Market mechanism
	4. Administrative rules	4. Financial instruments
	5. Administrative wages	5. Worker decided wages

6. All-embracing state budget	6. Decentralized state budget for economic operations
7. Consumption as residual	7. Consumption as an independent priority or factor in development
8. Collectivization of agriculture	8. Business cooperation of peasants

The difficulty was not so much in principle as in implementation. Centralized economies cannot be dismantled overnight. The first actual steps toward a self-managing socialist economy were cautious. The idea was not well understood, and in the beginning, workers controlled very little. Medium-range goals of the system remained much the same—extensive and rapid industrialization emphasizing infrastructure—as did the problems of capital accumulation and distribution. Some feared that instead of the best of both worlds, Yugoslavia had taken the worst.

Consequently, there began a see-saw centralization/decentralization/centralization pattern that has characterized the Yugoslav economy ever since. This pattern reflects a basic conflict between the proponents of more emphasis on the "market" aspects of self-managing socialism, economic rationalizers rather inaccurately often considered "liberals," and their opponents. At stake are fundamental conflicts over the nature of regional development, social priorities, and at bottom, the question of who must pay the cost of change.[12]

Thus from the moment the LCY rejected Stalinism for self-managing socialism, the party has been faced with conflicting political-economic demands in circumstances where the LCY had abdicated the right to decide by fiat. In the long run this shift proved more important for Yugoslav politics than did the fluctuating international environment, marked by the collapse of Khrushchev's 1955–56 reconciliation attempts, the Polish and Hungarian crises of 1956, caused in part by the Soviet leader's campaign to bring Yugoslavia back within the fold, and the 1958 Soviet-Yugoslav dispute over the nature of Yugoslavia's road to socialism and its legitimacy within the post-Stalin international Communist movement. For by the 1960s it was clear that a serious political struggle was underway in the guise of economic debates. Moreover, the party itself was divided on these issues. Hence they were not resolved and continued to fester into the 1970s.

The Economic Issues and Actors[13]

Economic rationalizers within and outside the LCY assumed not only that economic Stalinism was distasteful for political reasons but also that Yugoslavia had reached a "take-off" stage in terms of the economy. At this stage artificially depressed standards of living in order to finance basic industrial infrastructure were considered harmful rather than helpful. Basically, the complaint of the economic rationalizers in the early 1960s was that Yugoslavia suffered from enormous waste, unnecessarily low personal consumption, and unutilized industrial capacity; all of these factors provided workers with no incentive to work. The economic rationalizers' solution was to make reality out of the fiction of market socialism. According to their scheme, individual enterprises, in conjunction with banks, were to be given greater control over earnings, pushed to make profitable investments, and allowed to go out of business if they could not earn a profit. Personal consumption would be gradually allowed to increase. The credit system would be reorganized. Prices would be moved in the direction of reflecting supply and demand. Monopolies would be allowed in those sectors where they were necessary to an economic scale of production.

By 1964 the Yugoslav leadership appeared to have accepted this platform for rationalization almost intact. Tito personally spoke of the need to raise standards of living. The trade unions came out in favor of the plan. The program was forcefully reiterated at the Sixth Central Committee Plenum. Yet implementation still appeared bogged down. The problem was not so much the resistance of economic "conservatives" but that a genuine "socialist market economy" had drastic implications for the well-being of several sectors of Yugoslav society. For our purposes these groups will simply be called the opposition.

The opposition reflected national-regional differences in the most graphic, painful way. First, as might have been expected, people in unprofitable enterprises and those in underdeveloped regions of the country were flatly against the reform. Although the two categories were not always synonymous, there was considerable overlap because of earlier policies favoring "political" factories in underdeveloped areas of Serbia, Montenegro, Macedonia, and Bosnia-Hercegovina. These were factories established as rewards (sometimes for wartime performance), as incentives for development in poorer regions, or as personal/political favors. Since these factories had never been assumed to have an economic base, the likelihood of their survival under the proposed reforms was small. However, whether or not a factory had been established for political reasons, potentially all factories in the less industrialized, formerly disadvantaged areas of the country would be in trouble.

Whereas economic rationalizers operated on the assumption that the Yugoslav economy had reached the point of economic take-off, the opposition disagreed. Those opposed to do the reforms emphasized that even if one could make such an assumption with respect to

Croatia, Slovenia, and the Vojvodina, the same could not be said for the less industrialized south. They insisted that in Kosovo, Macedonia, Montenegro, and Bosnia-Hercegovina forced investment be maintained for the sake of equalization.

Opposition arguments were based on social priorities rather than economic rationalism. Oppositionists argued that the reforms were antisocialist. A state with welfare commitments could not accept the consequences of unemployment, restricted social services, and a widening of the gap between developed and underdeveloped regions of the country. In individual rather than regional terms, the consequences implied increasing wage differentials at a time when food prices were rising. It stressed capitalist norms of competition rather than socialist egalitarianism. Ideological objections aside, the opposition pointed to some uncomfortable economic realities. The economy could not survive the simultaneous collapse of many enterprises in terms of either the economic or the social consequences that would surely occur if the subsidized factories were forced to do without their subsidies and show a profit.

Those who would feel the weight of the economic cost of reforms found allies among those who would have to face a political cost. The ranks of middle- and lower-level party and government functionaries stood to lose significant power with any depoliticizing of the economy. These bureaucracies stubbornly resisted implementation of the reforms despite approval at the top of the party. Thus the opposition found its strength in national, regional, and bureaucratic bastions. At the highest level, vice president and head of the security service (UDBA) Aleksandar Rankovic served as the protector of these forces, and only after his fall in 1966* did the program of the rationalizers push ahead.

The result was much as had been predicted. The party responded to increased unemployment by allowing large numbers of Yugoslavs to work abroad. This massive labor migration eased the pressure of unemployment and brought much needed foreign currency into the economy. Yet it had a variety of undesirable side effects. The foreign workers, particularly those working in more industrialized European nations such as West Germany, Austria, and Sweden, raised the standard of expectations within Yugoslavia. The workers came home to marry, to take a cousin abroad with them, or to show off a new car.

*Formerly considered Tito's successor, Rankovic was ostensibly removed for letting his UDBA agents go too far in bugging Tito's bedroom. However, the commission investigating the charges against him was headed by the subsequent head of the Croat CP, Miko Tripalo, and there is reason to think that Rankovic's economic policies played not a little role in his political retirement.

Such rising expectations only intensified frustration with Yugoslav economic reality. As one economist rather bitterly expressed it, "We can't have a West German standard of living on the basis of a small, backward Balkan economy. And everyone now wants one."

As the consequences of the economic reforms began to surface in severe social-political dislocation in 1968, international events intervened. In August the Soviet Union and its more orthodox East European allies invaded Czechoslovakia to put an end to the Dubcek regime's experiment with "socialism with a human face." By September that action had been expanded into the Brezhnev doctrine, by which Moscow reserved the right to intervene militarily or otherwise if developments in any other socialist country threatened either (1) socialism within that country or (2) the basic interests of other socialist countries.[14] Again Yugoslav security was directly threatened.

Not since 1948 had the country appeared so united. The LCY attacked the invasion of Czechoslovakia as a violation of socialist norms and reminded all parties involved that in case of need the Yugoslav army was ready to defend Yugoslavia's borders. Domestically, party membership went up, with more young people joining than at any time in recent years. Militarily, the Yugoslav People's Army (JNA) adopted a mixed partisan strategy called "all people's defense," and accepted Territorial Defense Units (TDUs) as partners of the regular armed forces. The National Assembly passed a law declaring it treason for any citizen to fail to resist foreign occupation. In 1969 Tito, euphorically and, as it turned out, prematurely, pronounced the "national question" solved.[15]

In sum, the fundamental economic/political conflicts that had intensified with the economic reforms of 1966 remained unsolved. Pushed aside by international crisis, these tensions returned in full force in the 1970s, complicated by an organizational power struggle, this time between the federal center and the republic party/bureaucratic elites. Despite Tito's personal intervention to stem the centrifugal forces, and what appears to have been a temporary victory for supporters of federal control at the Tenth Party Congress in 1974, these same fundamental policy choices are at the heart of the political debate dominating post-Tito Yugoslavia. Once again substantial political energy is focused on how best to change the Yugoslav political system; there is an on-going tug-of-war between those favoring centralism and those advocates of the market as the answer referred to as economic rationalizers.[16] Moreover, in the 1980s the dramatic expansion of self-managing institutions to include some 20,000 Basic Organizations of Associated Labor (BOALS)—the smallest of the self-managing units in the economy—substantially complicates the problem of doing whatever is decided upon. For the BOALS have contractual rights and, partly as a result, in some cases appear unresponsive to market forces. To understand these developments, they must be seen in the present political context.

CURRENT POLITICAL STRUCTURE AND DYNAMICS

Yugoslavia is a federation composed of six republics and two autonomous provinces. Five of the republics are the territorial bases of the Yugoslav nations identified in the first part of this chapter—Serbia, Croatia, Slovenia, Montenegro, and Macedonia. The sixth, Bosnia-Hercegovina, is divided roughly equally between Serbs, Croats, and Moslems with no single ethnic group having a majority. Nor are the "national" republics ethnically homogeneous. In 1981 Croatia had a Serbian minority of 11.5 percent. This drop from the 14.2% registered as Serbs in the 1971 census is partially explained by the jump from 1.9% to 8.2% in the number of residents of Croatia who, instead of opting for an ethnic designation, registered as "Yugoslavs."[17] Serbia includes the autonomous provinces of the Kosovo, with its majority of ethnic Albanians, and of the Vojvodina, where there are large Hungarian, Croat, and Slovak minorities. Albanian enclaves exist in both Montenegro and Macedonia. These overlapping ethnic and territorial boundaries create complex political problems.

The League of Communists of Yugoslavia is the only official political party. Each republic has its own party organization, however, creating regional party elites who, given the ethnic dimension of their political base, have interests that frequently conflict with one another and with the central party organization. Paralleling the party organization, there is a federal governmental structure involving a collective State Presidency, a federal assembly or parliament consisting of two chambers (the Federal Chamber and the Chamber of Republics and Provinces) with a federal executive council acting as the executive body of the parliament, federal agencies and courts. Each republic has its president, assembly, and governmental bureaucracy as well, with the assembly structure reaching down to the local government level in the form of commune assemblies.

The Twelfth LCY Congress in June 1982—the first party congress since Tito died in May 1980—billed itself as "the Congress of Continuity."[18] Thus until the 1986 congress, the Yugoslav party will be run by a 165-member Central Committee, and a 23-member Presidium with its own secretary and a number of executive secretaries. This is roughly parallel to the Central Committee, Politburo, and Secretariat in the Soviet and more orthodox East European party structures. Due to the manner of selection and the relationship of the individual republics to that process, however, the end result in terms of where power actually resides is very different.

The Yugoslav Central Committee is composed of 20 representatives from each republic: 19 plus the president of the republic; 15 representatives from each autonomous province, including the president of the provincial committee; and 15 representatives from the army party organization. The Presidium has three members from each republic, two from each autonomous province, and one from the army.

Elected for the first time by secret ballot, this is a truly collective leadership, based on a strict rotation schedule. The Slovene leader Mitja Ribicic was elected president of the Presidium for a one-year period that ended in June 1983. He was replaced by Dragoslav Markovic, a representative of Serbia, to be followed by representatives from Kosovo, 1984; Montenegro, 1985; Vojvodina, 1986; Macedonia, 1987; and Croatia, 1988. The party secretary, Nikola Stojanovic from Bosnia-Hercegovina, had a two-year term. He was replaced in 1984 by a representative from Macedonia to be followed by Serbia, 1986; Kosovo, 1988; Vojvodina, 1990; Slovenia, 1992; Croatia, 1994; and Montenegro, 1996.[19] The presidents of republic/province/and JNA party organizations participate as ex officio members of the Presidium. In short, the top hierarchy of the LCY has been firmly tied to proportional representation for the regional party organizations, while the role of the army has been formalized at the highest party levels.[20]

Although it is correct to see the Yugoslav party/state leaderships as an essentially interlocking directorate, the elections of 1982 left only Dr. Vladimir Bakaric of Croatia a member of both the party Presidium and the State Presidency. With Bakaric's death in January 1983 even this link was severed, showing a current preference for formal separation of these two governing hierarchies.* In Yugoslavia there is no tradition of a party secretariat comparable to the one in the Soviet system. Indeed, at the 1982 congress only three executive secretaries

---

*In February 1984, it was officially announced that seven of the eight members of the State Presidency would leave that job in May 1984. Five had served the maximum two five-year terms. Of the three who could have been renominated, only Radovan Vlajkovic of Vojvodina was put up again. The other seven members, whose confirmation was expected on May 15, 1984, were Stane Dolanc (Slovenia), Josip Vrhovec (Croatia), Branko Mikulic (Bosnia-Herzegovina), Veselin Djuranovic (Montenegro), Gen. Nikola Ljubicic (Serbia), Sinan Hasani (Kosovo), and Lazar Mojsov (Macedonia). Djuranovic was to replace Mika Spiljak (Croatia) as president of the State Presidency in the normal rotation cycle for that body. Both Dolanc and Mojsov held key positions on the Federal Executive Council, as the secretaries of Internal Affairs and Foreign Affairs, respectively.

were elected to assist Stojanovic in providing "liaison" between the LCY and republic/provincial parties, with the understanding that the Presidium reserved the right to add to that number at a later date "according to the spheres of work."[21]

Next to the party-state apparatus, the armed forces are the most significant all-Yugoslav institution. Indeed, the JNA has its own League of Communists, which in terms of numbers is larger than the party organizations of two of the republics. Given the historic image of the Yugoslav army as an instrument of Serbian hegemony, considerable effort has been made to assure multi-ethnic representation among the officer corps. These efforts appear successful at the top of the command structure, although it is impossible to tell to what degree they have penetrated the middle and lower levels, which in the early 1970s conservative estimates considered 70 percent Serbian. The political influence of the army is reinforced by that of the veterans' organization, SUBNOR, also statewide and because of the nature of the partisan struggle, most likely largely Serbian and Montenegrin, except perhaps in Slovenia.

The trade unions also provide an institutional framework that spans the republics and provinces, although it is difficult to estimate their importance as compared to the daily influence of administrative and economic institutions that exist on regional, local, and enterprise levels.

Lastly, the Socialist Alliance (SAWPY) is an umbrella organization that functions much like a primary system in single-party electoral systems. It includes officially sanctioned interest groups such as women's organizations, professional groupings, and students, and legitimate social-political organizations that may have issue-oriented impact but little systematic input into national policy.

The nature of these institutions and their interaction tends to be obscured by formal functional descriptions. Charts are misleading. Present-day political reality involves institutional jockeying for position in the struggle to determine not only who but what will control the future of Yugoslavia. Rooted in history, this confrontation is being fought out through conflicting interpretations of the experiment with self-management. It is a political drama motivated by the power of an idea that has swept the actors far beyond their intended goals, changed some parts, and willy-nilly introduced others. Self-managing socialism, as an alternative to Stalinism, has inadvertently legitimized ethnic politics within Yugoslavia.

Nation Versus Class: The Organizational Dilemma

When Yugoslavia split with Moscow in 1948, the Yugoslav leadership was demanding *national* emancipation from Soviet hegemony and *socialist* emancipation from CPSU ideological domination. The Yugo-slav road to socialism was to be a modernized version of the society Marx sketchily described in his analysis of the Paris Commune of 1871. Politically, self-management was to extend beyond the factory to the commune and the republic. It was a truly radical approach that gave legitimacy to wide-scale political participation at all levels and, despite sporadic attempts at back-tracking such as the determined recentrali-zation efforts at the Tenth Congress in 1974, irrevocably undermined democratic centralism as an organizing principle. The ongoing debate concerning the substance of democratic centralism in the 1980s not-withstanding, it is a hard fact that it is impossible to have issues de-cided at both the top and the bottom simultaneously. To quote one member of the Committee for Organization and Statutory Affairs of the LCY CC during preparation for the Twelfth Congress, "There is no point in invoking democratic centralism, if we have not provided con-ditions for the membership to take a creative part in determining stands, framing up decisions or directing things."[22]

The logical political implication of self-management was increased autonomy of decision making at the republic and commune levels with inevitably increased importance of the republican party organizations. Given the coincidence of key republics with certain "national" (ethnic) groups already discussed, this autonomy soon led to demands for na-tional self-determination, which was the last thing that the League of Communists of Yugoslavia had in mind. Soon, the contradiction of preaching the right of "national communism" at the international level and prohibiting it within Yugoslavia became increasingly hard for the party to live with.

For years the answer to this problem had been Tito himself. Unfortu-nately, Tito's personality cult guaranteed the appearance of state and party unity at the expense of negotiated settlement of basic conflicts. By 1970 the Yugoslav leader himself had become uncomfortable with a system that considered his person indispensable. Hence the mammoth constitutional amendments of 1971.

On the most basic level the amendments amounted to Tito's attempt to manage his own succession. Drafted by a mixed commission of political leaders and legal advisers, rather than by a commission of legal experts as with earlier constitutional amendments, their writing took two months. Tito himself presided over the final meeting. Yet the result surely was not what he had intended. Swept forward by demands once again for a genuine participatory federalism, the amendments reflected both national (ethnic) ambitions and bureaucratic power struggles, first, between federal (LCY) and republic party elites; sec-ond, between the state and party bureaucracies.

At first it almost seemed that the federation had disappeared in the process. Although the central government retained responsibility for defense, foreign policy, and a "united market" (no one seemed quite sure just what such a market meant), one might almost have said that the Yugoslav state had "withered away" into a confederation of co-equal republics. Interrepublican committees were set up to negotiate political and economic conflicts of interest. The rule was by consensus, so in effect each republic had a veto. A collective presidency consisting of members from each republic and each of the autonomous provinces was to replace Tito, who was allowed by amendment 36 to retain the position of president for life.

The interrepublican committees soon reached a stalemate over the unresolved issue of economic rationalization versus social priorities. Croatian nationalism became identified with the leadership of the League of Croatian Communists. Thirty thousand Zagreb students struck demanding revisions in the foreign currency regulations that, from their perspective, unfairly drained off foreign exchange that came into the country via the Croatian coast into Belgrade banks. Tito attacked the strike as "counterrevolutionary" activity. The nationalist (and, incidentally, economic reform-minded) Croat leaders Miko Tripalo and Dr. Savka Dabcevic-Kucar resigned. Heads rolled at all levels of the Croat party apparatus; high-ranking Croats in the army appear to have been purged as well.

At the time and for the most part in retrospect, these events have been considered a Croatian crisis, i.e., a nationalist-separatist move that failed.[23] From an organizational-political perspective, there was another crucial consideration. The unintended consequence of the constitutional amendments of 1971 had been to generate demands that self-management be taken to its logical conclusion in terms of the Yugoslav party organization itself. As the former head of the Croat Central Committee ideological commission put it:

He who is ready to accept the concept of Yugoslavia as a federative state composed of equal nations and national minorities, and not ready to discuss the LCY as a federation of national parties, shows his true attitude concerning the former concept. There cannot be a federation of equal, self-managing communities, if there are no possibilities for formation of the League of Communists both on the class and national basis.[24]

Bluntly, one may say that Yugoslavia had not one political party in 1971 but eight, representing each republic and the two autonomous provinces.

Tito's determination to end that situation was at the heart of the Croatian crisis of 1971. He struck in favor of a reformed, strengthened, and most importantly, *united* Communist party that had the power "to interfere" when necessary, and to which the republican Communist parties were to be strictly accountable. The emphasis on Croatia being only one of the offenders and the seemingly senseless expansion of the purge to other republics were a part of Tito's plan to recentralize the League of Communists of Yugoslavia, streamlining it until he felt secure that the party as an organization could survive him.

The Tenth Party Congress in 1974 ratified the party centralization. It is difficult to evaluate the long-term impact of that reorganization despite the apparent rehabilitation of the regional party organizations at the June 1978 Congress and their increasing dominance evident at the 1982 Twelfth Congress. A whole generation of republican party leaders who had political experience and credibility with their constituencies and who, despite strong differences, worked well together, was sacrificed for what turned out to be more of a flirtation than a return to Leninism. The departure of these leaders from the political scene is a logical place at which to consider the changing nature of the Yugoslav political elite.

POLITICAL LEADERSHIP AND CHANGING ELITE PATTERNS

Despite the formal renunciation of the party's monopoly on political life, political leadership in Yugoslavia remains the function of the League of Communists. The nature of that leadership is undoubtedly influenced by the other institutional interest groups already discussed. Nonetheless the decisions that determine high-level Yugoslav domestic and foreign policy take place within the League of Communists or such governmental organs as the collective presidency, which can best be understood as an interlocking directorate with top party bodies. It would be naive to assume that numbers equate with influence on policy in the Yugoslav party, yet they do provide information on access to the policy-making process. We know for sure that those outside the party do not make key decisions. Therefore the composition of the LCY can serve as a rough index of who decides the allocation of power and resources in Yugoslav society.

According to Yugoslav sources, party membership in absolute numbers grew as follows:[25]

1946	253,000	1971	1,025,000
1948	482,000	1973	1,076,711
1952	772,000	1977	1,400,000
1954	654,000	1980	2,041,272
1958	829,000	1982	2,117,083
1968	1,146,000		

If one assumes that the 1948 figure essentially reflects membership before the Soviet-Yugoslav split, by 1958 more than half the membership had joined the party after the break with Moscow. Notwithstanding a drop following decentralization and deemphasis of party power, 1958 membership had surpassed the 1952 mark. If one makes allowances for those who dropped out of the party or who were pushed out because they could not adjust to their new role, it is a fair assumption that the majority of the 1.1 million members in 1968 had been politically socialized into the values of self-managing socialism by a party organizationally and ideologically unique within the international Communist movement. At the top, where those most familiar with the Soviet model remained, personal political survival and the need to assure the party's domestic legitimacy continually necessitated public affirmation of the Yugoslav way.

In short, numbers tell us that with the exception of brief periods of disorientation—1952–54, during radical organizational change, and 1970–71, presumably due to political chaos and ambivalence of direction—the Yugoslav party has grown steadily. Spurts of membership followed perceived external threats, i.e., the Soviet-Yugoslav break in 1948, the "allied socialist" invasion of Czechoslovakia in 1968, and Tito's death in 1980. The majority of these members entered the party at periods that would strongly suggest continuing commitment to an independent, i.e., nonaligned, Yugoslavia. Self-management is accepted as an axiom of Yugoslav political life with the day-to-day substance of that symbolic commitment to expanding participation decided by political struggle.

The steady shift in social composition of party membership is even more striking than its growth. Figures are subject to dispute, but trends are clear. The sharpest is the drop in peasant members, who declined from more than 50 percent in 1952 to 6.7 percent in 1971. Manual workers fell slightly in the same period from 32.2 percent to 28.8 percent. Conversely, the most dramatic jump was in the catch-all category of white collar workers, which moved from 18.9 percent in 1952 to 45.5 percent in 1971. In a rough fashion, this confirms Branko Horvat's claim that as of the mid-1960s "employees" (white-collar workers such as administrative officials, academics, managers, and security personnel) have above average membership in all categories, whereas workers, whether skilled, semiskilled, or unskilled, are below average.[26] Moreover, not only has the rate of joining been three times higher among employees than among workers, but employees with only primary education outnumber skilled workers in the party.

Denitch's breakdown gives a concise picture of the current Yugoslav party.[27] Group I (heavily overrepresented in terms of percentage of the population) includes managers, technical and general intelligentsia, and students; as Denitch succinctly puts it, these are "the present and future cadres of society, its experts, and administrators, and the candidates for those roles." Group II (slightly over or slightly underrepresented) includes those who work in the modernizing sector and visibly benefit from the system created by the Yugoslav revolution. Group III (heavily underrepresented) consists of peasants, private craftsmen, housewives, and the unemployed. One out of every 10 Yugoslavs may be a party member (9.4 percent); nonetheless, some 50 percent of the population are still functioning in a primarily traditional society, outside the socialist and modern sectors of Yugoslav political/social life.

In thirty years, the Yugoslav political elite has evolved from an organization dominated numerically by peasants and ideologically by seasoned revolutionaries to a party of managers, administrators, technicians, and minor bureaucrats. Although Djilas's charge that the party had become a new class[28] is implicitly recognized by the sustained struggle against technocratism and the "red bourgeoisie," in all fairness, the LCY has served as a major channel for the upwardly mobile, while providing a political leadership possessing the skills needed to create and run a modern society. The steady rise of managers and professionals among parliamentary deputies was indicative of that trend; to what extent this has been reversed by the 1974 constitution remains unclear.

Yet the fundamental fact about the Yugoslav political elite is best captured in George Orwell's satiric phrase, "Some are more equal than others." The unifying reality/myth of partisan struggle has had major political consequences. Indeed from 1945 until Tito's death in 1980, a core of revolutionary elites known as the "Club of 1941" dominated Yugoslav politics. Legitimized by their role in the national liberation struggle, these former partisans controlled the levers of power both at the federal center and within the republics/autonomous provinces. Despite visible casualties at the top of the party (Djilas in 1954, Rankovic in 1966, those such as Koca Popovic who resigned in protest at the fall of the Serbian Party Chairman Marko Nikezic in 1972, Kardelj who died in 1979, and Tito himself in 1980), the "Club of 1941" continued to provide an infrastructure of Yugoslav political leaders during the transition to a collective leadership who could no longer fall back on the godfather of Yugoslav communism to arbitrate national (ethnic) or bureaucratic crises. They provided a kind of solution during a vulnerable, politically sensitive period. Subsequently, as will be discussed below, they have become a visible part of the problem.

Then there is what one might call a loyal opposition. These are the Marxist humanists associated with the intermittently banned journal *Praxis,* who support the general principles of self-management, while pointing to flaws in implementation. They are the critics, political gadflys whose questions point to some of the most painful problems of Yugoslav political and social life. Not surprisingly, they are frequently unpopular. Despite the dismissal of the Belgrade Eight from their teaching posts at Belgrade University by an act of parliament in 1975, the *Praxis* group has a natural constituency among the most idealistic students and a strong international support group, which from the regime's point of view makes their ideological challenge potentially dangerous and continually embarrassing.[29]

As for changing elite patterns, perhaps the most notable shift in the 1970s was the skyrocketing power of the republic party elites vis-a-vis the federal center, its temporary forced decline, and the simultaneous rise of the military to positions of party prominence. One result of Tito's drive to recentralize the LCY, ridding the party of Communists who were "nationalist-minded," has been to strengthen the political significance of the army. At the Tenth LCY Party Congress in May 1974, twenty-one generals and other high ranking officers became members of top party bodies. Not only did this level of participation hold firm at the Eleventh LCY Congress in 1978, but the armed forces' right to political access was essentially institutionalized in an explicit power-sharing arrangement whereby the party organization of the JNA was guaranteed representation on the LCY Central Committee equal to that of the autonomous provinces. This territorial/organizational quota system survived the post-Tito Twelfth Party Congress in June 1982, as did the incorporation of a representative of the Yugoslav military on the party's 23-member Presidium.

This is a far cry from the army takeover fantasized in the Western press as one post-Tito political alternative. However, the importance of the military as a political actor in post-Tito Yugoslavia should not be underrated. In the 1982 party Presidium only seven members were held over from 1978. Nine of the twenty-three are ex officio, i.e., on the highest party body in their capacity as president of a republic/province or the JNA party organization. Certainly, with the January 1983 death of Dr. Vladimir Bakaric—long considered by many observers to be the most important Yugoslav leader after Tito and Kardelj—the military men at the top of the LCY are among its most senior members. Indeed, Bakaric's warning that any attempt by the army to seize power would unleash civil war notwithstanding,[30] this is considered natural and right by such prominent Yugoslav spokesmen as Professor Jovan Djordjevic, who bluntly wrote: "the army always remains one of the important organs of the system, an instrument not only of the country's defense but also of its politics."[31]

Although I would not go so far as to assume that there has been a fusion of party-army leadership roles at the highest level, if one uses Huntington's index of interpretation by the military of other social institutions,[32] military influence on civilian power structures in Yugoslavia has steadily increased since the Ninth LCY Congress in 1969. Indeed, there are currently three generals on the LCY Presidium: Dane Cuic selected to represent the party organization in the armed forces; Franjo Herljevic—the former head of the State Security Service— occupying one of the Bosnia-Hercegovina slots; and Petar Matic from the Vojvodina. This underlines the reality that, power-sharing arrangements aside, politicians in uniform have an advantage in that they can represent territorial units as well as participate in party bodies in their military capacity. The new defense minister, Branko Mamula, is not on the Presidium, but will undoubtedly work closely with that body. His predecessor Nikola Ljubicic has taken over as state president of Serbia. Ljubicic's new job signals determination to take a firm stand against further violence in that republic's autonomous province Kosovō.[33] His subsequent nomination to the Collective State Presidency (February 1984) expanded the military's role still further. Nor is the increased military participation limited to upper party echelons. Under the 1974 constitution army delegations officially sit in communal and republic assemblies, raising the question of whether it may become appropriate to think in terms of a party-army elite in Yugoslavia much as one would for many of the developing countries of the Third World.

SPECIFIC PROBLEM AREAS

Thus far this chapter has provided a context for understanding the fundamental problems facing Yugoslav policy makers, their perspectives, and the structure of the political environment. Here we will look briefly at the interaction of these problems before turning to their international dimension.

Yugoslavia is plagued with four major internal dilemmas:

1. Economic tensions created by the need for austerity to pay the principal and interest due on Yugoslavia's $20 billion debt to the West, exacerbated by differences in regional levels of development.
2. Political/social pressures generated by the deep-rooted, national (ethnic) antagonism inherent in Yugoslav political cultures.
3. Organizational/ideological struggle over the nature of the post-

    Tito League of Communists and its relationship to republic/
provincial parties.
4. Sociological/political difficulties centering on the age
   homogeneity of the Yugoslav revolutionary elite.

The early 1980s is a time of troubles for the Yugoslav economy. Like
Poland, Yugoslavia is caught in the vice created by the burden of large
Western debts that must be serviced in hard currency. In view of declining Yugoslav exports and the negative impact of the worldwide
economic slump on Yugoslav tourism, the needed Western currencies
are increasingly unavailable. Roughly half of the $20 billion came due
in 1982/1983 ($7 billion repayment was expected in 1983).[34] Thus, the
most immediate problem for Yugoslav policy makers attempting to
negotiate a post-Tito political transition was and is the economic imperative: how to come up with enough hard currency to avoid default
and keep the country's credit good? No easy task for an, at best, newly
industrialized Balkan country plagued by an estimated 30 percent inflation, with some 888,000 workers unemployed.[35]

By the summer of 1981 Yugoslavia found itself in an absurd position
of buying raw materials in the West and due to lower quality controls
selling in the East for what amounted to "play money" (at least in terms
of repaying Western debts) or elaborate barter arrangements. According to some official estimates, inflation that summer topped 50 percent.
Strenuous efforts were made to turn the situation around, such as the
establishment of the Kraigher Federal Commission for Economic
Stabilization. Hard currency imports were sharply curtailed; priority
given to clamping down on runaway domestic investment[36] and
stimulating export enterprises with hopes of selling in the West.

This meant that the economic well-being of individual Yugoslavs
declined. Coffee, an absolute must for traditional hospitality in those
parts of the country under Turkish domination for 500 years, became
prohibitively expensive and harder to get. Prices shot up. There were
shortages of such basic items as laundry soap and cooking oil. These
annoyances were aggravated by wide differences in policies and levels
of efficiency in local distribution. From the viewpoint of an ordinary
housewife, the official price freeze was a joke. Indeed, there were so
many exceptions that at best one could say the policy slowed formerly
galloping inflation to a trot.

After the Twelfth Party Congress, the government pushed forward
with still more stringent economic measures in an effort to prove to
Western bankers that Yugoslav decision makers could bite the bullet.
In October 1982 the dinar was devalued again, this time by 20 percent,
a move justified by the Yugoslav Prime Minister Milka Planinc as

needed to improve Yugoslav exports. Other austerity measures followed.[37] In 1983, there was food rationing in many parts of Yugoslavia.[38] Gasoline could be bought only for coupons, and Yugoslavs wishing to travel abroad had to deposit 5,000 dinars (about 100 dollars) for one year in a no-interest government account. To take such belt-tightening measures was all the more difficult given the developmental disparities between Yugoslav republics and autonomous provinces. Moreover, the process was complicated by the fact that the policy makers involved were simultaneously wrestling with the political fall-out of Albanian Yugoslav national/ethnic protests far more violent than the Zagreb student strikes and demonstrations in the early 1970s.[39]

By 1981 there were 1.7 million ethnic Albanian citizens of Yugoslavia, more than double the number of Montenegrins and more than the 1.3 million Macedonians. Indeed, more than half as many Albanians lived in Yugoslavia as in neighboring Albania. Most such Albanian Yugoslavs lived in the Kosovo, an autonomous province within the republic of Serbia, where they were 78 percent of the province's 1.5 million inhabitants. At the same time some 378,000 Albanians lived in Macedonia (20 percent); another 37,000 in Montenegro. Thus both these republics have significant Albanian minorities as well. The key political question remains that of republic status for the Kosovo. The existence of neighboring Albania aside, how can 1.2 million Albanians be denied the right to be a republic when there are far fewer Montenegrins with that right?

Numbers and time would appear to be on the side of the Albanians. Today this minority is the fifth-largest ethnic group in Yugoslavia after Serbs, Croats, and Bosnian Moslems, and tallying just 20,000 below the Slovenes. Moreover, the Albanian birthrate is the highest in Yugoslavia (estimated at 3.7 percent). Since the Slovenes have a much lower birthrate, and a suspected larger number of Bosnian Moslems register as "Yugoslav," it may not be long before the Albanian "national minority" will be the third-largest ethnic group in Yugoslavia.

Yet this demographic logic is undermined by both historical and political considerations. From the Serbian viewpoint, the Kosovo is historically Serbian. Here the medieval Serbian kings were crowned. Here in the town of Prizren, Tsar Dusan established his empire in the fourteenth century. Here in 1389 Serbs fought Turks in the famous battle of the Kosovo, a battle whose spirit still lives in the Serbian epic *Kosovo Polje*. Here in the dusty town of Pec, the Serbian patriarchate was founded in 1346 and the Serbian church became independent of Constantinople. In short, the Kosovo is sacred to the Serbs.

From the Serbian perspective, Albanians are interlopers forced on them by the Turks, who favored Muslim Albanians above Christian

Serbs. Albanians came as "colonizers," forcing Serbs from the region in the seventeenth and eighteenth centuries. Albanians, in turn, date their claim back to the seventh century when the Kosovo was inhabited by the Illyrians, ancient ancestors of the Albanians. Here in 1878 the League of Prizren was established, marking the beginning of Albanian national consciousness. In short, as Peter Prifti has eloquently documented, both Serbs and Albanians claim title by virtue of (1) possession and (2) historic-symbolic significance.[40]

The decentralizing reforms of the late 1960s excited hopes of increased local autonomy throughout Yugoslavia. Open Albanian nationalism flared in the Kosovo. Rioting ensued, and there were demands that the province be granted republic status, use of the Albanian language at all levels, and a "national" university, and that Albanians living in the Macedonian republic should be protected. Soon violence spread to the Tetovo district of Macedonia.

Although the Kosovo has not received republican status, a number of concessions to Albanian nationalism was made. By 1970 Albanian was an actual rather than a token language in the Kosovo. Albanians had the right to fly the Albanian flag, an overwhelmingly sensitive issue, and they soon were to achieve the demand for a "national" university (one where the language of instruction was Albanian) at Pristina. There were economic improvements as well. Downtown Pristina, capital of the Kosovo, became a showcase of urban renewal, frequently featured on Yugoslav television. Yugoslav leaders were justly proud of their efforts to modernize the province. This pride only intensified the backlash of shock and bitterness that followed the spring 1981 outbursts of Albanian nationalism and frustration at the continued discrepancy between living standards in the province with those enjoyed by the rest of Yugoslavia.[41]

Set off by a student demonstration on March 11, 1981 against bad food in the University of Pristina cafeteria, a wave of riots and violent disorders swept the province. Estimates of the number of rioters ranged from 10,000 to 20,000, many of them armed. Shopwindows were smashed, cars overturned, and, according to some sources, 40 people were killed and over 1,000 wounded.[42] Reportedly workers, and in some cases Albanian provincial party members as well, joined the student rioters in openly nationalistic demands that at the moderate end of the spectrum focused on republic status for the province while the more extreme wanted outright secession, by implication favoring union with Albania.

The Yugoslav army backed up by security detachments restored an uneasy calm, although sporadic incidents of violence continued to occur. In spite of attempts to blame the crisis on subversive activities directed from Tirana and by "others" who would like to see Yugoslavia fall apart in ethnic chaos, calls for investigation and "differentiation" (a euphemism for party purges) on the part of the provincial League of Communists underlined recognition of indigenous unrest. Despite the somewhat tardy replacement of the former head of the Kosovo party organization, Mahmmut Bakali—presumably for not having anticipated and defused the nationalist agitation—self-criticism, "administrative punishments," and expulsions of those party members judged to have been grossly negligent or actually rioters, there is considerable evidence of footdragging and less-than-enthusiastic cooperation by the provincial party in the demanded "renewal."[43] At least on the part of many knowledgeable observers in Belgrade there is an unofficial but openly expressed fear that the Kosovo Communist party and provincial security apparatus are themselves hopelessly infected with nationalism, and that the provincial party-controlled press is unreliable. This has led to political demands for more "objective" reporting in the province and to an increasing number of Serbian reporters who are intent on getting at the true story, most especially of the situation of Serbs and Montenegrins still living in the region.[44]

All of which brings me to what may be considered the ripple effect of nationalist manifestations in Yugoslavia. As with the Croatian events in December 1970, Albanian rioting in the spring of 1981 and the subsequent failure of efforts to "pacify" the province, in turn, have intensified Serbian nationalism, often characterized as chauvinism by non-Serbian Yugoslavs. For Serbs, to accept republic status of the Kosovo would be to cut out the heart of Serbia. Such a solution has been described by Stane Dolanc, at the time a member of the LCY Presidium, as "impossible" within the framework of Yugoslavia.

Moreover, Serbian fears of reverse discrimination for Serbs and Montenegrins in the province are not simply paranoid. Not only did the 1981 census reveal that some 18,000 Serbs and more than 4,500 Montenegrins had left the Kosovo since 1971, but in the turmoil of 1981 that exodus visibly increased amid charges of Albanian pressure on its Slavic neighbors to get out. It is exceedingly difficult to stem the tide once an ethnic group feels increasingly politically/economically disadvantaged (never mind unsafe) in any particular location, as the commissions directed to monitor Serbian/Montenegrin outmigration are painfully aware.

The explosiveness of this issue is exacerbated by media coverage. The mandate from Belgrade for full information aside, outside journalists are handicapped in their reports on events in the Kosovo by lack of local contacts, by reliance on visibly biased sources, and by what might be characterized most kindly as inexperience with investigative reporting.[45]

In this context it is perhaps understandable that solving the Kosovo crisis took on an overwhelming importance for both ordinary Serbs and their political representatives. Conversely, the single-mindedness of that approach annoyed non-Serbian Yugoslavs, particularly in the other Serbian autonomous province of Vojvodina, where it was feared with some justification that Serbian attempts to reassert authority vis-a-vis the Kosovo would be accompanied by attacks on Vojvodina autonomy. Quite apart from reports of sympathy for the Albanians among the Hungarian population of this region, even high-ranking Serbian members of the Vojvodina party demonstrated considerable impatience. As I was told in the Vojvodina capital, Novi Sad, "it is not up to Yugoslavia to solve the Serbian national question at the expense of all other political and economic priorities."[46]

Although officially strongly supportive when it came to Serbian territorial fears, observers in both Zagreb and Ljubljana (capital cities of Croatia and Slovenia respectively) felt that federal and Serbian politicians alike should have seen the writing on the wall. After all, as symbolically appropriate as an Albanian language track at Pristina University might be, where were the 37,000 students attending that university to find jobs on graduation? The Kosovo could not absorb them. Indeed, with unemployment in the province reaching 27.5 percent by 1981, it was more important than ever that Albanian Kosovars also be proficient in Serbo-Croat.[47]

In terms of the unresolved conflict between the economic rationalizers and their opposition discussed earlier, the Kosovo riots of 1981 and their aftermath emphasize the political need to eliminate the gap between economic conditions in the Kosovo and those in the more prosperous parts of Yugoslavia. Yet it is not possible to achieve anything approaching equalization and simultaneously to allow the northern, more developed areas of the country to advance at the pace they are capable of. In Ljubljana or Zagreb, which approach West European standards of living, demands for equalization are seen as economic exploitation.

This issue was as intense in the summer of 1981 as it had been ten years before during the rising tide of Croatian nationalism. If anything, Croat and Slovene resentment at perceived misuse of federal development funds in the Kosovo sharpened. Subsequently, the question of who would pay the ongoing bill was also a matter of dispute. Take, for example, the openly negative Slovene reaction to the unexpected increase in the Yugoslav defense budget by some $350 million dollars for 1983, requiring a 30 percent increase in Ljubljana's 1982 contribution if this amount were spread among the republics/provinces.[48]

At the same time pressure has become more insistent that non-Slovene Yugoslavs working in that republic in a service capacity make an effort to learn Slovene instead of resting on the knowledge that most Slovenes understand Serbo-Croat. In short, language remains a key component of ethnic politics in Yugoslavia, increasingly even in Slovenia, long the most low-keyed of Yugoslav republics in terms of "national manifestations." Religion is also becoming more sensitive in this regard if regime attacks on Catholics and Moslems alike are any indication.

However, in my view, economic nationalism remains the fundamental, long-term threat to Yugoslav political and economic life. Nationalism intensifies debates over resource allocation, while socialist economic rhetoric becomes a vehicle for expressing national/ethnic grievances otherwise repressed as illegitimate within the Yugoslav system. In this manner questions of economic reform not only open the back door to ethnic politics, but themselves become bogged down in conflicting nationalisms.

Given the nature of both "national" and economic dilemmas, conflicts of interest among republic/provincial party leaders as well as between these territorially based party organizations and the LCY can hardly be expected to disappear. Although Tito forced a resolution of the Croatian crisis in 1971/1972 that favored the federal center, now the tables are turned. Ironically, Croatia subsequently achieved many of the demands that led to the purge of the LCC leadership at Karadjordjevo. Despite these gains and the increased acceptance of the need for national/ethnic as well as territorial representation on top party/state bodies, the manner in which the 1971 crisis was resolved is publicly repressed but not forgotten. At best a paper-thin trust exists between the two major nations occupying Yugoslavia.

Moreover, although republic elites suffered a major setback at the Tenth Party Congress of 1974, the logic of self-managing socialism continues to support them. In one sense, such Croat leaders as Mika Tripalo and Savka Dabcevic-Kucar were captured by their republic's political constituency, not by a "counterrevolutionary mass movement." A similar process inhibits the drive for "differentiation" in the Kosovo in the 1980s. Undeniably, Albanian national/economic grievances have taken a violent, explicitly antisystem form in some cases. Nonetheless, the Kosovo Party organization is only the most extreme example of the fact that—temporary solutions notwithstanding—in the 1980s Yugoslav party leaders are subject to both genuine and increasing pressures from below.

This brings us to the overlapping problem of the nature of the post-Tito Communist party and tensions created by the demand for expanded access to political power. In retrospect, it is evident that Tito failed to create/or recreate the revolutionary party that he had in mind with his mini cultural revolution of the early 1970s. The reversal implicit in renewed emphasis on the "pluralism of self-managing interests" at the Eleventh LCY Congress in 1978[49] raised the possibility that after more than a quarter of a century of stressing the party's "educational role" in society, it is no longer possible to return to the "commanding role" sought by the 1971–72 purges. While the top party leadership supported Tito personally, they did not support his interpretation of democratic centralism. Then in 1982 the first post-Tito Party Congress "of continuity" ratified the transitional collective leadership based on a complex territorial/ethnic quota system that once again tilts the balance of organizational power away from the federal party apparatus to the republic/provincial parties.

Formal commitment to democratic centralism aside, organizationally the League of Communists of Yugoslavia is essentially a confederation of its republic, provincial, and armed forces party organizations. These parties held their own congresses before the federal Twelfth Party Congress. Delegates selected at regional congresses and that of the armed forces went to Belgrade in June 1982 representing their territorial or JNA organizations. While the Twelfth Congress must be considered a masterpiece of organizational interaction, the journalistic impression that it elected a new party leadership is misleading. In reality the federal congress ratified republic/provincial/JNA choices for who would represent them at the top. Whether or not party leaders from other republics/provinces might have preferred a different choice of colleagues, there was no veto power over the regional lists such as existed by virtue of Tito's authority during his lifetime. The policy consequence is significant for the content of democratic centralism, for with central party policy largely a matter of negotiated solutions, democratic centralism becomes more an instrument of implementation than an organizing principle.

The nature of Yugoslav collective leadership is also marked by another of Tito's political initiatives in his declining years. In his determination to stage-manage his own succession, Tito tried to strengthen party institutions that he had come to personify. It was the party as an organization that would survive. In short, there must be no more Titos. At the seventh session of the CC Presidium on October 19, 1978, that body adopted new standing rules providing for a "chairman of the Presidium" to stand in for Tito (who remained president of the party for life) for one year and no longer. With Tito's speech to the Eighth

Congress of Yugoslav Trade Unions the next month[50] it became clear that the demand for collective work was intended to penetrate all levels of party organization. Tito called for one-year terms for party presidents and secretaries in the commune and republic/provinces organizations as well as at the top of the federal party.

The irony of the great leader of Yugoslavia attacking "leaderism" aside, this was a bold attempt to combine collective responsibility with constant rotation of leading positions designed to prevent "unhealthy ambitions of single persons" or the monopoly of power by informal groups. It struck at the longstanding problem that Yugoslav politicians tend to cluster in political cliques whose members move back and forth between key/party/state/trade union posts in their regions. In such instances, genuine political participation runs into the bottleneck of the same ten prominent officials playing musical chairs with the top local political jobs.[51]

Tito's initiative firmly tied "collective leadership" to deprofessionalization of politics. It is not an intrinsically obvious combination despite the strong ideological bias against professional politicians inherent in Yugoslav self-managing socialism. There were constitutional problems as well, for Tito rather blithely ignored the fact that the constitution of 1974 had set two-year terms for presidents and secretaries of local communities and self-managing sociopolitical agencies. Not too surprisingly, the campaign set off a determined political struggle between proponents of the one-year mandate and those within the party who felt that such frequent rotation was politically too disruptive to allow for orderly government. The fear was that the amount of time spent on deciding who was in charge would lead to nothing being done at all. This debate continued after Tito's death, and the issue was side-stepped rather than resolved at the Twelfth LCY Congress.[52]

To some degree political energies directed to sorting out the content of collective leadership in post-Tito Yugoslavia have obscured a fundamental demographic problem of party rank and file. The tendency for LCY membership to become disproportionately white collar has swelled the ranks of administration at all levels. Many Yugoslavs with whom I talked in 1981 and during the summer of 1982 feared that endemic bureaucratization had not only hardened the arteries of revolution but severely restricted political reforms needed to weather the ongoing economic crisis.

Moreover, the question of fair distribution of political benefits is just as acute in Communist as in noncommunist political systems. In Yugoslavia the discrepancy of workers' self-management led by a party with fewer and fewer workers could become politically explosive. Although the lesson of Poland, where the Polish working class attempted to bypass the party to assume its own "leading role," intensifies awareness of potential consequences, this is not a new problem. The Belgrade student strike in 1968 focused on highly sensitive demands to eliminate social inequality and unemployment and to democratize the League of Communists. At that time, Tito supported the students' priorities if not their methods. He pledged to restore unity and appealed to the strikers to help him. The initial response was euphoric; it was a masterpiece of cooptation. Yet in the political/economic context that came to dominate Yugoslav politics, even Tito could not deliver.

Without Tito, Yugoslav policy makers intent on stabilizing the country's staggering economy are substantially more vulnerable to potential challenges from the Left. Students of the 1980s, like those of 1968, are the children of the partisans, some of whom learned only too well the ideal of "egalitarian socialist society." Through no fault of their own, they do not belong to the "Club of 1941." Still, there is no true substitute for that trial by fire. To attack from the Left is the only legitimate challenge to a governing party that is charged somewhat harshly by the young with having both won and abandoned the revolution. Their anger is a potential weapon available to the opponents of the market socialism that some economists in Yugoslavia and the West alike see as the only way out of the country's present economic troubles.

These days, the problem of "gerontocracy"—impossible to discuss openly during Tito's lifetime—is frankly admitted by party leaders and debated in the Yugoslav press.[53] One does not need to go so far as to agree that "sclerosis has taken over the political blood stream" to recognize the need for an orderly departure of the partisan generation to make way for new political talent and leadership. Indeed, steps are being taken in that direction. The ages of the members of the 1982 Federal Executive Council show clearly that this government is younger than previous ones. It is also heavily weighted on the side of technical, most especially economic, expertise. At the same time, the party leaderships in the republics/provinces are younger than the average age of the LCY CC Presidium, in some cases by as much as ten years.[54] Therefore it can be assumed both that republic/party apparatuses will serve as increasingly mandatory political apprenticeships for federal responsibilities and that some clashes between the LCY and the territorially based party organizations will be fueled by a conflict of generations. As an interesting aside, here too the Yugoslav Armed Forces is held up as an organization that has successfully replaced old leaders; a political model to be followed.

It is to the credit of the power-sharing arrangement worked out at the Eleventh Congress in 1978 that even in the shadow of martial law in Poland there is less emphasis by political observers on the army as a temporary or not so temporary substitute for party cohesion. I would still argue, as I did in the late 1970s,[55] that the Yugoslav armed forces have been successfully engaged in the day-to-day running of the country in a manner that reduces the temptation for political intervention by military elites.

This does not mean that the military is unconcerned. The current Yugoslav defense minister, Admiral Branko Mamula, has emphasized the army's contribution as a "breeding ground of brotherhood, unity, and Yugoslav socialist patriotism," lauding it as an important factor "of security, internal cohesion, and stability" of the country. He is blunt about the negative reaction of the army to "slowness and certain inconsistencies in implementing agreed policy" and the tendency to favor special interest "at the expense of common, general Yugoslav interests."[56]

These concerns could intensify if the civilian party leaders are unable to reach a concensus on the substance of the political changes that it appears generally agreed must accompany the economic program for recovery, or, conversely, if complaints about defense spending were allowed to erode Yugoslavia's military budget. Military leaders in Yugoslavia have been willing to go along with what in my view amounts to a party/army partnership in post-Tito Yugoslavia. Yet as all around the world, the ability of the civilian partners to remain in control depends on party cohesion and political performance. Thus in Yugoslavia the future party/army dynamic is not so much a question of political ambition as of the skill of Yugoslav party leaders in riding out the economic heavy weather of the 1980s, institutionalizing the current collective leadership, and navigating the ship of state in terms of Yugoslav foreign policy.

THE FOREIGN POLICY COMPONENT

Nonalignment is a tricky concept.[57] Both East and West have seen it as a vague, primarily symbolic stance, each suspecting that to be nonaligned meant tilting toward "the other camp." From both sides of the ideological fence, it was viewed as a nonpolicy, a slightly immoral nonpolicy at that. By contrast, in the Yugoslav perception, nonalignment meant buying in, not opting out. Tito did not invent nonalignment. Yugoslavia joined in a process already existing in Asia and Africa, whereby newly independent states were attempting to change international priorities away from East-West ideological differences to the problems of what it is politically fashionable to call the North-South split, i.e., the differences between the "haves" and "have nots" on a continuum of modernization-development-industrialization. In this process ideology was only as relevant as its contribution toward these goals. To the developing countries, nonalignment meant more than their refusal to be surrogates in superpower conflicts marginally related to their national interests. It meant an active policy of influence-seeking whenever problems of special concern for their young, fragile societies were involved. This amounted to a policy of ad hoc, issue-oriented collaboration, pragmatically rooted despite the rhetoric surrounding efforts to find common platforms.

Yugoslavia moved toward nonalignment in answer to the isolation imposed by the Cominform break. That move came in part as a consequence of the Yugoslav election to the U.N. Security Council in 1949, when for the first time Belgrade experienced prolonged close contact with the newly emerging nations of Asia and Africa. Nonalignment maximized Tito's influence and options in an otherwise unpromising international environment. Nonalignment satisfied the psychological need to keep a window open for future contacts with the socialist East while simultaneously keeping open that essential door to economic relations with the West. Nonaligned allies had an additional advantage. They left Tito free to put forward the "Yugoslav model" within the international Communist movement, thereby potentially leaving room for the revolutionary expansionism that he had reluctantly abandoned with the Cominform split.

As the postwar bipolar international system moved beyond the cold war into the "limited adversary relationship" between Moscow and Washington in the 1960s, East European countries came to be seen less as satellites than as client states. There was *de facto* acceptance of the Yugoslav principle of national roads to socialism, that at least until the invasion of Czechoslovakia in 1968 blurred the distinctiveness of the Yugoslav path. The nonaligned states of Asia and Africa took to fighting among themselves. In 1979 nonaligned Vietnam invaded nonaligned Cambodia. In the 1980s mutual Moslem bloodletting in the Iran-Iraq war with all its disastrous consequences for the economies of other nonaligned nations continues to resist mediation. These are only the most recent examples of the degree to which the movement is plagued by internonaligned violence. One by one the first generation of nonaligned leaders died: Nehru (1964), Nasser (1970), and now Tito (1980).

Moreover, the other side of successful recruitment has been the organizational dilemma of coordinating policy and finding a common denominator from which to approach such issues as the North-South dialogue. For as nonaligned membership grew from the 25 states that attended the founding Belgrade Conference in 1961 to the 101 members that participated in the seventh Nonaligned Summit in New Delhi in

March 1983, so did the differences that divided these states: how to respond to Soviet military occupation of Afghanistan; who should fill Cambodia's seat; and how to relate to the deteriorating situation in the Middle East? Such divisions cut across both policy and ideological lines.

In the 1980s the intensity of U.S.-Soviet hostilities, which foreign policy elites in Belgrade agree with many Third World scholars and diplomats should be considered as "the second cold war," has answered the question raised by the era of detente—nonalignment between whom? The renewed urgency of defusing potential superpower confrontations interacts with open concern about the influence of superpower proxies such as Cuba which takes the position that the socialist countries are the "natural allies" of the nonaligned.[58] Despite the shift in leadership of the movement from Havana to New Delhi and Fidel Castro's replacement as chair by Indira Gandhi, the question of the membership criterion—i.e., who is nonaligned—remains the question of the 1980s.

The Yugoslav commitment to nonalignment has been substantially more consistent than the movement's international environment or collective political behavior. As the concept appeared increasingly fuzzy during the heyday of detente, even those Yugoslav spokesmen who conceded that nonalignment might be the wrong label were firmly convinced that for Yugoslavia it was the right policy. In their view, nonalignment is fundamentally a demand for democratization of the international system to allow small and medium-sized states to operate as independent political actors rather than as superpower clients.

Thus, throughout the 1970s, the target of nonalignment shifted from the Third World to Europe, where the snail-like progress toward a European security conference provided a vehicle for Belgrade's efforts to achieve a common denominator of interests among small and medium European states.[59] Whatever it was not, the 1975 Helsinki Conference on European Security and Cooperation was at least a partial victory for Yugoslav foreign policy. These efforts have subsequently focused on the drawn-out CSCE sessions in Madrid, with visible results in terms of a closer relationship between the neutral and nonaligned states in Europe.[60]

Nonalignment also strikes a balance acceptable both to those Yugoslavs who would prefer closer ties with the Soviet bloc and to those who favor a more Western orientation. In this sense, Yugoslav dedication to the nonaligned alternative is a domestic compromise as well as a foreign policy. Particularly given the increasingly confederal nature of the Yugoslav party faced with its present political/economic imperatives, there is little doubt that nonalignment will continue. This policy maximizes Yugoslav influence in Europe and the Third World. It strengthens Yugoslavia's hand in the East-West game and intracommunist politics alike.

Since Tito's death, the Soviets have played a waiting game with respect to Yugoslavia, substantially refraining from attempts to influence political direction. Unlike former President Carter, Brezhnev went to Tito's funeral. His successor's readiness to help Yugoslavia is expressed in the guidelines for long-term economic cooperation (until 1990) signed between the two countries during Soviet Prime Minister Nikolai Tikhonov's visit to Belgrade in March 1983.[61] Moscow's share of Yogoslav trade has been steadily going up. In 1981 the Soviets accounted for 18.8 percent of Yugoslav imports and absorbed 33.3 percent of Yugoslav exports—increases of 5.3 percent and 11.6 percent respectively over 1977 figures.[62] With an estimated $35 billion in turnover expected for 1981–85, it is not an exaggeration to call the Soviet Union Yugoslavia's most important trading partner.[63]

Even before Tikhonov's visit, fears that such economic dependency could have political repercussions were being openly discussed in Belgrade and other Yugoslav capitals. Nonetheless, it had not been forgotten that despite Tito's Order of Lenin, the 1972 honeymoon in Soviet-Yugoslav relations soured, and credits reportedly promised during Soviet enthusiasm for the campaign to recentralize the LCY never materialized.

In short, Yugoslav political observers have a healthy skepticism about "fraternal assistance," while Yugoslav policy makers are both sophisticated and experienced in balancing between Moscow and other policy options. In Marxist jargon, it was undoubtedly "no accident" that, the very day the Yugoslav-Soviet guidelines were signed in Belgrade, it was announced that Yugoslavia had reached an agreement with 15 Western banks on a $2 billion loan as part of a $5 billion Western package to assist the Yugoslavs with their debt-servicing difficulties. Shortly thereafter, the May 10–15, 1983 visit of the Chinese Communist party Secretary-General Hu Yaobang and his fifty-member delegation underlined the post-Tito leadership's intention to remain nonaligned between Moscow and Beijing.

Politically Yugoslavia can be expected to continue to clash with the Soviets over both Afghanistan and Poland. Moreover, the Yugoslav view that Eurocommunism is "nonaligned communism" and that nonaligned principles apply to intracommunist politics is just as unpalatable to Brezhnev's successors as it was to Brezhnev.

How these differences influence Yugoslav foreign policy will continue to be a function of what other political and most importantly economic options exist. It is no secret that Western currency can do a lot more to help shore up the struggling Yugoslav economy than can barter arrangements with the Eastern bloc. Yet clashes of Yugoslav and U.S. policy interests can be expected on issues ranging from Washington's vision of what it takes to make Europe secure, attitudes toward Eurocommunism, and Yugoslavs' nonaligned preferences for the Middle East to the even more sensitive matter of pressure for freedom of the press as we understand it in post-Tito Yugoslavia. The manner in which U.S. policy makers respond to these situations will influence not only American-Yugoslav relations but potentially, Yugoslav strategic choices. In turn, how such issues are resolved will have an impact upon the domestic ideological-organizational struggle—strengthening some contenders, weakening others.

Overall, Yugoslav foreign and domestic policy problems are hopelessly entangled. Indeed, there is a pattern of Yugoslav foreign-domestic policy interactions dating from the Soviet-Yugoslav split in 1948 whereby foreign policy imperatives first created, then consistently reinforced, Yugoslav commitment to expanded political participation, i.e., socialist pluralism. Had Tito and the top Yugoslav leadership not desperately needed an alternative to the Stalinist model, Yugoslav self-managing socialism would not exist. The drive to recentralize the LCY after the Djilas affair in the mid-1950s was cut short by the second Soviet-Yugoslav dispute when Khrushchev dumped Tito in favor of Chinese support for the Soviet "leading role" in the international Communist movement at the 1957 Moscow Conference of ruling Communist parties. To justify their continued defiance, the LCY came out with the party program of 1958, thereby strengthening the first tentative steps toward self-management. The 1958 program was pointedly reaffirmed at the June 1978 LCY Congress, a symbolic rehabilitation of the pluralistic ideas that had been consistently played down since the "Croatian events" in 1971.

This shift away from the party recentralization of the early 1970s was symbolically connected with Soviet-Yugoslav polemics over the nature of the Eurocommunist challenge to Moscow. The end result of contending with Soviet ideologies over whether Eurocommunism represented nonaligned politics or anti-Sovietism strengthened the position of Yugoslavs in and outside the party to whom socialist self-management meant increasing local autonomy, genuine market socialism, legitimation of interest aggregation, and the right to criticize without fear. Nonaligned principles reinforced the concept of collective responsibility and the urgency of seeking a political solution in the Kosovo that would not undermine Yugoslavia's foreign policy credibility.

Nor are foreign-domestic linkages limited to the broad cycles of attempting to sort out the relationship of the LCY to self-managing political organs within Yugoslav society. The "national question" is made more difficult by the fear that foreign powers can and will exploit terrorist elements of emigre subcultures, while territorial, ethnic-based irredentist demands exacerbate Yugoslav relations with neighboring Balkan states. The economic debates are fueled by squabbles over foreign credits. At the same time, attempted economic solutions open the door to mass labor migration, which has major domestic and foreign policy consequences. As one Yugoslav graphically put it, to separate these issues is like trying to unravel a pig's intestines. This chapter can at best identify the issues.

PROSPECTS FOR THE FUTURE

Although I do not agree with those scholars who believe that Yugoslavia has created a "socialist political culture," on balance I do consider Yugoslav self-management a grand political experiment. Dedication to that ideal, for all the problems of making it work, has been at the heart of Yugoslav politics for more than thirty years.

Every year thousands and thousands of ordinary Yugoslavs have had to cope with managing their own political and economic lives. Expanding the pool of those educated enough to bring needed skills to that process has been a priority. Indeed the nature of Yugoslav party membership indicates that most modern sectors of society have a real stake in their system and in continuing the experiment. As for foreign policy, Yugoslavia's most successful product has been its skillful, sophisticated diplomats. To whatever degree the experience of the Yugoslav diplomatic corps is diluted by applying republic/provincial quotas, the number of Yugoslavs entering the ranks of the country's foreign policy elite has nevertheless increased.

In my judgment, the process of trying to bring responsible participation out of the reality of Balkan apathy has given contemporary Yugoslav society strengths that were sadly lacking in the interwar Kingdom of Serbs, Croats, and Slovenes. Whether or not today's society can sustain the frustrations generated by economic hardships and drastic decline in the standard of living for most Yugoslavs remains an open question. There are prophets of doom in and outside Yugoslavia.

To retain perspective, it is useful to remember that this is hardly the first instance of such pessimism concerning Yugoslav options. For ten years before Tito's death in 1980, Yugoslavia-watchers speculated, "After Tito—what?" Their predictions were predominately gloomy scenarios of political collapse, ethnic-generated civil war, military coups, disintegration of the country with Croatia and Slovenia becoming mini-West European nations and the rest of Yugoslavia sliding into the Soviet bloc, or, at best, indirect Soviet domination of a demoralized League of Yugoslav Communists. Although I would in no way minimize the problems facing Tito's successors, it is sometimes forgotten that these forecasts of doom did not materialize.

The initial slogan of the Yugoslav transitional team—"After Tito— Tito!"—meant a continuation of the ideals of brotherhood, unity, and self-management. During the nine months that I spent in Yugoslavia in 1981, even teenagers wore Tito T-shirts and intercity buses often displayed placards proclaiming, "We are guarding Tito's way." A workman talked to me at length and with great sincerity about the importance of Tito's legacy. At the same time inflation, shortages, backlash from the violence in the Kosovo, and the lack of any single authority figure significantly strained all sectors of Yugoslav society. There were many frustrated complaints about how life had been better under Tito, and about whom to blame for the current economic hard times.

These observations point to a basic dilemma for Yugoslav policy makers. Tito is the George Washington of Yugoslavia (try imagining an American history textbook if George Washington had been president for thirty-five years). He is a cornerstone of the founding myth of Communist Yugoslavia, haloed by political ancestor-worship that supports the legitimacy of the current Yugoslav leaders. Unfortunately, the reality is that for all his political shrewdness and genuine brilliance at maximizing Yugoslavia's importance in the world, Tito was a poor economist. For years he ignored sound economic advice and blocked needed devaluation of the dinar. The truth is that Tito himself was in large part to blame for today's economic situation. What is more, Yugoslav politicians and economists are well aware of this. Yet they cannot have it both ways; Tito cannot simultaneously be the hero of Yugoslavia and a political scapegoat, no matter how justified his successors might be in saying, "we told him so." To criticize Tito publicly is a crime.[64] Nonetheless there are attempts to overcome this dilemma in the form of economic analysis that emphasizes that all economic factors have been deteriorating for the past *eight years,* i.e., a time period within which Tito can be implicitly held responsible.[65]

This process of indirect de-Titoization has also involved upgrading the image of Edvard Kardelj and pairing the Slovene theorist with Tito in such a way as to imply that these political leaders were equally important to developing the Yugoslav alternative.[66] It surfaced still more openly with the criticism made by intellectuals and party officials of the elements of personality cult reflected in the 1983 celebration of Tito's birthday.[67]

To whatever extent Tito's unifying myth is brought into a more balanced perspective, the need for effective political institutions increases. Perhaps because the post-Tito organizational solutions are
poorly understood in the West, Yugoslavia gets little credit for what is
a substantial political achievement. Its complex territorial/ethnic/army
quota system is a broadly based power-sharing arrangement that substantially increases the chances for implementation of policy. The rotation schedules minimize the amount of political energy dissipated in
factional struggles at the top. No winner can take all; conversely there
are no total losers. At least potentially, the political roles of the prime
minister and the Federal Executive Council have been upgraded.

Admittedly with an economic gun to its temple, the government has
installed an unpopular austerity program and has made hard decisions
reasonably quickly despite the dire predictions about republic/
provincial consensus being synonymous with policy paralysis. These
accomplishments have increased public awareness of the need for economic integration even among those most opposed to centralist political solutions.[68] In my judgment, the problem of the Kosovo cannot be
solved, but in an economically stabilizing Yugoslavia it can be lived
with and perhaps gradually defused.

Nonetheless there are a number of political pitfalls over which the
Yugoslav leaders have some but by no means total control. First,
under the strain of being considered what is sometimes referred to as
"the sacrificed" political generation, Yugoslav policy makers must resist the temptation to get sidetracked into confrontations with the
Yugoslav press over media criticism of mistakes, inconsistencies, and
the inevitable examples of poor performance. Whether or not those
political leaders who find the hard-hitting reporting of the post-Tito
media unhelpful and even harmful are right, efforts to muzzle the press
only hurt their credibility at home and abroad.

Secondly, there is an inherent danger in the ongoing agonizing over
whether Yugoslavia should change its political system or those running
it, with the implication sometimes being that both are necessary.[69] This
is the 1980s variant of the historic debate over whether Yugoslavia
needs more or less economic/political self-management. It focuses on a
genuinely fundamental problem for all collective leadership—how to
avoid the logical consequence that if everyone is responsible then no
one can be held accountable.[70]

Undoubtedly, reforms are needed. However, the craving for a total
solution, a panacea that will somehow miraculously wipe out economic
conflict, ethnic hostility, and social inequality at one blow, has been a
generic weakness of the Yugoslav revolution. In the 1940s the solution
was perceived to be the catharsis of partisan struggle, then in 1952 the

turn to self-management, later the 1961/1965 economic reforms, the 1971 constitutional amendments, and the 1974 recentralization of the party. The real importance of the 1978 congress was that it signaled the recognition that a political mechanism was needed, and not a miracle or a new personality cult. That mechanism, which has survived Tito's death and the 1982 LCY Congress, desperately needs to be institutionalized and improved, but not abandoned. For in the end self-managing socialism, if it is to exist at all, must find ways to establish accountability within the framework of collective responsibility. It is appropriate to remember that the Yugoslav economy is in its current condition largely because Tito could not be held accountable.

Self-managing socialism, like other attempts at democracy, is basically incompatible both with charismatic authority and, in the Yugoslav context, with any major recentralization.[71] The present and future Yugoslav leaders' success in synthesizing the norms of self-management with the post-Tito personality cult will be a major factor in future political outcomes, further complicated by the country's stark economic needs.

Perhaps most imminently, there is the bleak possibility that austerity measures to meet the demands of Western bankers will eventually cut so deeply into the second/grey economy that keeps most ordinary Yugoslav families going that the economic cure could precipitate popular revolt and political collapse. This would be analogous to the situation of the Dominican Republic in 1965—a World Bank version of the medical homily, "the operation worked but the patient died." Should this happen, the after-Tito prophets of doom may prove to have identified the right scenarios if for the wrong reasons. Yet Yugoslav leaders are not naive in this respect, and Yugoslavia has an impressive survival record against bad odds. Thus even those who consider the Yugoslav system most fragile should take comfort in the fact that history does not repeat itself without the help of men and women who make policy.

NOTES

This chapter benefited greatly from the research assistance of Rada Vlajinac of the Massachusetts Institute of Technology Center for International Studies. Its revision is based on field research in Yugoslavia made possible by a Fulbright Faculty Research Abroad Grant, May–December 1981, an American Council of Learned Societies East European Summer Fellowship to return to Yugoslavia during the 1982 LCY Twelfth Party Congress, and the writing time supported by a University of Missouri-Columbia Graduate Research Council Summer Fellowship, 1982. I am grateful to Alex N. Dragnich for his comments on the first edition.

1. Quoted by Vladimir Dedijer, *With Tito Through the War: Partisan Diary, 1941–1944* (London: A. Hamilton, 1951), p. 39.

2. See M. George Zaninovich, *The Development of Socialist Yugoslavia* (Baltimore: Johns Hopkins Press, 1968), pp. 44–50.

3. Population figures from *NIN (Nedeljne Informativne Novine)* (Belgrade), February 28, 1982. In reality, which peoples are considered nations is essentially a matter of Yugoslav public policy resulting from a mixture of both foreign policy and domestic concerns. The Macedonian and Moslem nations exist for political reasons. Dennison I. Rusinow provides a concise account of how in Yugoslavia "Muslim" became an ethnic rather than a strictly religious designation, "Yugoslavia's Muslim Nation," Universities Field Staff International (UFSI) Report, 1982, no. 8, Europe.

4. See Bogdan Denis Denitch, *The Legitimation of a Revolution: The Yugoslav Case* (New Haven: Yale University Press, 1976), pp. 34–36. My intention is not to imply that this is the only political legacy that the Serbs brought to interwar Yugoslavia. For the story of the Serbian struggle for constitutional rule, see Alex N. Dragnich, *Serbia, Nikola Pasic and Yugoslavia* (New Brunswick, N.J.: Rutgers University Press, 1974).

5. A. Ross Johnson, "The Role of the Military in Yugoslavia: An Historical Sketch," in Roman Kolkowicz and Andrzej Korbonski, eds., *Soldiers, Peasants, and Bureaucrats: Civil-Military Relations in Communist and Modernizing Societies* (London: George Allen & Unwin, 1982), table 8.3, "Nationality of the Officer Corps," p. 198.

6. This was particularly true in Croatia and is a pattern that has continued. According to unofficial estimates in 1971, individuals who were ethnically Serbian living in the republic of Croatia accounted for roughly 35 percent of the Croatian Communist party as opposed to 15 percent of the republic population.

7. Note there were substantial outside contributions both in terms of British and American aid to the partisan war effort and later during the war when the Soviet Red Army liberated Belgrade. Subsequently, Djilas's protest concerning the behavior of these Russian soldiers in Yugoslavia was to become a factor in the Soviet-Yugoslav dispute. See Milovan Djilas, *Conversations with Stalin* (New York: Harcourt, Brace, & World Inc., 1962), pp. 87–88.

8. See Branko Horvat, "Yugoslav Economic Policy in the Post-War Period: Problems, Ideas, Institutional Developments," *The American Economic Review* 61 (June 1971), supplement, p. 73.

9. See Robert Bass and Elizabeth Marbury, eds., *The Soviet-Yugoslav Controversy, 1948–1958: A Documentary Record* (New York: Prospect Books, 1954). For a subsequent Yugoslav version, see *White Book on Aggressive Activities by the Governments of the USSR, Poland, Czechoslovakia, Hungary, Rumania, Bulgaria, and Albania towards Yugoslavia* (Belgrade: Ministry of Foreign Affairs, 1951).

10. I am grateful to Alex N. Dragnich for drawing to my attention the role of the U.S. Embassy in this regard. See also Jozo Tomasevich, "The Immediate Effects of the Cominform Resolution on the Yugoslav Economy," in Wayne S. Vucinich, ed., *At the Brink of War and Peace: The Tito-Stalin Split in Historical Perspective* (New York: Columbia University Press, 1982), pp. 100–101.

11. Horvat, pp. 80–81.

12. Deborah D. Milenkovitch, *Plan and Market in Yugoslav Economic Thought* (New Haven: Yale University Press, 1971), pp. 54ff.

13. For an excellent analysis, see Dennison I. Rusinow, "Yugoslavia's Problems With Market Socialism," American Universities Field Staff Report (AUFS) (now known as Universities Field Staff International), Southeast Europe Series, XI, 4 (May, 1964).

14. Michael M. Milenkovitch, "Soviet-Yugoslav Relations and the Brezhnev Doctrine," *Studies for a New Central Europe,* no. 4 (1968–69), pp. 112–121.

15. *Borba* (Belgrade), September 22, 1969.

16. Professor Najdan Pasic's letter to the party Presidium calling for a "competent and authoritative" commission to review the functioning of the Yugoslav political system in response to the demands for more rationality and effectiveness at the LCY Twelfth Congress signaled an official return to the issue of systemic reform. Formerly president of the Serbian Constitutional Court, Pasic was elected to the Central Committee at the June 1982 congress. *Politika* (Belgrade), September 29, 1982.

17. In terms of the country as a whole, the number of self-identified "Yugoslavs" grew by a dramatic 450 percent from 273,077 to 1.2 million, an unexpected and politically controversial increase. Given deep-seated hopes and fears centering on the issue of national integration, this demographic indicator is understandably sensitive. Note the polemics set off by Professor Dusan Bilandzic's negative interpretation and the suggestion that to search for a Yugoslav nation is an "illusion." Bilandzic interview with *Vjesnik* (Zagreb), May 8, 1982.

18. See Dennison I. Rusinow, *Yugoslavia's First Post-Tito Party Congress: Part II,* "The Congress Copes," UFSI Report, 1982, no. 40.

19. *Politika* (Belgrade), July 1, 1982.

20. Undoubtedly this solution reflected political struggle, for it in no way resembled the rumored streamlined seven-member executive committee that some party officials were talking about the summer before. The *Times* (London) June 2, 1977; for analysis see Slobodan Stankovic, "Top Party Hierarchy to be Reorganized," RFE Background Report 108, June 6, 1977.

21. *Borba* (Belgrade), June 20, 1982.

22. *Borba* (Belgrade), July 2, 1981. The warning of the new chairman of the LCY CC Presidium, Mitja Ribicic, that declining party cohesion might necessitate a stricter interpretation is among the most straightforward statements in the subsequent postcongress debate. *Borba* (Belgrade), September 15, 1982.

23. See F. Stephen Larrabee, "Yugoslavia at the Crossroads," *Orbis* (summer 1972); Dennison I. Rusinow's four-part analysis, "Crisis in Croatia," AUFS (June–September 1972); and Viktor Meier, "The Political Dynamics in the Balkans in 1974," in *The World and the Great Power Triangles,* edited by William E. Griffith (Cambridge, Mass.: MIT Press, 1975), pp. 61ff.

24. *Vjesnik* (Zagreb), February 11, 1977. For the Serbian interpretation see Alex N. Dragnich, *East Europe,* October 1971.

25. *NIN* (Belgrade), October 1972; *Borba* (Belgrade), March 30, 1977; *Start* (Zagreb), March 26, 1983. For a look at the problem posed by the composition

of this membership, see Slobodan Stankovic, "Tito's Successors Prepare 'Silent' Party Purges," RFE/RL Background Report, April 8, 1983.

26. Branko Horvat, *An Essay on Yugoslav Society* (White Plains: International Arts and Sciences Press, 1969), p. 201. This trend has continued into the 1980s. According to the Presidium's report, of the 622,427 (29.4 percent) workers in the party, only 8.8 percent are unskilled. *Vecernje Novosti,* June 17, 1982.

27. Denitch, pp. 92–93. Note the implications of the fact that of almost 1 million members who joined the party between 1973 and 1980, 72.3 percent were young men under 27 years old and predominantly high school or university students. *Borba* (Belgrade), July 2, 1981.

28. Milovan Djilas, *The New Class: Analysis of the Communist System* (New York: Praeger, 1957).

29. See Gerson S. Sher, *Praxis: Marxist Criticism and Dissent in Socialist Yugoslavia* (Bloomington: Indiana University Press, 1977). Intermittent harassment and temporary denials of passports have continued into the post-Tito period. However, despite some political sniping, the new leadership's desperate need for Western credits relegated the Praxis issue to the backburner during the early 1980s.

30. Interview with *Frankfurter Rundschau,* December 17, 1971.

31. Jovan Djordjevic, *Politicki sistem—Prilog nauci o coveku i samoupravljanju (The Political System—A Contribution to the Science of Man and Self-Management)* (Belgrade: Privredni Pregled, 1973), p. 606.

32. Samuel P. Huntington, *The Soldier and the State: The Theory and Practice of Civil-Military Relations* (New York: Praeger, 1957). This process reached a high point in the latter half of the 1970s. From 1974 until 1982 General Herljevic directed the civilian security apparatus. During this period, officers sat on the party statutory commission and an army general served as public prosecutor. In 1978 there were five generals on the National Defense Council, while both Defense Minister Ljubicic and General Herljevic were members of the Federal Council for Protection of the Constitutional Order. A Slovene general occupied the post of secretary-general of the Collective State Presidency until the Twelfth Congress when he was replaced by a civilian. In the spring of 1979, an army colonel took over as editor-in-chief of the party's chief theoretical journal *Komunist.*

33. For coverage of his June 1982 session with the Kosovo leadership, see *Politika* (Belgrade), June 25, 1982.

34. *NIN* (Belgrade), October 17, 1982. For Western analysis of Yugoslavia's economic plight see the *Wall Street Journal,* December 7, 1982 and the *New York Times,* December 8, 1982.

35. This is roughly 13 percent unemployment. *Ekonomska Politika* (Belgrade), April 4, 1983 and Zdenko Antic, "Yugoslavia to Revitalize Small Private Business," RFE/RL Background Report, April 22, 1983.

36. This was a function of excessively low interest rates. Reportedly Yugoslav banks were still making short-term credit available at 9.7 percent and long term investment credits at 5.5 percent while inflation soared to 30–40 percent. *Vjesnik* (Zagreb), March 7, 1982.

37. Attempts to eliminate redundant and unprofitable state enterprises combined with strong encouragement of the private sector in order to encourage more Yugoslavs working abroad to return and invest their money at home. The *New York Times,* July 31, 1983.

38. Rationing was not favored by the federal government, but local commune decision makers, desperately trying to deal with distribution problems, have resorted to it increasingly despite warnings of the secretary for Internal Affairs, Stane Dolanc, that this would serve as a "provocation" and in defiance of a Constitutional Court ruling that rationing is illegal. *NIN* (Belgrade), January 30, 1983; Zdenko Antic, "Imbroglio Over Food Rationing in Yugoslavia Continues," RFE/RL Background Report, February 25, 1983.

39. For detailed analyses see Pedro Ramet, "Problems of Albanian Nationalism in Yugoslavia," *Orbis,* vol. 25, no. 2 (summer 1981): 369–388; and Mark Baskin, "Crisis in Kosovo," *Problems of Communism,* (March/April 1983): 61–74.

40. Peter R. Prifti, "Minority Politics: The Albanians in Yugoslavia," *Balkanistica: Occasional Papers in Southeast European Studies, II* (1975), p. 10.

41. By 1980 per capita income in the Kosovo had dropped to 27.8 percent of the national average despite absolute improvement in standard of living as a result of the federal money poured into the province. *Tanjug,* December 4, 1980.

42. The *Times* (London), April 4, 1981.

43. It appears that by September 1981 only some 365 of the 4,000 party members at Pristina University had been expelled and fewer than 1,500 of the 92,000 Kosovo party members purged. *NIN* (Belgrade), September 6, 1961; Baskin, op. cit., p. 65.

44. For official admission that such reporting sometimes slips into one-sided sensationalism that worsens interethnic relations in the province see the statement by the president of the Serbian Committee for Information, Dr. Vojislav Micovic, *Politika* (Belgrade), June 22, 1982.

45. Take the events surrounding the extensively publicized murder of Danilo Milincic, a Serbian youth killed by alleged Albanian attackers shortly before the 1982 Twelfth Congress. The municipal council of the Socialist Alliance of the region where the violence occurred protested that the Belgrade press had reported that the boy's father, Slavoljub, had been killed 15 years before by an undetected murderer, leaving the impression of a history of harassment of this Serbian family by Albanians; in fact, another son, Miroslav, and Slavoljub's own father-in-law had been convicted of that crime. *Vecernje Novosti,* June 11, 1982. In their response to this charge, the journalists involved admitted that the information concerning the father's death had come from the Milincic family, that they had not checked it, and had seen no reason to do so as no one in the village had told them the reasons for the murder of the father. *Vecernje Novosti,* June 13, 1982.

46. Interviews in Novi Sad, June 1982.

47. On the unemployment level, see *NIN* (Belgrade), February 28, 1982. The importance of language learning to good relations among Yugoslavs living

in the Kosovo was emphasized by the new state president of Serbia, Nikola Ljubicic, in his session with Kosovo party leaders. To his credit, Ljubicic stressed that Serbs must learn Albanian as well as Albanians learning Serbo-Croat. *Politika* (Belgrade), June 25, 1982.

48. *Delo* (Ljubljana), December 4, 1982. Nor was this the only public complaint at the prospect of a 24.3 percent increase in the JNA budget that many Yugoslavs undoubtedly believe is linked to meeting security needs in the Kosovo. See Slobodan Stankovic, "Yugoslavia's Army Budget Comes Under Fire," RFE/RL Background Report, December 30, 1982.

49. The 1978 Congress Theses were based primarily on Edvard Kardelj's controversial book, *The Roads of Development of the Socialist Self-Management Political System* and the historic LCY program of 1958. The best single discussion of these complex developments is Dennison I. Rusinow's "Yugoslavia's Domestic Developments," paper prepared for a conference on "Yugoslavia: Problems and Accomplishments," Woodrow Wilson Center, Washington, D.C., October 16, 1977.

50. *Borba* (Belgrade), November 22, 1978.

51. *Borba* (Belgrade), January 7, 1979.

52. *Komunist,* July 9, 1982.

53. *Danas* (Zagreb), November 23, 1982.

54. When Milka Planinc became prime minister in 1982 she was 57 years old. In her 29-member government, 18 members were in their fifties, 6 in their forties. Only 5 had been members of the former government. Twelve were economists from economics faculties, and another was president of a major auto industry. In 1982 the average age of the LCY CC Presidium was 58.6 as compared to republic/provincial leaderships ranging from 51.6 in Bosnia-Hercegovina to 48.2 in Macedonia. Ibid.

55. Robin Alison Remington, "Civil-Military Relations in Yugoslavia: The Partisan Vanguard," *Studies in Comparative Communism,* vol. XI, no. 3 (autumn 1978): 250–264.

56. *Narodna Armija,* April 14, 1983; Slobodan Stankovic, "Yugoslav Defense Minister Calls the Army 'Backbone of the System'," RFE/RL Background Report, April 28, 1983. As political polemics over systemic changes escalated in fall 1983, military leaders expressed blunt concern. Note the warning by chief of the General Staff, Colonel General Petar Gracanin that "the people's trust" in state and party leaders might "vanish" if the situation did not improve. *Narodna Armija,* November 3, 1983.

57. Alvin Z. Rubinstein, *Yugoslavia and the Nonaligned World* (Princeton: Princeton University Press, 1970) and Leo Mates, *Nonalignment: Theory and Current Policy* (Dobbs Ferry, N.Y.: Oceana Publications, 1972).

58. This viewpoint was put forward by former Soviet leader Leonid Brezhnev at the Fourth Nonaligned Summit in Algiers, 1973.

59. See Radovan Vukadinovic, "Small States and the Policy of Nonalignment: The Yugoslav Position," *Southeastern Europe,* II, Part 2 (1974), pp. 202–212. Also Ljubivoje Acimovic, *Problems of Security and Cooperation in Europe* (Alphen van den Rijn, Netherlands: Sijthoff & Noordhoff, 1981).

60. Note the September 1982 meeting of these nonbloc countries in Belgrade.

61. *New York Times,* March 26, 1983.

62. *Direction of Trade Statistics-Yearbook* (International Monetary Fund, Washington, D.C., 1982), pp. 401–402.

63. AP Belgrade, March 25, 1983.

64. As demonstrated by the 1981 arrest of a leading young Serbian poet, Gojko Djogo, for making allusions to Tito that "rudely offended his personality." For analysis see Milorad M. Drachkovitch, ed., *East Central Europe: Yesterday, Today, Tomorrow* (Stanford, Calif.: Hoover Institution Press, 1982), p. 388ff.

65. *NIN* (Belgrade), December 5, 1982 (italics mine).

66. *Danas* (Zagreb), June 30, 1982.

67. *Vjesnik* (Zagreb), June 8, 1983.

68. Based on 1981/1982 interviews most particularly in Ljubljana and Novi Sad.

69. Yugoslav leaders are not unaware of this problem. During the Tenth CC Plenum in October 1983, fear was expressed that discussion about reform is "diverting our activity from concrete tasks," *Vecernje Novosti,* October 26, 1983. This plenum publicly revealed the depth of ideological/political differences at the top of the LCY concerning the nature of proposed changes.

70. Dramatically underlined by the resignation of Rade Koncar from his party posts during the 1982 Twelfth Congress. *Politika* (Belgrade), June 30, 1982. The son of a partisan war hero, Koncar has become a symbol of those political forces favoring more strict party accountability and implicitly "a firm hand."

71. This conclusion substantially agrees with A. Ross Johnson's *Impressions of Post-Tito Yugoslavia* (Santa Monica, Calif.: A Rand Note N1813, January 1982).

BIBLIOGRAPHY

Acizes, Ichak, and Mann Borgese, Elisabeth, eds. *Self-Management: New Dimensions to Democracy.* Santa Barbara, Calif.: ABC-Clio Press, 1975.

Burg, Steven L. *Conflict and Cohesion in Socialist Yugoslavia: Political Decision Making since 1966.* Princeton, N.J.: Princeton University Press, 1983.

Campbell, John C. *Tito's Separate Road.* New York: Harper and Row, 1967.

Carter, April. *Democratic Reform in Yugoslavia: The Changing Role of the Party.* Princeton, N.J.: Princeton University Press, 1982.

Dedijer, Vladimir. *Tito.* New York: Simon and Schuster, 1953.

Denitch, Bogdan Denis. *The Legitimation of a Revolution: The Yugoslav Case.* New Haven and London: Yale University Press, 1976.

Djilas, Milovan. *Conversations with Stalin.* New York: Harcourt, Brace, 1962.
———. *The New Class: An Analysis of the Communist System.* New York: Praeger, 1957.

Doder, Dusko. *The Yugoslavs.* New York: Random House, 1979.

Drachkovitch, Milorad M. "Yugoslavia: The Dangers of Political Longevity" in Milorad M. Drachkovitch, ed., *East Central Europe: Yesterday, Today, Tomorrow.* Stanford, Calif.: Hoover Institution Press, 1982, pp. 349–398.

Horvat, Branko. *An Essay on Yugoslav Society.* Translated by Henry F. Mins. White Plains, N.Y.: International Arts and Sciences Press, 1969.

Johnson, A. Ross. *Impressions of Post-Tito Yugoslavia: A Trip Report.* Santa Monica, Calif.: A Rand Note N1813, January 1982.

———. *The Transformation of Communist Ideology: The Yugoslav Case, 1945–1953.* Cambridge, Mass.: MIT Press, 1972.

Markovic, Mihailo. *From Affluence to Praxis: Philosophy and Social Criticism.* Ann Arbor: University of Michigan Press, 1974.

Mates, Leo. *Nonalignment: Theory and Current Policy.* Dobbs Ferry, N.Y.: Oceana Publications, 1972.

Milenkovitch, Deborah D. *Plan and Market in Yugoslav Economic Thought.* New Haven: Yale University Press, 1971.

Moorthy, K. Khrishna. *After Tito What?* New Delhi: Radiant Publishers, 1980.

Ramet, Pedro. *Nationalism and Federalism in Yugoslavia.* Bloomington: Indiana University Press, 1984.

Robinson, Gertrude Joch. *Tito's Maverick Media.* Urbana: University of Illinois Press, 1977.

Rubinstein, Alvin Z. *Yugoslavia and the Nonaligned World.* Princeton: Princeton University Press, 1970.

Rusinow, Dennison I. *The Yugoslav Experiment.* London and Berkeley, Calif.: Royal Institute of International Affairs and University of California Press, 1977.

Sher, Gerson S. *Praxis: Marxist Criticism and Dissent in Socialist Yugoslavia.* Bloomington: Indiana University Press, 1977.

Shoup, Paul. *Communism and the Yugoslav National Question.* New York: Columbia University Press, 1968.

Singleton, Fred. *Twentieth Century Yugoslavia.* New York: Columbia University Press, 1976.

Stojanovic, Svetozar. *Between Ideals and Reality: A Critique of Socialism and Its Future.* New York: Oxford University Press, 1973.

Wilson, Duncan. *Tito's Yugoslavia.* Cambridge: Cambridge University Press, 1979.

Zaninovich, M. George. *The Development of Socialist Yugoslavia.* Baltimore: Johns Hopkins Press, 1968.

Zukin, Sharon. *Beyond Marx and Tito: Theory and Practice in Yugoslav Socialism.* New York and London: Cambridge University Press, 1975.

East European Economies: Achievements, Problems, Prospects

10

Paul Marer

The aim of this chapter is to describe the most important trends and forces that have determined and will continue to shape the economic achievements, problems, and prospects of the countries of Eastern Europe. A basic theme is the fundamental diversity among the eight countries of this heterogeneous region. Eastern Europe includes the German Democratic Republic (GDR) and Albania, whose per capita income levels differ from each other by a factor of at least ten. It includes an economic alliance system, the Council for Mutual Economic Assistance (CMEA), led by the Soviet Union, of which Bulgaria and Romania are both members even though each has a different kind of "special" relationship with the USSR. Eastern Europe embraces Yugoslavia (not a full member of the CMEA) with its unique, worker-oriented market socialism; Hungary with its New Economic Mechanism (NEM), under which enterprises are no longer assigned a compulsory plan; the GDR, Poland, and Czechoslovakia, whose economies depart in varying degrees from traditional, Soviet-type central planning; and Albania, whose economy today is more "Stalinist" than perhaps any East European economy ever was, including that of the Soviet Union during the 1930s. Perceiving the nature and extent of this diversity is the key to understanding the economy of Eastern Europe.[1]

The chapter will also treat the conceptual and practical problems of measuring economic performance. Since no single indicator of performance exists, five of the key economic indicators customarily relied on by economists to evaluate a country's performance will be described and, where possible, quantified. Also to be discussed are the problems of obtaining standard statistical information for Eastern Europe and of interpreting both official data and statistics compiled in the West on Eastern Europe.

A third theme is Eastern Europe's economic relations with the

USSR; a discussion of this subject will show how these relations have evolved during the postwar period and identify the critical issues of today and tomorrow.

A fourth theme is Eastern Europe's economic relations with the industrial West. In recent years, this relationship has become increasingly dominated by the surprisingly rapid and large accumulation of foreign debt by the CMEA—about $80 billion at the end of 1982. A section of the chapter will explain why and how this large increase in Eastern Europe's indebtedness occurred, identify which East European countries could not meet their payment obligations, discuss present efforts to deal with the problem, and suggest its implications for the future.

A further aim is to demonstrate, as specifically as possible, the particularly close linkage between economics and politics in Eastern Europe. With respect to external politics, the key, of course, is Soviet policy vis-a-vis Eastern Europe, which will be examined in some detail and from the perspective of Eastern Europe. Domestically, the political factor is particularly important in discussing such questions as whether and how each country's traditional, centrally planned economic system can be modified, and the nature of the forces both seeking and resisting economic reforms.

I. THE ECONOMIC "ENVIRONMENT" IN EASTERN EUROPE

The East European countries differ with respect to size, resource endowment, historical and cultural experience, nationality, language, level of economic development, direction and speed of changes in their economic systems, development strategy, economic performance, and political orientation. The variation is great even if the region is defined narrowly to include only the six core states of Bulgaria, Czechoslovakia, the German Democratic Republic, Hungary, Poland, and Romania; if Albania and Yugoslavia are included, the heterogeneity is even more pronounced.

To give the reader a flavor of the region's economic diversity, this section outlines, first, the different *initial conditions* under which central economic planning was introduced in the eight East European countries after World War II, and, second, the important *postwar events and circumstances that created or accentuated diversity* among these countries, even as they all introduced a somewhat similar "socialist" form of economic organization, which may loosely be called "central planning."

Initial Conditions After World War II

Size. Most striking is the difference in size between the relatively small, resource-poor countries that make up Eastern Europe and the continent-sized, resource-rich USSR, whose economic model was imposed upon the region after the war. In terms of population and land area, the East European economies range from tiny Albania to medium-sized countries like Poland, Romania, and the GDR.

Level of development. At the end of World War II, the region consisted of industrialized nations (the GDR and Czechoslovakia); countries at the beginning stage of industrialization, but already possessing a developed industrial sector (Hungary and Poland); and very poor, essentially agricultural societies (Romania, Bulgaria, Yugoslavia, and, the poorest country by far in all of Europe, Albania).

Statehood. In assessing initial environmental conditions, one must consider how long each nation-state had been in existence. A political unit with a history of territorial integrity and effectively functioning governments in a stable nation-state provided a more solid base for economic development than a unit where these conditions were largely absent. With respect to territorial integrity, only two East European countries, Bulgaria and Albania, have been located on essentially the same territory since before World War I. The nation-states corresponding to today's Hungary, Czechoslovakia, Yugoslavia, and Romania were formed only after World War I. By contrast, Poland was transformed after World War II with respect to its geography and the composition of its population; the GDR was formed as a nation-state in the late 1940s, and was subsequently diplomatically isolated from much of the Western world for about two decades.

Regional disparities and nationality problems. Many economic difficulties involved in the mobilization and allocation of resources can be avoided if a country does not suffer from sharp conflicts among different nationalities or other minorities within its borders or from serious regional inequalities. In both respects, Yugoslavia was (and still is) the most heterogeneous; significant ethnic and regional differences also existed (and still do) in Czechoslovakia. The other countries are more homogeneous in this respect, although in Romania, 13 percent of the population consists of minority nationalities (9 percent of whom are Hungarians). In Bulgaria, at least 10 percent of the population are Turks, Greeks, Romanians, Armenians, and others. The remaining East European countries, with the exception of the GDR, also have minority national groups and backward regions.

Resource endowment. The natural resource endowment of a country inevitably influences economic structure, industrial location, investment policy, and foreign economic relations. The possession and exploitation of natural resources are important for the domestic economy and may provide significant export earnings. Ranking the countries from those with the best to those with the least-adequate endowment, we find that the relatively well-endowed are Poland (black and brown coal, copper, sulfur, lead, zinc, iron ore, aluminum, natural gas); Romania (oil and gas, coal, bauxite, salt); Yugoslavia (iron ore, copper, timber, lead, coal, bauxite); and Albania (chromium, timber, bitumen, lignite, crude oil, gas, copper, iron ore). By contrast, relatively poorly endowed with natural resources are the GDR (although it has brown coal, potash, iron ore); Czechoslovakia (coal, antimony, magnesite, pyrite, fluorspar, iron ore, copper, manganese); Hungary (bauxite, coal, natural gas, sulfur); and Bulgaria (low-grade coal, lead, zinc, copper, chromium, manganese ore, asbestos).

An important aspect of resource endowment is the suitability of the country's soil and climate for agriculture. Quite well-endowed in this respect are Hungary, Romania, Bulgaria (reasonably self-sufficient in food and some possible net exports), and, to a lesser extent, Poland and Yugoslavia. However, the amount of resources devoted to agriculture and agricultural organization (especially with respect to ensuring the stability of institutional arrangements and providing a good incentive system) are as important as, if not more important than, soil and climate. East European countries differ from each other also in how they organize their agriculture; as a result, there is considerable diversity in agricultural performance.

Location and climate are also important for attracting tourists, who tend to seek sun and water. Yugoslavia, Bulgaria, Romania, and Hungary have exploited this advantage since the mid-1960s by specializing in providing tourist services, while Albania has not taken advantage of its tourist potential. With respect to location, another significant factor is whether a country is landlocked, like Hungary and Czechoslovakia, or whether it has a long seashore and good seaports, like the GDR, Poland, and Yugoslavia.

War damage, reparations, and other unrequited transfers. The war had different effects on the countries of Eastern Europe in terms of the destruction of physical and human capital and of postwar reparations obligations. In terms of war-related destruction, the greatest damage was suffered by the territory that subsequently became the GDR and by Poland, whose capital and other large cities were largely destroyed. Reparations, which were made principally to the USSR, were accompanied by outright economic exploitation by the Soviets under Stalin. The GDR carried the largest burden by far, but substantial economic resources were also extracted from several other East European countries. A rough estimate, based on careful assessment but rather incomplete data, suggests that until Stalin's death in 1953, the size of the unrequited flow of resources from Eastern Europe to the Soviet Union was of the same order of magnitude as the flow of resources from the United States to Western Europe under the Marshall Plan, around $14 billion.[2]

Lack of regional cooperation. In addition to being isolated from much of the outside world after World War II, Eastern Europe lacked a strong historical tradition of regional economic or political cooperation. As noted by Aspaturian, historically, Eastern Europe has been comprised of small, relatively weak states, many divided from one another by ancient animosities; they have traditionally been manipulated and exploited by neighboring great powers for their own ends. In addition to the problems posed for these countries by Soviet domination after the war, lack of a tradition of regional cooperation made it all the more difficult to adjust to the new conditions. In addition, the Soviet Union under Stalin actively discouraged economic and political cooperation among the East European countries.

Further Differentiation During the Postwar Period

Ownership Patterns in Agriculture. There was a striking dissimilarity among the East European countries, first, in regard to the postwar implementation of land reforms and, second, after the initial collectivization drives had begun, in regard to the eventual decision to permit the private sector to remain dominant (Poland and Yugoslavia) or to transfer agriculture into predominantly socialized forms (all other countries). But even among the latter group, there are significant differences in the relative importance of the residual private sector.

The East European countries also differ in the form under which socialized agriculture functions. State farms are relatively the most important in Romania and Czechoslovakia (tilling approximately one-third of the arable land) and are least important in the GDR and Bulgaria. Moreover, "collective farms" vary with respect to size, organization, scope and extent of local initiative permitted, and the system of incentives and remuneration, to mention just a few of the relevant factors.

Defense burdens. East European countries vary in the size of the military expenditures that they decided, or were asked, to shoulder. During the 1950s Czechoslovakia carried a particularly onerous burden. During much of its postwar history, Yugoslavia also allocated a relatively large slice of its resources to national defense. Even today, under conditions of relative peace, the burden of defense expenditures, including the role of the police force, border guards, and other control mechanisms, varies considerably from country to country.[3]

Critical events. Dramatic political events have served as important backdrops to economic policy. These have included the 1949–52 embargo of Yugoslavia by the Soviet Union and by the other East European countries; the embargo by the West (which was the direct consequence and manifestation of the cold war) aimed principally against the USSR but causing greater economic difficulties for the countries of Eastern Europe; the 1953 uprising in East Berlin; the 1956 riots in Poland and the revolution in Hungary in the same year; the Twentieth Congress of the Communist Party of the Soviet Union in 1956 where Khrushchev criticized Stalin and changed Soviet internal and external policies; the erection of the Berlin Wall in 1961 to stem the large outflow of professionals and skilled labor (between 1949 and 1961 more than two million residents—more than 10 percent of the population—emigrated to West Germany); the Soviet bloc's break with China during the early 1960s; the 1968 Soviet invasion of Czechoslovakia; the 1956 upheavals and the 1970 and 1976 resistance to retail price rises in Poland; the nearly complete political and economic realignment of Albania with China during the early 1960s and the severing of their links in 1978; the upheavals in Poland, leading to the imposition of martial law in December 1981; and the economic crisis in the region, leading to debt-rescheduling by Poland and Romania and economic austerity in all countries.

Special links with particular countries. Among the environmental considerations that have brought significant economic benefits to one country but much smaller benefits or none at all to others are the following special political and economic links between particular countries.

Bulgaria and the USSR. The Soviets have granted substantial aid to Bulgaria in various forms; for example, several large, long-term, subsidized credits at an average interest charge of 2 percent—some in hard currency. The bulk of the loans were or are to be repaid with products of industrial complexes newly established with the aid of these credits.

Albania and the rest of Eastern Europe and China. Until 1961, the Soviet Union and all East European countries gave large, subsidized credits and other forms of aid to Albania. According to one Western estimate, economic aid by the USSR totaled $156 million and technical and military assistance approximately $100 million, while Eastern Europe (excluding Yugoslavia) provided $133 million in economic aid. (Yugoslavia aided Albania only during 1947–49, when a confederation between the two countries was planned). In addition, hundreds of Albanians were sent to Eastern Europe for study or technical training, and the East European countries sent engineers and other experts to Albania. After 1959, the principal donor, of course, became China; according to one Western estimate, Albania had received $838 million in aid from its new ally by 1975. But China's abrupt change of policy, including its opening to the West and to Yugoslavia after the death of Mao, caused the two countries to sever their links in 1978. Today, Albania is isolated from all socialist countries and has only weak and tenuous commercial links with a few West European countries.

GDR and the Federal Republic of Germany. Under a protocol of the 1957 Rome treaty that established the European Economic Community (EEC), West Germany's trade with the GDR was classified as "intra-German" and is therefore exempt from the tariffs and levies that fall on trade with other non-EEC countries. The benefits that the GDR derives from this arrangement include the following items: tariff exemption for GDR exports to West Germany; exemption from levies raised on agricultural imports from all other non-EEC countries; extra scope for price increases allowed by special arrangements for value-added tax; savings on interest payments owing to the interest-free swing credit provided by West Germany to finance trade between the two countries; and a fixed exchange rate between the two German currencies that leaves the GDR unaffected by the Deutschmark's repeated revaluations. Since intra-German trade has been rising rapidly in recent years the GDR's gain from this special relationship is undeniably substantial.

II. CALCULATING AND INTERPRETING ECONOMIC PERFORMANCE INDICATORS

Data Availability and Measurement Concepts

For many years after World War II, few economic data were published by the East European countries. Those published tended to extol, often in a propagandistic fashion, the achievements of central planning under "socialism." Gradually, however, the volume of published economic statistics increased, and the quality and reliability of the data improved. This change was brought about principally by the need to base economic research and planning decisions on reasonably accurate data. At the same time, the pressure to show good performance tended to lead to exaggerations in reporting by the producing units (especially for those indicators on which bonuses are based) and sometimes also by the control organs, such as the ministries, as well as by the central compilers of the statistics. Notable differences remain among the countries in the details and quality of their official statistics, but the shortcomings—notably, the tendency to hide the economy's weak points—are still substantial, and the data disclosed still fall short of those commonly available for the Western industrial nations. In most countries there are no meaningful data on retail price increases and income distribution.

Accurate assessment of Eastern Europe's economic performance is further hindered by differences in the Eastern and Western concepts of national income accounting and growth-rate calculation, so that meaningful international comparisons require methodological adjustments of official East European data. These considerations, combined with the necessity of estimating missing data and making subjective choices and judgments regarding different statistical series, preclude the development of a fully defined, objective set of accounts on Eastern Europe's economic "performance."

A further difficulty is that "economic performance" is multidimensional, although this is so for any economy. The five indicators most often relied on to measure performance are: economic growth rates; production efficiency (i.e., how much input is needed to produce a unit of output, which, over time, is measured by the growth of productivity); improvements in the standard of living and the distribution of income among individuals, groups, and regions (a very important aspect of which is the rate and nature of inflation); the rate of unemployment; and the status of the balance of payments. Sometimes a comparatively good performance with respect to one indicator can be achieved only by a concurrent or postponed weaker performance in some other area of the economy. Discussed below are problems of calculation and interpretation of each of the five economic performance indicators, presented, when possible, with supporting data.

Economic Growth Rates

Meaning and interpretation. Perhaps the most important—certainly the most frequently cited—statistic is economic growth performance, i.e., how rapidly the aggregate output of goods and services produced by the economy is growing. A rapid growth in *real production* (in contrast to the money value of production, which may rise as a result of inflation) tends to make other economic targets easier to attain. These targets can be improving the standard of living; bettering the distribution of income by giving a larger slice of a growing pie to the poorest groups or regions; providing jobs to whose willing and able to work; and increasing exports to pay for needed imports.

Generally, the higher the growth rate, the better the economy's performance, but sometimes that interpretation may not be accurate. One reason for this is that unusually high growth rates tend to create troublesome imbalances in the economy; a good example is Poland during the 1970s, to be discussed below. The nature of the imbalance depends on how a high growth rate was achieved: if it was financed from internal sources, through a high investment rate, then consumption (i.e., the standard of living) tends to suffer—as was typical of all East European countries during the 1950s; if the growth was financed mainly from external sources, i.e., by borrowing, then future growth rates may be impaired, as exports must go to service the foreign debt rather than to pay for current imports. Another typical problem with an unusually high industrial growth rate is that it pollutes the environment. This has been the case throughout Eastern Europe, as also in the West, and most notably in Japan. The impact of industrial growth on environmental quality is not yet reflected in standard economic statistics collected and compared among nations.

Measurement problems. Growth rates depicting the output of an economy and its various sectors are published in greater or lesser detail by the central statistical offices of all East European countries. The growth rates officially claimed to have been achieved or planned show from moderate to spectacular results, depending on the country, economic sector, and period. Western experts consider the figures to be somewhat exaggerated because they are based on reports by enterprises subject, except in Hungary and Yugoslavia, to strong pressures to fulfill the plan. A further bias is caused by a reporting system that permits and encourages the pricing of "new" products so that the value of gross output is artificially increased. The exaggeration varies not only from country to country and sector to sector but also from year to year. The upward bias is believed to be the greatest in the official statistics of the less-developed countries, although the statistics of even the more-developed countries, especially those of the GDR, are not immune from this problem.

Western recomputations of East European growth rates employ definitions and methodologies and weight the component series in accord with standard Western approaches; but, of course, they must contend with the scarcity of published data.* Still, most Western experts believe that the recalculated series are better indicators than the official series of long-term economic growth trends.

Findings. A comparison of the officially published Net Material Product (NMP) and Gross National Product (GNP) output series calculated in the West is presented in Table 1 for each of the seven East

---

*Recalculated production indices by sector are based largely on officially published output series in physical units, an approach that may have a conservative bias because data in physical units do not reflect model changes and other quality improvements over time. This method also incorporates new products in the index with a certain lag after these products have been introduced.

Table 1 Average Annual Growth Rates of East European Countries' Net Material Product, Officially Reported (O) and Gross National Product, Recalculated (R), 1965–82

Period	Bulgaria		Czechoslovakia		GDR		Hungary		Poland		Romania		Yugoslavia	
	O	R	O	R	O	R	O	R	O	R	O	R	Oᵃ	R
1965–69	8.7	4.7	6.9	3.5	5.2	3.2	6.8	3.1	6.0	3.8	7.8	4.6	6.1	5.2
1970–74	7.8	4.5	5.7	3.4	5.4	3.5	6.2	3.4	9.8	6.6	11.3	6.2	6.3	6.2
1975–80	6.1	1.2	3.7	2.2	4.1	2.4	3.2	2.3	1.2	0.9	7.3	3.9	6.5	7.0
1979	6.6	3.7	3.0	0.9	3.8	2.7	1.9	0.6	−2.3	−1.7	6.2	3.8	6.5	7.0
1980	5.7	−3.1	2.9	2.1	4.2	2.2	−0.8	0.9	−6.0	−2.4	2.9	−1.6	5.7	5.7
1981	5.0	3.0	−0.4	−1.1	4.8	2.4	2.0	0.4	−12.1	−5.4	2.2	0.6	1.5	2.0
1982	3.8	2.8	0.0	0.5	2.5	0.5	2.4	1.7	−8.0	−4.0	2.6	2.7	0.9	1.5

ᵃ Social product defined according to the material product approach.

Sources: Official, 1965–75: CMEA Data 1979 (Vienna: Vienna Institute for Comparative Economic Studies, 1979); 1975–80: Economic Survey of Europe in 1981 (New York: United Nations), Tables 2.2.1 and 3.1.1; 1981–82: Wharton Econometrics, Current Analysis (news release of March 17, 1983). Recomputed: Thad P. Alton, et al., Economic Growth in Eastern Europe, 1965, 1970 and 1975–1981 (New York: L.W. International Financial Research, Inc. 1982), Table 16, and Occasional Paper No. 75, Table 16.

European countries, as available, for sub-periods between 1965 and 1982 and annually for 1979–82. The tabulation includes data for Yugoslavia and none for Albania.

The official NMP figures measure, in constant prices, gross output by sector less material costs, excluding the so-called nonmaterial service sectors. The recalculated GNP figures measure aggregate economic activity, including the service sectors, by summing indices of sectoral output in constant prices, using factor cost weights. Because NMP and GNP differ in coverage, methodology, and bases of valuation, the two series are not expected to present the same performance picture. The official NMP series, while biased upward, is believed to be one of the most important indicators used by the leadership in the East European countries to judge their own economic performance. The recalculated GNP series is the best Western estimate of how rapidly the East European economies are growing.[4] Although Table 1 shows the growth of output only since 1965, if the series were extended back to the early 1950s, it would reveal that for approximately three decades, from the early 1950s until the late 1970s, the East European countries were able to grow at a rapid pace. The least-developed countries grew faster than the more-developed ones, so that the development gap has narrowed. One reason for the relatively good growth performance is that a traditional, Soviet-type centrally planned economy is able to mobilize unemployed and underemployed resources that, for a time, can generate impressive increments in output. But in the case of Eastern Europe, a further reason was that until the end of the 1970s, the countries were able to rely on three consecutive but temporary support mechanisms.

During the early 1950s, the regimes used extreme methods to mobilize resources and to squeeze agriculture and the consumer to finance a rapid growth in investments. Eventually, however, the strong-arm methods to increase inputs proved to be economically and politically counterproductive. Political excesses and the absence of material incentives undermined political stability and the economic efficiency of resource use.

During the 1960s, the East European countries (except Albania) were boosted by increased trade with the USSR (for Yugoslavia, increased trade with the West was more important). Energy and raw materials imported from the USSR at low cost were exchanged for machinery and other manufactured products. However, by the early 1970s the Soviet Union concluded that large increases in energy and raw material exports for East European manufactures were no longer in its economic interest, for reasons to be explained below. During the 1970s the annual increments of Soviet exports to East Europe slowed;

by the early 1980s their absolute level began to stagnate (in volume, not value terms). Lack of incremental supplies, along with rapidly rising prices of these goods, has put further economic pressure on Eastern Europe.

East European growth rates were boosted in the seventies by Western government and private bank credits. By the end of the 1970s the indebtedness of the East European countries reached dangerously high levels (except for Czechoslovakia and Albania) as exports to the West lagged behind imports owing partly to the shortcomings of the centrally planned economic system, mistakes in policy, and unfavorable economic and financial conditions on the world markets. The pressures became very substantial. In 1981 Poland was forced to reschedule debt repayments; in 1982 Romania joined Poland. During 1982–83, Hungary and Yugoslavia also encountered especially serious debt-servicing problems, joining the ranks of many less-developed and some more-developed market-economy countries facing similar difficulties.

Table 1 shows that during the second half of the 1970s the growth rates of all the East European countries had decelerated significantly. Since 1979 there have been one or more years of absolute declines in total production in Poland, Hungary, and Czechoslovakia, according to official data; based on Western computations, production declines were also experienced by Bulgaria and Romania. Poland's problems were the most severe and persistent, since output in that country declined in each of the four years between 1979 and 1982.

It is unmistakably clear that by the beginning of the 1980s the East European countries had entered a fundamentally new economic era. The economic pressures they faced were not merely cyclical or temporary but fundamental with no easy or obvious ways to overcome them.

Table 1 summarized the growth rates of output. If a country has a significant inflow (outflow) of resources from (to) foreign countries, then a distinction must be made between the growth of production and the growth of domestic utilization. Net foreign borrowing makes it possible for domestic utilization—private and public consumption plus investment—to increase faster than production. A net outflow of resources—which occurs if the sum of debt service payments and the deterioration of the terms of foreign trade exceed the sum of new loans obtained from abroad—means that domestic utilization must grow slower than production. Whereas during the first half of the 1970s the domestic utilization of the East European countries exceeded the growth of output owing to foreign borrowing, sometime during the latter part of the decade the opposite situation developed in most countries. This is shown in Table 2, which juxtaposes official statistics on

Table 2. Average Annual Official Growth Rates of Net Material Product Produced (P) and Domestic Utilization (U), 1971–82

Period	Bulgaria		Czechoslovakia		GDR		Hungary		Poland		Romania		Yugoslavia[a]	
	P	U	P	U	P	U	P	U	P	U	P	U	P	U
1971–75	7.8	8.6	5.7	6.1	5.4	4.7	6.2	5.6	9.8	11.6	11.3	n.a.	6.3	n.a.
1976–80	6.1	2.8	3.7	2.2	4.1	3.6	3.2	1.9	1.2	−0.2	7.3	6.9	6.5	4.5
1981	5.0	7.7	−0.4	−4.5	4.8	1.7	2.0	0.1	−12.1	−12.3	2.2	−4.9	1.5	−0.8
1982	3.8	4.2	0.0	−3.0	2.5	0.5	2.4	−2.0	−8.0	−12.0	2.6	−1.5	0.9	−4.8

[a] Social product defined according to the material product approach.

Sources: same as Table 1.

the growth of production (P) and the growth of domestic utilization (U).

A decline in the growth *rate* or in the absolute *level* of production is one type of adjustment an economy that has borrowed excessively or faces a prolonged deterioration in its terms of trade eventually must make; forcing domestic utilization significantly below current production levels is a further adjustment that becomes necessary in such situations. The real story of what has been happening in Eastern Europe is not so much the declining growth of production as the much more substantial cuts in domestic utilization, as shown in Table 2.

When domestic utilization must be cut, the choice is between reducing consumption, or investment, or both. Since the late 1970s the East European countries have drastically cut the absolute level of investment (by about 75 percent in the case of Poland!) and in most cases some cut in real consumption also could not be avoided. Stagnating or declining consumption causes serious political problems for governments. A substantial and prolonged cut in the level of investment undermines prospects for rapid economic growth in the future.

The current and future unavailability of the temporary support mechanisms that have propped East European growth rates before the second half of the 1970s and the difficulties created for the future by several lean investment years are the bases for concluding that in the absence of successfully implemented systemic reforms, East European growth rates during the rest of the 1980s are unlikely to return to levels achieved prior to the second half of the 1970s.

Standard of Living and the Distribution of Income

This indicator is the yardstick whereby a typical citizen measures and compares the performance of an economy. Two things matter: the demonstration effect of the higher living standard found in the industrial West—which is one of the most important factors pressing the decision makers in Eastern Europe—and the rate of improvement from year to year.* One runs into serious difficulties in trying to measure, and especially to compare with Western figures, East European living standards, and changes thereof, on the basis of official data. One difficulty is that, typically, a much larger share of a family's consumption is comprised of "communal," i.e., public goods, such as education

---

*The issue of comparative living standards is especially important in the GDR, whose population compares its standard of living with that of the people in West Germany, especially since both can watch West German TV. Generally, the more mobility across national frontiers, the more direct the comparisons between absolute living standards.

and the nominally "free" health care (although under-the-table payments to those delivering health care and other services have become the norm, not the exception). These countries also offer low-cost (i.e., subsidized) living accommodations and public transportation. This makes a comparison of wage, salary, and income tax *levels* as well as wage and salary *increases* across countries much less meaningful than in market-economy countries.

Still another difficulty in assessing living standards is the wide and growing differences among the East European countries in the availability of consumer goods. Thus, if one looked at the rapid increases in recent years of the average zloty wage paid to Polish workers and found also that the Polish consumer price index hardly changed during this period, one would be justified in concluding that the Polish standard of living had improved considerably in recent years. But when traveling in Poland, one finds that the queues in front of most food stores and other retail establishments are long; that regardless of the number of zlotys a family has in its pocket or in the bank, it typically has to wait eight to twelve years or longer for a decent apartment and four or five years to buy a car; and that certain highly prized consumer durables, including many Polish-produced ones, are available in the stores *only* for dollars or other Western currency—but not everyone has access to foreign currency and thus to these goods. As everyone, including the Poles, would admit, this situation has contributed to the tensions that have exploded in Poland.

The availability of consumer goods is much better, for example, in Hungary than in Poland. This is noteworthy because aggregate data show that the two countries are at approximately the same level of per capita income. This difference in the availability of consumer goods in the two countries reflects in part a much larger allocation of the GNP pie to consumption in Hungary than in Poland, and in part the greater efficiency of Hungary's economic performance.

More fundamentally, however, the availability, quality, and choice of consumer goods are largely a functions of a country's level of per capita income. Thus, we find the consumer in a much better situation in the GDR, in Czechoslovakia, and in the northern republics of Yugoslavia (especially in Slovenia) than in Romania, Bulgaria, the southern republics of Yugoslavia, and of course in that poorest of all European countries, Albania. To be sure, there are significant differences also between Bulgaria and Romania, with the availability of consumer goods and services being notably better in Bulgaria.

Although there are large differences among the East European countries in living standards, the distribution of income, and the cost of access to goods and services, from the late 1960s until the late 1970s consumer welfare had improved significantly in all countries. Since then, living standards have declined substantially in Poland and Romania and modestly in most of the other countries, for the reasons mentioned above. The fact that similar difficulties have been experienced in many West European and less-developed countries may have mitigated somewhat the adverse political impact of stagnating or declining living standards in Eastern Europe.

A very important factor in comparisons of the standard of living in the East European countries with those in other countries is that in Eastern Europe a wide range of unpublicized economic and travel privileges are granted to the political, managerial, military, and scientific elite. This is an especially important consideration in those countries where the availability of consumer goods through the normal distribution channels is poor. These privileges are carefully differentiated by type of position and are greater for those holding politically sensitive posts. The economic value of privileges, such as obtaining desirable apartments quickly and access to well-stocked special stores, can exceed the recipient's money wages. The power to grant and take away highly prized economic perquisites is one of the primary levers in the hands of the party organization to secure loyalty to the regime from key people.

Unemployment

The number of workers without jobs is uniformly low, hovering near zero, in all East European countries except Yugoslavia, where unemployment is high, comparable to Western levels. The wiping out of unemployment (and the elimination of the most extreme forms of poverty) may well be the most significant economic and social achievement of the postwar regimes of Eastern Europe. However, this achievement is not without its costs and problems, mainly because practically all blue- and white-collar workers are guaranteed not only employment but the particular job that they hold at a given moment. Because the state does not allow inefficient enterprises to go bankrupt and because inefficient workers cannot (except in the most flagrant cases) be fired, there is less incentive for workers and more limited opportunity for managers to improve labor efficiency than in a market economy.

Balance of Payments

This measure indicates in any given year whether a country is a debtor or a creditor vis-a-vis foreign countries. A sizable deficit is generally considered a "problem," especially if the deficit persists year after year, while a surplus is viewed as positive, a signal of the economy's fundamental strength, which makes it possible for the country to "earn" more than it "spends" abroad. But as with any simple assessment of a borrower-debtor relationship, the real situation is more complicated. Just as it is for an individual or a business, being a borrower country can be a wise decision if (1) the borrowed resources are put to a productive use, providing a rate of return in excess of the interest rate paid; and (2) the debt-service obligation (interest plus repayment of the principal falling due) does not exceed the borrower's capacity to pay it.

All East European countries have been heavy borrowers from the outside world since the early 1970s. But an assessment of the status of their balance of payments as an economic performance indicator is complicated by special factors. Their currencies are not "convertible" like the currencies of most Western countries. This means, on the one hand, that neither the citizens of the individual East European countries nor foreigners can exchange zlotys, levas, etc., for foreign currency, or convert foreign currency into zlotys, levas, and so on (with the exception of tourists under carefully controlled conditions or illegally on the black markets), and, on the other hand, that foreign holders of East European currencies (with the exception of tourists) cannot automatically command goods produced in these countries. Which goods can be imported from the East European countries is determined by their central plan (except in Yugoslavia and in Hungary), and not by the amount or type of currency a foreign buyer may hold.

Commerce among the socialist countries is arranged and settled, almost as if on a barter basis, bilaterally. The combined flows of trade and services (such as tourism and shipping) tend, in the aggregate, to be in balance; any imbalance that remains between two countries at the end of a period is normally settled by further shipment of goods from the deficit to the surplus country. (Certain interesting new deviations from this practice will be discussed in Section III.) Thus, East European balance of payments data should focus only on their transactions with the rest of the world, i.e., with the nonsocialist countries.

The situation in East-West commerce is as follows. All the East European countries have been borrowing principally from the industrial West, and in convertible, i.e., "hard" currencies, to import Western goods greatly in excess of their exports to the West. At the same time, the East European countries have been lending large sums—mainly to finance their own machinery exports—to Third World countries, which principally have nonconvertible "soft" currencies. These two kinds of debit and credit transactions (in hard and soft currencies) cannot be used to offset one another. The critical issue for these countries' balance of payments is their payment status with the hard-currency, principally the industrial Western, countries. Because their payment status is so intimately tied to the broader issues and problems of East-West commercial relations, East Europe's hard-currency payment figures will be presented and discussed in Section IV, which focuses on East-West commercial relations.

There is one other important difference in the approach and interpretation of balance-of-payments statistics for market economies with convertible currencies and East European (and other) economies with nonconvertible currencies. For a country with a nonconvertible currency, it is not enough to put the borrowed resources into productive use; it must also convert the increased production into convertible currencies, by increasing its exports only to countries that can pay in convertible currencies, i.e., principally to the industrial West. But the East European economies encounter problems in this respect, both in their own economies' inability to produce goods that are easily salable on Western markets and in the tariff and nontariff barriers their goods still face in Western countries. Thus, the East European countries find the "conversion" of their increased output into convertible currency a difficult task indeed, a problem that will be discussed in some detail in Section IV.

III. EASTERN EUROPE'S ECONOMIC RELATIONS WITH THE USSR

The most significant general factor in the relations between the Soviet Union and the countries of Eastern Europe is the large disparity between the population, territory, resource endowment, and military power of the USSR and those of the countries of Eastern Europe, individually and collectively. Given these differences, and given the objectives of Soviet policy, intrabloc relations involving the USSR are inevitably asymmetrical. They are, in the most general terms, marked by the dominance of a superpower and the dependence of six relatively small client states. Yugoslavia's relationship with the Soviet Union has differed in substance from those of the other six since the Stalin-Tito break in the early 1950s, when Yugoslavia first became politically and economically independent from the USSR; although relations were subsequently reestablished, Yugoslavia has carefully guarded its independence. The USSR and Albania severed practically all contact in the early 1960s.

Any relationship of asymmetrical interdependence offers opportunities for the strong to take advantage of the weak. In the political-military sphere the six East European nations have certainly been subordinated to the Soviet Union, although Romania has been able to achieve much greater elbow room to maneuver and is one of the two East European CMEA countries with no Soviet troops stationed on its soil (the other country is Bulgaria). An interesting question is, therefore, has the Soviet Union also asserted its power to dominate the East European countries economically? Has the Soviet Union exploited its political-military position for its own economic advantage? The historical logic of the situation would seem to support an affirmative answer to both questions, as do the well-documented cases of economic coercion by the Soviets under Stalin, and of Soviet military intervention in East Germany in 1953, in Hungary in 1956, and in Czechoslovakia in 1968.

Until after Stalin's death in 1953, the Soviet Union's political domination of Eastern Europe was accompanied by conventional types of economic extraction, such as reparations transfers (mainly from East Germany and also from Bulgaria, Hungary, Romania, and, indirectly, from Poland); by so-called joint stock companies in Eastern Europe, through which the Soviet Union took some of these countries' resources; and by the Soviet practice of paying unfairly low prices for East European exports (particularly well documented in the case of Poland).[5]

During the post-Stalin period, the economic relationship between the Soviet Union and Eastern Europe has changed substantially. Since the mid-1950s, the Soviet Union apparently has not obtained large unrequited resource transfers from Eastern Europe. In fact, some specialists argue that in recent years the USSR has actually been paying an economic price for the continued dependence of the East European countries on the Soviet Union. The essence of this argument is that a large share of Soviet exports to Eastern Europe consists of energy and raw materials that the Soviet Union could readily sell to the West for hard currency with which to buy urgently needed machinery and other commodities from Western countries, goods that the East European countries are unable to supply to the USSR.

Relations Under Stalin and the Adoption of the Soviet "Model"

Let us look at the question of Soviet-East European economic relations from the point of view of the East European countries. After the postwar reconstruction had been completed, by 1948–49 (later in the GDR), the development strategy of all East European countries followed the Soviet model: the share of investment in national income was increased to very high levels, mostly at the expense of consumption; investment was concentrated in industry and, within industry, on machine building and metallurgy. As a result, these countries achieved good-to-spectacular growth rates, with fluctuations, but at the same time generated serious imbalances by building high-cost, quickly obsolete industries that left a legacy of serious economic problems.

Was the adoption of the extreme version of the "Soviet model" by national Communist leaders voluntary or imposed? We do not as yet have enough information to provide unqualified answers, yet the evidence points toward the latter. Countless eyewitness accounts testify to the decisive role Soviet advisers and shopping lists played in choosing development strategies in Eastern Europe during 1948–53, and perhaps beyond. Such Soviet actions can be explained in part by the USSR's desire to assure the dependency of these countries on the Soviet Union. In the case of Czechoslovakia and the GDR, Soviet industrial-strategic considerations also played a role. In these two countries in particular, there was a disproportionately large investment in machine building and in other industrial branches whose products were exported to the Soviet Union. In the GDR, war destruction and dismantling by the Russians in metallurgy and in the chemical and engineering industries left the country's manufacturing capacity predominantly in the light and food industries and in light machine building. Yet while these latter industries were often operating below capacity because of supply shortages, and in 1958 were still producing far below 1939 levels, branches founded or expanded to produce for Soviet export (shipyards, railroad equipment plants, precision machinery, electrical machinery, and heavy industrial equipment) were operating above 1939 levels.[6] Available data are consistent with the hypothesis that at least in Czechoslovakia and the GDR, postwar development strategies were significantly influenced by Soviet strategic priorities.

A Hungarian economist arrived at a similar conclusion for Hungary:

> Decisions which shaped the economic structure of individual countries were based on bilateral economic relations, primarily the relations with the Soviet Union. This was so not only because the Soviet Union had a decisive share in each country's foreign trade but also because only Soviet industry was able to produce or to share the technical documentation of large metallurgical and machine-building projects and to supply the basic raw materials; and also because its prestige and experience served as an example to every socialist country. However, given the known distortions of Stalinist policy, this [approach] frequently resulted in one-sided decisions even in questions of detail.[7]

We tentatively concluded that during the first postwar decade the USSR was instrumental in forcing the development of high-cost industrial branches in some countries, possibly throughout Eastern Europe, probably for several interrelated reasons. First, Soviet leaders probably did believe that their own pattern of industrialization was ideologically correct and did have universal applicability for the new socialist states. Second, this model also had the beneficial political ramification of placing limits on the East European states' interaction with one another, and thereby heightened each state's dependence on the Soviet Union. Third, this dependence was beneficial to the Soviet Union as a means of supplementing its requirements for investment and strategic goods from the more advanced East European countries, and for other products from the less industrialized East European countries, during the Western embargo.

The Decade of Transition: 1956–65

During the second postwar decade (approximately 1956–65), the USSR must have realized that the political cost of economic extraction probably exceeded the economic benefits gained; hence extraction was discontinued in most cases. Also, as the embargo was relaxed and as the more-developed East European trade partners gradually fell behind Western technological standards, the USSR probably considered imports from Eastern Europe less crucial. It is conceivable that during this period the USSR had no clear notions and no definite policy regarding what commodity composition could provide it maximum benefits from intrabloc trade. To be sure, large and very useful blocwide projects had been completed, such as an electricity grid and pipeline. But much discussion was also heard of the need for improved blocwide specialization and integration.

As a consequence of the development strategy followed in Eastern Europe, the region's poor endowment of natural resources, and the wasteful use of materials during the postwar years, net import needs of raw materials and energy grew rapidly during the 1960s. The smaller countries absorbed an increasing share of their total output of primary products domestically and redirected some raw material exports to the West. The USSR became a large supplier of their needs, to the extent of about $2.5 billion worth of raw materials and energy by 1970. Today, the Soviet Union imports mainly machinery and equipment, industrial consumer goods, and food products from Eastern Europe but often complains that many of the imports are not up to world standards.

Sometime during the late 1960s, the USSR had come to the conclusion, judging from its position in CMEA debates, that the exchange of raw materials for manufactures with Eastern Europe was disadvantageous because it limited the USSR's ability to import technology and other goods from the West, for which it had to pay predominantly with primary products, chiefly raw materials and fuels.

*Prices, Commodity Composition, and Bilateralism
in Intra-CMEA Trade*

Intra-CMEA prices are based on those in effect on the world market in earlier years (averaged over a certain period), because such prices represent alternative opportunities to CMEA buyers and sellers and also because, given arbitrary domestic prices, CMEA countries have been unable to come up with an alternative to world prices acceptable to all members. There is no question, however, that considerable bargaining does take place over prices, if for no other reason than that "world market price" is an ambiguous concept. World prices are said to be adjusted to eliminate the influence of speculation and monopoly and to take into account CMEA demand and supply. Until 1975, intra-CMEA prices remained fixed for five years and were based on average Western world prices of an agreed-upon earlier period. For example, an agreement was reached among CMEA countries in 1970 that intra-CMEA prices would remain fixed from 1971 through 1975 and would be based on the average world market prices of 1965–69. This rule, however, was changed in 1975; in recent years a five-year moving average of world prices has been the basis for setting intra-CMEA prices.

In interpreting empirical studies of CMEA prices, it is important to note that individual commodity prices and quantities traded are determined not by single buyers and sellers in relative isolation from the prices of other commodities, as in the West, but by government agencies that bargain over a whole range of export and import prices at once. Bargaining power in such a situation may be exerted through prices (obtaining high prices for exports and paying low prices for imports) and also through quantities (supplying small or zero quantities of goods whose prices are disadvantageous and forcing the trade partner to supply specified kinds of goods in specified quantities, if prices are advantageous). Thus, if a Western observer finds the price of a particular commodity high or low relative to current world prices, this may be because the CMEA price has remained fixed while the world price has changed or, alternatively, because the price that is "out of line" may be compensated by offsetting deviations in the prices or quantities of other export and import items.

This leads to the very important question of the commodity composition of trade within CMEA and especially in Soviet-East European commerce. Trade is balanced bilaterally. The transactions are denominated in so-called *transferable rubles* (Western world prices converted into transferable rubles at the official ruble/dollar rate) that play only an accounting role; export "earnings" do not represent real purchasing power within CMEA because they can be spent only on goods that the other country is willing to supply. This is an inflexible system that leaves open the question of how the kinds and quantities of goods to be imported and exported to the other CMEA countries are determined. This question can be approached only by bearing in mind that the real value of commodities traded within CMEA is judged by each country's planners, not primarily by what the commodity "costs" in CMEA but by how strongly it is in demand, either because it alleviates shortages and bottlenecks in the domestic economy or because it can be sold in the West for "hard" currency which in turn can be spent to purchase practically any good sold anywhere on the world market. Accordingly, goods produced in the CMEA countries are ranked according to the strength of demand for them. Goods in greatest demand are called "hard" goods; commodities in surplus that few countries would want are called "soft" goods. Different commodities have different degrees of hardness or softness and their ranking can change from time to time, as changing production and priorities alter the demand-and-supply picture. Speaking in terms of broad commodity categories, the ranking of goods from "hardest" to "softest" is generally as follows: (1) energy and raw materials that can be sold readily on the world market; (2) modern machinery, equipment, and spare parts that can be exported to or, alternatively, must be imported from Western countries; (3) products of the food and light industries needed in a CMEA country to alleviate domestic supply problems in the consumer sector; (4) standard machinery built in CMEA countries for which there is demand by the importing country; and (5) all other commodities.

Standard procedure within CMEA is for each country to try to balance not only total exports and imports with each trading partner, but also the sale and purchase of goods within each category of "hardness" or "softness." This is a very imperfect substitute mechanism used in the CMEA "market" where prices and money balances do not play the allocative role that prices and money usually play in a "real" market situation. We do not have enough information to calculate how successful this balancing between each pair of CMEA countries is, but our understanding is that bilateral balancing by types of commodities is pretty much the rule in all CMEA links *except* those between the USSR and the individual East European countries. This is evident from even a cursory glance at the trade data, which show that the Soviet Union is the principal supplier of energy and raw materials (ranked first in terms of hardness) to the East European countries while it mainly imports from them commodities that are ranked lower in terms of hardness (with the possible exception of Poland—a large exporter of coal to the USSR).

Toward a Balance Sheet of Eastern Europe's
Commercial Relations with the USSR

As to the benefits, or "gains," from trade, it is useful to distinguish between static and dynamic considerations. One issue with respect to the static gains from trade is whether or not CMEA countries trade according to their short-run comparative advantage. A substantial part of CMEA trade within the bloc is probably not according to this criterion, partly because Eastern Europe's capacity to export has been shaped decisively by its pattern of industrialization during the first postwar decade, and partly because opportunity costs are not fully known due to inadequacies in the system for determining domestic prices.

Another issue concerning the static gains from trade is whether prices are higher or lower in CMEA than the opportunity cost on the world market. Even if comprehensive information on intra-CMEA prices were available so that direct comparisons could be made with world-market prices, the results would be difficult to interpret because intra-CMEA prices, as well as quantities of traded goods, are tied to the prices and quantities of other export and import items. For this reason, and also because many manufactured goods traded in CMEA are not readily salable on the world market, there is not a great deal of opportunity in the short run to reorient trade from the CMEA to the world market, especially not for the East European countries. Nevertheless, some calculations can be made and certain conclusions drawn concerning gains and losses that arise from the way in which CMEA prices are determined.

Intra-CMEA prices can be established relatively easily for energy, raw materials, and other primary products because these are mostly standardized commodities traded on world markets at published prices. After 1973, the world prices of energy and many raw materials rose sharply; intra-CMEA prices, because of the price rule, increased more slowly. Thus, as net exporter of energy and raw materials, the USSR obtained for those goods prices lower than current world prices, resulting in what may be called implicit subsidies to Eastern Europe.

Consider this situation with respect to the most important commodity traded in CMEA: crude oil. Whereas in 1972, the intra-CMEA and world-market prices of crude oil were about the same, between 1973 and 1982 the world-market price rose more rapidly than intra-CMEA prices. For any period, the difference between the world-market price and the intra-CMEA price, multiplied by the quantity of net exports, yields the amount of implicit subsidy, since the Soviet Union could have sold the crude oil on the world market at or close to the prevailing world-market price.

Detailed computations covering the period 1971 to 1978 show that on trade in fuels, nonfood raw materials, semimanufactured goods, and agricultural products combined, the Soviet Union implicitly provided a net cumulative subsidy of about $14 billion to the six East European CMEA countries. This amount was somewhat greater than 10 percent of cumulative total Soviet exports to these countries during the period.[8] The distribution of this subsidy total by country was the following:*

	Total (Billion $)	Per capita ($)
Bulgaria	3.5	390
Czechoslovakia	2.6	170
GDR	4.8	290
Hungary	1.0	100
Poland	2.1	60
Romania	−.1	−.5

The amount of implicit subsidy is determined largely by the bilateral commodity structure of trade that has evolved gradually during the postwar period and the extent to which an East European country depends on trade with the USSR, but it may also be influenced by politically determined preferences or dispreferences of the USSR. It seems that for all of these reasons Bulgaria has been favored, since the amount of subsidy received by that country, especially in per capita terms, is substantial. Particularly notable is the contrast with Romania, which has been much more oriented toward the West and was self-sufficient in energy until the late 1970s (though political considerations may have played a role also) in that it apparently did not receive subsidies in primary product trade with the USSR.

Since through 1982 the world price of crude oil rose, if computations were available through 1982, a period during which the world price of crude oil rose, the amount of Soviet subsidy to Eastern Europe would be significantly greater. The value of subsidies on other raw materials declined much earlier than on crude oil. In 1982 crude oil and other fuel prices began to decline sharply whereas intra-CMEA prices continued to rise. If fuel prices were to stabilize at their early 1983 level of about $28 per barrel, then intra-CMEA prices would equal and then exceed world market prices sometime around 1985; if the world market price were to decline to about $25 a barrel, then intra-CMEA prices would

*Prices in trade with Yugoslavia, not a CMEA member, are much closer to prevailing world market prices.

equal and then exceed world market prices sooner so that subsidies would begin to flow from Eastern Europe to the USSR.

Calculating the extent of subsidies for manufactured goods is difficult since, for most such products, there is only a world market price range for similar but not identical products. There is little reliable information on intra-CMEA prices of manufactured goods; what there is suggests that prices may be relatively high, though much of the evidence is drawn from data for the 1960s.

On the question of dynamic gains from trade, important trade benefits are foregone by the exporter if the preferential or "sheltered" CMEA market absorbs over a long time poor-quality goods and obsolete equipment, thereby reducing the incentive to innovate and produce "for the market," causing the exporter to fall further and further behind its competitors. This is the cost that appears to fall disproportionately heavily on the smaller and relatively more advanced CMEA countries like the GDR, Czechoslovakia, Hungary, and Poland. The importer of shoddy goods and equipment loses potential productivity gains, too; yet the importing country may not be able to resist buying such goods if its own producers are dependent on the same CMEA suppliers for their export market. This is why in a bilateral, state trading framework, terms-of-trade considerations (i.e., changes in the export price index compared with changes in the import price index) cannot be divorced from the commodity composition of trade.

At this point the reader may well pause and conclude that it must be very difficult to draw up an accurate balance sheet showing who benefits and by how much in Soviet trade with Eastern Europe. The reader may wonder also whether the CMEA countries themselves have a good idea of where these matters stand. This is, indeed, the case.

One might also note parenthetically that public opinion in most of the East European countries—in Poland most emphatically—believes that the Soviet Union continues to exploit them economically. Unscientific as this opinion may be, it reflects some combination of the public's distrust of its leadership which it considers subservient to the USSR, skepticism that the Soviets would discontinue economic exploitation (well documented for the Stalin era), desire for a scapegoat to blame for the country's economic problems, and a fundamental belief that the Soviets ultimately are responsible for maintaining an inefficient economic system. By contrast, the Soviet view appears to be that in recent years the USSR has provided significant subsidies to Eastern Europe, the amount being a function of the volume of energy and raw materials sold at below current world-market prices.

Several other issues are also very important in assessing economic relations between the Soviet Union and Eastern Europe.

One of these is East European participation in CMEA investment projects, the largest ones located in the USSR. East European investment in Soviet resource development is not new. But whereas during the late 1950s and 1960s these credits were typically small, bilateral, and designed mainly to increase the capacity of existing projects, since 1971 (the signing of the so-called Comprehensive Program of the CMEA), there has been a dramatic increase in the size and number of these projects, and in multilateral participation (but not ownership). The largest and by far the most important project is the $5 billion (that is the initial cost estimate—actual costs were significantly higher) Orenburg natural gas pipeline, channeling gas from Soviet fields to Eastern Europe. Each East European country except Romania agreed to build a section of the pipeline (Romania provided only pipe and equipment), supplying labor and above-plan deliveries of equipment, technical services, and the hard currency with which to import the pipes and other machinery purchased in the West. One form in which convertible currency was supplied by the East Europeans for this project was to assume their share of the convertible currency obligations of CMEA's International Investment Bank (IIB). Between 1976 and 1978, the IIB borrowed $2.05 billion, in four loans, on the Eurodollar market for the Orenburg project and provided these funds to the USSR, which made purchases, largely of pipe, for the entire project.[9] The East Europeans owe the IIB for their share of the Soviet hard-currency purchases and, according to IIB rules, must repay in hard currency at world-market rates of interest.

Direct participation by Eastern Europe in construction projects in far-away Soviet territory has proved to be difficult and very expensive. Hungary, for example, is devoting 4 percent of its investment budget to such joint ventures. Part of the money goes to sending workers to these projects. But to compensate for the hardship, and to provide incentive and special support facilities, the wages of a typical worker sent from Eastern Europe to these inhospitable regions of the USSR can be up to five times what the worker would be paid at home, making direct labor participation increasingly difficult to justify economically. There are further problems in providing the needed technical services plus labor skilled in pipeline construction.

Because CMEA lacks a price and monetary system that would make possible more meaningful economic calculations (so that CMEA trade and specialization decisions could be made on a more rational basis), a convertible currency financial subsystem has gradually developed within CMEA. One aspect of this subsystem is the hard-currency transactions of the two CMEA banks, the International Bank for Economic Cooperation (IBEC) and the IIB. Another aspect is that today a certain portion, estimated at between 5 and 15 percent of intra-CMEA trade, is *valued* at current world market prices and is *settled* in convertible currencies.

The rise of a convertible currency subsystem since about 1970 reflects several developments. As the world market prices of certain commodities rose sharply after 1973 while intrabloc prices in CMEA remained unchanged for a time, it became uneconomical for the suppliers of such goods, mainly the USSR, to sell them to the CMEA countries, but they were obligated to do so under long-term agreements or contracts. Hence, so-called above-quota deliveries would often be made only against convertible currencies, at current world market prices. Another factor was the rising share of Western components—inputs, technology, and investment resources—acquired, mainly by the East European countries, for convertible currencies and incorporated into products supplied to the USSR and other CMEA countries, normally for transferable rubles. More and more, the East European countries are seeking to receive a certain percentage of the value of such exports in convertible currencies.

Conclusions and Prospects

The evolution of Eastern Europe's economic relations with the USSR can be summarized as follows:

(1) Soviet-East European economic relations underwent a fundamental change in the post-Stalin period: outright Soviet exploitation was discontinued by the mid-1950s, as economic relations were placed on a more equitable footing.

(2) Eastern Europe's postwar industrialization policies, copying—at Soviet insistence it seems—the Soviet model of the 1930s, did not follow these countries' comparative advantage, which would have been dictated by their resource endowment, i.e., lack of raw materials and relatively small size. It was not economical to build an extensive and often duplicative heavy industrial structure in each of the nations.

(3) One important consequence of postwar industrialization policies was that each East European country became locked in, to a greater or lesser extent, with the Soviet market, which was serving both as supplier of increasingly scarce energy and raw materials and as buyer of East European manufactures, a significant share of which had never reached, or had gradually fallen behind, world standards.

(4) The bottom line on the economic balance sheet of Soviet-East European relations is difficult to calculate. The Soviets' claim that for some time they have been subsidizing Eastern Europe appears to be correct, although the large implicit subsidies are significantly offset by various forms of East European subsidies to the USSR. Moreover, economic and political interaction with the USSR imposes (unevenly

distributed) long-term costs on the CMEA countries of Eastern Europe, although interaction provides certain benefits also.

(5) Tangible advantages of membership in the CMEA trading bloc notwithstanding, the shortcomings and problems of too heavy reliance on each other's closed markets gradually became obvious to all CMEA members by the early 1960s. Foremost among these shortcomings are: the general unavailability of advanced technology from CMEA suppliers; lack of stimulus to produce quality products; and serious obstacles—inadequate price and monetary relations foremost among them—standing in the way of intrabranch specialization agreements that could provide large and badly needed productivity gains to CMEA economies. One by one, these countries must increasingly depend on improved productivity as the backbone of their economic growth (in the so-called new, intensive phase of their development) because they can rely less and less on rapid growth of industrial employment, and large additions to their stock of capital, financed by holding down consumption standards (which were the main sources of growth in the earlier, so-called extensive phase of their development), or on foreign borrowing.

(6) One by one, each CMEA country, including the Soviet Union, adopted a new policy and program to reorient part of its trade from CMEA to Western countries. The timing, speed, and extent of this reorientation were geared to each country's own needs, perceptions, and possibilities. For the East European countries, critically important in this process of reorientation was the beginning of detente, first, because a Soviet rapprochement with the West automatically provided the green light for the East European countries to do likewise, and second, because it made the Western countries more receptive to trade, to lend money, and to enter into long-term industrial cooperation deals with the CMEA countries.

(7) The Soviet Union's rapid expansion of trade with the West during the 1970s increased the opportunity cost of being a large net supplier of energy and raw materials to Eastern Europe, as did the rising domestic cost of extracting and transporting these goods from the remote Siberian oil and gas fields and mining regions. An important mitigating circumstance was the large windfall gain the USSR enjoyed because of its improved terms of trade with the West, the rising price of gold (it is a large producer and exporter), and its ability to tap into the OPEC surplus by selling military hardware to oil-exporting countries. Nevertheless, during the 1970s the rate of growth of the *volume* of Soviet energy and raw material exports to Eastern Europe declined steeply, prompting the East European countries to step up purchases from the world market.

(8) During the rest of the 1980s the Soviet Union will face increased

economic problems, caused by the low and declining growth rates in its labor force, fall in productivity growth rates typical of a "mature" centrally planned economy, further steep increases in the cost of extracting and transporting raw materials and energy, sluggish agriculture that does not respond to traditional central planning methods, and declining world prices of energy and raw materials (these goods provide much of its hard-currency export earnings). Thus, the Soviet Union does not appear to be in a position to provide significantly increased quantities of energy and raw materials to Eastern Europe in exchange for manufactured products or to give price subsidies anywhere near the scale it had provided until the early 1980s. The Soviet Union appears to have decided to give reduced priority to meeting Eastern Europe's economic needs during the rest of the 1980s. For some time, it has been encouraging the East European countries to set moderate growth targets and to turn to the world market to obtain items in short supply in the CMEA countries. At the same time, a new factor has become increasingly important in Soviet calculations: the growing economic weaknesses of the East European countries and the related political instability, actual or potential. This situation has prompted (and probably will continue to prompt) the Soviet leaders to proceed cautiously in raising export prices too steeply or curtailing energy and raw material shipments too precipitously.

IV. EASTERN EUROPE'S ECONOMIC RELATIONS WITH THE INDUSTRIAL WEST

Expansion of Trade and Rising Indebtedness

All East European countries boosted sharply their imports from the industrial West during the 1970s to help modernize their economies with Western technology. They also required large increases in industrial material purchases from the West to compensate for a slowdown in the growth of such imports from the USSR and from each other. Because the rate of growth of exports was considerably slower than the tempo of imports, all these countries borrowed heavily from the West, pushing the total gross hard-currency debt of the six East European countries from $8 billion at the end of 1970 to about $66 billion at the end of 1980; two years later the debt was slightly lower. If Yugoslavia is included, the debts of the seven East European countries rose from $9 billion in 1970 to $83 billion by 1980 (Table 3). This huge increase in debt was partly planned—a deliberate policy of borrowing resources to modernize, which in turn was supposed to generate increased output with which to repay the funds—and partly unplanned. The unplanned

Table 3 Gross Hard-Currency Debt of the East European Countries and the USSR, 1971–82 ($ Billions)

	1971	1975	1980	1981	1982[a]
Bulgaria	0.7	2.6	3.5	3.1	2.8
Czechoslovakia	0.5	1.1	4.9	4.4	4.0
GDR	1.4	5.2	14.4	14.7	13.1
Hungary	1.1	3.1	8.8	8.7	7.8
Poland	1.1	8.0	25.1	25.5	24.8
Romania	1.2	2.9	9.5	10.2	9.8
EE-Six	6.1	23.0	66.2	66.5	62.2
USSR	1.8	10.6	17.6	20.9	20.1
CMEA-Seven	7.9	33.6	83.8	87.4	82.3
Yugoslavia	2.7	8.0	16.9	18.3	18.3
EE-Seven + USSR	10.6	41.6	100.7	105.7	100.6

Note: An alternative debt series would be net hard currency debt = gross hard currency debt to Western banks, governments, and international financial organizations minus deposits in Western banks reporting to the Bank for International Settlements (if the debtor does not provide deposit information) or minus total foreign exchange deposits (if the debtor provides this information). Other published figures on net debt may be smaller if the debtor's gold holdings, hard-currency credits granted to LDCs, and deposits in Western banks not reporting to the BIS and other items are also subtracted.

Categories of debt included: long-, medium-, and most short-term debt (data on some short-term debt, such as credits granted by some supplies, are not readily available); for the GDR, swing credit from the FRG (cumulative, noninterest-bearing liability with no fixed repayment schedule) is also included.

All debt is evaluated at year-end foreign currency/dollar exchange rates. Thus, the dollar value of debt denominated in a currency other than the U.S. dollar may change owing to exchange-rate fluctuations.

[a] Preliminary, calculated by adjusting previous year's debt by estimated current account balance, changes in foreign exchange rates, and known hard-currency transactions.

Sources: 1970, 1975: Wharton Econometrics, *Current Analysis* (News Release of April 27, 1982); 1980–82: Wharton Econometrics, *Current Analysis* ((News Releases of March 23, 1983 and September 17, 1982) and *Centrally Planned Economies Outlook* (Washington, D.C., March 1983); Allen J. Lenz, "Controlling International Debt: Implications for East-West Trade," unpublished paper (1983).

increase in debt was the result of soaring world energy and commodity prices, the economic recession in the West (which made it more difficult for Eastern Europe to export to Western hard-currency markets), the extraordinary grain imports necessitated by repeated poor harvests throughout much of the bloc (which also reduced or eliminated Soviet grain exports to Eastern Europe), and the need to buy more materials and spare parts for the newly acquired Western technology than had been planned when the technology was first purchased.

The growth of individual countries' hard-currency debt from 1970 to 1982 is presented in Table 3, which also includes, for comparison purposes, the debts of the Soviet Union and Yugoslavia. The figures presented are gross, which means that indebtedness is not reduced by the amount of convertible-currency deposits each country has in banks located in the West.

Between 1961 and 1977, Albania was also a large borrower—or grantee—from the People's Republic of China. Although exact figures are not available, it may have obtained the equivalent of about $1 billion, but not predominantly in hard currency. The fact that much of the credit Albania had received had been forgiven or simply will not be repaid, whereas the rest of Eastern Europe will have to repay what it has borrowed, is an important distinction when considering the *burden* of indebtedness, but not its *contribution* to growth, in the short run.

By the end of the 1970s several East European countries had run into severe difficulties of debt service. Poland in 1981 and Romania in 1982 were forced into debt rescheduling; in 1983 Yugoslavia had to receive a financial "rescue" package to avoid formal rescheduling. Before examining the current situation by country, let's consider how and why Eastern Europe's debts could rise to such high levels.

Causal Factors in the Growing Indebtedness

Several events in combination helped to bring about the present situation of increasing indebtedness. First, detente made improved East-West economic relations possible. Second, the Communist countries changed their cautious credit policy and were willing to borrow large sums. Third, much of the huge trade surplus generated by the OPEC countries was deposited in Western banks, which were seeking opportunities to lend these funds profitably. Since borrowing by Western businesses was sluggish (due to the oil-price-rise-induced recession), East European as well as LDC borrowers were courteously accommodated. Fourth, the recession in the West created excess capacity and high unemployment, which made Western governments eager to promote exports to willing buyers, and a crucially important means of promotion was providing government-backed (guaranteed and sometimes subsidized) credits. Fifth, strong competition among Western exporters and government credit agencies for Eastern orders practically eliminated earlier restraints on loans to Communist countries. The United States stands alone among Western countries in restricting (via the Jackson-Vanik amendment to the Trade Act of 1974) government-backed loans to Communist countries (except to Yugoslavia, Poland, Romania, and, since 1978, Hungary).

Servicing the Debt

What factors determine a country's ability to service its current and probable future level of debt (i.e., its ability to pay the interest charges and the principal due)? Six considerations are of importance: (1) the level, growth, and structure of debt; (2) the possibilities for commodity exports (on both the supply and demand sides); (3) the possibilities of generating net hard currency from sources other than commodity exports; (4) the possibilities for reducing imports; (5) world inflation rates and changes in the debtor's terms of trade; and (6) international credit market conditions and the country's standing in the international credit community.[10] A brief examination of how these considerations apply to the countries of Eastern Europe will help elucidate the forces that shape East-West commercial relations.

(1) *Level, growth, and structure of the existing debt.* The larger the debt, the larger tend to be the interest payments; how large depends, of course, on the rate of interest charged. Much of Eastern Europe's debt is owed to commercial banks in the form of "Eurocurrency" loans, on which interest charges are tied to prevailing rates on the international financial markets. A dramatic rise in interest rates between 1978 and 1982 has contributed significantly to increasing the debt-service burdens of the East European countries. The maturity structure of the debt refers to the timing of the repayment obligations; the greater the amount of repayment due in the *near* future (because the money was borrowed short-term or because long-term debt is coming due), the greater is the current debt-service burden. Since most countries rely principally on their export earnings to generate money to service their debt, one way to standardize and compare the current burden of debt among countries is to calculate their debt-service ratios, i.e., the share of current exports that must be devoted to pay the interest and the principal on medium- and long-term debt falling due (which may, however, be refinanced, so that the actual burden in any given year can be less than the implied burden shown by these ratios). Short-term debt is not included because of the assumption that it can be refinanced automatically. If a country runs into debt-servicing difficulties, the assumption may no longer be correct, so that the real burden of debt service becomes higher than indicated. Table 4 shows the estimated 1970–82 debt-service ratios of the East European countries and the USSR; only hard-currency (i.e., Western) exports, rather than total exports, are used in the denominator.

Debt service ratios and other commonly used indicators of external indebtedness (such as total debt to export ratios) cannot unfailingly predict a country's debt-servicing problems because each indicator focuses on only one dimension of the debt situation and the information it provides is historical, giving no clue to the current and prospective economic policies of the country. Such indicators do, however, offer some insight and direct attention to countries whose economic situations require comprehensive and careful analysis. For example,

Table 4 Eastern Europe and the USSR:
Estimated Debt-Service Ratios (Percent)

	1970	1975	1980	1981	1982
Bulgaria	30	44	30	24	20
Czechoslovakia	9	11	23	26	24
GDR	13	24	36	35	29
Hungary	14	20	26	42	38
Poland	19	32	107	102	64
Romania	36	21	38	43	46
Yugoslavia	17	19	20	25	27
USSR	7	13	7	7	7

Sources: 1970, 75: Wharton Econometrics, *Current Analysis* (News Release of April 27, 1982); 1980–82: Wharton Econometrics, *Centrally Planned Economies Outlook* (Washington, D.C., March 1983), Table 5. Certain adjustments were made for individual countries to improve comparability over time and across countries. For explanation, see sources cited.

Poland's debt-servicing difficulties were clearly foreshadowed by the extremely rapid increase in its debt-service ratio between 1975 and 1980, but the problems of Romania and Yugoslavia—the other two East European countries that were forced to reschedule—were less evident on the basis of this indicator.

(2) *Possibilities for commodity exports to hard-currency countries.* Many factors shape a country's export performance. In the first place, much depends on development and trends in the domestic economy. The fundamental question is whether the debtor country can effectively transform borrowed resources into import substitutes or exports. This involves, in the first place, how large a share of borrowed resources is devoted to investment rather than to consumption: the larger the share that goes to investment, the more likely that productive capacity will be enlarged, creating the potential to generate exports; if money is borrowed to import consumer goods, this does not create additional capacity (unless these consumer goods are essential to motivate workers to produce).

The next important link is the rate of return on investment: has the money been used productively, or has it gone into worthless show projects, unfinished construction, or unnecessary or unwanted inventories? Unfortunately, mistakes of planning and shortcomings of the economic system make the East European countries susceptible to spending *some* of their resources in this manner, Poland and Romania perhaps to a greater extent than the other countries.

The third step in transforming borrowed resources into hard currency is the ability to shift output into substitutes for hard-currency imports or into hard-currency exports. Can East European countries produce modern, high-quality semimanufactures and machinery as well as attractively packaged and marketed consumer goods for which there is demand in the West? Even in Poland, which has coal, sulfur, and copper, the *increase* in its Western exports must come largely from manufactures. This is also the case for all the other East European countries. (The USSR, by contrast, is richly endowed with energy and raw materials, if it can extract and transport them, but this is a difficult task without more Western participation.) The East European countries' record in producing such manufactures is mixed; a strict supply-, rather than a demand-, oriented central planning system is not very conducive to the production and marketing of modern, high-quality manufactured goods.

This mixed record results from the fact that under traditional central planning, many decisions are made at the top of the hierarchy. But because the big, unwieldy bureaucracies have inadequate information and too many contradictory pressures and goals, they make many mistakes. Subordinated units have little incentive to correct the mistakes because they must fulfill the plan. Whereas product mix and product characteristics should respond to demand, especially in the case of manufactures exports, the isolation of producing enterprises makes them unaware of, and generally uninterested in responding to, demand pressures. This, in turn, leads to increasing difficulty in exporting manufactured goods to hard-currency markets. The answer, sooner or later, is that the economic system must be "reformed."

Since the 1950s, all the East European countries have experimented at one time or another with reforms of various kinds, but only Yugoslavia (in the early 1950s) and Hungary (since 1968) have made a genuine commitment to comprehensive *economic* decentralization. Yugoslavia introduced a unique, worker-oriented economic system that is clearly more market-oriented and flexible than traditional central planning. Unfortunately, however, for economic efficiency and the balance of payments, economic decisions have become excessively decentralized and politicized, especially in recent years, so that Yugoslavia has also been facing a continuous and difficult struggle to generate sufficient hard-currency exports (and save on imports) to maintain an equilibrium in its balance of payments.

Hungary is the only CMEA country that has introduced comprehensive reforms that make its economic system significantly different from those of the other East European countries. In some areas the reforms have yielded excellent results (notably, agriculture); in other areas, such as the promotion of hard-currency exports of manufactures, the results so far have been modest.

A crucial question for exports is the absorptive capability of the

Western market of East European goods. Assuming that the East European countries can overcome the domestic hurdles to their exports mentioned above, will the West be willing and able to buy increased quantities of East European manufactures? The degree of Western *willingness* is influenced by the status of East-West political relations: the greater the difficulties, the greater the legislative and psychological resistance to imports from Communist countries. And Western *ability* to buy East European goods is largely the function of Western economic performance: the more rapidly these economies grow, the greater the demand—the more room—for Eastern imports. The prolonged recession and slowed growth rates in the West following the 1973–74 energy price explosion have diminished Western ability and willingness to purchase East European goods, especially manufactures, but the East European countries' lack of flexibility and timely adaptation to changing world market conditions are contributing factors also.

(3) *Possibilities of generating hard currency from sources other than commodity exports.* There are several other such sources. One is *exporting armaments* to certain Third World countries (armaments exports are not included in published commodity export data; it is believed that these are of importance for Czechoslovakia and the GDR and of course for the USSR). Another source is *exporting tourist services,* which is of considerable significance first and foremost to Yugoslavia, but also to all East European countries, with the exception of Czechoslovakia, which has not tried to attract Western tourists for political reasons, since 1969, and Albania, which has been openly xenophobic.[11] A third source is *exporting shipping services* (of great importance to Poland, the USSR, and also to Bulgaria), and a fourth, *remittances* from migrant workers (to Yugoslavia) or from relatives (mainly to Poland).

Finally, mention should be made of the so-called *internal exports.* This latter revenue source is a complex institution that is growing in importance and often requires that the authorities close their eyes to, and in some countries actively encourage, black-market currency operations. The basic idea is to sell certain goods and services within the country for hard currency only, but the variations on this theme are almost infinite. Initially, so-called hard-currency shops were set up to sell imported Western goods, such as liquor, to Western tourists, for hard currency. Subsequently, certain high-quality domestically manufactured and handicraft goods were also made available in these shops to Western tourists or to citizens earning or receiving (e.g., from relatives in the West) hard currency. In some countries, as in the USSR, the elites are rewarded with special coupons to enable them also to shop in these stores for goods unavailable for local currency.

The new twist in some countries is that a growing number of the scarcest goods and services desired by the population—such as automobiles and apartments, for which the waiting time can be several years—are offered by the state against immediate delivery for hard currency, with no questions asked as to the source of the foreign money. This policy is the most notable in Poland, where a large segment of the population devotes considerable effort to acquiring, nominally illegally, dollars and other convertible currencies from tourists and other sources. The policy appears to be rather short-sighted, with many undesirable longer-term economic and social consequences, including a growing lack of respect for a government that discriminates against the holders of its own currency, not to speak of the arbitrary nature of the income distribution that results because many citizens are unable or unwilling to acquire hard currency illegally.

(4) *Possibilities of reducing imports.* Conventional wisdom holds that this is the ultimate weapon whereby the planners in a centrally planned economy can control their balance of payments. While this statement contains some truth, the flexibility of the planners to control imports is limited. To what extent it is limited depends on the composition of imports (the more they consist of such essential commodities as energy, raw materials, and basic consumer goods such as grain, the less flexibility there is), and on the politically acceptable reduction in the rate of economic growth and in the availability of consumer goods that a reduction of imports tends to bring about. The individual East European countries differ greatly from one another in these respects. Until the imposition of martial law, the leadership in Poland appeared to be the most constrained by a combination of domestic economic and political considerations. On the other hand, if imports are not reduced, there is a possibility of not being able to meet the country's debt-service obligations on time, as shown by recent events in Poland and Romania.

(5) *World inflation rates and changes in the terms of trade.* Other factors being equal, a high rate of world inflation should make it easier for the East European countries, as for all other debtors, to service their debts. But high rates of inflation tend to be reflected in high rates of interest charged on the outstanding commercial and all newly acquired debts. Most important to any country are changes in its terms of trade, i.e., changes in the price level of its exports as compared with the price level of imports. A significant deterioration in the East European countries' terms of trade with both the West and the USSR have taken place during the past decade, which is one important cause of their growing indebtedness and debt-service problems.

(6) *International credit conditions and the debtor's credit-worthiness.* Another extremely complex set of factors to evaluate, this

variable, like the stock market, can change rapidly from one year to the next. As long as Western governments are willing to lend to promote exports, as long as Western commercial banks are flush with money that they must lend out to make money, as long as debt rescheduling is confined to a few small countries in remote world regions, and as long as the East European countries as a group are viewed as creditworthy, in part because the lenders believe that they are protected by the USSR's "credit umbrella," international credit conditions are supportive of the East European countries' desire to run trade deficits and to refinance portions of debt coming due. But the situation changed by the late 1970s and then dramatically worsened during the first few years of the 1980s as, one by one, all of the conditions just listed were altered. The rapid deterioration in the East-West political environment in the wake of events in Afghanistan and Poland contributed to changing Eastern Europe's international trading and credit conditions.

Recent Developments and Prospects by Country

Between 1970 and 1980, the East European countries had run substantial deficits in their trade with the West. During the early part of the 1970s, the deficits of the East European six combined (excluding Yugoslavia) were only a few hundred million dollars; beginning in 1973, the deficits leaped into the billions and began rising rapidly. The deficits peaked in 1976 at $6 billion, enabling these countries in that year to import from the West about one-third more than they were able to finance via exports. This was made possible by Western credits.

The causes of the large import surpluses were many and varied from country to country. For the net importers of energy (in 1977 Poland and Romania joined the others in becoming net energy importers), deterioration in their terms of trade was very important. Unwillingness to curtail overly ambitious investment plans and projects, requiring large Western imports to complete and to operate, also played a crucial part, as did the overoptimism of planners about their country's ability to pay for Western machinery by eventually exporting the resulting products. Maintaining excessive growth rates in the face of increasingly serious balance-of-payments problems was responsible for diverting to consumption some goods that could otherwise have been sold for hard currency; it also pushed up imports. There were, however, major differences among the countries in how they expanded their economic relations with the West and in the timing and mode of responding to the rapidly cumulating economic problems. Table 5, presenting the hard-currency exports, imports, and trade balances of the seven East European countries for 1977–83, reveals some of these differences.

Bulgaria. Although the country has been depending on trade with the

Table 5 Hard-Currency Exports, Imports, and Trade Balances of the East European Countries, 1977–83 ($ Billion)

Year	East European Six	Bulgaria	Czechoslovakia	GDR	Hungary	Poland	Romania	Yugoslavia
Exports (f.o.b.)								
1977	18.2	1.3	2.7	3.0	2.7	4.9	3.6	3.6
1978	21.0	1.6	3.1	3.4	3.2	5.5	4.2	3.8
1979	25.9	2.3	3.7	4.0	4.1	6.4	5.4	4.5
1980	32.3	3.0	4.5	6.0[b]	4.9	7.5	6.4	4.8
1981	31.7	3.3	4.3	6.7[b]	4.9	5.4	7.1	5.7
1982	31.3	3.2	4.1	7.9[b]	4.9	5.2	6.0	5.9
1983[a]	31.4	2.9	4.1	8.7[b]	4.9	5.3	5.5	6.6
Imports (f.o.b.)								
1977	22.9	1.3	3.4	4.5	3.0	7.0	3.7	7.4
1978	25.9	1.4	3.5	4.4	4.0	7.4	5.2	7.9
1979	30.2	1.6	4.1	5.8	4.2	8.0	6.5	10.2
1980	35.2	2.0	4.5	7.6[b]	4.6	8.5	8.0	10.5
1981	30.0	2.7	4.0	6.6[b]	4.4	5.4	6.9	10.6
1982	25.0	2.6	3.6	6.4[b]	4.1	3.7	4.6	9.6
1983[a]	24.6	2.3	3.5	7.0[b]	4.0	3.9	3.9	8.8
Trade Balance								
1977	-4.7	0	-.7	-1.5	-.3	-2.1	-.1	-3.8
1978	-4.9	.2	-.4	-1.0	-.8	-1.9	-1.0	-4.1
1979	-4.3	.7	-.4	-1.8	-.1	-1.6	-1.1	-5.7
1980	-2.9	1.0	0	-1.6	.3	-1.0	-1.6	-5.7
1981	1.7	.6	.3	.1	.5	0	.2	-4.9
1982	6.3	.6	.5	1.5	.8	1.5	1.4	-3.7
1983[a]	6.8	.6	.6	1.7	.9	1.4	1.6	-2.2

[a] Preliminary, estimated on the basis of mid-year data and projections.

[b] Adjusted for estimated undervaluation of dollar value of intra-German trade. Unadjusted figures in 1980 were: exports, $5.3 billion; imports $6.9 billion.

Sources: East European countries other than Yugoslavia, Wharton Econometrics, *Centrally Planned Economies Outlook* (March 1983 and September 1983 and News Release of December 7, 1981). These sources are based on official statistics in some way adjusted by Wharton or the author to improve comparability over time or across countries; Yugoslavia, 1977–79: [Tyson and Eichler].

USSR to a much greater extent than any other East European nation, during the first half of the 1970s Bulgaria ran relatively large trade deficits with the West. As a result, by 1975 it had the highest debt-service ratio among the East European countries (Table 4). But in 1977 it began and by 1982 it had successfully completed a remarkable adjustment program. It was the first East European country to eliminate the trade deficit, in 1977, and thereafter to run sizable surpluses each year. As a result, the absolute level of Bulgaria's debt has declined since 1980 so that by the end of 1982 Bulgaria's debt-service ratio appears to have become manageable. There is evidence that the Soviet Union has helped Bulgaria considerably (e.g., shipping it relatively large quantities of crude oil at subsidized prices, some of which Bulgaria reexported for hard currency), possibly in payment for political services rendered. Be that as it may, Bulgarian policy makers deserve credit for bringing their balance of payments under control sooner and more decisively than most of the other East European and less-developed countries. Overall, Bulgaria appears to be among the better-performing economies in Eastern European.

Czechoslovakia. Up to now this country has relied on Western credits to a relatively modest extent only: its total outstanding debt is comparatively small (Table 3) and its debt-service ratio is within a reasonable range (Table 4). Czechoslovakia's caution can be seen also in the relatively small trade deficits it ran up to 1979 and the modest surpluses it has achieved since 1980 (Table 5). Nevertheless, Western experts consider the country's economic prospects rather poor because much of its capital stock and the technology it embodies are increasingly outdated and because there are few signs that meaningful economic reforms are in the offing.

GDR. In contrast to Czechoslovakia, the GDR has been running large trade deficits and has been borrowing aggressively: it owes about three times as much as Czechoslovakia, even though the size of the two economies is comparable. This difference can be explained in part by the special economic relationship the GDR enjoys with the FRG, one aspect of which is its ability to tap large interest-free "swing" credits from West Germany. By 1981, however, serious questions were raised in the international financial community about the creditworthiness of the GDR. Whether as a preventative measure, or because it was unable to raise loans to finance further deficits, in 1981 it jerked its hard-currency trade account into balance and in 1982 ran a very substantial trade surplus (Table 5). Overall, however, the discipline of the German worker and bureaucracy seems to be able to compensate, at least in part, for the inefficiencies of central planning.

Hungary. In 1982 Hungary came within a hairbreadth of joining Poland and Romania in being unable to meet its external debt obligations. Relative to the size of its economy and hard-currency exports, the country has been running uncomfortably large deficits since 1974, requiring substantial new borrowing year after year, capped by an exceedingly large deficit in 1978. In recent years it has been running very substantial convertible-currency export surpluses within the CMEA, mostly with the USSR, which have helped its balance of payments with the West significantly. (This trade is included in Table 5).

Early in 1982, in the aftermath of the Polish and Romanian payments crises (see below), Western bankers, governments, and suppliers instituted a tight credit squeeze on Eastern Europe and Arab countries withdrew large deposits from Hungary because they needed the money. Hungary came face to face with a severe balance-of-payments and liquidity crisis. Although the unforeseen "environmental" factors certainly played a role in triggering the crisis, the fundamental cause was its inability to bring its balance of payments under control in time. Fortunately for Hungary, its application to the IMF and the World Bank was accepted in early 1982, which made it possible for it to obtain a bridging loan of $300 million from the Bank for International Settlements (BIS) and then a medium-term loan from the IMF ($600 million), which—along with a $270 million World Bank loan and some other credits it secured, and severe belt-tightening at home to curb imports and to free resources for exports—enabled it (or so it appeared in the winter of 1983) to weather the crisis without having to reschedule. In 1979 Hungary also began to institute significant new economic reforms that held out the promise of improved economic and trade performance during the second half of the 1980s.

Poland. Between 1970 and 1976 Polish decision makers not only went on an international spending spree, but they also lost control over the running of their economy. Thus, in the strict sense of the designation, Poland could no longer be called a centrally planned economy since plans and projection had little causal relationship to economic reality.

Poland first approached Western creditors to renegotiate its debts in late 1980. (Debt renegotiations take place on two semi-independent tracks: Western governments, under the auspices of the so-called Paris Club, negotiate the rescheduling of debts owed to governments; the much larger number of commercial creditors use separate negotiating forums. Poland has an interest in orderly rescheduling because the alternative would be to default. That would cause Polish assets outside Poland to be attached by creditors, so that it would be able to import only through complicated and costly barter arrangements. Furthermore, the country would be unable to obtain any kind of credit from the West for a long time to come and would be unlikely to be admitted to the IMF and the World Bank. Outright default would also have serious adverse repercussions on the other East European countries and the USSR since Western governments and banks would be under pressure to cease lending to them. Western lenders have a financial interest in rescheduling to assure that they will receive at least partial payment regularly and to keep alive the hope of eventually receiving full payment. These are the reasons why today there is a net flow of resources from Poland to the West, as indicated by that country's $1.5 billion surplus in 1982 (Table 5) plus whatever surplus Poland might be generating through invisible exports (tourism, shipping, etc.) and remittances.

What economic role is played by the USSR and the countries of Eastern Europe in Poland? Although we don't have the full picture, evidence suggests that during 1980 and 1981 the USSR provided substantial economic assistance to Poland in the form of additional deliveries to and reduced imports from Poland and loans of substantial amounts of hard currency. The East European countries—while clearly being hurt economically by the disruptions in Poland that affect Poland's export delivery obligations—do not appear to have provided large-scale economic assistance. After the imposition of martial law, the Soviet Union seemed to have reduced sharply its economic assistance to Poland. This may well have been a move motivated by political as well as economic considerations: to blame Poland's economic hardships on Western sanctions and lack of credits, which Poland's leaders have been doing publicly since introducing martial law.

It is extremely difficult to make plausible economic forecasts for Poland. As long as the domestic political situation remains unsettled, the chances of a healthy economic recovery do not appear to be good. Moreover, a healthy economic recovery would require major economic reforms, which take time to design, to implement, and to yield results. Even if a viable reform blueprint were to be found and accepted by the leadership, its successful implementation would require a meaningful political consensus.

Romania. An excessively paced and across-the-board industrialization drive and other mistakes in economic policy (such as the building of a large petrochemical industry just as domestic oil reserves were declining rapidly), combined with unforeseen changes in the external economic and political environment, created a serious balance-of-payments crisis by 1981. Although for years Romania has not been punctual in settling its international financial obligations, during 1981 it fell so substantially behind its payments to foreign creditors and suppliers that new government and commercial credits effectively became unavailable. Romania was even forced to renegotiate the disbursal of a previously approved loan by the IMF. In July 1982 Western governments rescheduled 80 percent of unpaid principal and interest on medium- and long-term debt due in 1982, and in December 1982 commercial creditors agreed to reschedule. Both rescheduling agreements were on terms that required Romania to run a substantial trade surplus, partly to settle arrears on obligations from earlier years. The Romanian leadership decided on large increases in net exports of food products, contributing to a significant deterioration in the domestic food supply situation, already poor even by East European standards. This led to the introduction in 1981 of food rationing and draconian decrees against hoarding, measures which naturally did not improve market conditions. Romanian hard-currency imports also declined from $8 billion in 1980 to about $4.6 billion in 1982(Table 5).

During the last few years Romania thus has made a large and painful external adjustment. Under a more prudent domestic leadership and with calmer international circumstances, the adjustment might have been spread over a much longer period. Romania has the potential for good economic recovery; the greatest uncertainty revolves around the quality of its leadership and economic decision making.

Yugoslavia. The extremely large hard-currency deficits Yugoslavia has been running year after year (Table 5) are not directly comparable to those of the other East European countries because a significant portion of Yugoslavia's trade deficits is financed by earnings from tourism and remittances from its nationals employed outside the country. Nevertheless, Yugoslavia also postponed too much the economic adjustment needed, until it was almost too late. During 1982 Yugoslavia faced severe balance-of-payments pressures, due in part to the general restriction of lending to Eastern Europe following the Polish and Romanian requests for rescheduling. Part of the problem could also be found in the organization of the Yugoslav banking system, which is so decentralized that there is no effective mechanism to allocate foreign exchange earnings from one bank or region to other banks or regions that must meet foreign payment obligations. This in turn has contributed to delays in settling the international liabilities of certain banks, seriously impairing the creditworthiness of the country. Were it not for a $7 billion "rescue package" negotiated during the first half of 1983, including a partial rescheduling of its debts, Yugoslavia today would be in a much more difficult economic situation and its prospects would be bleak.

The amount involved and the speed with which the agreements with commercial creditors, Western governments, and international organizations were reached when it became clear that Yugoslavia would not be able to meet its obligations show that the West does not put Yugo-slavia in the same category as the rest of Eastern Europe.

In addition to political considerations, the fact that Yugoslavia appears to have decided to implement a new set of reforms to introduce more economic rationality to its present unwieldy system of economic decision making may have been a factor also in Western willingness to provide large, new, medium-term credits. Yugoslavia's current economic situation is quite precarious; much will depend on the successful implementation of proposed systemic and policy changes.

CONCLUSIONS

Although many similarities exist in the reasons for the rapid increase of East European countries' debts during the 1970s and debt–servicing difficulties in the early 1980s, there are also important differences. Albania's leaders did not take advantage of credits or loans from the West and chose to remain economically and politically isolated. Czechoslovakia pursued a more cautious credit policy than the rest of Eastern Europe. In the CMEA, Romania in 1972 and Hungary in 1982 joined the IMF and the World Bank—independent policy decisions of significance, considering the strong opposition to these institutions by the hard-line regimes of the USSR, the GDR, and Czechoslovakia.

The relationship between the availability of Western credits and economic reforms is worth consideration. The argument is often made in the West that the ready availability of external financing has allowed CPEs to postpone fundamental economic reforms because their mistakes and inefficiencies can be "financed." The implication of this line of reasoning is that, had fewer credits been available, basic reforms would more likely have emerged. Although the many pressures for and against economic reforms suggest that a single-cause theory should not be advocated, it is worth noting that the two countries that had borrowed the least—Albania and Czechoslovakia—so far have retained a rather rigid CPE system, whereas the two countries that have gone the furthest with reforms—Yugoslavia and Hungary—are among the most heavily indebted nations in the region. I conclude from this that there is no obvious causal relationship between the availability of Western credits and economic reforms. While it is true that Western credits help to finance systemic inefficiences and policy mistakes, increased trade with the West and the eventual need to service a large debt also create significant reform pressures. Resolution of the pressures for and against reform is country specific.

Interesting political implications arise from consideration of the sources of aid to the East European countries in serious debt-servicing difficulties. It is striking to note how quickly and decisively Western countries came to the aid of Yugoslavia in 1983, with the United States playing a significant though not too visible role, in putting together a financial rescue package. The principal motive appears to have been recognition that Yugoslavia's collapse could provide an opening for Moscow to draw the country back to its orbit.

There does not appear to be a similar readiness to help the other East European countries. This policy is in marked contrast to that applied to LDCs, many of which belong to Western economic, political, or military alliance systems; hence, significant efforts to assist them are usually made. It is doubtful whether Romania would obtain significantly more help from the West even if it had a more efficient leadership (but with the same foreign policy orientation). To be sure, membership in the IMF and the World Bank is an important lifeline for those member countries.

Conventional wisdom held until recently that the Soviet Union would come to the aid of any CMEA country in debt-servicing difficulty, as anticipated by the "umbrella theory." Recent events show that, as a broad generalization, this is not necessarily the case, although it has held true in specific situations. Both Bulgaria and Poland had received from the USSR temporary balance-of-payments assistance. More generally, Soviet economic policy vis-a-vis Eastern Europe can be characterized as both conservative and cautious. On the one hand, it is not "pulling out the rug" from under these countries by reducing sharply its energy and raw material deliveries or increasing prices too precipitously, actions which would be in the USSR's economic (but not necessarily political) interest, but which could trigger debt rescheduling if not defaults in some cases. On the other hand, neither is the USSR willing to subsidize Eastern Europe permanently by charging less than world-market prices for energy and raw material exports.[12] Be that as it may, Bulgaria appears to have been helped by the USSR relatively more than the other East European countries.

Turning to Eastern Europe's economic prospects, the combination of its high levels of debt—and therefore debt service—and the economic, financial, and political uncertainties means that each of the seven East European countries can anticipate several more years of austerity, resulting in slow growth and lack of improvements in living standards. To be sure, a speedy economic recovery in the industrial West, lower real rates of interest, and an easing of East-West political tensions would lighten significantly Eastern Europe's adjustment burdens.

NOTES

1. A comprehensive compilation of studies on the economies of Eastern Europe, including studies on each of the eight countries, is the 1,427-page *East European Economies Post-Helsinki* (A Compendium of Papers Submitted to the Joint Economic Committee, Congress of the United States) (Washington, D.C.: US GPO, August 24, 1977). Sections I and II of this chapter make extensive use of the author's contribution to that volume, "Economic Performance, Strategy, and Prospects in Eastern Europe." Approximately every third year the joint Economic Committee of Congress publishes a new compendium of studies on the economies of Eastern Europe. See *East European Economic Assessment,* Part 1 published in 1980 and Part 2 in 1981.

2. Paul Marer, "Soviet Economic Policy in Eastern Europe," in *Reorientation and Commercial Relations of the Countries of Eastern Europe* (A Compendium of Papers Submitted to the Joint Economic Committee, U.S. Congress) (Washington, D.C.: US GPO, 1974).

3. See T. P. Alton, et al., "Defense Expenditures in Eastern Europe, 1965–1976," in *East European Economies Post-Helsinki.*

4. Methods of calculating the indices, the definitions used, as well as the many problems and pitfalls of making intertemporal and international comparisons are found in Thad P. Alton, "Comparative Structure and Growth of Economic Activity in Eastern Europe," in *East European Economies Post-Helsinki.*

5. For details, see Paul Marer, "Soviet Economic Policy in Eastern Europe."

6. Edwin Snell and Marilyn Harper, "Postwar Economic Growth in East Germany: A Comparison with West Germany," in *Economic Developments in the Countries of Eastern Europe* (A Compendium of Papers Submitted to the Subcommittee on Foreign Economic Policy of the Joint Economic Committee, U.S. Congress) (Washington, D.C.: US GPO, 1970), pp. 567, 570.

7. Sandor Ausch, *A KGST-egyuttmukodes helyzete, mechanizmusa, tavlatai* [CMEA Cooperation, Situation, Mechanism and Perspectives] (Budapest: Kozgazdasagi es Jogi Konyvkiado, 1969).

8. Michael Marresse and Jan Vanous, *Soviet Subsidization of Trade with Eastern Europe: A Soviet Perspective* (Berkeley: Institute of International Studies, University of California, 1983).

9. *East-West Markets,* August 7, 1978, p. 8.

10. For a more detailed discussion of these issues and the political context of Eastern Europe's debt, see the thoughtful and provocative article by Richard Portes, "East Europe's Debt to the West: Interdependence is a Two-Way Street," *Foreign Affairs,* vol. 55, no. 4 (April 1977).

11. For an approach to the estimation of Eastern Europe's tourist revenue, see Paul Marer and John Tilley, "Tourism," in *Reorientation and Commercial Relations.*

12. See Marresse and Vanous.

11 The Soviet Union and East Central Europe: Crisis, Intervention, and Normalization

Jiri Valenta

The Hungarian revolution of 1956, the Prague Spring of 1968 and the Polish crises of 1956 and 1980–81 have been the most traumatic events for the Soviets in Eastern Europe since the Soviet-Yugoslav break of 1948. When examined in a comparative perspective these crises provide a unique opportunity to analyze revolutionary change in the region; the Soviet response in the form of military intervention, both direct and indirect; and so-called normalization, the long-term process whereby the Soviets have sought a reversal of revolutionary change. These three theoretical concepts will provide the framework for comparing each case study with the others.

Revolution as used here corresponds to the Aristotelean *metabole* or change of a systemic nature. Walter Laqueur cogently defined "revolution" as "an attempt to make a radical change in the system of the government." This "often involves . . . the use of force," but not of necessity. Revolution may also mean "any fundamentally new development in the economy, culture or social fabric. . . ."[1] As such, revolution is distinguishable from *coup d'etat* or revolt.

The revolutionary upheavals in Eastern Europe after World War II conform to Laqueur's broad definition in that they expressed the desire to bring about, through violent and/or peaceful methods, profound and fundamental changes in a society's dominant values and politico-economic structures. In the Communist countries of East-Central Europe, the revolutions that have occurred in twelve-year cycles since 1956 assumed both violent and nonviolent modes. Accordingly, Soviet writers distinguished between violent revolution or "counterrevolution" and nonviolent revolution or "creeping counterrevolution."

The revolutions in Eastern Europe might have succeeded in bringing about fundamental and profound changes had they not been halted by intervention conducted or sponsored by the USSR. Intervention is usually defined in the language of international politics as an act that involves force. According to Percy Winfield, it occurs "when one state interferes by force or the threat of force in the affairs of another state."[2] Soviet interventions in Eastern Europe have involved direct as well as indirect use of military force. A direct intervention is the massive deployment of Soviet armed forces either alone or in the company of allied WTO (Warsaw Treaty Organization) forces with the clear purpose of occupying a country and reversing revolutionary change (Hungary in 1956 and Czechoslovakia in 1968). Indirect intervention refers to the deployment of Soviet and WTO forces on the borders of and within another WTO country, to elicit fear and to pressure the leadership of the country into initiating the same reversal process *on its own,* short of occupation (Poland in 1956, 1980–81). While the means differ, both types of intervention share the same objective. In both instances threatened or actual military coercion has usually been preceded and reinforced by diplomatic and economic pressures brought to bear by the Soviets.

The term "normalization" is borrowed from the Russian since there is no phenomenon quite like it in Western political vocabulary. In Russian *normalizatsiia* describes the complex policies developed and fostered by the Soviets, under specific national conditions and over a period spanning a decade or more, to reverse partly or fully revolutionary change in a given East European country.

Since World War II, Hungary, Czechoslovakia, and Poland have been important links in the security *cordon sanitaire* (known since 1955 as the Warsaw Treaty Organization) along the USSR's western flank. They also form part of a less visible but no less vital political and ideological *cordon sanitaire* guarding the Soviet Union against hostile political and philosophical incursions and, because of their ideological alliance, generally enhance the USSR's international respectability. However, while Moscow was equally sensitive to revolutionary changes in Budapest, Prague, and Warsaw, postinvasion normalization policies in these countries have been markedly different, particularly as concerns the greater emphasis on preserving ideological orthodoxy in Czechoslovakia as opposed to Hungary and Poland.

In Poland—a WTO country where the Soviets in the past permitted a great degree of internal autonomy—the course of normalization for the 1980s remains to be seen. This chapter makes note of the peculiarities of the Polish situation and points to some possible scenarios for ensuing normalization. As this study will show, differing conditions and historical circumstances and the personalities of individual leaders (both Soviet and East European) have helped to shape the various normalization processes. From this fourfold comparative perspective, one can also make deductions about general Soviet behavior in Eastern Europe.

REVOLUTIONARY CHANGE IN EAST CENTRAL EUROPE: 1956, 1968, 1980–81

The incipient transformations witnessed in Poland and Hungary in 1956, Czechoslovakia in 1968 and Poland in 1980–81 correspond to the previously given definition of revolution. In all four instances the attempt was made, if only briefly, to adapt communism to the social and cultural fabric of the northern portion of what, until recently, was known as Central or East-Central Europe. In spite of existing differences, the countries in this region share significant historical and cultural ties with Western Europe. Thus it was no accident that revolutionary ferment took place mainly here and, with the exception of Yugoslavia, to a much lesser degree in the Balkan countries of Eastern Europe.

In spite of the complex interaction of a number of different internal and external factors, the revolutionary ferment in these countries was similar. Each time broad segments of the population had become dissatisfied with political and economic conditions, especially the suppression of individual liberties, the Sovietization of the way of life, and the inefficiency of the centralized Byzantine economic system. These conditions, as well as power struggles culminating in factional polarization of the leadership, were the most significant internal factors that led to revolutionary upheaval.

However, there were also many important differences. In Poland in 1956 the revolutionary situation gained momentum because of the policy of de-Stalinization initiated by Nikita Khrushchev at the Twentieth Congress of the CPSU in February 1956. This in turn accelerated democratization of the Polish party, increased the demands for radical reforms, and intensified the power struggle between various groups in the Polish leadership. Discredited politicans who had been closely identified with Stalin's era such as Jacob Berman and Hilary Minc were leaving the scene. Meanwhile two other groups in the leadership, the relatively liberal-minded versus the more conservative and pro-Soviet, were contending for power. The workers' strike of Poznan in June of 1956, when the state security and military restored order with brutal force resulting in hundreds of casualties, was a turning point in the unfolding Polish drama.

In the months following the Poznan revolt, yet another group of "centrist" Polish politicans led by the formerly imprisoned Wladyslaw

Gomulka staged a comeback. Gomulka favored more relaxed domestic policies but within a Leninist framework. Supporting him were numerous reform-oriented party officials and intellectuals who had hoped initially that Gomulka would support radical changes leading to a far-reaching democratization of Polish society. On the same day Gomulka and his three associates were elected to the Central Committee of the Polish Workers' Party (PZPR)—October 19, 1956—the demands for radical democratization, the relaxation of censorship, and factional struggle in the Polish party had reached such proportions that a four-member Soviet Politburo delegation, led by Nikita Khrushchev, and accompanied by eleven Soviet generals, arrived unexpectedly in Warsaw. Khrushchev resented Gomulka's proposed candidacy as new first secretary of the Polish party. He also viewed the situation in Poland as "counterrevolutionary" and threatened military intervention.[3]

The Hungarian revolution was not the climax of a gradual process of reform, as were the peaceful revolutions in Poland in 1956 and certainly in Czechoslovakia in 1968 and Poland again in 1980–81. Instead, it was a sudden, violent explosion in response to a Soviet threat to intervene against the new regime of Gomulka in Poland. Popular sympathy for Poland, Hungary's traditional ally, was the catalyst. Emotions reached a critical high during a peaceful student demonstration in Budapest on October 23 and provoked the first outbreak of violence. However, the stage had been set for the radicalization of Hungarian society months before when optimism generated by Hungarian Premier Imre Nagy's "New Course" (including among other things, the abolishment of police terrorism and political prison camps and the promotion of policies favoring economic consumerism) quickly gave way to frustration after his Soviet-supported removal in early 1955. Like most revolutions, the one in Hungary did not come at a time of popular despair but rather after a sharp reversal from a period when the expectations of the people for rapid social change were running high.

Further Soviet mismanagement of the Hungarian situation contributed to the conflagration. Following Nagy's removal the Soviet leaders chose the discredited politician Rakosi to implement de-Stalinization in Hungary. When this solution failed, they selected another equally disreputable politician, Erno Gero.[4] Finally Nagy was restored to the premiership after the first wave of street violence on October 23. In response to the violence the Soviet military intervened with a few tank batallions already stationed in Hungary. This first intervention was resisted by demonstrators who were joined by several Hungarian military units. The intervention was ill-planned and poorly executed, and it only aggravated the situation. After four days the Soviets concluded a ceasefire with the Nagy government and agreed to withdraw their troops from Budapest, giving an illusion of victory to the rebels. Subsequently, as had happened in Poland several days earlier, a Soviet Politburo delegation (A. I. Mikoyan and M. I. Suslov) was sent to Budapest to negotiate, if possible, a diplomatic solution to the crisis.

A somewhat romantic Communist of humanist tendency, much like Czechoslovakia's Alexander Dubcek, Nagy did not want a revolution and was completely unprepared for his new role.[5] His supporters convinced him that a new program of sweeping political reforms exceeding the original "New Course" might be implemented successfully. However, the revolution soon went far beyond the radical reforms envisioned by Nagy and his advisers. When Nagy became prime minister for the second time, it was to restore order, but by then the revolution had assumed its own momentum. The party organization, once a vehicle for control, had disintegrated almost entirely. The revolution meanwhile had become a spontaneous mass movement, often without leadership and marred by incidents of mob violence. Nagy's name was frequently lent to actions he did not know about and would have opposed.

The revolutionary changes in 1968 in Czechoslovakia were of a very different nature. The Czechs' enthusiasm did not match the revolutionary temper and elan of the Hungarians in 1956. Correspondingly, the so-called Prague Spring was more gradual, legalistic, and tolerant. Unlike the feverishly sketched Polish and Hungarian platforms of 1956, the revolution in Czechoslovakia was a broad and very thorough program, initiated from above and implemented peacefully over a period of several months.

In all three countries factional struggles within the leadership served as catalysts for subsequent developments. The power conflict in the Czechoslovak Communist party resulted in the replacement of First Secretary Antonin Novotny by Dubcek in January 1966.[6] In contrast to their efforts on behalf of conservative elements in Poland and Hungary, the Soviets did not attempt to back indefinitely ·the discredited Novotny, who had desperately sought their support to prevent his ouster. Recognizing that Novotny's position was untenable, the Soviet leadership did not try to prevent his fall. Nor did they dictate his successor.

The power struggle leading to Novotny's fall (as well as those of Nagy and Gomulka's opponents earlier) was conditioned by mounting internal discontent. The domestic sources of the crisis were a belated de-Stalinization program, the economic problems of 1962–63 and the ensuing economic reforms, the unresolved Slovak question, the slow process of political rehabilitation, and the open expression of dissent from reform-minded intellectuals in the party.

During the several months preceding the invasion, the factional struggle evolved into a broader battle for the democratization of Czechoslovak society. The protracted nature of the political crisis, the continued resistance of Novotny and his supporters to Dubcek in 1967–68—a resistance that paralleled that of Rakosi to Nagy in Hungary, and the relaxation of censorship allowed further mobilization of public support.

In April 1968, reformist leaders of the Czechoslovak Communist party incorporated their pluralistic concept of socialism "with a human face" into the "Action Program," which became the Magna Carta of Dubcek's new leadership. It was more comprehensive and went much further than the initial program of Nagy in Hungary. The main domestic features were greater intraparty democracy; more autonomy for state bureaucracies, other political parties, and the parliament; restoration of civil rights (freedom of assembly and association); investigations of secret police excesses; greater national rights for Slovaks and other ethnic minorities within a new federal structure; and comprehensive economic reforms. In addition, Dubcek permitted the establishment of new political clubs and subsequently abolished censorship. In foreign affairs the "Action Program" pledged to pursue increasingly autonomous policies, but, mindful of the lessons of 1956, it did not advocate policies that would threaten Soviet security interests such as a change in Czechoslovakia's foreign policy orientation or WTO status.

Though fanned by uninhibited news media and not always under control, the Czechoslovak revolution was not a spontaneous mass movement. It was not anti-Soviet or even anticommunist but clearly socialist in nature. Whereas in Hungary the party had disintegrated and in Poland (both in 1956 and 1980–81) it was unable to reform itself, in Czechoslovakia the party was the vanguard of the revolution and the primary vehicle for change. Limited pluralism did not cause the party to lose general control; although somewhat diffused, power remained in the hands of the party leadership.

Yet developments in Czechoslovakia, no less than those in Poland and Hungary in 1980–81, directly challenged Soviet political and ideological interests. While in Czechoslovakia reforms were only gradually introduced and their outcomes were far from certain, from the Soviet point of view the revival of freedom of the press, in particular, created a dangerous political precedent with possible repercussions in Eastern Europe as well as the Soviet Union.

The revolutionary ferment in Poland in 1980–81 was similar to the Prague Spring in that it came about gradually and was self-limiting. However, it was initiated by workers outside the party rather than by party intellectuals. In Czechoslovakia in 1968 the workers were largely apathetic to radical reforms until the Soviet invasion. In contrast to both Hungary and Czechoslovakia, the Polish workers in 1980 had had experience with strikes and revolts directed against government policies. The workers' revolts in 1956, 1970, and 1976 served as a springboard for revolutionary changes in 1980–81. While on previous occasions strikes had taken place in one Polish city or region, the August 1980 strikes swept through the entire country, leading to a national workers' revolt.

As in 1956 and 1970, in 1980 the party first secretaries were forced to resign. This led to First Secretary Edward Gierek's replacement by Stanislaw Kania. The national workers' organization, Solidarity, was established with the help of intellectuals who bridged differences that had surfaced during the workers' protests in 1956 and 1970. The Catholic church also played an important role by helping to bring about a national coalition of workers and intellectuals. The role of the Catholic church in Hungary in 1956 and in Czechoslovakia in 1968 was not remotely comparable to that of the Polish church. Subsequently, other new organizations consisting of peasants (Self-Ruling Trade Union for Individual Farmers) and students (Independent Students' Union) were formed. Though not the principal vehicle of revolution, as in Czechoslovakia, even the Polish party did not remain immune to revolutionary change. Radical reformers in the party built horizontal structures, as opposed to vertical structures of Leninist democratic centralism, and fostered genuinely free debates among the party branches without asking the leadership's permission. These reformers also pushed for negotiations with the moderate wing of Solidarity.[7]

Like the Prague Spring, the popular revolt in Poland in 1980–81 was neither violent nor a direct challenge to Soviet security interests. On only a few occasions were the Soviets moved to express concern about those interests. However, from the Soviet perspective, developments in Poland were unpredictable. Moreover, had the situation been allowed to evolve, the Polish armed forces eventually might have become less reliable, thereby weakening important bonds within the Warsaw Treaty Organization.

The Soviets' fundamental concern was that their East European politico-ideological and economic *cordon sanitaire* would be corroded by unrestricted change. A truly successful workers' revolution, originating "from below," was even more threatening to the USSR than the revolutionary program of reform instigated "from above" by Czech party intellectuals in 1968. Soviet acceptance of Poland's free trade unions would have amounted to nothing less than recognition of a mass, non-Leninist working class organization rivaling the Communist party's self-proclaimed monopoly of political power. East German and

Czechoslovak leaders shared the Soviets' fear that Solidarity's legalized right to strike would undermine the party's authority and lead to the establishment of a dual power base in Poland, with detrimental spillover effects in their own and other East European countries. Thus they conducted vitriolic campaigns against "counterrevolutionary" forces in Solidarity and "revisionists" in the party and pressed for military intervention.

A unique aspect of the Polish crisis concerns its economic dimensions. In contrast to Poland and Hungary in 1956 and Czechoslovakia in 1968, in Poland in 1980–81 there was not only popular dissatisfaction with economic and political conditions but also a dramatic economic collapse. Poland's hard-currency debt to the West reached $22 billion in 1981. Although the principal culprits were Poland's outdated centralized economic system and years of economic mismanagement, strikes by Solidarity members in 1980–81 contributed to declines in coal output and machinery production, aggravated existing shortages, and had a disruptive effect on long-term plans of the Council for Mutual Economic Assistance (CMEA). Furthermore, the Polish crisis happened at a time when other CMEA countries, some of them with serious debts to the West, were similarly experiencing serious economic problems.

PATTERNS OF SOVIET INTERVENTION

Poland and Hungary 1956: Different Solutions
A number of crucial factors led to the Soviet decisions to invade Hungary and not Poland in 1956. The Soviet ruling elite was undoubtedly united in its belief that developments in both countries constituted politico-ideological and security challenges to the USSR and practically all of Eastern Europe. Although Hungary probably figured lower on the list of security priorities than did Czechoslovakia and certainly Poland, the Soviets, nevertheless, felt that their security and above all political and ideological interests lay in preserving their East European alliance system.[8]

In Poland, Soviet leaders originally threatened to use military force to stabilize the situation and to prevent Gomulka's election as new party leader. The deployment of Soviet armed forces in Poland and along the East German and Polish borders and the deployment of Soviet naval ships in Polish ports were meant to intimidate and force the Poles to comply with Soviet demands. However, the Soviet leadership accepted Gomulka's victory when Gomulka and his supporters decided to deploy the armed workers' militia and a loyal security corps detachment to the outskirts of Warsaw. The Poles' willingness to resist had an impact on the perceptions of Soviet leaders. As acknowledged by Khrushchev:

> . . . as we began to analyze the problem in more detail and calculate which Polish regiments we could count on to obey [Soviet Marshall Konstantin] Rokossovsky [minister of defense of Poland but a Soviet citizen], the situation began to look somewhat bleak. Of course our arms strength far exceeded that of Poland, but we didn't want to resort to the use of our own troops if at all avoidable.[9]

The Soviet Politburo decided, at least temporarily, against the invasion. A provisional agreement was concluded between the Polish and Soviet leaders on October 20, although the tension continued. On October 23, however, Soviet attention was diverted, unexpectedly, to the new crisis in Hungary.

The Hungarian revolution, with its anti-Soviet undertones, harbored grave and immediate political and ideological consequences for Hungary as well as the rest of Eastern Europe and the USSR. Unlike Gomulka, Nagy did not succeed entirely in restoring order, and occasional acts of brutality against secret police created an impression of chaos. During the revolution Khrushchev is reported to have emphasized with emotion whenever he referred to Nagy: "They are slaughtering Communists in Hungary."[10] Since there was considerable support in Poland for the Hungarians and substantial interest and curiosity in other East European countries, the Soviet leadership feared that the revolution might spill over into these and other countries and perhaps undermine the Soviet hegemonic system. Indeed, the hard-line regimes in Romania, Czechoslovakia, and East Germany viewed Soviet inaction with alarm and pressed for a speedy solution. Meanwhile, in the Soviet Union intellectuals and students in large cities such as Moscow avidly followed developments in Hungary and Poland via the Voice of America and other Western radio stations.[11]

Evidence clearly points to considerable indecision and debate in the Soviet Politburo during the ten-day ceasefire in Hungary. Some pushed for an invasion while others such as Khrushchev preferred to "seek a political solution, if such a solution was still possible." During this period Soviet leaders conducted extensive talks with other WTO allies, and with Yugoslavia and China. Although the Soviet leaders were united in their belief that something had to be done in Hungary, they differed, for specific domestic, bureaucratic, and personal reasons, about the means to be used. They could not agree initially about the likely response of the West. Moreover, according to subsequent admissions by Khrushchev, there were "internal" factors leading to the invasion. He believed that his rivals would blame him personally for the Soviet "defeat and the loss of Hungary."[12]

October 30 was a turning point in the crisis. Under popular pressure, Nagy proclaimed the establishment of a multiparty political system organized around a coalition of several parties as existed in 1945, thereby violating the first commandment of Soviet rule that predicates political control by the local Communist party. Almost immediately the Soviet debate began to focus on a commonly perceived set of security, political, and ideological stakes. Simultaneously, the costs of an invasion were lowered by new international developments. The United States, preoccupied with the coming presidential elections, gave clear signals that it would do nothing in the event of an invasion. Even more important was a Soviet-perceived major split in the Western "camp," when the United States firmly opposed military intervention by Britain, France, and Israel in Suez, Egypt on October 30, 1956. This factor, according to Khrushchev, created a "favorable moment" for the second Soviet military intervention in Hungary.[13]

On the night of October 31, Soviet armed forces stationed in Hungary were reinforced with units from the USSR and Romania, a move that contravened an earlier Soviet-Hungarian agreement about the partial withdrawal of Soviet troops from Budapest and signaled active preparation for the invasion. On November 1, Nagy, desperate and probably suspecting Soviet deception, announced that Hungary would withdraw from the Warsaw Treaty Organization and assume neutrality. On the same day, Janos Kadar, the new first secretary of the Hungarian Socialist Workers' Party and a member of Nagy's government, left Budapest, apparently separating himself from the government. He would later be chosen to serve as head of the new "revolutionary government of workers and peasants" established after the invasion.

The invasion came after three days of tactical deception during which the Soviets, while pursuing further negotiations with a Hungarian governmental delegation, were in fact putting the final touches on the invasion plan. The invasion, preceded by the arrest of the Hungarian delegation, was a complete surprise. Whereas the first intervention involved only 6,000 troops, the second was undertaken by 120,000—those already deployed in Hungary and new troops from the Ukraine and Romania. Hungarian resistance was wiped out, except at two or three points, in only twenty-four hours.

Why did the Soviets adopt a "soft" solution in Poland and not in Hungary? The accepted rationale is that Gomulka was in better control of the domestic situation in Poland than was Nagy in Hungary and that Gomulka did not break Soviet rules by establishing a pluralistic regime or withdrawing from the Warsaw Treaty Organization. These were important differences, but there were also many others.

The Polish and Hungarian upheavals occurred almost simultaneously, the developments in Poland triggering the Hungarian revolution, which, in turn, influenced developments in Poland. Nagy, apparently following Gomulka's lead, seemed to believe that he could wear the mantle of national communism and force the Soviets to compromise. But, in the Soviet mind, Hungary was not Poland. In Hungary there was bloodshed during which members of the secret service and party officials were killed. More important, Nagy did not succeed in uniting his leadership as Gomulka had done.

Another key factor was the differing military considerations in both countries. It could be argued that the Soviets, confronted with crises in both Poland and Hungary, saw Hungary as an easier target for invasion. Obviously, military invasions of both countries would have produced a tremendous upheaval in Eastern Europe with unforeseeable regional and perhaps even worldwide consequences. The Soviet leaders must have known that the smaller, less populated Hungary, whose party was severely split, would be more easily subdued than Poland. In Hungary, unlike Poland, security forces had disintegrated, and Soviet advisers had succeeded in dispersing the armed forces, thereby preventing their potential deployment against Soviet troops. Moreover, in Hungary many pro-Soviet military officials were not dismissed and continued to sabotage the building of a new army.

Soviet military doctrine prescribes the use of strategic surprise and deception when undertaking military invasion. Doubtlessly the Soviet generals realized that strategic surprise could be more easily effected in Hungary—where most strategic centers and airfields were already surrounded by Soviet armed forces on October 31—than in Poland. In Poland, Gomulka was supported by a loyal Secret Service Corps, many units of armed forces, and armed workers in Warsaw. He signaled to the Soviets that the Poles would fight if Soviet troop maneuvers continued around Warsaw. In this respect, Gomulka "deviated" more than Nagy.

Khrushchev's October 20 compromise with Gomulka's leadership was very likely resisted by foes in the Politburo who linked the Polish crisis with Khrushchev's de-Stalinization program.[14] Soviet generals, in particular, must have been furious, since the compromise included a reduction in Soviet military personnel in Poland. (This affected the Polish Minister of Defense and Soviet Marshall Rokossovsky, thirty Soviet generals, and hundreds of officers.) The Soviet generals were determined not to be "humiliated" again several days later in Hungary.

It is not clear how the Soviets would have responded to the Polish crisis had the Hungarian revolution not erupted. Gomulka's effective preparations for military resistance were one factor in the equation. However, the almost simultaneous revolution in Hungary might have been an even greater deterrent to any contemplated invasion of Poland. Indeed, Khrushchev informed Gomulka that the Soviet forces would return to their Polish bases only on October 23—the first day of the Hungarian revolution.[15] As Khrushchev would say, perhaps, this was no coincidence.

Czechoslovakia, 1968, and Poland, 1980–81

Soviet behavior during the Czechoslovak crisis combined hostility with a spirit of compromise.[16] Because of the gradual and nonviolent nature of the Czechoslovak revolution, it took the Soviets longer (not days but months) to agree about the best way to deal with the threat in Czechoslovakia. Only in May 1968 did the Politburo seriously begin to contemplate invasion as a viable option to be warranted only, as Brezhnev later explained, by "extreme circumstances."[17] As in Hungary, although more persistently, some Soviet leaders sought a nonmilitary solution. This became clear in negotiations with the Czechoslovak leaders—at the Politburo-to-Politburo summit conference in the Slovak town of Cierna-nad-Tisou in late July 1968—during which Soviet officials began to exert pressure on Dubcek and his colleagues to curb reforms. While political pressure was applied at the conference, the Soviets also exerted psychological pressure on the Czechs (as they would on the Poles twelve years later) by conducting military exercises around and within the country. In July, under the guise of WTO military maneuvers, the Soviets deployed invading forces of 400,000 men on Czechoslovakia's borders and several thousand men inside the country, despite the Czechoslovak leadership's insistence that they be withdrawn immediately.

The Bratislava declaration of August 3, 1968, drafted at the end of the protracted negotiations between Czechoslovakia and its WTO allies, was a seeming confirmation of the last-ditch effort made at the earlier Cierna negotiations by those Soviet leaders who feared the costs of an invasion and hoped to find an alternative solution.[18] The Soviet leaders, still divided and uncertain about further developments, regarded the results of the talks in Cierna and Bratislava in the same light in which their predecessors had viewed the 1956 Warsaw and Budapest talks—provisional accounts allowing the option to intervene should the situation deteriorate further or the Czechoslovak leaders fail to implement the agreements reached. From August 3 until August 20, Czechoslovakia, like Hungary between October 31 and November 4, lived out the last moments of a fragile independence, to which Dubcek (like Nagy before) was seemingly oblivious.

Dubcek and Nagy were men of integrity. However, they were incapable of a Machiavellian approach to politics. Dubcek and his supporters did not have a firm grip on the domestic situation. The Czechoslovak leadership was divided between those who supported the reforms and those who opposed them, with a sizable number of centrists. Fearing their defeat at the forthcoming party congress on September 9, the Czechoslovak antireformists intensified their efforts during the summer to discredit Dubcek and his supporters.[19] Although both Dubcek and Nagy showed considerable expertise in domestic politics, they were inexperienced in foreign affairs, Dubcek particularly so.

Dubcek's continued implementation of radical reforms was the factor that tipped the balance toward the ultimate Soviet solution. The Soviets did not fear a dramatic change in Czechoslovak foreign policy for it was clear, particularly after Cierna and Bratislava, that the Dubcek government would not deviate from the basic Soviet foreign policy line. Moreover, they knew that Czechoslovakia was not really threatened by NATO or West Germany, in spite of Soviet propaganda to the contrary. What Kremlin leaders did fear was the threat to the Soviet Union itself from "creeping counterrevolution" in Prague.

Soviet leaders' shared image of the stakes in Eastern Europe, such as cohesion among the WTO countries and preservation of the security, political, and ideological status quo, were important issues during the August 1968 Politburo debate. Soviet fears were not that Czechoslovakia would withdraw from the Warsaw Treaty Organization or Council for Mutual Economic Assistance, but rather that (like Poland in 1980–81) it would continue to belong to these organizations and influence other members. If Czechoslovak reformism were validated at the forthcoming party congress, the repercussions would be felt by other WTO members and perhaps ultimately by the Soviet Union.

The Soviets were not alone in their apprehension about the spillover effects of the Prague Spring. Walter Ulbricht of East Germany and the now-conservative Gomulka of Poland (who was again battling for political survival) both complained that Dubcek was not complying with the agreement and warned Soviet leaders that no guarantee of political stability in their respective countries could be forthcoming unless the Warsaw Treaty Organization used military force to restore order in Czechoslovakia.

As in the case of Hungary, Soviet leaders were also influenced by internal considerations. Foreign radio broadcasts kept Soviet intellectuals, would-be reformers, and, most alarmingly, dissidents in the Ukraine apprised of the crisis in Czechoslovakia. Events in that country were closely followed and there was a measure of sympathy and support for the Czechs. The Soviet leaders responsible for domestic affairs, such as the first secretary of the Ukrainian Central Committee, P. E. Shelest, especially feared the spillover of "Dubcekism" and pushed for a radical solution. Brezhnev, cognizant of Khrushchev's position in 1956, could ill afford to tolerate the image of Czechoslovakia as a "second Hungary."[20]

As in Hungary, the decision to intervene was the result of a complex cost-benefit analysis. In the end, the Soviet Politburo concluded that invasion, from a military standpoint, would be a low-risk operation. Dubcek's unwillingness to fight and the clear U.S. noninvolvement noticeably increased the chance of success. The United States— caught up in the Vietnam War, racial disturbances, and presidential politics—was unwilling to do anything on behalf of Czechoslovakia. This position was implied in the public statements of Secretary of State Dean Rusk in 1968, and by President Johnson's strong interest in the early start of SALT negotiations.[21]

During the night of August 20–21, 1968, twenty-three Soviet divisions, together with two divisions from the Polish and East German armies, one from Hungary, and a token brigade from Bulgaria, boldly took Prague and other vital centers. The Soviet generals had learned from the Hungarian experience of 1956, when the first small-scale military intervention, solely by Soviet troops, was ineffective. The invasion of Czechoslovakia was a surprise action, rapid, and overwhelming. The Czechoslovak armed forces were unprepared. Furthermore, they were given orders not to resist by Dubcek, who was anxious not to take any action that might be construed as unfriendly to the Soviets. In twenty-four hours Czechoslovakia was an occupied country. The Soviets immediately set about establishing a new "revolutionary government."

In the beginning the Soviet response to the revolutionary challenge in Poland in 1980–81 resembled Soviet behavior in Czechoslovakia. During the summer and fall of 1980, the Soviets supported the new first secretary of the Polish Party, Stanislaw Kania, who sought to contain Solidarity through a strategy of "socialist renewal" allowing for bargaining and limited concessions. However, as Solidarity made greater demands during the fall and the winter of 1980, the Soviets began to consider the military option. In behavior reminiscent of the Czechoslovak crisis, the Soviets and their WTO allies conducted a menacing military buildup along the Polish borders in December 1980. Simultaneously, a hostile campaign, similar to that preceding the invasion of Czechoslovakia, was launched in neighboring countries. One of its apparent functions was to establish ideological justification for "fraternal assistance."

What probably dissuaded the Soviets from invasion was the realization that Poland, unlike Hungary and Czechoslovakia, could not be easily stabilized by direct military intervention. As in 1956, the Soviets had reason to believe that an invasion would be resisted by at least some Polish military units. Moreover, they knew, given the size of Poland, its armed forces, and the traditional Polish propensity to resist foreign intruders, that such an operation was risky and fraught with high international costs. Furthermore, militarily it would be difficult, given the Soviets' military operations in Afghanistan. Finally, they were impeded in some measure by the preemptive diplomacy of the Carter administration that advised the Poles openly about the Soviet military buildup via public media. This information prepared the Poles, focused worldwide attention on the crisis, and helped deny the Soviets the advantage of surprise.[22]

The Soviets decided to forego a direct military intervention not because they tolerated Polish events but rather because they thought they could better achieve their objectives through a long-term strategy of indirect interventionism. Their decision to implement this strategy using the Polish armed forces—an institution more highly esteemed than the party by Poles and the only force capable of stabilizing the situation—suggests considerable insight on the part of the Soviet Politburo. Polish Minister of Defense and prestigious military figure General Wojciech Jaruzelski was considered the individual most able to impose the tough solution the Soviets had in mind. Kania by this time (spring-summer 1981) had been discounted as weak and ineffectual.

The imposition of martial law required meticulous physical as well as psychological preparations and would have been impossible without the help of Soviet military and security advisers in Poland, particulary Soviet Marshall Viktor Kulikov, who visited Jaruzelski shortly before martial law was declared. Military maneuvers in the spring and summer of 1981 afforded the Soviets the opportunity to introduce surveillance teams and install monitoring equipment in Poland. Several other large-scale military maneuvers conducted in 1980–81 along the borders of Poland, in the country's interior, and on its adjacent waters produced almost constant psychological pressure. Capitalizing on the fear of invasion, the Soviets and the Polish fifth column urged Kania to crack down on Solidarity.

The first opportunity to declare martial law occurred in March and coincided with the large-scale WTO maneuvers in and around Poland, when the Polish secret police tried to provoke a confrontation between the militia and Solidarity in the town of Bydgoszcz. In spite of pressure on Kania and his new prime minister, Jaruzelski, by Politburo rivals Stefan Olszowski and Tadeusz Grabski, martial law was not implemented at this time. This was a turning point in that it marked the beginning of a Soviet-backed campaign against Kania. Newly formed conservative groups, such as the Katowice Party Forum, attacked Kania for tolerating "counterrevolution" while other groups, such as the Grunwald Patriotic Union, claimed that Solidarity was under Zionist influence. The campaign reached a peak prior to the Polish Party Congress in June, when Grabski made an unsuccessful attempt to organize a coup against Kania. On June 5, in a letter similar to that sent to Dubcek prior to the invasion of Czechoslovakia, the Soviets sounded the political death knell for Kania by accusing him, but also Jaruzelski, of having succumbed to counterrevolutionary pressures. All the while WTO exercises in Poland continued.

In significant contrast to what happened in Czechoslovakia, the reformist wing of the Polish party, which wanted to renovate the Leninist party structure along horizontal lines and favored cooperation with Solidarity, was defeated through political maneuverings before and at the Party Congress. By using the threat of Soviet intervention, which he considered probable, Kania was able to prevent the election of a large number of radical reformers as congress delegates. This assured the victory of many conservative members of the Central Committee of the Congress. In spite of this balancing act, Kania failed to establish a strong leadership or limit the unfolding Polish revolution. This led to an intensification of the Soviet threat with mammoth war games in September 1981.

What finally tipped the balance in favor of martial law was the decision at the first Solidarity congress in September to adopt a program of economic reform and self-management by elected workers instead of party-appointed officials. Moscow called this congress an "anti-Soviet orgy" since it resulted in, among other things, the call by radical Solidarity members to expel party officials from the factories. This challenge to the party's monopoly over industrial production alarmed conservative elements in the party apparatus both in Poland and the Soviet Union. The congressional call for support of free trade unionists in Eastern Europe also alarmed party conservatives in neighboring countries. During and after the congress radical elements in Solidarity continued to push for freedom to conduct political activities and for a relaxation of censorship.

In response to the congress and growing Soviet intimidation, the Committee of National Salvation, headed by Jaruzelski, was secretly established in the fall. On October 18, 1981 at a meeting of the Central Committee, Jaruzelski replaced Kania as first secretary of the Polish party. At this session Kania's policies of renewal were criticized sharply and twelve Central Committee members, who had become members of Solidarity, renounced their union membership. Although contingency planning probably had begun beforehand, available evidence suggests that the decision to impose a state of war was made jointly by the Soviets and Jaruzelski shortly after Kania had been replaced. This explains the relaxation of Soviet pressure and attacks on Poland around that time. Cooperation replaced coercion as the dominant feature of Soviet-Polish relations from October through December, even though Jaruzelski was probably forced by the Soviets to accept the martial law solution.

Contingency plans for the military takeover were already being implemented in late 1981. Tactical considerations were an important element in the debate that shaped the decision. The Soviets and Jaruzelski realized that the severe winter would provide the best time for a crackdown by minimizing opportunities for resistance. Moreover, in the fall of 1981 there were strong signs of polarization within Solidarity, an indication that Poland's "silent majority" was becoming impatient with severe economic conditions and perhaps disillusioned with the union. The Soviet policy of indirect intervention culminated on December 13, 1981 with the declaration of martial law and the surprise arrest of Solidarity's leadership by Polish security and armed forces.[23]

POSTINTERVENTION NORMALIZATION

Hungary and Czechoslovakia

Normalization policies are those developed and encouraged by the Soviets under specific national conditions and over a long period to reverse what they view as "counterrevolutionary" change in East-Central Europe. Normalization differs from consolidation. The latter refers to the immediate postintervention measures initiated or supported by the Soviets in Hungary between 1956 and 1959 and in Czechoslovakia between 1968 and 1971. While comparing normalization processes, preliminary observations will be made regarding possible scenarios for the unfolding process of normalization in Poland in the 1980s.

During the years of consolidation, the policies of the Hungarian and Czechoslovak regimes were greatly influenced, if not almost wholly determined, by the Soviets. In both countries the Soviets were committed to the policy of eliminating all political opposition, even if this necessitated using coercion and terror. Thus in Hungary, Nagy and some of his associates were tried and executed, while others were jailed. In Czechoslovakia, on the other hand, the Soviets did not impose exemplary punishment on Dubcek and his supporters. However, whereas in Hungary political repression lasted only a few years, in Czechoslovakia it mounted insidiously and dragged on into the late 1970s.

Although the original Soviet plan was to replace Dubcek with his pro-Soviet foes Indra and Bilak, it was the centrist Gustaf Husak whom the Soviets eventually backed. Husak, like Kadar, had been imprisoned during the Stalin era and this undoubtedly strengthened his candidacy.

Though the consolidation processes in Hungary and Czechoslovakia had similar features, the long-term processes of normalization have differed considerably. In both countries the Soviets closely monitored events and encouraged subservience to the USSR in foreign policy matters. Although neither country has deviated from Soviet foreign policy guidelines, a close look suggests that among Soviet allies Hungary occupies a middle ground while Czechoslovakia, since 1969, is among the most conformist.

In domestic affairs, however, the pattern of normalization in Czechoslovakia fortified a regime acceptable to the Soviets but not to most Czechs and Slovaks, while in Hungary the pattern of normalization led to a flexible regime tolerated not only by the Soviets but also by most Hungarians. Kadar's famous slogan of 1961—"Who is not against us is with us"—reflects his strategy for building national alliances and achieving domestic liberalization.[24] He did this without compromising Hungary's status as a Communist state in which strategic policy making is in the hands of the ruling elite. Normalization in Hungary brought an end to terror and ushered in political relaxation and even cautious pluralism. It provided for a general amnesty for political prisoners, the relaxation of censorship, and the uninterrupted transmission of Western radio broadcasts (which had been jammed prior to this). It resulted in such political innovations as increased duties for parliament, limited multiple-candidate competition in national elections, and greater responsibilities for social organizations such as trade unions. Such political liberalization has been accompanied by increasing economic and cultural relaxation as well as greater contacts with the West, including active reconciliation with the Hungarian diaspora.

The greatest strides were of an economic nature. The New Economic Mechanism (NEM) implemented in 1968 took "Kadarization" beyond what Khrushchev used to call "goulash socialism"—contemporary consumer satisfaction often bought at the cost of future productivity and economic growth. This new policy, which was tolerated by Brezhnev's leadership even after the invasion of Czechoslovakia, advocated not only a shift in economic priorities favoring consumer and agricultural sectors but also considerable decentralization of the command economy including autonomy for individual enterprises and aspects of the market-type economy, such as a new system of pricing. As a result of the cautious economic liberalization under Kadar's leadership, Hungary in the 1970s became one of the most prosperous East European countries, with a kind of social contract between society and the Communist regime.

The reverse of Kadar's slogan describes the process of normalization in Czechoslovakia in the 1970s: "Whoever is not with us is against us." Normalization in Czechoslovakia under Husak proceeded slowly from an unsuccessful search for compromise and a fictitious endorsement of the continuation of Dubcek's democratization to a policy of open repression and continuous purges. The main targets of the repression were the reform-minded Communist party members who were the main force behind the 1968 peaceful revolution. As a result, about 30 percent of party members were expelled and most suffered economic sanctions. Fifteen years after the Soviet invasion, the Czechoslovak regime still relies on Soviet methods of detention, forced exile, and political trials to deal with dissidents and maintain stability.

In the 1970s, while Hungary continued on the path of market-oriented reform, Czechoslovakia, at Soviet insistence, gradually returned to centralized economic planning. (Some limited economic measures needed to improve efficiency were introduced in 1978.) The regime placed primary emphasis on achieving stability and constantly improving the standard of living. In its ability to foster a "socialist consumer society," supported by Soviet economic aid which included hard currency loans, the Czechoslovak regime was successful until the late 1970s.

A complex configuration of factors conditioned the evolution toward domestic liberalization in Hungary and the retardation of the same process in Czechoslovakia. Among the most important were the changing political climates in the USSR and Eastern Europe, Soviet perceptions of the overall domestic situations in the two countries, actual Soviet policies, Husak's and Kadar's personalities, and factional struggles within their leaderships.

The political environment in the USSR and Eastern Europe changed significantly between 1956 and 1968. Reformism under Khrushchev actually helped to advance Kadar's normalization process in Hungary. (Also helpful, though marginally so, were U.S. policies. In 1962 at the United Nations, the Soviet Union, Hungary, and the United States worked out an understanding, ending a political boycott of then Hungarian Premier Janos Kadar's postinvasion regime in exchange for internal liberalization in that country.) Normalization in Czechoslovakia, in contrast, was conditioned by the more restrictive environment in the USSR and East-Central Europe beginning in 1968–69. Brezhnev's relatively conservative politics and such foreign policy considerations as the perceived need to forestall the erosive influence of detente in the 1970s all contributed to this new environment. During this period, Eastern Europe, in terms of Western policy concerns, became a "forgotten region" and Czechoslovakia a "forgotten country."

Another factor that favored Kadar's policies was the Soviets' perception of the domestic situation in Hungary, particularly the memory of the bloody conflict of 1956 when the Soviets suffered several thousand casualties. (In Czechoslovakia in 1968 there were very few Soviet casualties.) The Hungarian temper and willingness to fight commanded respect and perhaps softened Soviet policies toward Hungary. Following the revolution and the disintegration of the Hungarian party, the Soviets basically had two policy choices regarding Hungary: a reign of terror or toleration of gradual liberalization. Kadar, for whom 1956 was not merely a "counterrevoltuion" but a "national tragedy,"[25] sensed that Khrushchev would eventually opt for the latter. Apparently, the costs incurred by the Soviets in 1956 were a bargaining chip that Kadar played skillfully in subsequent negotiations with the Soviet leaders regarding normalization. The Soviets, who did not want a recurrence of the 1956 bloodshed, were compliant.

A third reason for Soviet tolerance was Kadar's personality.[26] He is an extraordinarily skillful and pragmatic politican with a gift for survival. Not an intellectual, Kadar is a simple and humble man of modest upbringing and education. These qualities have made him a relatively popular figure in Hungary. This is a remarkable achievement for any East European politician, and even more so in the case of Kadar since he was considered a traitor by most Hungarians during the period of consolidation. At the same time, he convinced the Soviets of his reliability and of Hungary's stability under his leadership. Soviet leaders have confidence in Kadar and in his ability to control the reforms instituted in Hungary.[27] Such was not the case with Nagy and Dubcek.

Though not Khruschev's first choice in 1956, Kadar was able to gain the former's confidence because he was a "centrist" politician, reform-minded yet tough against all extremism, and possessing an impeccable anti-Stalinist background. Under Khrushchev's patronage, Kadar became the sole acceptable choice for Hungary. This support enabled him to remove from his leadership the conservative elements that had opposed his policies of national reconciliation.[28]

The Soviets' grudging tolerance of the NEM after 1968 contrasts sharply with the rejection of comparable economic reforms in Czechoslovakia and with the Soviet attempt to stifle similar reform measures in the USSR. To date, Kadar's regime in Hungary has managed to preserve domestic flexibility, despite Soviet insistence on a return to orthodoxy in Czechoslovakia. Notwithstanding certain setbacks and slowdowns, the core of Kadar's reform program has survived.

Normalization in Czechoslovakia was also a result of changing Soviet political conditions and preferences, the personality of the Czechoslovak leader Husak, factional politics in the Czechoslovak leadership, and linkages between Czechoslovak and Soviet politics. The most important of these factors appears to have been the changing political environment in the USSR and Eastern Europe during the last two decades. In the 1970s, under Brezhnev, there was a marked retreat from reform in the USSR and Eastern Europe. This stand favored Soviet *Westpolitik,* which necessitated closer ideological coordination along orthodox lines among the East European countries.

Second, in contrast to Hungary, the Soviet military victory in Czechoslovakia was "easy." The Czechs and the Slovaks confirmed an almost unbroken tradition of unarmed resistance against foreign invaders. Only a few dozen Soviet soldiers were killed and most of the fatalities were accidental. Soviet memories of Czechoslovakia in 1968 are less traumatic than their memories of Hungary. In short, the Czechoslovak pattern of normalization was shaped by a political, socioeconomic, and psychological climate quite different from that of 1956.

Third, the different patterns of normalization were conditioned by the contrasting political positions of Husak and Kadar. When he came to power in April 1969, Husak was viewed by many observers as a possible "Czechoslovak Kadar." Neither man had compromised himself as a politician. As Kadar had supported Nagy, so Husak had championed Dubcek during the Prague Spring. Both possessed certain anti-Stalinist credentials. Despite these similarities, Husak's and Kadar's positions on assuming power were very different. Husak did not wield the same capital as Kadar. In other words, Husak's bargaining position was weakened by the Soviets' knowledge that the Czechs and Slovaks, who had not resisted the invasion, would not resist the imposition of harsh normalization policies. Furthermore, though Husak was the best candidate from the Soviet point of view, Czechoslovakia had other politicians with "centrist" leanings who could have replaced him. Kadar, in Hungary, however, was indispensable.

Other important differences between Husak and Kadar pertain to their personalities and styles. Though both are good politicians with an instinct for survival, Husak is more conservative. Unlike the proletarian, jovial Kadar, Husak, a trained lawyer, is an ambitious individualist and, some would say, an arrogant intellectual with a messianic sense of mission. He is not a member of the dominant Czech nationality, and in the past vigorously resisted Prague's traditional centralism, more so than most other Slovak Communist leaders. He is more committed to protecting Slovak national interests than to instituting genuine reforms. This may explain why in Slovakia normalization took a much milder form than in the Czech lands.

Unlike Kadar, Husak has at times been challenged and even over-ruled, with support from some Soviet quarters, by leaders more conservative than he, such as Bilak, Indra, and Antonin Kapek. Nevertheless, there are signs that Husak would like to emulate some of Kadar's normalization policies or at least display greater flexibility. For example, during the early stages of normalization, he is credited with having resisted the attempts of his more conservative colleagues to put Dubcek and his supporters on trial as well as Soviet efforts to make direct arrests in Czechoslovakia.[29] Nevertheless, the trials of dissidents, some of them reform-minded former party officials, took place in the late 1970s. Obviously, the stringent policies of the Czechoslovak hard-liners were not considered too high a price for the stability the Soviets were seeking in Czechoslovakia.

Polish Normalization

Although the patterns of Hungarian and Czechoslovak normalization can be used as a measuring stick to estimate what developments can be expected in Poland in the 1980s, an equally important gauge is the forgotten Polish experience with normalization after 1956. In 1980–81 revolutionary changes were a continuation of the 1956 experience. In 1956, like in 1980–81, the Soviets preferred to use indirect forms of intervention in Poland. Because of the absence of direct Soviet force, Polish normalization after 1956 followed a pattern that may be repeated in the 1980s.

In contrast to Hungary, in Poland there was no repression by occupying forces. Indeed, some of the achievements of 1956 were preserved: the rejection of forced collectivization of agriculture, the maintenance of the independent-minded Catholic church (in sharp contrast to Hungary), and the heightened class consciousness and assertiveness of the working class.

However, other achievements of the Polish October of 1956 were supressed by Gomulka's government under Soviet pressure. Gomulka used the Soviet invasion of Hungary as a reason for curbing revolutionary changes in Poland. Though he tolerated some relaxation and contact with the West, freedom of speech was curtailed already in 1957. In the following years, Gomulka, unlike Kadar who integrated the reform-minded wing of his party, purged party reformers while tolerating conservative party elements. At the same time freely elected, independent workers' councils were liquidated. In spite of the existence of excellent theoretical work on the socialist market economy by Polish economists, the market-oriented program was never implemented as in Hungary.

A complex of external and internal factors also conditioned Polish normalization. The political environment in both the USSR and Eastern Europe during the late 1950s and early 1960s was so restrictive as to prohibit domestic experimentation. True, Khrushchev determinedly would not accept genuine political pluralism in Eastern Europe, but he did tolerate limited political liberalization and far-reaching economic reforms. Actually, Gomulka was in a much better position to pursue more independent domestic policies than were Kadar in the late 1950s and early 1960s or Husak in the 1970s.

The main causes of the more restrictive Polish normalization in the 1950s and 1960s were, in addition to Soviet pressures, the unique political and socioeconomic climate in Poland and Gomulka's personality. While encouraging false hope about democratization, Gomulka willingly did away with some of the October achievements.[30] When he came to power, Gomulka, like Kadar and Husak, was not a compromised politician. His incarceration during Stalinist time was looked upon in Eastern Europe and in the Kremlin as an impressive credential.

Like Kadar, Gomulka was not an intellectual but a self-taught man. However, Gomulka was much more conservative and dogmatic. As he grew increasingly arrogant he became isolated from the radical-reform forces who had supported him in October 1956. Gomulka's dependency on the Soviet leadership grew in proportion to his mounting isolation. His isolation was manifested in 1968 when he advocated the Soviet invasion of Czechoslovakia and in 1970 when he apparently asked the Soviets to intervene militarily against Polish workers whose revolt in the Baltic cities was deemed a threat to his leadership.

Obviously, the factor most conditioning Polish normalization in the 1980s is economic conditions. The economies of Czechoslovakia and Hungary never approached the disastrous state of the Polish economy in the early 1980s. Moreover, an expanding world economy enabled the Hungarian economy to recoup quickly from the effects of the 1956 revolution and subsequent Soviet invasion. Hungarian political normalization was accompanied by relative economic achievements. In contrast, as a result of economic catastrophe and a major economic indebtedness to the West, Poland may not recover financially for years to come. Definitely the major factor of success in Kadar's normalization program is missing today: the ability of the party leadership to improve the standard of living and thereby enter into a social contract with a majority of the population.

Although radical reforms in Poland are long overdue, it is questionable whether they can be introduced while the general climate in Eastern Europe (with the exception of Hungary) and the USSR remains basically inhospitable to radical economic reform. However, because Poland represents a very heavy burden on the USSR and current economic conditions in the Communist bloc are deteriorating rapidly, the Soviet leadership may be forced to support experiments with radical economic reforms in Poland. Also lacking in Poland are the brutal shock and aftereffects of invasion that were felt acutely in Hungary and, to a lesser degree, in Czechoslovakia. Although the military coup in Poland weakened the revolutionary forces it did not have the complementary effect of preparing the way for national reconciliation. In Hungary extreme national catastrophe prepared for Kadarization.

As in Hungary in 1956 and Czechoslovakia in 1968, there is an ongoing factional struggle in 1984 within the Polish party that is closely related to the future course of normalization. On the one hand there are Jaruzelski and his supporters who as of fall 1983 had not convinced the Polish people that they were capable or sincerely desirous of achieving national reconciliation. On the other hand, there are his opponents, Politburo members Stefan Olszowski, Albin Siwak and, more openly Tadeusz Grabski, who, though demoted, is active as their front man. The latter group has urged that dissidents be brought permanently under control, using methods employed earlier in Czechoslovakia. These and other advocates of a tough policy consider the more reform-minded Deputy Prime Minister Mieczyslaw Rakowski and Politburo member Kazimierz Barcikowski—who favor a political course similar to the one adopted by Kadar—to be too liberal.[31]

The personality of Jaruzelski is an important factor. Although little is known about Jaruzelski or even whether he will continue for any lengthy period to head the Polish party, he clearly is neither a simple Polish nationalist nor Moscow's stooge. Whether he has Kadar's ability to conceive and implement a long-term strategy of reconciliation is questionable. It is useful to recall that Kadar was considered a quisling in 1956 and managed to become a popular leader only much later. Hence it would be premature to write off Jaruzelski.

One of the basic differences between the three previous cases of normalization and the current one in Poland is that the military is ruling the country instead of the party. It remains to be seen whether the military will be able to govern as effectively as it seized power and whether the Soviets, traditionally fearful of Bonapartist tendencies in the military, will tolerate General Jaruzelski as head of the party. There are other features peculiar to the Polish situation such as the powerful Catholic church, which has traditionally forced the Polish Communist government to exercise restraint. Finally, the long and persistent struggle of the working class, culminating in the emergence of workers' independent trade unions, is unique to Poland. Thus, they may not be easily eradicated.

If he remains in power, will Jaruzelski, like Kadar, prevail over the conservatives? Or will Jaruzelski, like his predecessors Gomulka and Husak, tolerate these elements? Even if Jaruzelski defeats his conservative opponents, will the Soviet leadership allow him to follow Kadar's example of reconciliation or will it insist on a return to orthodoxy as Brezhnev did in Czechoslovakia? Whether Poland moves toward the Czechoslovak, the Hungarian, or earlier Polish pattern of normalization will depend on the unfolding of events during the next several years.

What have been the immediate effects of Jaruzelski's takeover? With Soviet backing, Jaruzelski used coercion and terror to suspend Solidarity and other organizations created in 1980–81 and to halt the revolutionary changes being sought and instituted in Poland. Detention of Solidarity's leaders and purges of thousands of "unreliable elements" were carried out on every political level. The suspension of martial law in July 1983, though objected to by conservative elements in the Polish leadership, did not bring significant political relaxation. It is difficult to predict the future course of Polish events; conditions may become markedly worse before they stabilize or vice versa.

However, future developments will follow one of three possible lines: the situation will remain essentially the same, for the short run at least; increased disorder and pressure will lead to greater repression and an approximation of the Czechoslovak variant of normalization; or dialogue between the government and Solidarity will result in an eventual coming to terms that will lead gradually to a moderate course similar to Hungarian normalization, while significantly different because of Poland's experience after 1956 and particularly because of its economic problems.

The first scenario, which envisions little change in the status quo, may not be the most likely line of development. The second and third scenarios are more plausible and as of fall 1983 the Czechoslovak scenario appeared to be more likely than the Hungarian one. However, this may change. One of the key factors mitigating against the Czechoslovak solution is that the introduction of martial law did not halt the economic decline as hoped. Although there have been no major strikes, passive resistance continues to undermine the discipline and productivity of the Polish worker. The Poles' long tradition of armed struggle against foreign rule and those whom they perceive as foreign agents may emerge once again if the government continues its repressive policies. If he chooses to follow a more moderate course of normalization, Jaruzelski's strongest bargaining chip in dealing with the Soviets may be Poland's unique political and economic situation. The Soviet leadership, at least in the long run, has to choose between a repressive normalization, which may yet culminate in direct Soviet intervention, or one allowing Jaruzelski to formulate and implement cautious reforms.

CONCLUSIONS

As demonstrated, Soviet leaders have political, ideological, and economic stakes in Eastern Europe that are conditioned by history and Leninist belief: the region is vital to the security, political, ideological, and economic well-being of the Soviet Union. To maintain maximum influence in the region, the Soviet Union must prevent the spread of what it views as anti-Soviet tendencies, be these "bourgeois," "revisionist," or "Eurocommunist." Accordingly: (a) the withdrawal of an East European country from the Warsaw Treaty Organization (WTO) (Hungarian scenario of 1956) is not permissible;[32] (b) the revolutionary restoration of a genuinely multiparty system in any of the WTO countries (Hungarian scenario of 1956) or the existence of genuinely pluralistic forces such as independent trade unions (Polish scenario of 1980–81) would jeopardize the control of the Communist party and therefore cannot be tolerated; (c) the weakening of a regime's loyalty (Czechoslovakia in 1968) or the inability of a regime to contain pressures for revolutionary change within acceptable limits (Poland, 1956 and 1980–81, Czechoslovakia, 1968) cannot be tolerated.

When confronted in Eastern Europe with revolutionary changes such as those described above, Soviet leaders believe that they have the right to intervene, using military force if necessary, to protect their interests. If this can be done by pressure and intimidation, forcing the country's leadership to crack down on its own people, so much the better. The Soviet self-perceived right to intervene in Eastern Europe under these conditions has been labeled the "Brezhnev doctrine." This may be inaccurate since Brezhnev was not the first to inaugurate such a policy. Rather he seemed to follow the "Khrushchev doctrine" (if not the Leninist or Stalinist doctrine), inasmuch as his justification for the invasion of Czechoslovakia was similar to Khrushchev's justification for the invasion of Hungary.[33]

One can only speculate as to what the Soviet leaders may have learned from the Hungarian, Czechoslovak, and Polish crises and how they will respond to similar challenges. Soviet decisions about the future "normalization" in Poland—which is, at the time of writing, far from being resolved—will undoubtedly provide more definitive answers. One thing that can be ascertained from the events in Hungary, Czechoslovakia, and Poland is that the Soviets are determined not to permit pluralistic socialism. Another is that Soviet responses to such developments and the subsequent normalizations are not predetermined. As shown, the postinvasion periods in Hungary and Czechoslovakia have been markedly different, with greater importance attached to the preservation of political orthodoxy in Czechoslovakia than in Hungary.

The outcomes of the 1956 and 1968 invasions suggest that direct Soviet interventionism can be advantageous to the USSR. In both cases substantial benefits in terms of East European stability accrued to the USSR. The invasions demonstrated the limits of autonomy set by the Soviet leadership and served as warnings to other ruling Communist parties. The invasion of Hungary made the invasion of Poland unnecessary in 1956. Because of what happened in Czechoslovakia in 1968, no Soviet invasion was necessary in Poland in 1981. Instead, fear fostered by Soviet military exercises prompted a Polish military coup.

The direct and indirect interventions in 1956, 1968, and 1981 are evidence of the Soviets' continuing difficulty in maintaining Communist rule in Eastern Europe. What makes these interventions necessary for Moscow is the special nature of the Soviet Union's security interests in Eastern Europe—concerns that are quite unlike the United States' security interests in the Caribbean Basin. Both superpowers still use military force directly and indirectly to stabilize crises in their strategic backyards. In this, the Soviet exercises on Poland's borders in 1980–81 are no different from recent United States maneuvers around Nicaragua. Their motives, however, are quite different. The United States' concern is with actual or potential military alliances—in this case, increasing Soviet and Cuban military ties with Nicaragua. In contrast, the Soviets' foremost preoccupation is ideological deviation—and its possible spillover from neighboring countries into the Soviet Union. Above all, the Soviets are concerned that a more humanitarian form of government may "infect" the Soviet people and weaken the regime from inside.

What the Kremlin still does not seem to understand is that Leninism is radically unsuited to Central Europe. Soviet politics are rooted in the despotism of tartar and czarist rule and the messianic pretensions of Byzantine and Leninist dogma. In contrast, the Central European countries have inherited a predominantly Western political and cultural tradition, and all have practiced some kind of constitutional government at one time or another.

The irony is that Soviet insistence on ideological orthodoxy undermines Central Europe's effectiveness as a military buffer. The repressive "normalization" of Czechoslovakia in the 1970s rendered that nation, which was traditionally friendly to the Soviet Union, totally unreliable in any warlike situation. Similarly, the coup in Poland humiliated and preoccupied the Polish army.

The post-Brezhnev succession introduced another important element of ambiguity in Soviet behavior in Eastern Europe during the 1980s. As in the past, Soviet transference of power may produce an absence of clear direction with resulting irresolution and contradictions in policies. The Soviet successions of 1982 and 1984 may soon be followed by successions in some East European countries. This event could contribute to instability and augment political infighting.

The new Soviet leader has two basic choices. The first is to work gradually toward a more voluntary relationship with the region—implementing economic reforms such as those implemented in Hungary in the 1960s, followed by cautious political liberalization. This is unlikely. All Soviet leaders are greatly restrained by domestic politics and by the ideological fears at the heart of the Soviet security doctrine. After all, how can the Soviet Union grant the Poles and Czechoslovaks what is denied the Russians? Other options are more of the same: maintaining Leninist hegemony in the face of continued revolt. The price, clearly, will be more retaliation that in turn heightens international tensions and sours superpower relations.

Finally, Soviet policies toward Hungary, Czechoslovakia, and Poland in the 1980s will be influenced, as in the past, by the general nature of Soviet relations with the West. Prudent U.S. policies toward the USSR and East-Central Europe might have a marginal impact. The West could use its economic leverage in negotiating directly with the Kremlin as it did in 1962, when Washington agreed through a tacit understanding to lift its boycott of the Soviet-installed Hungarian regime in exchange for internal liberalization in Hungary. However, any Western policies could hardly pry the regimes of East-Central Europe from the Soviet sphere of influence.

NOTES

Parts of this chapter dealing with Hungary and Czechoslovakia are based on my chapter in Sarah Terry, ed., *Soviet Policies in Eastern Europe* (New Haven: Yale University Press, 1984). An earlier version of this chapter appeared under the title, "Revolutionary Change, Soviet Intervention and 'Normalization' in

East Central Europe," *Comparative Politics,* vol. 16, no. 2 (Jan. 1984), pp. 127–51. The author is indebted for their comments to, among others, Robert Legvold and Sarah Terry. He acknowledges interviews with numerous Soviet, Czechoslovak, Hungarian, and Polish officials, scholars, and dissidents and is grateful to Virginia Valenta and Elizabeth Rosdeitcher for their insightful readings of the manuscript.

    1. Walter Laqueur, "Revolution," in David I. Sills (ed.) *International Encyclopedia of the Social Sciences* (13) (New York: The Macmillan Co. and The Free Press, 1966), 501–507. Laqueur's definition differs somewhat from that developed by Huntington and Johnson who thought of revolution primarily as a violent act. Samuel Huntington, *Political Order in Changing Societies* (New Haven: Yale University Press, 1968), 264; Chalmers Johnson, *Revolutionary Changes* (Boston: Little, Brown, 1966), 7.

    2. Percy H. Winfield, "Intervention," *Encyclopedia of the Social Sciences* (8) (New York: The Macmillan Co., 1932), 236–239.

    3. *New York Times,* October 21, 1956.

    4. Although the Soviets did not anticipate the revolution, shortly beforehand they assessed Hungary as "the weakest point in the socialist camp." A few days before the revolution, the Soviets placed their units in Hungary and Romania on a state of alert. "The Report on Hungary," *United Nations Review,* vol. 4, no. 2 (August 1957), 7; J. M. Mackintosh, *Strategy and Tactics of Soviet Foreign Policy* (London: Oxford University Press, 1962), 165–178.

    5. The most comprehensive analysis of the Hungarian revolution is that by Bill Lomax, *Hungary 1956* (New York: St. Martin's Press, 1976).

    6. For the most comprehensive and well-balanced analysis of the Czechoslovak peaceful revolution, see H. Gordon Skilling, *Czechoslovakia's Interrupted Revolution* (Princeton: Princeton University Press, 1976).

    7. For an account of the revolutionary changes in Poland in 1980–81 see Stewart Stevens, *The Poles* (New York: Macmillan Publishing Co., 1982).

    8. As Khrushchev explained to the Yugoslav Ambassador to Moscow Veljko Micunovic on October 25, 1956: "Anti-Soviet elements have taken up arms against the 'camp' and the Soviet Union. . . . The West is seeking a revision of the results of World War II and has started in Hungary, and will then go on to crush each socialist state in Europe one by one." Veljko Micunovic, *Moscow Diary* (New York: Doubleday, 1980), 134–35. Micunovic was the Yugoslav Ambassador to the USSR from 1956 until 1958.

    9. *Khrushchev Remembers,* Strobe Talbott (ed.) (Boston: Little, Brown and Co., 1970), 203

    10. Micunovic, *Moscow Diary,* 127.

    11. Julian Gorkin, "Young People Look to the Future (Hungary, Poland, and Spain)," *The Review* (Brussels) (Imre Nagy Institute for Political Research), vol. 3, no. 4 (October 1961) and Micunovic, *Moscow Diary,* 153.

    12. Micunovic, *Moscow Diary,* 134 and 153–154; Mohamed Heikal, *The Sphinx and the Commissar* (New York: Harper & Row, 1978), 92.

    13. *Khrushchev Remembers,* 362.

    14. See Roy Medvedev, *Khrushchev* (Garden City, N.Y.: Anchor Press, 1983), 106.

15. Konrad Syrop, *Spring in October* (New York: Frederick A. Praeger, 1957), 143.

16. For a comprehensive analysis see Jiri Valenta, *Soviet Intervention in Czechoslovakia, 1968: Anatomy of a Decision* (Baltimore: Johns Hopkins University Press, 1979); Valenta, "Soviet Bureaucratic Politics and Czechoslovakia," *Political Science Quarterly,* vol. 94, no. 1 (Spring 1979), 55–76.

17. Zdenek Mlynar, *Nightfrost in Prague: The End of Human Socialism* (New York: Karz Publishers, 1980), 162. Mlynar was a former secretary of the Czechoslovak Communist Party Central Committee.

18. As such the Bratislava Declaration resembles the Soviet declaration of October 30, 1956. The Bratislava Declaration, however, contains "escape" clauses to justify, if necessary, an invasion. During the conference at Cierna, First Secretary of the Ukrainian Central Committee P. E. Shelest reportedly attempted to break up the negotiations by insulting some Czechoslovak leaders and accusing them of actively supporting separatist tendencies in the Transcarpathian Ukraine. In contrast, Politburo member M. A. Suslov reportedly tried to find a political solution to the crisis. Valenta, *Soviet Intervention in Czechoslovakia,* 71–92.

19. They tried to secure Soviet "fraternal assistance" by providing "proof" of "counterrevolution" in Czechoslovakia (supplied to the Politburo by Soviet Ambassador S. V. Chervonenko and KGB operatives in Czechoslovakia). Such "proof" was essential to convince those in the Soviet leadership who had resisted an invasion. Ibid., 123–128, 136.

20. Valenta, *Soviet Intervention in Czechoslovakia,* 139–145.

21. At this point it was not important whether Brezhnev, as he told the Czechoslovak leaders in Moscow, had actually received President Johnson's assurance on August 18 that the United States still honored the Yalta and Potsdam agreements and, by implication, would not try to resist an invasion. (This was reported by the eyewitness Mlynar, *Nightfrost in Prague,* p. 214, but it was denied by Secretary of State Dean Rusk and by Walter Rostow, national security advisor to President Johnson, in interviews with this author.) By this date, the Soviet Politburo already had enough signals from the U.S. government to know that it would not take action on behalf of Dubcek's regime.

22. Jiri Valenta, "Soviet Options in Poland," *Survival* (London) (March–April 1981), 50–59; "Soviet Use of Surprise and Deception," *Survival* (London) (March–April 1982), 50–61.

23. Jiri Valenta, "Explosive Soviet Periphery," *Foreign Policy* no. 51 (Summer 1983), 87–100.

24. Kadar's interview with *L'Unita* (Rome) (December 1, 1969).

25. Kadar's speech in Denis Sinor, ed., *Modern Hungary: Readings from the New Hungarian Quarterly* (Bloomington: Indiana University Press, 1977), 42.

26. Charles Gati, "The Kadar Mystique," *Problems of Communism,* vol. 23, no. 3 (May–June 1974), 23–27; William Shawcross, *Crime and Compromise: Janos Kadar and the Politics of Hungary Since Revolution* (New York: E.P. Dutton, 1974).

27. See Soviet praise of Kadar's able struggle on two fronts, *Pravda*, November 25, 1970.

28. For a detailed discussion see the study of William F. Robinson, *The Pattern of Reform in Hungary: A Political, Economic, and Cultural Analysis* (New York: Praeger, 1973).

29. Vladimir Kusin, *From Dubcek to Charter 77: A Study of "Normalization" in Czechoslovakia, 1968–1978* (New York: St. Martin's Press, 1978), 161.

30. Maria Turlejsha, "Wladyslaw Gomulka and the Achievements of October 1956," unpublished paper, The Wilson Center, July 11, 1983.

31. For a more extensive discussion see Jiri Valenta, " 'Normalization'?: The Soviet Union and Poland," *The Washington Quarterly* vol. 5, no. 4 (Autumn 1982), 105–19.

32. It should be noted, however, that Albania withdrew from the Warsaw Treaty Organization in 1968. This was a special case because of its small size, its geographical location, and its willingness to fight the Soviets.

33. The ideological justification for the invasion, formulated as the Soviet right to "defend the achievements of socialism" in Eastern Europe, can be found in the WTO letter to the Czechoslovak leadership of July 1968 and as an "escape clause" in the Bratislava Declaration. It is also clearly stated in an article by S. Kovalev in *Pravda*, September 26, 1968 (published after the invasion). Brezhnev implicitly endorsed it in a manner similar to the manner in which Khrushchev had justified the Soviet invasion of Hungary 10 years earlier. Compare Brezhnev's speech (*Pravda*, November 4, 1968) with Khrushchev's speech (*Pravda*, April 1, 1958).

Nationalism and Integration in Eastern Europe: The Dynamics of Change

12

Teresa Rakowska-Harmstone

The dynamics of political life in post-1945 Eastern Europe have been shaped by the interplay of two key sets of political forces: the presence and policies of the Soviet Union as the superpower dominant in the region, and social forces for change within East European states emergent from the national traditions and political culture of each. Among countries discussed in this book, only Yugoslavia and Albania have escaped direct Soviet tutelage—in 1948 and in 1960, respectively. But even these two countries cannot avoid the effects of Soviet influence as it radiates through the region; for the other countries, it has been, and ultimately still is, even now, a determining variable. The two sets of forces work at cross-purposes more often than they complement each other, an incongruity that has found its reflection in the region's endemic instability. In the 1960s, the 1970s, and the early 1980s this instability was augmented by the impact—within the Communist fraternity—of the dispute between the USSR and China, and, in social relations generally, by growing pressures for change, and by the opening up to the West, started by Nikita Khrushchev's "peaceful coexistence" policy and continued under Leonid Brezhnev's "detente." But the 1980s, with "detente" fading and the cold war seemingly revived, promised no relief for Eastern Europe.

The Soviet presence in Eastern Europe has been responsible for the establishment and maintenance of a Communist political system in each of the countries concerned,[1] and has largely determined the form, if not necessarily the substance, of each regime's policies, particularly with respect to the promotion of economic and social transformation aimed at the establishment of "socialism," and "internationalist" foreign policies. Also, it has imposed limits to change for the states within the reach of the Soviet armed might. Indigenous political forces, on the other hand, caused the initial deviations from the Soviet model,

360

and have shaped national attitudes to the system, as well as social responses to the Communist policies and demands that confront each national regime. Outside influences encourage the deviant patterns. Western influence reinforces traditional Western elements in the political culture of most East Europeans, while the challenge to Soviet leadership and to the universality of the Soviet model within the Communist movement strengthens the drive for national self-determination of all East European parties.

As Eastern Europe entered the 1970s, it seemed that the ability—and will—of the Soviet Union to enforce strict conformity were in decline, despite the 1968 intervention in Czechoslovakia. The patterns of change developed in the sixties implied further differentiation, as East European systems were responding broadly to each country's specific demands in three areas: the search for domestic legitimacy in the wake of the "loss of faith" crisis that followed de-Stalinization; the search for an economic management formula that would break through the barrier between an extensive and an intensive growth pattern; and the assertion of national *raison d'etat* in domestic and foreign policies. As I wrote in 1972:

> The resurgent nationalism and the pressures demanding the freedom to pursue one's "own thing," including political liberalization and economic rationality, all point to particularistic solutions. Moreover, and despite appearances, these tendencies operate in an increasingly favorable environment, characterized by an overall decline in Soviet influence, effectiveness, and credibility, and by the corresponding need of local elites to establish their credibility and legitimacy in local, national terms. This in the general framework of competing universalist claims of the two communist superpowers, which negate the old claim to one ultimate truth, and open new alternatives for the smaller states. . . . In addition there . . . is the change in the style of Soviet leadership, its frequent lack of resolution and consensus, and the consequent absence of the "will to act."[2]

But as the seventies unfolded and the trends toward change continued, a new countervailing force emerged in the form of a Soviet policy to consolidate the "world socialist system," namely to integrate Eastern Europe with the Soviet Union, aiming over the long range at the establishment of an organic relationship that would incorporate East Europeans into the Soviet body politic beyond the point of return. First moves toward integration started apparently in the early sixties, and they were given fresh impetus by the events of the Prague Spring of 1968. A coherent new Soviet theory of bloc integration emerged in the early seventies and has been consistently implemented since. Thus a new and powerful element has emerged that stands in the way of further emancipation of East European states, as the Polish developments of 1980–81 clearly demonstrated.

The dynamics of interaction between national forces for change and the new Soviet thrust for integration will shape conditions in Eastern Europe in the 1980s, with the effects also felt in the international arena. On the face of it, the two forces are on a collision course. The direction of East European change patterns is rooted in national self-assertion and seeks modifications in the Soviet-imposed political model that would respond better to national political cultures and developing social demands. The policy of bloc integration, on the other hand, reasserts the Soviet leading role and aims at an eventual total submergence of East European variants into the Soviet model. The room for maneuver left to East European leaders within the new blueprint has been shrinking, and it has been increasingly difficult for them to negotiate successfully national demands. The aging Soviet leadership, faced with social, economic, and national problems at home while at the same time playing for high stakes in the global arena, has not been receptive to differentiation and nonconformity within its own camp. Leonid Brezhnev's death and the accession to the post of general secretary of the Communist Party of the Soviet Union (CPSU) of, first, Yuri Andropov (1982), and, second, Konstantin Chernenko (1984), did not seem to have brought any policy changes toward Eastern Europe. The tenure of both was limited from the outset by age and health problems, and the emergence of a new and younger Soviet leadership in the 1980s and thus, perhaps, of a new policy, was only a matter of time.

SOVIET PRESENCE

The Soviet Union's presence in Eastern Europe is the result of the Allied victory over Nazi Germany in World War II and of the subsequent polarization of political and military strength between the two superpowers—the USSR and the USA—that left the former dominant in Eastern Europe. A "secure" Eastern Europe has been a Soviet strategic target of first priority since 1943–45, dictated by the perception of the importance of the region both as a defensive buffer zone in case of another attack from the West, and as the staging area for the extension of influence westward into Europe, the dual perception that has had strong roots in Russian and Soviet history. The basic asymmetry of power between the Soviet Union and the East European states and a consistently low priority assigned to the region in Western strategic considerations were key factors that allowed for the establishment of undisputed Soviet hegemony there.

The three initial postwar years (1945–48) served to consolidate Soviet power in the region, a task that was enormously facilitated by the Red Army's occupation of most of the area. By 1948 Communist parties were firmly in control, and Eastern Europe entered a period of enforced conformity known as the "Stalinist" period, which ended with the dictator's death in 1953. Under Stalinism, and led by the "Muscovites" within each East European party,[3] each country was transformed into a mini-copy of the Soviet system. Each was run directly by Soviet "advisers" located strategically within party, police, and military bureaucracies. Each followed identical economic and social policies (minor variations were allowed reflecting specific conditions) and spoke with a Soviet voice in foreign policy. Each was tied to the Soviet Union by bilateral ties and was economically exploited, as, for example, in the case of the notorious joint companies. The Yugoslav party's successful resistance to these arrangements, possible only because it had an independent power base at home, resulted in that country's expulsion in 1948 from the Cominform. The expulsion, a shock to the Yugoslav Communists at the time, proved to be a blessing in disguise. It launched Yugoslavia on its "own road to socialism" that survives to this day, and released it (along with geographically isolated Albania which, nonetheless, remained faithful to Stalinism) from direct Soviet tutelage. In the captive states, the "nationalist deviation" of Tito served as an excuse to purge, in the late forties and early fifties, his alleged would-be imitators. The purge decimated the "native" factions in the East European parties. It was only after Stalin's death in 1953, when Soviet leaders became involved in the struggle for Stalin's succession, that the "Muscovites," most of whom were Stalinists, were gradually eased out of power.

Khrushchev's victory ushered in a new phase in Soviet policy toward Eastern Europe, one of relative relaxation. But the sudden decompression that accompanied the jockeying for power within the leadership of the CPSU between 1953 and 1956 released the suppressed nationalist elements in Hungary and Poland. These forces erupted in 1956 in the Hungarian revolution (which attempted to remove Hungary from the Soviet orbit altogether), and in a workers' revolt in Poland that brought Gomulka, one of the purged "native" Communists, back to power. Notwithstanding the armed suppression of the Hungarian revolution, Khrushchev confirmed the new autonomy gained by the East European parties in the chaotic period of succession to Stalin. Soviet "advisers" were withdrawn, and East European Communists were allowed to develop policies that would respond to their countries' needs, provided that none of the basic Soviet policies and requirements were undermined. This new Soviet emphasis on "viability"[4] resulted in the strikingly differentiated evolution of the East European states.

Far-reaching innovations were introduced. Poland de-collectivized and is now the only country within the bloc (except for Yugoslavia outside) with agriculture largely based in peasant-owned holdings. The autonomy of Poland's Roman Catholic church was reasserted, a price the Polish United Workers' Party (PUWP) had to pay for the episcopate's cooperation in preventing political explosions; the price included concessions to Polish national culture, of which the church has traditionally been a guardian. Even so, another round of workers' riots—in December 1970—resulted in a change in the Polish leadership, with Gomulka replaced by Edward Gierek. Economic reforms took the form, on the one hand, of a decentralized command planning model of the New Economic System (NES) adopted in the GDR, and on the other, of a socialist market model of Hungary's New Economic Mechanism (NEM). Nationalism became enshrined in Romania's official Communist orthodoxy under Nicolae Ceausescu, and in Romanian foreign policy. In Czechoslovakia, Alexander Dubcek and his collaborators established "socialism with a human face." The latter, however, proved to be too much for the post-Khrushchev CPSU leadership of Leonid Brezhnev and Alexei Kosygin. The Czechoslovak party's permissive attitude to political pluralism and freedom of expression, and above all its claim to have found a new model to fit developed Communist societies,[5] triggered another military intervention in August 1968. This time it was a collective endeavor by members of the Warsaw Treaty Organization, an early byproduct of the new integration policy as it began to take shape in the military sphere. The 1968 intervention provided a background for the enunciation of the keynote of the new policy, the "Brezhnev doctrine" of limited sovereignty.

BLOC INTEGRATION POLICY

The "viability" phase of Soviet policy in Eastern Europe ended conclusively with the invasion of Czechoslovakia. But first signs of the new emphasis on integration appeared in the 1960s. Of these the most important was a new pattern of military exercises designed to foster cohesion of Warsaw Pact forces. This system combined East European with Soviet units under a joint (overall Soviet) command, thus denying to the East Europeans an effective operational independence and an opportunity to train for the defense of their national territory.[6] Stalin and Khrushchev both pursued integration policies earlier: Stalin, through direct penetration of East European polities by Soviet agents; Khrushchev, by using the instrumentalities of multilateral regional organizations: the Council for Mutual Economic Assistance (CMEA) established in 1949 and the Warsaw Treaty Organization (WTO-Warsaw Pact) set up in 1955 as a counterpart to NATO. Brezhnev's new policy borrowed from both of his predecessors: it revived the bilateral ties between Moscow and East European capitals but under a multilateral umbrella; and it avoided Romania's veto, which stymied Khrushchev, by dropping the unanimity principle and by pursuing integration by sectors and in selected target areas.

A fully developed blueprint of the new policy emerged after 1968.[7] Still in force in the 1980s, this policy envisages simultaneous steps toward integration in four basic areas: political, military, economic, and cultural. Objectives of the policy are implemented through a largely invisible power grid that links the CPSU with the East European parties. The formal framework is provided by the WTO-CMEA regional state system. The primacy of politics, characteristic of Communist systems, permeates the arrangements. Soviet and East European sources are unanimous in emphasizing that the unity of the "socialist community" (sotsialisticheskoe sodruzhestvo), as the bloc is officially called, is based in the members' common Marxist-Leninist ideology and in the leading role Communist parties play in their societies. They speak of the "intensive convergence of socialist countries" and of the "determining role" of interparty collaboration "in arranging the whole complex of political, economic, ideological, and cultural interconnections between fraternal states."[8] Because of its "seniority" and "experience" (not to mention the power it wields), the CPSU runs the whole system. In each sphere the integration machinery follows existing structural arrangements.

Political integration is carried out within the familiar party-state structural dichotomy. Interparty integration proceeds on the basis of the multiplication and institutionalization of contacts between leaders as well as between lower-level functionaries of the ruling parties, in order to coordinate policies and to synchronize technical aspects of the parties' multifaceted activities. The contacts are multilateral and bilateral, and take place at the international, national, and sub-national levels. The leaders meet formally once a year, usually in the Crimea, in addition to numerous other contacts. Functionaries meet frequently in various locations throughout the region to coordinate specific activities or campaigns; a recent example has been a blocwide campaign of political socialization. Coordination of "fraternal" parties' activities below the top level is the task of the CPSU Central Committee's Department for Liaison with Communist and Workers' Parties. Meetings between top leaders tend increasingly to be bilateral (the CPSU General Secretary and East European party chiefs), a practice which effectively deprives a would-be dissenter of an opportunity to register a veto. Multilateral gatherings of all leaders are reserved for official occasions such as the CPSU congresses (every four or five years), and the rather infrequent meetings of the Political Consultative Committee (PCC) of the Warsaw Pact. This body, officially the supreme authority in matters of bloc coordination, has served so far to formalize the decisions but not to make them.

Apart from its special function of military coordination, the Warsaw Pact serves to orchestrate policy at the state to state level, particularly in foreign policy. Formal sovereignty of member states is strongly emphasized at this level in recognition of the national sensibilities of all the states, but particularly Romania, the one openly recalcitrant member. The degree of compliance varies widely, but progress in political integration has been reflected in the synchronization, throughout the bloc, of constitutional instruments to formally enshrine the "leading role" of the Communist party in society, as well as a constitutional, or treaty, commitment to a common, Soviet-directed, foreign policy. In Poland (the last to comply), the action, in the form of constitutional amendments adopted in January 1976, generated political protests that forced modifications in wording to make the amendments more palatable. Nevertheless, the ferment invoked by the amendments was fueled by another round of workers' protests over price increases in the summer of the same year. The resulting coalition between the intelligentsia and the workers led to open, although illegal, political opposition in the late 1970s, and eventually to the massive wave of strikes in the summer of 1980 that paralyzed Poland's economy, again toppled the leader, and gave birth to the remarkable phenomenon of Solidarity.

Military integration mechanisms under the Warsaw Pact command were started first, and seemingly progressed the furthest, reflecting Soviet concern over internal security of the bloc after 1956 and in the aftermath of Romania's withdrawal from joint military arrangements in 1963. The military-administrative and political socialization mechanisms include a joint command system, integrated officer and troop training, integrated bilateral or multilateral operational deployment of forces including interchangeability of national formations down to the unit level, and synchronized equipment, logistics, and communications. All members (except Romania) share a Soviet-inspired military doctrine that has no relevance to their defense needs as sovereign national entities. The political education networks and the main themes of indoctrination are coordinated by the Military Political Administration of the Soviet Armed Forces. Access to command positions for East European officers depends on their having been trained in Soviet staff schools and is subject to political approval (the *nomenklatura* system). Soviet officers occupy all key command positions in the pact structure. Although in peacetime national armies are nominally under the control of their respective ministers of defense, lines of command actually run along the network of Soviet liaison officers from Moscow where the joint command is located. The pact's backbone consists of Soviet forces stationed on the territory of all pact members except Romania (which opted out) and Bulgaria (where apparently there is no need for them). The fragmentation of East European force structures in the operational sense has served as the basis for their reintegration into bilateral or multilateral entities under Soviet command. Apart from Romania, none of the East European member states appears to have operational control over its armed forces sufficient to mobilize them for the country's defense.[9] Thus, it is unlikely that the imposition of martial law in Poland in 1981 was an act of independent Polish national will. Rather, it appears to have been the result of twenty years of operational and command integration and of indoctrination in "socialist patriotism," an achievement that spared the Soviet Union the necessity of direct intervention.

State-to-state linkages do not depend solely on the WTO system but are secured by a network of bilateral treaties of friendship and cooperation concluded between the USSR and other pact members, and by pact members with each other. The first round of these treaties was signed in the 1940s; the second and third, in the 1960s and the 1970s. The Soviet Union also has status-of-forces agreements with Hungary, Poland, Czechoslovakia, and the GDR, which regularize the stationing of Soviet troops in these countries. Thus, should the Warsaw Pact be dissolved, the political and military integration mechanisms of the bloc would nevertheless remain firmly in place.

CMEA is the instrument of *economic integration,* envisaging a "socialist division of labor" as well as joint planning, technological integration, and joint projects, some of them of supranational character. Objective economic forces strongly favor integration: the necessary economies of scale are feasible only on an integrated basis. Moreover, East Europeans depend heavily on imports of Soviet fuels and raw materials and on Soviet markets for their manufactured goods, the quality of which is inadequate for Western markets. Economically, Eastern Europe is increasingly a burden to the Soviet Union, but the political trade-offs involved are obviously considered to be worth the costs. At the same time some economic compensations for the Soviet Union have also been introduced, such as annual renegotiations of prices paid for Soviet products by CMEA partners, and East European investments in the development of Soviet natural resources. Because the CMEA economic integration proceeds under a nonmarket model (despite the Hungarian anomaly), decision making can easily be delegated upward to supranational bodies, a trend which has been resisted by Romania and less explicitly by others, because it preempts national sovereignty. So far CMEA has proceeded on the basis of coordinated planning, but the pressure from Moscow to institute joint planning has been mounting.[10]

Cultural integration, which envisages the development of "internationalist" and "socialist" attitudes, depends on the growth of contacts and is the least developed as well as the least likely to succeed, because it implies an imposition and dissemination of Soviet (Russian) culture regarded by most East Europeans as inferior to their own. Cultural integration is nevertheless vigorously promoted by the Soviet Union, particularly in its efforts to coordinate and dominate social science research and historiography. An attempt to "internationalize" history has been visible in more than one East European country, as has been an emphasis on the study of the Russian language. Voices from Moscow have been heard discussing future integration of the bloc's educational systems. Resistance to cultural integration has been pronounced and widespread but an institutional framework to promote it has already been developed. The major instruments appear to be the academies of sciences of East European countries, under the leadership of the Academy of Sciences of the USSR. It is, perhaps, not accidental that the positions of the president and academic secretary of the Polish Academy of Sciences are within the *nomenklatura* of the party's Politburo.[11]

Mindful of lessons of the past, the regional integration policy that emerged in the seventies aims at a gradual long-term integration from below, that will accrue piecemeal in selected areas, and thus will not trigger East European defense mechanisms. It relies on persuasion and incentives more than on force. The incentives are designed to operate within the range of autonomy still left to East European regimes but in the context—to be sure—of overwhelming Soviet political, economic, and military preponderance. A promise of economic benefits and international contacts and status secured under the Soviet umbrella is designed to balance the erosion of national sovereignty implied in common arrangements; the erosion is further obscured by the principles that adherence to each of the multiple types of joint endeavors is strictly voluntary. Finally, as a trend outwardly parallel to that currently pursued in Western Europe, the policy of regional integration is internationally highly respectable, particularly in its economic aspects.

The existence of an elaborate Soviet blueprint for integration carries no assurance that it will succeed. Forces of nationalism in Eastern Europe, socioeconomic pressures for democratization, particularly in the northern tier, and the prevalent Russophobia are formidable obstacles. Moreover, the East European regimes' enthusiasm for and participation in joint arrangements varies with their perception of how these would affect their countries' national interest, and progress made toward real integration has been slow in all spheres except the military. Nevertheless, the policy is a good indicator of the current and future thrust of Soviet policy. Economic pressures for integration and their long-range impact should not be underestimated. Neither should the quality of relentless pressure generated by the "senior partner" in conditions of basic asymmetry of power in the region, especially if one keeps in mind that Soviet support is the ultimate guarantor of the survival of most, if not all, East European Communist regimes.

DOMESTIC PATTERNS

The Soviet presence guarantees the survival of Communist systems in the bloc countries (the two independent Communist states, Yugoslavia and Albania, also benefit here indirectly), but the guarantee is a liability in most parties' relations with their own societies, because with few exceptions the Russians have traditionally been hated and communism distrusted through the region. Consequently, in the seventies and eighties, each party has been preoccupied with efforts to generate legitimacy of its own based on a national consensus. In doing so, the East European parties have had to acknowledge and to make an attempt to respond to three basic types of pressures that have been in the forefront of social demands in their societies: the pressure for national sovereignty; the pressure for political democratization and pluralism; and the pressure for an improvement in the standards of living.

But, given the geostrategic factors and the characteristics of Communist political systems, none of these demands can actually be met. Soviet power and Soviet pretensions to regional and global leadership preclude genuine sovereignty for any state within the bloc, and place enormous pressure on the two mavericks—Yugoslavia and Albania, the first of which also faces critical ethnic nationalism at home. Leninist characteristics of Communist political systems—the monopoly of power appropriated by each Communist party on the strength of its ideologically legitimated role as the vanguard of the working class and exercised on the operational principle of democratic centralism—are incompatible with either pluralism or democratization. The com-

mand planning system, typical of Leninist systems, is highly
dysfunctional to the development of the technological-intensive stage
of economic growth that is required for a meaningful improvement in
the living standards.

Within these limits, nevertheless, some dialogue at least has developed between Communist regimes and their societies, to find accommodation in one or more areas of these demands. Patterns of
change and adaptation have taken different forms depending on each
country's political culture, its level of development, the abilities and
perceptions of its leaders, and the magnitude of outside stimuli.
Superficially, it has been easy to accommodate nationalism in most
countries, and economic experimentation has taken place, if not always effectively. Concessions in the political sphere have proven to be
the most difficult, however, because of the threat that pluralism carries
to the systems' survival.

Historically Russophobia affected most of the East Europeans, with
the exception of the Bulgarians, the Yugoslavs (mainly Serbs), and the
Czechs. The Soviets' entry into the region and their subsequent behavior in 1948, 1956, and 1968 only served to aggravate anti-Russian hatreds and lost them the few friends they had had. Also, only a few
states in East-Central Europe between the wars had strong indigenous
Communist movements and, as is well remembered throughout the
region, the postwar Communist systems there were imposed from the
outside, with Yugoslavia and Albania as the two exceptions, and
Czechoslovakia as a partial exception. For all of these reasons it has
been imperative for East European Communist regimes to
"nationalize" themselves as much as possible, a policy that became not
only possible but also indicated when "native" factions came into
power; nationalism has grown to be progressively more important for
regime maintenance with the passage of time.

Appeals to national traditions and invocations of national interest
find an immediate response among the populace as much as among the
parties' rank and file, and nationalism affects not a few of the leaders
despite their avowed loyalty to "internationalism." In ethnically
homogeneous states such as Poland, Hungary, or Albania, or in the
states with small but troublesome national minorities such as Romania,
nationalism has been vital in generating popular support for foreign and
domestic policies. The value of national symbols is readily recognized:
the royal palace in Warsaw, virtually destroyed during World War II,
was reconstructed, and the return of the Crown of St. Stephen to
Budapest by the United States in 1978 was accorded all the pomp and
circumstance deemed essential for a national treasure. National symbols are also important in multi-ethnic societies, such as Yugoslavia or

Czechoslovakia, as signs of national unity, but particular ethnic nationalism there (as in the Soviet Union), has been a major stumbling block on the road to national integration: it has been a destabilizing political force and a vehicle for decentralization, inclusive of separatism, for example on the part of the Croats and the Slovaks.

The image of an outside "enemy"—basically the Soviet Union in the local context, although a traditionally hostile neighbor also serves—has been particularly functional to the cause of national unity, as in the case of Yugoslavia. But for the bloc parties the stress on nationalism carries an ever-present danger of bringing to the surface latent anti-Russian feelings. A policy or a statement that implies "standing-off" to the Russians carries an immediate pay-off in popular approval, although few East European leaders have felt secure enough openly to pull the bear's whiskers; Romania's Ceausescu has been an outstanding exception. The Romanian party has openly legitimized its rule in nationalism, a decision that has been reflected in unique (within the bloc), ideological formulae (national communism as a supreme value as well as the denial of the leading role to the CPSU), in an independent foreign policy, and in assimilationist policies toward national minorities. The GDR is a special case, because it represents only a part of the German nation; the SED therefore found it both difficult and frustrating to manipulate nationalist symbols. The stress has been on the emergence of a socialist German nation, as an entity distinct from and superior to the bourgeois German nation represented by the Federal Republic of Germany; the future of GDR is said to be "indissolubly" connected with that of the other socialist nations.

Invocations to national unity have frequently and not incidentally tapped sources of national chauvinism and have emphasized intolerant and undemocratic features of traditional nationalism. This trend is superbly summarized by a Polish dissident writer; his emphasis on an "outside" approval for the revival of this type of nationalism and, obliquely, on the dangers of being swallowed up by Russia are worth noting:

> Nation, fatherland, patriotism are the words uttered frequently and willingly in the press and on television. Today in Poland the needs of national consciousness are satisfied mostly by visual methods. Films are made of the Piast [the first Polish dynasty, 8th–14th century] period, or else the novels of Sienkiewicz [famous 19th century patriotic writer] are remade for the screen. For three hours a viewer can watch a Polish hero wearing a breastplate bearing the image of the Virgin Mary and bearing a sword whom neither the Tatars nor the Swedes can conquer. He is thus confirmed in his "Polishness" and is strengthened by historical traditions. After leaving the theater he may read a review of the movie that will further perk up his self-

esteem: a review permeated by the Old Polish spirit, sentimentally patriotic. But a viewer will not find in any newspaper a review that would tell him that there is no contemporary patriotism without a consciousness of human rights, and that freedom of the nation depends on the realization of these rights. The show has been successful. Sons of workers, peasants, and working intelligentsia sit in rows gaping at a shadow—in sound and color—of a mounted knight, wearing a breastplate. Really, this is weird. Especially if one considers when and where the spectacle is taking place: in Poland, thirty years after the reform camp took över. . . . For a foreigner it is too complex to comprehend new conditions and manipulations as a result of which the filming of the defense of Czestochowa [a 17th-century siege by Swedes of a sacred cloister] has become a patriotic alibi for the power structure. . . . What bothers me most is that today in Poland *sarmatyzm* [the nobility's code of martial virtues] has been licensed, that it is obviously needed by someone, for some reasons, and that *it has been approved from outside.* It is not only the sword and the breastplate, but also the new military paraphernalia: September (1939) battles, helmets of the revolts, and forest camps . . . and anti-Semitism. Sometimes I am very much afraid that very soon all of this would become a *Polish folklore,* an equivalent of a *lezginka* [Caucasian dance]: and our virile nationalists will catch on too late and without batting an eyelash, when they, and the rest of us, will be swallowed up together with all this folklore; then our traditions of national struggle will be good-naturedly tolerated, as was the coat of the nobility [*kontusz*] in royal-imperial Galicia, or as the Cherkess ensembles are now tolerated in Russia. Because possibly all of this has been agreed upon, and somewhere some bureaucratic heads have known for a long time that it will be necessary to include in the accounts also this small, *internal,* nationalism, one more to be added.[12]

This passage, written in the mid 1970s, now sounds strangely prophetic in its concern over the manipulation of Poland's martial traditions. It is precisely this manipulation that facilitated the suppression of Solidarity by the Polish armed forces. It was the myth of the uniform, of "roga-tywka" (the traditional officer's cap) and the Polish eagle perched on it, and of General Jaruzelski as "our general" that served to disguise the Soviet hand behind the successful reimposition of Communist orthodoxy on the rebellious society.

The Polish example illustrates the success in the use of nationalism as a legitimizing device in the service of communism. Nevertheless, it has been a double-edged sword, from Moscow's points of view, as demonstrated in the case of Romania, where nationalism has indeed been used to legitimize a Communist regime, but on the basis of barely disguised anti-Russian sentiments. East European national communism—pioneered by the Yugoslavs—has contributed to polycentrism in bloc relations, and it has been a major force behind the post-Stalinist autonomization and a source of conflict between bloc members; it poses constant challenge to the Soviet leadership and a major road-block to integration. One dimension of nationalism, however, remains unexplored: would Communist elites continue to espouse the national-ist cause if by doing so they created a threat to their survival as the ruling group?

Pressures for democratization and pluralism are generated as much by elements of traditional political culture as they are stimulated by economic development and modernization. The latter inevitably re-sults in a higher degree of social politicization, and the demands for political participation increase in proportion to improvements in eco-nomic standards and in access to social services. It appears, however, that the intensity of political demands is directly related to the type of political culture: the more authoritarian it is, the fewer demands there are for basic political changes and the easier it is to accommodate the pressures under the party's umbrella. But if democratic or antiau-thoritarian elements exist in a political culture, they reinforce the im-petus toward democratization fostered by modernization to form an explosive political mix. It is no accident therefore that growing social pluralism has been more readily controlled by the party in the countries where the political culture is more congruous with the system, as in the case of the GDR, Romania, or Bulgaria, and that pressures for demo-cratization have repeatedly led to explosive political situations in the countries with political cultures incompatible with Leninism, as in the case of Czech democratic traditions or the Polish and Hungarian indi-vidualistic and aristocratic political heritage.[13]

As pointed out above, the leading role of the party (i.e., the party's monopoly of power, which cannot be shared with other social groups) creates an insurmountable obstacle to democratization. Inevitable corollaries of the leading role of the party, i.e., its monopoly to aggre-gate social interests as well as to assign social priorities, are the denial of the very existence of social conflict and sub-system autonomy, and consequently the absence of any machinery for conflict resolution; the application of the principle of democratic centralism to the total range of social relations; and the maintenance of the monopoly of communi-cations and monopoly at enforcement. None of the ruling elites has been able to compromise on the party's leadership principle (and that includes the League of Communists of Yugoslavia) because of their need to retain power. The range of accommodations, however, has been very broad—the most far-reaching changes took place in Yugo-slavia, where additional constraints imposed by the CPSU's vigilance have not been enforceable.

The key question of how to deal with the problem of interest articulation and conflict resolution has been in the forefront of the attention of the party elites as well as of the revisionists; the spectrum of approaches to the problem on the basis of Marxist-Leninist positions has ranged from neo-Stalinism, through the "reactionary left," "Marxist-humanism" (a moral stance), and "socialist pluralism," to "efficient authoritarianism."[14] In practice the latter model has been preferred, and a range of techniques has been developed to substitute for institutionalized pluralism, all of them under the party umbrella: bureaucratization of major interests ("institutional" pressure groups); partial transformation of the "transmission belts" (party-directed social organizations such as the trade unions) into interest articulators but not quite into Western-type "associational" groups (in Yugoslavia and to a limited extent also in Hungary); the technique of cooptation and consultation of professional and technical elites (pioneered in the GDR but adopted throughout the bloc), and party-run mass "participation" techniques, practiced by all.

The two most centralized systems, Romania and Bulgaria, have made the least accommodation to social interests; the GDR has successfully practiced bureaucratization, cooptation, and participation techniques; the Hungarian variant, which also included limited transformation of transmission belts into interest-access channels, is the most far-reaching in the bloc, and has also been the most successful. In the devolution of power, however, it lags far behind the Yugoslav experiment in self-management and decentralization. The Czechoslovak venture into socialist pluralism was cut short by Soviet intervention, and Czechoslovakia has returned to the ranks of neo-Stalinists. In Poland, all the orthodox techniques have been tried but none of them worked and the conflict between the regime and society has erupted in 1980–81, leading temporarily to the establishment of genuinely free trade unions and to the reemergence of pluralism and a civil society outside Communist political structures. But the Polish party's acceptance of changes proved to be a temporary tactic imposed by its weakness. When sufficient forces for repression were marshalled, a *status quo ante* 1970 (not 1980) was restored by the military coup of 13 December 1981, while Soviet and other "fraternal" troops deployed in and around Poland poised for an invasion, should Jaruzelski fail. It remains to be seen whether conditions in Poland develop on a Hungarian or on a Czech pattern. Judging by a continuous stalemate between the regime and the society, prospects for a national rapprochement seemed poor. The disastrous economic situation seemed to preclude even the Czech variant of consumerism as a price for political conformity.

In general, there have been four major variants in the practical approach to the articulation of social interests and the handling of the problem by the authorities:

1. Interest articulation is allowed only within the party through bureaucratization and cooptation; this approach has been pioneered by the GDR and is utilized by most of the others;

2. Interest articulation is permitted within a somewhat broader circle of social organizations; this has meant some, but not substantial, diminution in the scope of the party's leading role (Hungary);

3. Interest articulation is permitted within a wide spectrum of social organizations; this has resulted in a substantial erosion in the exercise by the party of its leading role (Yugoslavia and "Prague Spring" Czechoslovakia);

4. Interest articulation emerges totally outside institutional channels and is not controlled by the party. This has taken the form of spontaneous riots and unrest ("anomic" pressure groups, e.g., GDR, 1953; Poland, 1956, 1968, 1970, and 1976; Hungary 1956; Romania's workers' strike, 1978), and of opposition groups and social organizations organized from below on a country-wide basis but totally outside the existing political system (Poland post-1976 but especially in 1980–81). The latter phenomenon proved to be a function of the weakness of the ruling party and its total lack of legitimacy; thus it was allowed to exist for a period of time. Ultimately, however, the fate of the Polish Solidarity was the same as that of all other challenges to the Communist party's monopoly of power: suppression by force.

Because of the basic incompatibility between the Leninist political system and political pluralism, there are no prospects for democratization going beyond the current Hungarian model within the bloc (to wit, the experiences of Czechoslovakia and Poland), or beyond the Yugoslav model outside the bloc.

Attempts at economic reform—to keep up a high rate of growth and to satisfy consumerism—have produced two variants: a market-type reform with indicative rather than command planning and decentralized economic management (Yugoslavia, Czechoslovakia prior to 1968, and, in a more modest version, Hungary); and a decentralized command planning system, pioneered by the GDR. The latter variant is preferred by the Soviet Union for the bloc, but it has failed, by and large, to deal with the problems of transition from an extensive to an intensive growth pattern. In the early 1980s there were signs that most East European regimes were thinking again of economic reforms; a matter of necessity more than preference, as their economies continued to deteriorate.

The Soviet party has been the most cautious and the least pressed to

provide channels for interest articulation, and the Soviet perception
still enforces the limits for the East Europeans. For the CPSU the
acceptability of innovations is directly proportionate to the perception
of the threat of "infection" they carry, thus the minimization of the
probable impact of any innovation affecting the party's leading role is
in the interest of the innovators.[15] The techniques used by the Soviet
Union to deal with various types of innovations range from direct
suppression to assimilation. In cases when, for whatever reason, suppression appears to be inconvenient or infeasible, an isolation technique has been used—a given phenomenon is judged to be a peculiarity
of a given country and is allowed to continue, provided it will not
spread to "fraternal countries." An example has been the tolerance of
the position of the church and the aberrant agricultural pattern—as
well as, for a time, of open opposition—in Poland; also the tolerance of
Romanian independence in foreign policy, and of the Hungarian market-type New Economic Mechanism. Ultimately, however, it is the
Soviet perception that sets the limits to change for the bloc as a whole.

INTERNATIONAL PATTERNS AND IMPLICATIONS

The Soviet presence in Eastern Europe has always been officially
justified in terms of defense and security requirements. The memory of
the World War II German invasion helped to create an image of a
revanchist Bonn in league with American "imperialists" within NATO,
nurturing aggressive designs. Initially, the image served well to cement
common Soviet and East European foreign policy, but it began to wear
out over time; by the late seventies the defensive justification for the
Soviet presence in Eastern Europe was no longer credibly tenable. The
West's recurrent hands-off attitude has resulted in the recognition that
the region belongs in the Soviet sphere of influence; moreover, the
Soviet Union's nuclear parity with the United States has effectively
precluded any such interference. At the same time, the new German
Ostpolitik signaled the acceptance by the Federal Republic of Germany
of the postwar territorial settlement, the validity of which has been
legitimized further by all the European states, the United States, and
Canada at the 1975 Helsinki Conference on Security and Cooperation
in Europe. In the period of detente the danger of an invasion from the
West has never been more remote. Nevertheless there has been no
parallel Soviet disengagement in Eastern Europe. On the contrary, the
seventies have seen both a major buildup of conventional military
power by the Warsaw Treaty Organization (far in excess of NATO's
conventional capabilities as well as of "policing" needs in the bloc) and
the launching of a new effort at integration between Eastern Europe

and the Soviet Union. Logic suggests that it is the region's *offensive* value that has come to be seen as of greater importance. The two aspects of Soviet-East European policy in the seventies—the massive buildup of conventional military strength and the emphasis on integration—would seem to combine at the basis of a new European and global "outreach": a quest by the Soviet Union for strategic, political, economic, and, last but not least, "ecumenical" influence as the leader of the world "progressive forces." Seemingly, the strategy has shifted, from securing the region for its own value, to transforming it into a staging area for further expansion, with East Europeans playing a role of junior partners in the endeavor.

In the early 1980s East-West tensions in Europe escalated again. This was due to several contributory factors. In December 1979 the Soviet Union invaded Afghanistan, and in December 1981 the Polish Solidarity movement, which evoked strong support not only from Western governments but from the Western labor movement, was suppressed. Demands for sanctions against the Soviet Union and the Polish military junta were spearheaded by the United States, led, after 1980, by the strongly anti-Soviet Republican administration of Ronald Reagan. The Reagan administration's main concern was to reverse the unfavorable trend in the "correlation" of strategic and military forces between the two superpowers, an aim that most West European governments supported, albeit discreetly. By 1983 the NATO decision to emplace the Pershing-II and cruise missiles in Western Europe as a counterpart to the Soviet SS-20s brought a threat of more Soviet missiles in Eastern Europe. The missile controversy, part of a broader armaments debate, spawned peace movements on both sides of the East-West division.

The Soviet shadow looms large in Western Europe and in the Balkans, as anyone can testify who has counted the comparative strength of the WTO and NATO divisions and hardware and who has tried to escape Radio Moscow signals on European airwaves. Increasingly, western observers point to a growing vulnerability of Western European states, particularly those of peripheral importance in the NATO system, and to Soviet pressures that fall short of open threats but that impose constraints on the pursuit of policies displeasing to the Soviet Union.[16] A none-too-subtle glimpse of Soviet military capabilities on terrain resembling their own was conveyed to representatives of Greece, Turkey, and Yugoslavia invited to Soviet military exercises in the Caucasus (Operation Kavkaz), and to Scandinavians in a similar invitation to exercises on the Finnish border (Operation Sever). Military exercises of the WTO Northern Tier at the time of the Polish crisis afforded an awesome display of Soviet power to the West Europeans.

But, the military strengthening of WTO forces had all the earmarks of a strategy of political blackmail rather than for direct military action, and it has created preconditions for a "Finlandization" of Western Europe, should the United States withdraw its strategic umbrella, for whatever reasons.

A strategy of economic integration of socialist states within the CMEA system is generally assumed to be incompatible with their developing strong bilateral economic ties with the West, an assumption that has provided some of the impetus in the West for the development of trade with the socialist countries. Although a multiplication of East-West trade exchanges carries the potential for a differentiation in the bloc's pattern of trade, there are also aspects of these exchanges that actually facilitate the bloc's integration.[17] Western technology transfer can be applied most efficiently on an integrated basis, taking advantage of economies of scale, and thus it promotes the "socialist division of labor"; also trade flows can be coordinated (as joint planning develops), fostering the same aim. The greater the success of the East Europeans in developing economic reciprocity with the West, the less of an economic burden they are to the Soviet Union without any significant decline in their ties to the bloc. But, if their vulnerability to Western price fluctuations, combined with high indebtedness to the West, results in a crisis (as in the case of Poland), the regime's dependence on Soviet support—economic and political—increases, thus blending it even more closely into the Communist state system.

Economic contacts are a channel for the penetration into Eastern Europe of unwelcome Western ideas, but they also facilitate transmission of "socialist" models westward. The East Europeans' old ties with Western Europe, and the image they project of "straining at the leash" of Soviet dependence, make them preferred partners for West Europeans and far more sympathetic and believable than the dour and "primitive" Russians—an ideal "Trojan horse" from the Soviet point of view. Overall, vigorous East-West commercial exchanges, particularly when combined with Western credits and other such initiatives as joint projects, tend to promote interdependence between the economies of socialist and capitalist Europe, opening up new avenues of political influence. In a "mirror image" perception, the Soviet leaders see the process as a means for extending "socialist" influence westward, just as Western politicians view the development of economic relations as an opportunity for the transmission of Western ideas eastward. The Soviet conviction, rooted in Marxist-Leninist ideology, that history marches toward "socialism" makes such a risk of Western "infection" supportable. East European countries have an interest in a regional dialogue between CMEA and the EEC. If successfully developed, cooperation between the two regional organizations would not only promote interdependence but would also further enhance the socialist bloc's cohesion and the Soviet's leading role within it. East-West economic ties that developed in the 1970s continued into the 1980s despite the increase in tensions.

In the seventies CMEA's economic role also acquired new dimensions in promoting relations with Third World countries, a significant if little noted development. The 1971 Comprehensive Program included a stipulation, directed specifically at the less-developed countries (LDCs), that nonmembers could join the organization, offering participation in the "international division of labor" as a new avenue to economic development (inclusive of scientific and technological cooperation, credits, and preferential status). A change in the CMEA charter in 1974 gave it a legal authority to enter international agreements as an organization. Thus CMEA may now conclude agreements with nonmembers (individual states or international organizations), enabling them to participate in the organization's economic system.

Economic partnership between CMEA members and the LDCs offers apparent advantages to both sides: it involves barter trade based in bilateral (or multilateral) clearing arrangements, guaranteeing market, supply, and price for a specific period of time (mostly one year). It assures a market and a supply of manufactured goods for the LDCs. For CMEA members, it provides an outlet for products that are nonmarketable in the West because of poor quality. Neither side has to use scarce hard currency. The arrangements are avertised by CMEA members as a developmental alternative to the dependence on capitalist countries and are therefore attractive to the LDCs, economically and ideologically. Some contracts, however, and in growing numbers, have stipulated payments in convertible currencies; moreover, CMEA members have shown consistent surpluses in their trade with the LDCs so far, thus rendering the image of economic advantage to the latter somewhat problematical. For the Soviet Union economic transactions under the CMEA label facilitate also a "political outreach," by developing long-range economic dependency ties with specific groups of developing countries. It should be noted that most Third World countries that have been attracted to a partnership with CMEA consider themselves to be socialist. Some, such as Vietnam and Angola, already had strong political and economic dependency ties with the Soviet Union and/or Cuba.

Eastern Europe has also been vitally important to the Soviet Union in political-ideological terms. The existence of a cluster of "socialist" states where Soviet hegemony is acknowledged validates the CPSU's claim to the universality of its model as *the* model for a future socialist world, in the face of competing Chinese claims and models of "national roads to socialism" developed by other autonomist parties. In Vernon Aspaturian's phrase, socialist Eastern Europe serves as a "fig leaf of communist internationalism"[18] for the Soviet Union and is therefore indispensable for the exercise of its "ecumenical" role. In the Soviet interpretation the "world socialist system" (the WTO-CMEA complex led by the Soviet Union) constitutes the leading element of the three contemporary "world progressive forces"; the other two are the "international workers' movement" and the "national liberation movement." All three are seen as evolving toward world socialism, the world's ultimate fulfillment and destiny.

Currently it seems that the international role assigned to the East Europeans under the new policy will allow them to retain a degree of flexibility in dealing with internal problems, notwithstanding the simultaneous emphasis on greater bloc cohesion. If the trends continue, a success in the extension of Soviet influence beyond the bloc may even reintroduce a new "viability" into intrabloc relations. But in the final analysis it is doubtful that the CPSU will ever willingly give up its claim to a hegemonial position within the bloc, or the movement, or its identification of the Soviet state's *raison d'etat* with the goals of world revolution. In the general context of Moscow's foreign policy the obvious liabilities that the control of Eastern Europe implies for the Soviet Union—endemic political instability and the "infection" value for domestic Soviet politics as well as the economic burden—appear to be outweighed by the advantages derived from integrating the region into the Soviet international system.

NOTES

1. Within a broader context this applies also to Yugoslavia and Albania. Soviet support for the development of the Partisan movement there was of significant, if not decisive, importance.

2. Teresa Rakowska-Harmstone, "Patterns of Political Change," in Adam Bromke and Teresa Rakowska-Harmstone, eds., *The Communist States in Disarray: 1965–1971* (Minneapolis: University of Minnesota Press, 1972), p. 346.

3. The leadership of each party was generally divided into three factions: the "Muscovites" (who spent the war years in Russia and frequently were long-term functionaries of the Comintern); the "natives" (who spent the war years in their own countries and participated in anti-German resistance movements), and "foreigners" (who spent the war years in the West).

4. J. F. Brown refers to the "Stalinist" period as the period of "cohesion," and to 1953–68 as the period of "viability." See "The Interaction Between Party and Society in Hungary and Bulgaria," A. C. Janos, ed., *Authoritarian Politics*

in Communist Europe (Berkeley: Institute of International Studies and University of California Press, 1976), pp. 109–114.

5. For an analysis of the "rules of the game" that apply here, see Zvi Y. Gitelman, *The Diffusion of Political Innovation from Eastern Europe to the Soviet Union* (Beverly Hills and London: Sage Publications, 1972).

6. See Christopher D. Jones, *Soviet Influence in Eastern Europe: Political Autonomy and the Warsaw Pact* (New York: Praeger, 1981). Only Romania was able to opt out of the military integration scheme after first joint maneuvers in 1963 and established a system of national territorial defense similar to that in Yugoslavia, with the defense of the nation enshrined as the core of its military doctrine.

7. For a discussion of the Soviet theory behind the integration policy see Teresa Rakowska-Harmstone, "'Socialist Internationalism' and Eastern Europe—A New Stage," *Survey,* no. 1 (98), winter 1976 and "Socialist Internationalism—Part II," ibid., no. 2 (99), spring 1976.

8. B. N. Ladygin, O. K. Rybakov, V. I. Sedov, *The Socialist Community of a New Stage* (Moscow: "Progress," 1979), p. 37.

9. For details, see Jones, op. cit., and forthcoming Teresa Rakowska-Harmstone and Christopher Jones with John Jaworsky and Ivan Sylvain, *The Warsaw Pact: The Question of Cohesion.*

10. I am indebted for this observation to Radoslav Selucky.

11. "Dokumenty: Nomenklatura" (Documents: the Nomenklatura), pp. 38–58, *ANEKS*—Political Quarterly (London), no. 26, 1981, p. 52.

12. Kazimierz Brandys, "Nierzeczywistosc (fragmenty)" [Unreality—fragments], *ZAPIS I* (London: Index on Censorship, first Polish edition, January 1977), pp. 33–34. Translation and bracketed explanations are by this author. Italics are in the original.

13. For the development of these themes, see Teresa Rakowska-Harmstone, "Aspects of Political Change," Teresa Rakowska-Harmstone, ed., *Perspectives for Change in Communist Societies* (Boulder: Westview Press, 1978).

14. For a discussion of these concepts, see Zvi Y. Gitelman, *Beyond Leninism: Political Development in Eastern Europe* (Pittsburgh: University Center for International Studies, University of Pittsburgh, October 1971), pp. 23–28.

15. For further discussion, see Gitelman, *The Diffusion of Political Innovation.*

16. See Walter Laqueur, "Perils of Detente," *The New York Times Magazine,* February 27, 1977.

17. See Carl H. McMillan, "Some Thoughts on the Relationship Between Regional Integration in Eastern Europe and East-West Economic Relations," to be published in F. Levcik, ed., *Internationale Wirtschaft: Vergleich und Inderdependenz,* Festschrift fur Franz Nemschak (Vienna).

18. Vernon V. Aspaturian, "The Political-Ideological Aspects," Charles Gati, ed., *International Politics of Eastern Europe* (New York: Praeger Publishers, 1976), p. 22.

CONTRIBUTORS

VERNON V. ASPATURIAN is Evan Pugh Professor of Political Science and Director of the Slavic and Soviet Area Studies Center at Pennsylvania State University. He is the author of *Process and Power in Soviet Foreign Policy, The Soviet Union in the World Communist System, The Union Republics in Soviet Diplomacy,* and coauthor of *Foreign Policy in World Politics* and *Modern Political Systems: Europe.*

WALTER M. BACON, Jr. is Assistant Professor of Political Science at the University of Nebraska at Omaha and editor and translator of *Behind Closed Doors: Secret Papers on the Failure of Romanian-Soviet Negotiations, 1931–1932.*

ARTHUR M. HANHARDT, Jr. is Professor of Political Science at the University of Oregon and Visiting Scientist at the Battelle Human Affairs Research Center in Seattle, Washington. He is author of *The German Democratic Republic* and has written on German politics in *Koelner Zeitschrift fuer Soziologie und Sozialpsychologie, The Journal of International Studies,* and *Societas.*

ANDRZEJ KORBONSKI is Professor of Political Science and Director of the Center for Russian and East European Studies at the University of California at Los Angeles. He is the author of *The Politics of Socialist Agriculture in Poland, 1945–1960,* and has written on various aspects of East European politics and economics, problems of East European integration, and East-West trade.

BENNETT KOVRIG is Professor of Political Science at the University of Toronto, the author of several books dealing with Hungarian politics and of *The Myth of Liberation: East-Central Europe in U.S. Diplomacy and Politics since 1941.*

PAUL MARER is Professor and Chairperson of International Business at the School of Business, Indiana University. He is the author of *Soviet and East European Foreign Trade,* editor of *U.S. Financing of*

East-West Trade, and coeditor of *East European Integration and East-West Trade* and *Polish-U.S. Industrial Cooperation.*

PATRICK MOORE is Special Assistant for Balkan Affairs and senior analyst for Bulgarian and Romanian issues, Radio Free Europe Research. He has written articles on political, diplomatic, and nationality questions for *Radio Free Europe Research* and *South Slav Journal.*

NICHOLAS C. PANO is Professor of History and Assistant Dean of the College of Arts and Sciences at Western Illinois University. He is the author of *The People's Republic of Albania* and of many articles dealing with various aspects of Albanian politics.

TERESA RAKOWSKA-HARMSTONE is Professor of Political Science at Carleton University, Ottawa, Canada. She is the author of several volumes dealing with Soviet nationalities, Soviet politics, and the governments of Eastern Europe. She is coeditor of *The Communist States in Disarray* and editor as well as coauthor of *Perspectives of Change in Eastern Europe.*

ROBIN ALISON REMINGTON is Professor of Political Science at the University of Missouri-Columbia and a research affiliate of the Massachusetts Institute of Technology Center for International Studies. Her publications include *Winter in Prague: Documents on Czechoslovak Communism in Crisis* and *The Warsaw Pact: Case Studies in Communist Conflict Resolution.*

OTTO ULC is Professor of Political Science at the State University of New York at Binghamton and the author of *The Judge in a Communist State, The Politics of Czechoslovakia,* and several other books and articles in the fields of comparative government and international relations.

JIRI VALENTA is Associate Professor at the U.S. Naval Postgraduate School in Monterey, California, where he serves also as Coordinator of Soviet and East European Studies. He is the author of *Soviet Intervention in Czechoslovakia: Anatomy of a Decision* and coeditor of *Eurocommunism between East and West* and *Soviet Decision-Making for National Security.*

INDEX